WESTERN DRAMA THROUGH THE AGES

WESTERN DRAMA THROUGH THE AGES

A Student Reference Guide

VOLUME 2

Edited by Kimball King

GREENWOOD PRESS
Westport, Connecticut • London

Library of Congress Cataloging-in-Publication Data

Western drama through the ages : a student reference guide / edited by Kimball King.
    p. cm.
Includes bibliographical references and index.
ISBN-13: 978-0-313-32934-0 (set : alk. paper)
ISBN-13: 978-0-313-32935-7 (vol. 1 : alk. paper)
ISBN-13: 978-0-313-32936-4 (vol. 2 : alk. paper)
1. Drama—History and criticism. 2. Theater—History. I. King, Kimball.
PN1721.W47 2007
809.2—dc22   2007010683

British Library Cataloguing in Publication Data is available.

Library of Congress Catalog Card Number: 2007010683
ISBN-10: 0-313-32934-6 (set)   ISBN-13: 978-0-313-32934-0 (set)
       0-313-32935-4 (vol. 1)   978-0-313-32935-7 (vol. 1)
       0-313-32936-2 (vol. 2)   978-0-313-32936-4 (vol. 2)

First published in 2007

Greenwood Press, 88 Post Road West, Westport, CT 06881
An imprint of Greenwood Publishing Group, Inc.
www.greenwood.com

Printed in the United States of America

The paper used in this book complies with the
Permanent Paper Standard issued by the National
Information Standards Organization (Z39.48–1984).

10 9 8 7 6 5 4 3 2 1

Contents

VOLUME 2

PART IV

Theater Movements and Issues

African American Drama

Kay E.B. Ruth

SETTING THE CONTEXT FOR THE BEGINNING: THE ORAL TRADITION AND PERFORMANCE

To understand any kind of writing by an African American, one must also understand the literary tradition from which it comes. The literature by blacks in this country started with the slaves who were hunted and captured or sold, chained and forced on great slave ships to make their way from Africa to America during the seventeenth, eighteenth, and nineteenth centuries. These slaves, who survived the miserable, treacherous, and often fatal journey, the Middle Passage, passed on to their descendants the oral tradition. This tradition consists of the use of song, dance, recitation, storytelling, and poetry as a means of entertainment, teaching, religious ritual, historical recording, and literary creation. Separated from their homelands, the slaves held on to their cultural traditions. And, because slaves by and large were not allowed to learn to read and write, their literature remained largely oral instead of written until the nineteenth century.

These beginnings are directly related to the written literature by African Americans who were able to produce even as slaves and those who produced afterwards. The oral tradition birthed the written literature of black Americans, and the literary lineage from this tradition can be traced to each genre of African American writing. For example, escaped slaves who found their freedom in the Northern cities of America continued the tradition of storytelling, sharing their life stories with others interested in freeing slaves. From many of these speeches and public communications on the abolitionists' stages came the most popular form of writing by African Americans during that time period: slave autobiography. In the same vein, African American drama is a direct descendant of the oral tradition as it is connected with storytelling, singing, and dancing. In Africa, one of the most prestigious positions in a tribe was that of the griot: the person who retained in his memory the history, literature, and religion of the tribe. During important community events, the griot took a place of authority and would often regale his audience with songs, dances, and storytelling to befit the occasion. In America, the slaves built on the oral and performance traditions of the griot. According to literary scholar William B. Branch, their taking on of the griot's role is the root of African American drama; oral texts created by the slaves were a continuation of "the ancient oral tradition of the [African] historian-storyteller, or 'griot'—with his elaborate, poetic 'praise song' monodramatizations, augmented by communal song and dance—which has come down through the centuries." The slaves would tell stories to pass time or even to convey coded messages of unhappiness or rebellion. Their audiences, learning by heart the repeated stories that were often accompanied by songs and dancing, would join in so that the performance, as it had been in Africa, was an oral and communal activity. Thus, just as in Europe the oral productions of the troubadours launched literatures in various countries, African oral productions provided the foundation on which African Americans built dramatic performances and creation.

Lucy Terry Prince (1730?–1821) is known as the first African American author. She was an African slave who was bought and freed by her husband and who was also a renowned storyteller who entertained the community with her narrative poems and songs. She is a direct link between Africa and the griot and African American dramatic performance. Her "Bars Fight," a narrative poem about a Native American massacre of colonists in Massachusetts in 1746, survives only in part. Still, it is evidence of an African American writing and using the text for performance. Prince's piece is important, too, because it shows how Africans transformed their creative productions into American texts. Adapting to their new surroundings—the colonial American landscape—understanding and learning American traditions and cultural values and taking them as their own, these newcomers to the New World merged oral tradition with American literary forms and themes. For example, "Bars Fight" graphically depicts the murders of several women, children, and men by Native Americans who use hatchets to brutally cut down their foes. Even though only a snippet of "Bars Fight" survives, it is important to note the empathy the narrative voice expresses for the colonists. Prince was a slave during the time she wrote the poem; however, she clearly sees herself in the same position as any other colonist who feared attack. Thus, Prince's narrative truly represents an American perspective and not just an African or African American perspective.

African Americans did develop certain themes in their literature that are distinct from the majority American culture. Depicting the reality of black life in America, voicing disgust and anger with political inequities and casting hope in, despair of, or apathy for the American Dream, African American writers have tried to capture the truth of being a minority with a slave heritage in a democracy. To express this truth from a black perspective, however, does not exclude them from the larger American literary tradition. As a matter of fact, while black dramatists acknowledge and incorporate these uniquely African American themes, they are voicing their perspectives on the same truths being pronounced by other writers of the times.

THE WRITTEN TRADITION: AFRICAN AMERICAN DRAMA

The Nineteenth Century

Of course, when one thinks of drama, one imagines more than one person standing in front of an audience reciting poetry or a story as Prince did. One thinks of a performance acted out on a stage separating the actors from the audience. One thinks of the lighting, scenery, characters in costumes and the breaking of action into acts and scenes, all of which allows one to understand that one is watching a story being performed live for the audience's illumination and enjoyment. The audience not only hears the story, but it also sees events unfold. The first known African American theater owner, William Brown, after first offering performances more in line with the oral tradition, adopted this traditional Western mode of playwriting for his acting troupe:

> Between 1816 and 1817, a Mr. Brown...opened a tea garden in lower Manhattan and, in doing so, launched a series of firsts in African American theatre. The popularity of the entertainment that Brown provided for his African American customers— songs, poetry, dramatic monologues—led to the formation of the African Grove Company, a performing troupe of Black actors....When Brown converted the upstairs apartments of the African Grove into a theatre seating 300–400 people, he established the first Black theatre in the country.[1]

As one can see, the actors' first performance pieces—"songs, poetry, dramatic monologues"—reflect the influence of the oral tradition on African American drama. However, these performers were also Americans, and they began to perform dramas that were popular within the larger American culture—one stemming from a European written literary tradition.

Mr. Brown is also known as the first American playwright of African descent in America. He wrote *The Drama of King Shotoway* for the African Grove acting company, and the troupe performed it in 1823. Unfortunately, the play was soon afterwards shut down for good, ostensibly because it was a public nuisance. In reality, these African Americans were considered a threat to a local theater run by white Americans. It did not help that *King Shotoway* portrayed the defense by slave descendants of the island, Saint Vincent, against colonization by the British.

In the play, these blacks were noble heroes and their cause was undeniably just—like that of the American colonists fighting against British tyranny during the American Revolution. It made a bold statement contradicting the racist attitude that Africans and their descendants were inferiors who could, as a consequence, be justifiably enslaved. In an America still struggling with the issue of slavery and the question of what to do with blacks, a drama showcasing the brave defiance by slave descendants against a white European power was, to a white audience, controversial at best and perhaps downright offensive and dangerous.

The beginning of African American drama was also highlighted by a curious dilemma black writers have universally experienced: they had the strong desire to participate in the majority culture and gain acceptance from both white and black audiences, but at the same time they were voicing their disillusionment with the status quo. To ignore social injustice would almost certainly alienate them from their black audience. However, to show disdain or to condemn America for its unequal treatment of blacks might cost them the approbation of their white audience. What happened to Mr. Brown is a case in point. Because he suggested that colonization should have been stamped out by armed rebellion by blacks, he was silenced; he lost his popularity with his white audience, and, thus, he lost his theater. Nothing more is known of the history of this Mr. Brown. His story ends with the closing of the African Grove.

William Wells Brown, who is the most well-known early African American dramatist, took up the mantle of political protest laid down by his predecessor. An escaped slave, Brown turned to writing literature as a means of calling America's attention to the horrible conditions of slaves in America. He was an abolitionist who had seen firsthand how dehumanizing, brutal, immoral, and degrading slavery could be for slave and slave master alike. As part of his political efforts, he wrote the play *The Escape, or A Leap for Freedom* (1858), in addition to several short stories and novels. Brown did not produce this play about a slave couple attempting to run away from their slave master in order to gain freedom, but he would often read it to captive audiences who had come to hear speeches against slavery. Again, here one sees the melding of the African oral tradition of performance and the Western dramatic tradition. Instead of producing the play for the stage, Brown presented the play more in the form of a lecture to protest the subjugation of blacks. In doing so, Brown is also part of a larger American tradition of the time in which authors like Mark Twain and Ralph Waldo Emerson toured America, giving lectures and dramatic readings of their works.

During the nineteenth century, a different kind of dramatic performance was also started by slaves on Southern plantations, albeit inadvertently. This type of performance is covered under the umbrella of minstrelsy. Today, the terms "minstrel" and "minstrelsy" carry negative connotations because of the stereotypes associated with the art form—stereotypes manifested in the use of black face, mispronounced speech, and images of ignorant-lazy-yet-happy slaves. However, it is important to note that minstrelsy started as a sign of the appreciation white entertainers had for the slaves' unique styles of dancing and singing. Minstrelsy began because often slaves were called to entertain their masters, mistresses, and guests by singing, dancing, or reciting poetry. White performers saw these "shows" and began to imitate the performances:

> White minstrel shows formally began in 1842 with the antics of Dan Emmett....In the forty years that followed, hundreds of white men donned hog fat and burnt cork to make thousands and thousands of dollars mimicking and distorting black music, black speech, black dance, and black culture, a tradition that was to last until the mid-twentieth century.[2]

As Hatch suggests, minstrelsy originated as a distortion of the slaves' art. Sincere performances became pieces at which to laugh; white audiences enjoyed, as high comedy, the antics and ignorance of "blacks" portrayed onstage.

However, black performers were able to reappropriate—that is, "take back and redefine"—the minstrel form in order to create serious, political art:

> After the Civil War, several black minstrel troupes appeared, but to succeed they had to imitate their imitators, and they too blackened their faces and drew white and red circles around their mouths and eyes. Pauline Hopkins in 1879 wrote *Peculiar Sam, or The Underground Railroad*...; she employed the current minstrel dialect as well as song and dance to engage her audience in the serious subject of emancipation.

It is ironic that these dramatists and performers felt the need to participate in the parody of black life portrayed by white minstrels. However, by using these accepted structures in order to critique them and prove their artistic failings, the black minstrels were able to create a parody of the parody. Moreover, they were able to present a serious matter, the desire for freedom and equality, for the audience's consideration.

The Twentieth Century

As in any genre of American literature, African American drama saw lulls between its major literary productions. Thus, the next major period of drama for African Americans came in the early twentieth century with the advent of the Harlem Renaissance. The giants who were to dominate this era in poetry and prose also were to dominate the stage. Langston Hughes, the most prolific writer during this period, wrote several timeless plays, such as *Mulatto* (1935), which ran on Broadway, and *Little Ham* (1935). *Mulatto* underscores the racial tension that still existed in America because of the heritage of slavery and the taboo of interracial sexual liaisons. It tells the story of a family of half black, half white children belonging to a rich white man and his black housekeeper mistress.

The youngest son both hates and reveres his father. Searching for the father's acceptance but denying the racism that causes his father never to marry his mother, the mulatto ends by killing his father and being killed by an angry white mob. The play begs the question of how America is to survive if it maintains the separation of the races and the oppression of African Americans. *Little Ham*, a much more lighthearted play in many ways, is still tragic in a sense. Here, as with all of Hughes' writings, the audience finds an everyday Joe, Little Ham, a black man searching for economic opportunities in order to survive in America. As with other American dramatists of the early twentieth century, Hughes offers critiques of the American Dream, the promise of opportunity for all Americans.

Hughes had many more successes in the theater, often incorporating song and dance into his productions for the stage. *Black Nativity* (1961), a favorite of audiences and churches at Christmastime, is a retelling of the story of the birth of Christ interspersing biblical narrative and action with spirituals and gospel songs. James Weldon Johnson, a poet and composer best known for writing the song, "Lift Every Voice and Sing," also acknowledged the artistry of slaves and the oral tradition. Though technically a collection of poems, his *God's Trombones* (1927) is imitative of slave sermons: oral productions meant to be recited dramatically to entertain and instruct the audience.

By 1955, when James Baldwin published *The Amen Corner*, a play that examines the roles religion and politics play in black lives, several famous novelists had turned their narratives into plays. For example, Richard Wright's novel *Native Son* (1940) was produced for the stage. Others rewrote their narratives by adding song and dance numbers as had Hughes. By this time, the written tradition of African Americans in drama had been long established as an entity that provided commentary on the lives of blacks struggling in America under racism as well as a close look at the workings of African American culture. Baldwin's play, for example, focuses on the inner workings of a close-knit community and the power struggle that ensues when two women in authority disagree. He shows that, within the black community itself, there live oppressive elements associated with human nature, not with racism. He also shows the struggles of one young man to become an adult others can respect. This identity quest is often echoed in both African American and American literature.

Perhaps the most renowned African American playwright of the 1950s and 1960s is Lorraine Hansberry, who reached Broadway with the production of *A Raisin in the Sun* (1959). As with writers before her—American and African American alike, such as Eugene O'Neill, Arthur Miller and Hughes—Hansberry wrote of the pursuit of and disillusionment with the American Dream. She shows that the American Dream is within blacks' grasp, though, in order to win it, they must often face and overcome not only institutionalized racism but also internal racist ideas. The story of the Younger family is an important acknowledgement that everyone—man, woman, and child; father, son, mother, and daughter—strives for recognition, love, and happiness. The family realizes that it must unite in order to fulfill each individual's needs. The play's title comes from a famous poem "Harlem" by Hughes. The poem begs the question, "What happens to a dream deferred," or a dream that goes unfulfilled. The play answers by saying that it does not have to "dry up like a raisin in the sun." Indeed, as black Americans were then discovering en masse during the Civil Rights Movement, happiness could be found by all Americans even in the midst of a racist society; not everyone was racist, and many wanted positive change. The play shows that while fulfillment is affected by the larger society, it can still be found and fought for if one has the support of family. Hansberry died at the very young age of 34 leaving the stage empty of her promise. Still, before she died of cancer, she wrote several more plays including *The Sign in Sidney Brustein's Window* (1964). *To Be Young, Gifted and Black* (1968) is a compilation of several of her writings her ex-husband put together after her death.

With the advent of the Civil Rights Movement came an increase in African American drama. Community centers sprang up to produce politically centered dramatic pieces that also presented the richness of African American life. During this period, writers were encouraged to create literature by, for, and about black life and to reject any major cultural ideology that denied the beauty of blackness. The Black Arts Movement—also referred to as The Black Aesthetic Movement or BAM—was born, and theater was a major part of it.

Playwright Adrienne Kennedy can be seen as one of the literary mothers at the forefront of this movement. Technically, Kennedy found her niche as a playwright before the BAM writers began to articulate their philosophy of art as it pertained to American literature, their place in it, and the politics of the larger world. However, her play *Funnyhouse of a Negro* (1960) does exactly what other poets, essayists, novelists, and playwrights of this movement insist should be done in literature: Kennedy experimented with form and accepted images of blackness while providing a biting commentary on the political institutions that have contributed to the degradation of the African American after slavery. The play's main character is of mixed race, and she is mentally torn between her European British heritage and her African heritage. She ends by committing suicide, an act that symbolizes how one part of humanity can abuse and brutalize another part just because they are racially different. This act can be seen as negative commentary on the colonization of countries, like Africa, by European nations, which used up the other countries' resources; as a representation of what racism does to communities; or as a look at the inner chaos one person faces as a result of being victimized by bigotry.

Kennedy's style of presentation was influenced by experimental and expressionist drama. For example, *Funnyhouse of a Negro* does not present the plot in the usual story pattern of a beginning, middle, and end. Instead, most of the play is in monologue form with much of it repeated over and over. Through this technique, the audience can come to understand the acute mental torment this character is in as well as the fragmented way she sees herself and her heritage. Other Black Arts Movement writers experimented with forms as well as Kennedy, borrowing ideas from the theater of the absurd as well as from ideas of the post-modernists, expressionists, and naturalists.

Amiri Baraka (Leroi Jones) has emerged as a spokesman for and leader of the Black Arts Movement. He is, as was Langston Hughes, a giant of his time and also of American literature. A prolific writer who has produced essays, poems, literary critiques, and political and social treatises, he is one of the best playwrights of African American drama. His *Dutchman* (1964) is a play about a young African American student, Clay, who encounters a beautiful white woman on the subway. He is both attracted to Lula, as she seductively eats an apple and strikes up a conversation, and repelled by her racist remarks and because of the cultural mores that tell him he, a black man, cannot trust a white woman. Clay stands as a symbol of the mindset of assimilation castigated by BAM writers. He, clearly, is a student who wants to learn how to be accepted by mainstream America, an act which Baraka considered as Clay's erasing his heritage. Clay also wants Lula to see him without stereotypes so that he will be acceptable to her. Reflecting Baraka's political philosophy that such behavior and desires are anti-black, the play ends tragically for Clay; he never makes his destination—Lula kills him— and the woman goes on to captivate another black youth. Baraka argues that assimilation into white society requires a loss of black identity, which conse-quently implies the destruction of black culture.

Baraka was not only producing other plays, such as *The Slave* (1964) and *Great Goodness of Life* (1969), but he was also galvanizing efforts to start theaters and schools of drama that would showcase the dramatic efforts of black authors. He started the Black Arts Repertory Theater/School in Harlem in 1965, and, in doing so, institutionalized his philosophy of writing: that black writers should write to black audiences in order to get them to reject mainstream America and its traditions; that African and African American cultural traditions were to be promoted; that art should be influenced by those cultural traditions in a rejection of American and Euro-American influence; and that the anger felt by black Americans, victims of history and racism, should be expressed loudly and passionately. His call for more black drama troupes and playwrights inspired African Americans all across America to step forward and to teach, act, and write.

Douglas Turner Ward's *Day of Absence* (1965) is one answer to Baraka's chal-lenge; it is a humorous drama with a political message about the power of the black working class. Set in a small Southern town, the play highlights the chaos that ensues when the white citizenry of the town realize they cannot function without their black domestics and blue collar workers, who have disappeared without a trace. The irony of the play is that the characters are caricatures of white Southerners played by blacks in white face. As such, this play is a parody of the minstrel tradition and the white performers who reinforced stereotypes of blacks, as well as a protest against how lower-class African Americans were often taken advantage of financially—even though they were the labor force that kept America going. Ward's play is a great example of the playwright's focus during the BAM. He, along with other playwrights such as Baraka, Alice Childress, Ed Bullins, Ntozake Shangé, and Kennedy, wrote about their world in a way to reappropriate African American images and to reject stereotypes of blacks perpetuated throughout American literary tradition.

Alice Childress's *Wine in the Wilderness* (1969) is her most famous play although she was writing successful plays much earlier. An actress, she had joined the American Negro Theater (ANT) along with such famous actors as Ossie Davis and Ruby Dee some twenty-six years before. As with her earlier plays for ANT, *Wine in the Wilderness* focuses on working class characters and how they are affected by a racist, capitalist society. Ever the realist, Childress uses the play to critique inner-racial bigotry as she reveals the hypocrisy many blacks saw in other blacks during the political upheaval of the 1960s and 1970s.

Going a Buffalo (1968) by Ed Bullins is another BAM drama that focuses on the lower classes of blacks. With its urban setting, the play dramatizes the desire for blacks caught up in a world of crime and poverty to find the wide open spaces of the American Dream. The play's characters—Mamma Too Tight, Curt, Pandora, and Art—inhabit a violent world that inhibits them and makes them long for a freer life. They are victims of their environment, a theme closely associated with the earlier naturalist American writers, including Richard Wright.

Ntozake Shangé's choreopoem *for colored girls who have considered suicide/ when the rainbow is enuf* (1971) is a melding of oral tradition, dance, and drama, as well as the black aesthetic espoused by Black Arts Movement writers. The drama, expressed through poetic monologues, music and dance, is the height of experimentation. The fusing of all of these types of expression is Shangé's nod to the BAM dictum of rejecting traditional dramatic forms; however, it is also a feminist text which takes on the politics of inner-racism and mistreatment based on gender. *for colored girls* exposes the violence and sexual exploitation black women face at the hands of black men. At the same time, it is a celebration of the African American woman who can endure this mistreatment and serve as the nurturing spirit of the race.

Movements in literature exist when a set of writers sees the world differently and expresses its views differently than the authors who wrote in earlier generations. Such is the case with neo-realist writers—writers who reject the extremism they see in the passion and politics of the Black Arts Movement in order to embrace their appreciation for realism. *The Colored Museum* (1986) by playwright

George Wolfe is a rejection of the feminist perspective of Shangé's works as well as a rejection of what Wolfe sees as unrealistic representations of black life in other writers. It is a pastiche of characters based on those one would encounter in African American and American literature and history. At the beginning of the play, as the museum opens, the audience is treated to its exhibits: characters who deliver monologues reminiscent of other characters in works by such authors as Hansberry and Shangé, as well as by characters who represent stereotypes in modern America. Wolfe shows that African Americans, especially men, are still being stereotyped as violent and criminal, even by black writers, and that these images are outdated and unrealistic. Therefore, these representations belong in a museum where the audience can see how antiquated and unreal they are. Wolfe also portrays African American women as castrating as they label and mistrust the black men in their lives. As with the other writers before him, Wolfe addresses the theme of African Americans and their historical and economic oppression as well.

The most well-known, produced, and studied playwright since Lorraine Hansberry is August Wilson. He stands not only as a great talent in African American literature but as an emerging talent of the American stage. Known for several plays, such as *Ma Rainey's Black Bottom* (1982); *Fences* (1987), for which he won a Pulitzer Prize; *Joe Turner's Come and Gone* (1988); and *The Piano Lesson* (1990), for which he won a second Pulitzer, Wilson focuses on realistically portraying African American life in each decade of the twentieth century. For instance, *Ma Rainey's Black Bottom* is about the influence of the blues on mainstream America as well as how the talented musicians who produced this music were exploited because of their color. Though it focuses on what American society does to blacks in terms of oppression, the play also turns its eye on what blacks can and will do to abuse or oppress other blacks. Even though each of Wilson's plays takes a different focus on black life, those two perspectives are always clearly in focus in order to show that African Americans can be victims, but they can also be victimizers as well. Again, this idea comes from a neo-realistic perspective, which recognizes the mixture of good and bad in everyone.

In contrast to Wilson, Suzan-Lori Parks generally holds white men responsible for black misfortunes. *The American Play* (1995), arguably her most famous work, depicts Abraham Lincoln as black man, possibly to suggest that a Caucasian would not benefit her race.

The Twenty-First Century

Wilson, Wolfe, Baraka, and others continue to write in the African American tradition, which is based on the slave's oral tradition, as well as American forms of literature. As they create, they realistically portray the African American experience throughout history. They define what it is to be black in a country that has historically held stereotypical views of blackness; they write about the culture, community, and traditions of blacks so that they are not only recognized as legitimate but also celebrated as culturally important; they show realistically that African Americans can contribute to American society, can attain the American Dream, and have to face the fact that if they do not, it may be their own fault. They write so that audiences may see that African Americans are humans, just like everyone else, with sterling qualities as well as flaws, and that, though their history within the nation may be different, they still retain the American spirit of endurance.

NOTES

1. This account of Mr. Brown is found in the anthology edited by James V. Hatch and Ted Shine, listed first in Further Reading.

2. Both quoted passages on minstrel shows are given by James V. Hatch in his introduction to *The Roots of African American Drama*, edited by Leo Hamalian.

FURTHER READING

Branch, William B. "Black Dramatists in the Diaspora: The Beginnings." Introduction. In *Crosswinds: An Anthology of Black Dramatists in the Diaspora.* Edited by William B. Branch. Bloomington: Indiana University Press, 1993.

Hatch, James V. and Ted Shine, eds. *Black Theatre USA: Plays by African Americans, The Recent Period 1935–Today.* New York: The Free Press, 1996.

———. "Those Who Left and Those Who Stayed." Introduction. In *Black Theatre USA: Plays by African Americans, 1847 to Today.* New York: The Free Press, 1996.

Hatch, James V. "Two Hundred Years of Black and White Drama." Introduction. In *The Roots of African American Drama: An Anthology of Early Plays, 1858–1938.* Edited by Leo Hamalian. Detroit: Wayne State University Press, 1990.

Marsh-Lockett, Carol. *Black Women Playwrights: Visions on the American Stage.* New York: Garland Publishing, 1999.

❧

Belief in Contemporary Drama

Gerald C. Wood

A HOMELESS SPIRIT

In his study of contemporary theater, *Modern American Drama, 1945–2000,* C.W.E. Bigsby asserts that many writers at the end of the twentieth century were reconsidering the need for religious perspectives, which Bigsby names "spirituality." Whether or not that was the case in the 1990s, in the beginning of this century many playwrights have observed the lost sense of the transcendent in contemporary life. While some of these dramatists have left their faith and others maintain a religious practice, they share a concern for the plight of human experience when the spiritual is denied, when life is reduced to the merely physical, wholly material. Their responses to such a predicament are various: sometimes the playwrights reassert belief as a primal source of meaning and order, sometimes they focus on the dehumanization of the isolated self, or sometimes they express the courage found in recovered faith. While the writers considered here—Conor McPherson, Neil LaBute, and Horton Foote—are in no way a definitive list of such playwrights, their recent work indicates some distinctive responses to the loss of religious assurance in the new millennium.

THREE IMPORTANT PLAYWRIGHTS

Conor McPherson

After many years of alcohol abuse, including one where, in his own words, his behavior had become "ridiculous," in the spring of 2001 Conor McPherson, the Irish playwright and filmmaker, was rushed to a hospital in London, where he endured a long coma induced by nearly complete organ shutdown. As he has summarized in an interview with Carol Vander, he was "in hospital in London for nine weeks. I ...nearly died. Alcohol ...almost destroyed my inner organs. I couldn't walk. I had basically tried to kill myself. Not consciously. But there was a drive deep inside me to finish my existence. It was uncontrollable and I was at its mercy." After such a frightening and temporarily debilitating experience, McPherson wisely took a sabbatical from his personal work in theater. He carved out an interim period of healing in which he would work in film, as writer and director, and adapt the work of others for both stage and screen. He restaged Eugene O'Brien's *Eden,* wrote and directed *The Actors* for Neil Jordan, from a story first imagined by Jordan. His play *Shining City* followed a three-year absence from the stage, a time of reflection on his own life and mortality.

Shining City is set on the north side of the Liffey, in a somewhat seedy, decadent Victorian section of Dublin, where a man in his 50s, John, arrives to see Ian, a therapist in his 40s. Initially John explains that he recently lost his wife, Mari, in an automobile accident, but then, somewhat hesitantly, he adds that he has been seeing her ghost as well. In the second scene, at the same therapist's office, Ian clumsily tries to break up with Neasa, his working class girlfriend, who is furious over Ian's abandoning her, and their child, at the home of Ian's brother and sister-in-law. During their argument it is revealed that he was training for the priesthood when they met and she had a brief affair, before their child was born and after Ian left the church. Scene three returns to another therapy session in which, more comfortable with the therapist, John confesses that childless and fearful of having missed something in his life, he began pursuing another woman, Vivien. But their tryst at Killiney is cut short by their clumsiness and guilt, and so he substitutes a trip to a brothel on the South Circular Road in order to, in his words, "connect with something, or someone." Following a long wait for his girl, he demands his money back but instead is beaten by a bouncer. Back home, he verbally and physically attacks Mari and withdraws from her. In the present he speculates whether she is appearing in ghostly form to attack or console him.

In scene four, Ian returns to his office with Laurence, a male prostitute from a nearby park. After Ian stumbles clumsily over offering drinks, playing music, and being intimate, the two embrace under Laurence's direction. In the final scene, five, Ian is preparing to move from his office, to Limerick, where he will join Neasa and their child and start a new practice, when John rings up. The ex-patient brings a gift, an antique lamp, and his thanks for Ian's help, declaring that he is moving into a new house "on the seafront...near St. Anne's Park." He adds that he is feeling more positive about his troubled relationship with his brother and has happily met another woman. He also saw Vivien once again, but this time he felt "like nothing had ever happened," that they "had *nothing* in common," that the whole experience was "Mad." The two men agree that, though John felt he saw things, there are "no ghosts," only feelings and minds which "just know nothing really." As John leaves, Ian begins tidying the room. As he closes the door through which John has just exited, revealed almost simultaneously to him and the audience is the ghost of Mari as described by John, in a filthy red coat and wet hair, as the lights go down.

In his earlier plays McPherson imagines the theater as a playful space to explore appearance and reality, entertainment and earnest inquiry, mischief and reason. In *Rum and Vodka, St. Nicholas,* and *This Lime Tree Bower,* for example, the speakers are aware of the audience, make fun of critics, and plead for a sensitive, humane response to their stories. For most of *Shining City,* this story seems different from the preceding ones, more of a traditional realist play. It follows the experiences of psychologist and patient as they both work through emotional issues. But in the last scene, the facade begins to disappear. First the writer briefly, in his words, "sticks a finger through the fourth wall" by making the audience conscious of itself in the theater.[1] John describes his date with a new girlfriend:

John: We're going to the theatre tomorrow night.

Ian: Oh!

John: I know! (*As though the theatre is rubbish.*) 'Good luck'

Then Conor McPherson turns even more deceptive. First he lulls the audience into believing they are following the conventions of mimetic and melodramatic theater toward a sense of closure. Ian reveals his commitment to marriage and heterosexuality. John has exorcised his demons by returning to the house he shared with Mari, followed by purchasing another, a more modern and forward-looking one on the seashore. But just as the provocations of the playwright's earlier productions seem tamed, the closing door reveals Mari in her red dress, wet and disheveled, beaten and terrifying. In the hands of a mischievous playwright, realism instantaneously dissolves before *Shining City's* spectators. And the audience, even against their better judgment, becomes believers, in ghosts and the magic of theater. No longer able to remain passive theatergoers, they are drawn into the anxious, uncharted physical and emotional space of Conor McPherson's unconventional drama.

This disorientation is not gratuitous theatricality. McPherson integrates such uncertainty into the rhetoric of *Shining City.* For example, John, a recent beneficiary of psychological healing, testifies to his mentor, Ian, that stability is found in worshipping feeling before all other gods: "even if I saw [a ghost], Ian, it's not... I mean, seeing something is one thing but...it's how it makes you *feel,* isn't it?" Embracing one's affective side isn't enough. The primordial call to order and comfort offered in religious belief haunts even the therapist.

In the final moments of the play, Conor McPherson is inviting his audience to join his ruminations on the phenomenology of belief. On the one hand, *Shining City* considers Ian's confusion, both sexual and emotional, as linked to his liberation from deliberating religious preconceptions. But the psychological explanation, that it is all emotion and point of view, is inadequate as well. If everything is true, then there is no place to stand. As McPherson himself explains in a statement quoted by Ian Johns, "The play is about life's uncertainties and the choices that face us . . . .about spiritual people who are faced with the possibility that everything they believe in is nonexistent and how difficult it is to accept the truth that we really don't know everything." The ghost is revealed in the play because the playwright wants the audience to experience belief as an animal need for a transpersonal grounding of individual experience.[2] But equally real is the association of belief with the uncanny, which has unavoidable ties to the disintegrating forces of illusion. If human beings are honest with themselves, McPherson writes, calm and anxiety are the twin children of belief. And so the playwright creates the liminal space of *Shining City*, where consciousness remains primitive and all ideology is unstable.

While the will to believe seems written into the DNA of these characters,[3] their desire for knowledge and comfort is grounded in the equally real presence of "a vast space we know nothing about," as reported in an interview with Carol Vander:

> To me a play, or any art is just like the paintings on the cave walls that the first human beings did. Those poor fuckers were the first ones to experience being conscious. What a bizarre experience it is to know that we are alive. And wonder if there is a God, and will something save us? To be alive and to understand the existence of pain is pretty frightening. And all I'm doing is drawing myself, or just people, up on the wall of the cave, just to have a look and try to understand the mystery of being here on this big rock in the middle of a vast space we know nothing about.

He hopes this play, like all this plays, inspires the people in the audience to feel closer to the playwright and each other by recognizing themselves in the cave, on the wall, at the theater.

Conor McPherson's plays work simultaneously in two directions. On the one hand, he chooses entertainment over the conventions of traditional theater. The dramas take the viewers on a playful ride to the edge of the permissible in theater. But McPherson is also an inquisitive and highly intelligent writer whose work is a form of conversation with his thoughtful self. As he confessed recently, "As a person, my inner life has always been turbulent, and I suppose the work I did was always a search for refuge, dry land, something to hold on to which had a kind of validity or self-evident truth to cling to. And that's a strong drive because it has always been so necessary."[4] Following such a personal path toward the authentic, he has reminded his audiences and himself that the world is unfixed, unknowable. Given this dark reality, his most contented characters embrace this uncertainty and control themselves in order to increase the chances they will be loved in the face of nothingness. Once they have learned the value of self-control, the characters seek acceptance without becoming the victims of their own desire. They reluctantly discover narcissism in both their early isolation and their subsequent impulses to fuse with the objects of their love. And now, in *Shining City*, McPherson offers his people, and himself, a form of belief which sanctifies life by wedding loving intention to the uncanny nature of all human experience.

Neil LaBute

Neil LaBute and Conor McPherson have much in common as contemporary dramatists. They both claim the early influence of David Mamet, who offered them a pattern of rapid-fire dialogue and intense, emetic self-assertion by anxious and sometimes violent characters, almost always men. They also share experimentation with the monologue form and a satiric view of contemporary life, emphasizing the self-absorption and alienation, the failure to love, of Irish and American males. They both focus on actors as creative collaborators in their writing, and they write and direct for film as well as theater. Less obvious is their shared ambivalence toward their religious experience. McPherson was raised in a Catholic home and educated in Catholic schools. Even though he has left the church, he admits to finding the stories and images of Catholicism arresting and aesthetically pleasing. LaBute became a Mormon after enrolling at Brigham Young University. And yet his plays, especially *Bash,* freely criticize the excesses of his church. While openly critical of their churches, LaBute and McPherson continue to interpret the material excesses of modern culture against the ethical standards established in Christianity.

Behind the disturbing violence of Neil LaBute's plays and films lies his concern with morality. As the writer himself explained to theater critic John Lahr in 1999, "The interesting thing about sin is that we've gotten a bit away from it. There's a right and a wrong that goes beyond the daily practice of living, and I think we have gotten away from that idea, yet it sort of hangs over all of us." Significantly, it is the "idea" of right and wrong, not its reality, that interests LaBute. That sense of usable limits is what attracted him to the Mormon faith. He says to Dinitia Smith, "The great thing about it, you can say definitely, 'This is what it is....I always liked things that had parameters, demarcation lines. And to see how far I can travel within those lines.'" The payoff for him as an artist is, he adds in a comment to Dona Kennedy, an internalized "moral tone" learned by working "within limits, pushing the boundaries to their very greatest within set limits." In a relativist society, freedom and identity rely, paradoxically, on a clear sense of social order, which allows the individual the choice of obeying the rules or rebelling and accepting the consequences.

This recognition that boundaries are essential to freedom is the central issue in his plays and films. For example, the church hymn that serves as one of the epigraphs to *Mercy Seat* points to the calm offered by a sense of the transcendent:

Approach, my soul, the mercy-seat,
Where Jesus answers prayers;
There humbly fall before his feet,
For none can perish there.

In the presence of a benign authority, the celebrant gains not only humility and liveliness but also the identity implied in the idea of "soul." According to LaBute, permissiveness makes the pursuit of identity more problematic, not easier. He says that in the film *Possession* "What I wanted to get at with Roland and Maud was the idea that the all-permissive society makes a person like a deer in the headlights. The ability to have it all can create this daunting sense that we don't know what we want." Similarly, his play *The Distance From Here* is not just about the violence it describes; its theme is "The more permissive the society, the more people become more confused," according to Daniel Zalewski. As John Lahr wrote in 2001: "LaBute dramatizes the sin of separation—human beings whose romantic imagination wills them to be strangers to themselves."

And strangers to others as well. Although LaBute has been criticized for the behavior of his characters, for the obscenity in his plays and stories, he is actually dramatizing the lack of restraint, of healthy boundaries. Most of the focus is on failed caretaking towards children. *Bash* involves two instances of infanticide. *The Distance from Here* ends with two young people deciding whether to recover the body of a baby who has been thrown into a zoo cage. And Ben, in *Mercy Seat*, while contemplating whether to fake his own death so he can abandon his family for his lover, imagines his twelve-year-old daughter crying over the loss of her father. Though he can imagine his child's anxiety and fear, he is too focused on himself to sacrifice for her well-being. At the most extreme, LaBute's short story "Maraschino," from the collection *Seconds of Pleasure*, describes a sexual encounter between a young woman and a man who apparently was once her stepfather, a relationship remembered by her but not the man. All of these abuses follow because in these families no one "acts like an adult or respects a boundary enough to set one," as pointed out in Lahr's 2002 play review.

In the broader, more satiric sense, this betrayal of boundaries becomes a national pathology. At its simplest and most personal, as explained by Mary Dickson, there is a kind of laziness about relationships, which LaBute identifies as part of "a disposable society. It's easier to throw things out than to fix them. We even give it a name—we call it recycling. Especially as relationships go, we're too quick to say the easiest way is to end it because we don't want to do the work." Stephen Holden adds that in sexual relationships, people treat each other as commodities, craving release from responsibility and choice, a drive which never brings peace:

"The utopian rhetoric of the sexual revolution combined with the commodification of sex to sell everything under the sun have guaranteed that millions of people conditioned to expect erotic salvation on demand are in for a bitter disappointment when it isn't delivered."

This lack of direction, self-control, and loving intention is the basis of the black humor of LaBute's plays, indicated in the dissonance between traditional ideas of "the good" and the aimless lives of the characters. For example, in *Your Friends and Neighbors* Cary can only think of being good in terms of sexual prowess; without a sense of morality, he can't understand the question, and ends by brushing off Barry's question as to whether Cary thinks he is a good person:

Cary: Hey, I'm eating lunch...

In *Mercy Seat* Abby extends her fantasy of dog-style sex with Ben's wife into a surreal blend of sadomasochistic sex and religious apocalypse: "Maybe that's what Hell is, in the end. All of your wrongful shit played out there in front of you while you're being pumped from behind by someone you've hurt. That you've screwed over in life. Or worse, worse still...some person who doesn't really love you anymore. No one to ever look at again, make contact with. Just you being fucked as your life splashes out across this big headboard in the Devil's bedroom." Both the dark comedy and the morality rely on the dissonance between contemporary physical license and the memory of ethical injunctions from a higher power.

Horton Foote

Horton Foote is a substantially different case from Conor McPherson and Neil LaBute, both in his lifelong adherence to Christianity and reliance on a subtext of religious implication. Raised in Wharton, Texas, in a family that valued church affiliation, Foote observed the strength his mother's family found in the Methodist church. He was especially attracted to the hymns his mother would sing and to the biblical stories he learned at an early age. After his mother moved to the Christian Science Church in the 1930s, her oldest son eventually followed. The emphasis on self-reliance and devout living in Christian Science was also attractive to Foote's wife Lillian Vallish Foote, who joined her husband in the faith. Such a history supports the writer's assertion that he is "a very religious" person who contends that all religious belief sustains people of whatever persuasion.

But as religious as he is, Foote also warns that his work is not written from that "point of view." There are, in fact, only a few religious characters in his plays and films. Ludie Brooks, a minister who struggles with grief in an early eponymous teleplay; Carrie Watts, the hymn-singing older woman in *The Trip to Bountiful*; and Rosa Lee, the Baptist wife in *Tender Mercies*, form a religious minority in the

Foote canon. Even fewer are the passages in which these characters assert specific religious notions, let alone ideologies. And among that small chorus, many of the loud voices express a fanaticism that is alien to the spirit of Foote's work. Mrs. Coons, the woman who confronts Horace on the train in *Lily Dale,* and Mabel and Vonnie, neighbors in *The Roads to Home* who bring religious instructions but little human help to Annie, often alienate the major characters and, by implication, the audience as well. Evangelism and secretly violent behavior, even when dressed as religious piety, is never normative in Foote's imaginative world.

Foote's own position is further camouflaged by his employment of found art from his home place, Wharton, Texas. He uses the language, characters, and stories of that particular place, reproducing as truthfully as possible the facts of their history. The people of Wharton are, he asserts, "the real mythmakers" because they are living realities "rooted in a time and place."[5] His primary goal is to reproduce their stories without any conscious religious agendas. And yet his plays and films establish remarkably rich subtexts, whose textures rely on "something" asserting "itself" from his "sense of living." While he does not write from a religious perspective, the tension between his desire to report accurately and his own deeply felt religious convictions creates Foote's unique form of mythic realism.

Take, for example, the issue of disease. There are no Christian Scientists in Foote's work, faith healing is not a choice for his characters, and the medical profession is treated respectfully. The rhetoric of his religious persuasion is not part of the text of his stories. And yet many of them are about the emotional component in sickness. In *The Road to the Graveyard,* for example, the fighting in the Darst family is linked to the mother's systolic abnormalities. As Lyda explains, "Mama is red in the face and got to choking and I had to nearly put my arm out of joint knocking her on the back. The others were too busy fighting even to notice she was about to fall out. We take her to the doctor to get her high blood pressure down and they come over and fight and raise it up again." In *Road to the Graveyard* conflicts lead to sinking spells, worry gives rise to rashes, and change stimulates "sick headaches," which cause upset stomachs. A similar neurasthenia appears late in *The Orphans' Home* cycle, only temporarily relieved by unnecessary operations. Although Foote does not explore the issue in any argumentative way, disease is linked with inward or possessive love. Implicitly, he suggests there are better paths to healing.

The most obvious alternative is that offered to Mac Sledge by Rosa Lee in *Tender Mercies.* Following the loving path of her God, Rosa Lee focuses on life, not death, and is thankful for every chance to offer her care. As Mac begins to experience one of his fits of anger and self-doubt after meeting with his ex-wife, Rosa Lee tries to comfort him with her reminder that "I love you, you know. And every night when I say my prayers and I thank the Lord for his blessings and his tender mercies to me, you and Sonny head the list." Her love, which she sees as a gift from God, is directed at Mac's alcoholism, portrayed as a sickness of body and spirit. His wife helps Mac set boundaries when she says he can't drink in her presence and can't express destructive anger toward her and Sonny. But mostly she feeds him emotionally, offering him graceful living and a home. God's loving nature expressed through Rosa Lee's devotion and care inspire healing in Mac and his new family.

Such love, Foote writes, inspires an intense desire for personal identity. Foote's most ambitious portrait of this need is the lives of Horace Robedaux and Elizabeth Vaughn in Foote's nine-play cycle *The Orphans' Home*. Orphaned at an early age by the death of his father and the remarriage of his mother to a man who rejects him, Horace lives an emotionally placeless life. Indicative are his sometimes comic attempts at placing a tombstone on his father's grave. No one, not even a cemetery caretaker, can tell him which grave is his father's. After many missteps and confusing attempts at orienting himself within his family and society, Horace finally develops a loving relationship with Elizabeth Vaughn. Their marriage gives him the emotional and spiritual sense of place which heals him. As he declares to Elizabeth in *Valentine's Day*, "I am no orphan, but I think of myself as an orphan, belonging to no one but you . . . . I've begun to know happiness for the first time in my life. I adore you. I worship you . . . and I thank you for marrying me." For her part, Elizabeth in *Courtship* elopes with Horace against the will of her father, the most powerful man in town. She is willing to risk rejection by and alienation from her parents in order to live as she desires. The love between Horace and Elizabeth inspires them to feel and courageously express their own personhood.

The final garden scene in *Tender Mercies* imagines this sense of self as god's will for mankind. Following the death of Mac's daughter in an automobile accident, he tends the garden as he confesses to Rosa Lee that he was once in a similar crash but survived. He continues that the previous night he prayed to God for an answer to why he lived and his daughter died. But he got no answer to his prayers, he says. Then, reflecting on his own experience, he adds,

> You see, I don't trust happiness. I never did, I never will.

Although Rosa Lee does have a response to Mac revealed earlier in her own prayer—that life is a mysterious course that we need not control—she does not comment on his genuine unhappiness. Instead she embodies the grace-inspired love that encourages Mac's self-reflection. In the midst of his confusion and despair, Rosa Lee comforts him as he explores his inability to have faith in an order beyond himself. Rather than deny or fuse with his pain, the wife inspires his growing clarity, courage, and responsibility.

While foregrounded in earlier works like *Tender Mercies* and *The Orphans' Home*, such images of identity and community are marginal in Foote's recent work. More typical in these dramas is the life of the spirit offered as an alternative to a broken physical and material world, as in *The Carpetbagger's Children,* which premiered at the Alley Theater in Houston in June of 2001. Written in homage to Anton Chekhov's *The Three Sisters,* the play is structured in imitation of Brian Friel's *The Faith Healer.*[6] It is the story of the Thompson family, told almost exclusively in monologues by three sisters, Cornelia, Grace Anne, and Sissie. Early in the first speech of the play, Cornelia focuses on the life of another sister, Beth, who died in her youth. Their deceased sibling was, according to Cornelia, "Papa's favorite. Mama's too. Mine. Everybody's." More than that, she was beautiful, stylish, and the natural leader of the family. When she became sick, the local doctors couldn't diagnose the malady, and so the family took her to specialists in New Orleans. Unfortunately, her disease was diagnosed there as incurable, a reality which the family and town conspired to keep from Beth.

And then in a passage reminiscent of Jesus's return to Jerusalem, Cornelia describes the final days of their sister, being carried off the train, and lifted onto a wagon on a street covered with straw so that the ride would be less jolting, and so that the wagons and horses passing the front of their house would be as quiet as possible:

And we all prayed day and night for God to make her well.

Although their prayers are not answered, the people of Harrison create a powerful sense of community in their love of Beth. Though Cornelia's worshipfulness toward her dead sister colors her impressions, the scene recovers the sense of a sacred place named in the Hebrew word *beth.* Without any religious declaration, and even with the denial of faith healing in the story, Foote sketches a version of how people would treat each other under a state of grace.

The seminal work for this physical hunger for the spiritual is *Alone,* an original teleplay written for Showtime and aired in December of 1997. It chronicles the life of John Webb, a farmer in his seventies, as he copes with the loss of his wife of 52 years, Bessie. John lives an emotionally rich and courageous life; he knows who he is and what he values. And he is grounded in family life. He enjoys as much as possible his nephews, Carl and Gus Jr., and their wives and children, even though they are obsessively interested in oil leases and the many distractions of popular culture, especially television. John's two daughters, Grace Anne and Jackie, and their husbands, Gerald Murray and Paul, are more loving. They return to help on the farm, with Paul becoming a caring companion to John, offering solace by recognizing the powerful and enduring love between Bessie and John.

But John is not finally sustained by this family any more than by his courageous identity. It is the faith he shares with two aging African Americans, Grey and Sarah Davis, that strikes the resonant final note of the film. Remembering that John always loved devil's food cake, they visit him to share that delicacy and memories of Bessie. Sarah remembers that the beloved wife always preferred the song "Shall We Gather at the River," which Sarah then sings, half to herself, in their shared moment of reflection. As the three aging people welcome a profound silence, Grey sanctifies it as a "Blessed. Blessed. Blessed quiet" and John echoes Sarah's words and sentiment in declaring that they all shall "gather at the river, The beautiful, the beautiful river." Lonely in their experience of mutability and death, the three believers share their memories in the service of comfort. In the process they gain a degree of transcendence by uniting the living and dead and looking to a river of eternity, which they believe will bring them peace.

Though separated by nationality, age, and personal religious views, these three playwrights share a concern for the alienation of contemporary life from the comfort of an ordering sense of the transcendent, the "Soul" asked to clap and sing in Yeats' "Sailing to Byzantium." But their responses to this absence are diverse. Conor McPherson in *Shining City* seeks to liberate belief from the reductive rules and clichés of religious, social, and psychological theories. Instead he invites his audience into the liminal space of his dramas, where belief is restored to its primal impulse—to draw one's vision on the walls of the uncanny. Neil LaBute is more anxious than McPherson over the loss of traditional morality's call to guilt and responsibility—toward family, community, and history. Without healthy religious controls, the self-absorption and opportunism of latter-day capitalism spins things out of control in his dramas. Like the other two playwrights, Horton Foote admits and reacts to the "nothing" and "nowhere" that surrounds many of his characters. And yet, unlike McPherson and LaBute, Foote finds solace in the order of the universe, a cycle imagined as loving and beneficent, beyond the chaos of individual lives.

NOTES

1. This insight and quote were obtained from Conor McPherson in an interview with the author on October 2, 2004.

2. From the October 2, 2004 interview.

3. From the October 2, 2004 interview.

4. This quote is from Conor McPherson's correspondence with the author dated June 16, 2003.

5. Taken from "The Artist as Myth-Maker." Lecture by Horton Foote at the University of Texas at Arlington, November 16, 1988; unpublished manuscript courtesy of Horton Foote.

6. These insights into *The Carbetbagger's Children* were conveyed by Horton Foote in a telephone interview with the author on February 11, 2002.

FURTHER READING

Bigsby, C.W.E. *Modern American Drama, 1945–2000*. Cambridge: Cambridge University Press, 2000.

Castleberry, Marion. "Remembering Wharton, Texas." *Horton Foote: A Casebook.* Edited by Gerald C. Wood. New York: Garland, 1998. pp. 13–33.

Dickson, Mary. "Who's Afraid of Neil Labute?" *Salt Lake City Weekly* Septempber 21, 1998: par. 1–35.

Foote, Horton. *"Roots in a Parched Ground," "Convicts," "Lily Dale," "Widow Claire": The First Four Plays of "The Orphans' Home" Cycle.* New York: Grove, 1988.

Holden, Stephen. "In Summer's Popcorn Season, Appreciating the Champagne." *New York Times* September 4, 1998, E1, E10.

Johns, Ian. "Shining in the Dark of Despair." *The Times* June 7, 2004.

Kennedy, Dana. "A Tranquil Authority on Degrees of Cruelty." *New York Times* August 16, 1998: AR 9, AR12.

LaBute, Neil. *The Distance from Here.* New York: Overlook, 2003.

Lahr, John. "The Makeover Artist." *The New Yorker* June 18 & 25, 2001: 170–71.

———. "Touch of Bad." *The New Yorker* July 5, 1999: 42–49.

———. "Whatever: Neil LaBute Turns Psychology into Behavior." *The New Yorker* May 27, 2002: 120–21.

McPherson, Conor. "Author's Note." *The Weir and Other Plays.* New York: Theatre Communications Group, 1999.

Smith, Dinitia. "A Filmmakers Faith in God, if Not in Men." *New York Times* June 23, 1999: E1, E4.

Wood, Gerald C. "Horton Foote: An Interview." *Post Script: Essays in Film and the Humanities* 10.3 (Summer 1991): 3–12.

———. "Old Beginnings and Roads to Home: Horton Foote and Mythic Realism." *Christianity and Literature* 45 (Spring/Summer 1996): 359–72.

———. *Horton Foote and the Theater of Intimacy.* Baton Rouge: Louisiana State University Press, 1999.

———. "The Physical Hunger for the Spiritual: Southern Religious Experience in the Plays of Horton Foote." *The World Is Our Home.* Edited by Jeffrey J. Folks and Nancy Summers Folks. Lexington: University Press of Kentucky, 2000. 244–58.

———. *Conor McPherson: Imagining Mischief.* Dublin: Liffey, 2003.

Zalewski, Daniel. "Can Bookish Be Sexy? Yeah, Says Neil LaBute." *New York Times* August 18, 2002: 10, 22.

❧

Biblical Drama in Britain and North America

Martha Greene Eads

Christianity is a dramatic faith. Jesus's directive to his followers to reenact his final meal with them shaped liturgical worship, and theater scholars have long concluded that this celebration of the Last Supper, also called Communion or the Eucharist, was the source from which Western religious drama sprang. Depicting the Christian concepts of Incarnation and Redemption—God's becoming the man Jesus in order to give His life for humankind—is a monumental challenge creative artists of all kinds, including painters, sculptors, composers, and poets, have relished.

EARLY BIBLICAL DRAMA IN EUROPE

The official relationship between Christianity and drama has, however, often been strained. With the rise of Roman Christendom came the decline of theater, a decline St. Augustine noted with approval in 400 A.D. Misgivings about the deceptiveness of acting and disapproval of actors' lifestyles contributed to the virtual eradication of formal theater in Christian Europe by the sixth century. Ironically, however, the Church itself celebrated Christianity's dramatic elements in increasingly complex ways, enhancing celebrations of the Eucharist by adding antiphonal exchanges and having priests adopt the roles of characters in accounts of Jesus's resurrection from the dead. Over time, as more scenes were added, liturgical Latin gave way to local languages and the dramatic services' popularity grew, the action moved from the cathedral choirs to the naves. By the early thirteenth century, many productions had moved outdoors to accommodate crowds. In 1210, Pope Innocent III ordered them out of the church entirely, and soon trade guilds began taking over the plays' production and moving them to community gathering places, sometimes on large wagons serving as stages. Although they added secular, comical features; local, anachronistic elements; and regional expressions, guild members retained the approval of local Roman Catholic clergy and continued to use the plays to illustrate events from the Bible and instruct audiences in Church doctrine and practice.

In their own day, these biblical scenes were often called "miracles," although most drama historians today reserve that term for discussing plays about saints' lives and use the term "mysteries" for dramas based directly on the Bible. The term's significance lies not so much in its relation to the plays' subject matter as it does their roots in the trade guilds. "Mystery" is derived from the French "mystere" or "metier," words associated with trade guilds. Alternatively, scholars sometimes refer to "cycle plays" because the guild productions generally featured a cycle of several short plays, rather than just one. Yet another term for these medieval biblical dramas is "Corpus Christi plays" because many were performed in honor of Corpus Christi, the Latin term for the body of Christ. In a papal bull in 1311, Pope Clement V directed communities to hold processions honoring the Eucharistic elements on the Feast of Corpus Christi, celebrated two months after Easter. In many communities throughout Europe as well as in England, guild members began presenting dramatic tableaux on Corpus Christi Day as displays of religious piety, civic duty, and organizational prosperity.

Often, a particular theme or concern unified individual cycles of plays. In *The Play Called Corpus Christi* (1966), V.A. Kolve shows that the individual plays within a cycle work together to illustrate salvation history. In other words, a cycle is not merely an "anthology" of evolved liturgical plays; it is a set of stories carefully chosen to a specific end. Kolve explains his view of the genre by linking it to the period's devotional practices:

> Drama in the later Middle Ages sought to increase the emotional richness and depth of man's existence as a creature under God....Men were taught that by feeling—by the experience of pity, grief, and love for Mary and Christ in their human roles—they could best come to an understanding of the Godhead, to a true awareness of the price of their salvation, and to an adequate sorrow for their own sin. They were invited above all to contemplate the human tragedy of the Passion, and through that contemplation to share in its transcendental victory.

Kolve attributes to the medieval dramatists the same focus that directs a preacher planning a sermon.

One of the plays' primary functions was almost certainly to promote repentance before communion. Scholar Eleanor Prosser explains the link between the plays and the religious practice:

> There would seem to be an intimate relation between the cycles and the text for the office for Corpus Christi: "Repent now. Partake not of Christ's Body unworthily." Recognizing this relationship is, I believe, essential if we are to approach the plays with an accurate understanding of their purpose. The cycles were not compiled by a loose following of chronology, from Creation to Judgment. Episodes have been carefully selected to fulfill a strictly theological theme: man's fallen nature and the way of his Salvation.

While she adds that she doubts that a complete repentance cycle "sprang full-blown from the Festival of Corpus Christi," Prosser nevertheless offers a persuasive and sensitive argument for the medieval biblical drama's unity and purpose. Although they also provide historians with fascinating clues about economic, social, and theological conditions during the eras in which they were produced, the medieval biblical plays' primary purposes were devotional.

Named for the towns and villages where they are believed to have been first performed, the surviving manuscripts of these plays were written collaboratively and thus have unknown authorship. Some of the most famous medieval English mystery cycles are *The Chester Plays*, composed as early as 1325 and first published from 1841 to 1847; *The Wakefield Plays*, composed around 1450 and first published in 1836 as *The Towneley Mysteries* (named for the family who owned the manuscript); *The York Plays*, possibly performed as early as 1376 and published in 1885; and *The N-Town Cycle*, composed around 1468 and published as *Ludus Coventriae* in 1841. Five of the thirty-two plays in the Wakefield cycle, including the often-anthologized "Second Shepherds Play," share a common vocabulary, a humorous yet devout perspective, and a distinctive nine-line stanza, leading scholars to conclude that the same "Wakefield master" wrote them.

As the gaps between these cycles' composition and publication dates suggest, biblical drama virtually disappeared from the English stage for several centuries. This disappearance took place for complicated theological and political reasons. Henry VIII began discouraging production of the popular Roman Catholic religious plays with the establishment of the Church of England in the 1530s, and their subsequent status depended on the convictions of his successors. In 1605, King James I proscribed naming God, Jesus Christ, the Holy Spirit, or the Trinity onstage, putting the events of Jesus's life completely off-limits to English dramatists. As a result, for most of the next three centuries, Christian playwrights in England and the countries under its political influence availed themselves of religious themes at will, but they kept a respectful distance from actual biblical stories and characters. The English Lord Chamberlain was given the authority to approve or ban plays based on their content in 1737, and that authority continued until 1968.

BIBLICAL DRAMA'S REVIVAL IN BRITAIN

Certainly, English dramatists continued to explore religious themes after the decline of the mystery play, and playwrights in the lands they colonized would eventually follow their lead. Plays ranging from Christopher Marlowe's sixteenth century *Doctor Faustus* to the many nineteenth century dramatizations of Harriet Beecher Stowe's *Uncle Tom's Cabin* were rife with religious meaning. Not until the end of the nineteenth century, however, did professional playwrights in both Britain and North America draw dramatic material openly and directly from the Bible. Drama critic Murray Roston speculates that critical biblical scholarship had posed so many challenges to Christianity by this time that dramatizing the Bible "was less an irreverence than an attempt at its defense."

Late Nineteenth Century to Mid-Twentieth Century

While he could hardly be described as a defender of traditional Christian faith, Oscar Wilde was the first of several playwrights to bring biblical material back to the English stage at the end of the nineteenth century. His *Salome* (1893) focuses on the first Christian martyr, John the Baptist, and was banned from London theaters not for its provocative themes but for its violation of the Jacobean proscription against naming Christ on stage. More cautiously than Wilde, Wilson Barrett only edged up to the Bible with his pageant melodramas *The Sign of the Cross* (1896), *The Daughters of Babylon* (1897), *Quo Vadis?* (adapted from Henry Sienkiewicz' novel in 1900), and *The Christian King* (1902). The popularity of such religious pageants, as well as that of the American film *From the Manger to the Cross* (1912) chipped away at opposition to plays about biblical characters, and in 1913 the Lord Chamberlain gave Beerbohm Tree permission to stage Louis N. Parker's *Joseph and His Brethren*. Playwrights who followed Parker's lead and adapted biblical and apocryphal stories included Arnold Bennett (*Judith*, 1919), E. Temple Thurston (*Judas Iscariot*, 1923), Clemence Dane (*Naboth's Vineyard*, 1925), D. H. Lawrence (*David*, 1926), James M. Barrie (*The Boy David*, 1926), and James Bridie (*Tobias and the Angel*, 1930; *Jonah and the Whale*, 1932; *Susannah and the Elders*, 1937; and *The Sign of the Prophet Jonah* and *Jonah 3*, both for radio in 1942). Along with these English playwrights, the Irish poet and dramatist William Butler Yeats published *The Resurrection*, one of his most haunting dramas, in 1931.

While these playwrights wrote for the commercial stage, British church dramatists made up a second group of early twentieth century writers to stage biblical stories. Although he was a successful commercial director, William Poel wanted to stage the late medieval morality play *Everyman* in London's Westminster Abbey cloister. Having been turned down by the Dean and Chapter, he then approached church officials at Canterbury. Granted permission to stage the play in the Master's Court of the Charterhouse, Poel presented *Everyman* and *The Sacrifice of Isaac* on July 13, 1901. *Everyman* then went to London's Imperial Theatre for a month and toured the United States. One of *Everyman*'s cast members, Nugent Monck, established the English Drama Society four years later, staging *The Interlude of Youth* and, a year later, nativity plays from the Chester Cycle in Chelsea and Chester. Monck prepared to revive the *Ludus Coventriae* in 1909, but he was charged with violating the Blasphemy Law and discontinued the English Drama Society.

Although his efforts to revive medieval religious drama met with considerable opposition, Nugent Monck won the respect of George Kennedy Alan Bell, who served as Dean of the Canterbury Cathedral in the late 1920s. In 1925, Bell proposed that the Cathedral begin staging a nativity play in the nave each year. Having won the support of his fellow clergy, Bell asked poet John Masefield to write a play for Canterbury and commissioned Gustav Holst to compose the music. Performed on the Cathedral's nave steps on May 28 and 29, 1928, Masefield's *The Coming of Christ* played to more than 6,000 people. With the success of this first play, Bell established the Canterbury Festival of Music and Drama and turned to Nugent Monck for the 1929 play: a revival of *Everyman*.

Unlike Nugent Monck, who was a professional actor and director, John Masefield was more interested in writing poetry and fiction than drama. Today, his plays receive little critical attention. He was, however, most definitely a writer of stature in his own day, being chosen poet laureate in 1930 over Rudyard Kipling, William Butler Yeats, A. E. Housman, and Walter de la Mare. Masefield had certainly been prolific by the time he became poet laureate, having already published thirty volumes of verse and verse drama, ten novels, six prose plays, and fourteen other prose works.

Although he was not an orthodox Christian, Masefield was nevertheless drawn to the Bible for dramatic inspiration, having already written the two biblical plays *Good Friday* (1916) and *The Trial of Jesus* (1922) for production at a private theater he and his wife had established. (*Good Friday* eventually opened in London in 1917, and *The Trial of Jesus* in 1932 after an initial rejection by the Lord Chamberlain.) Both plays focus on the historical figure of Pontius Pilate and his wife Procula, with the addition of Jesus and several other characters in *Trial*.

Masefield's Canterbury play, *The Coming of Christ*, focuses on Jesus' birth rather than on his trial and death. The first half of the one-act play is set in heaven and treats the debate of the pre-incarnate Christ, whom Masefield calls the Anima Christi, with four angels. Warning the Anima Christi against putting on flesh, the angels identify human greed as the cause of destruction and betrayal. The second half of the play focuses on Christ's coming to earth but nevertheless maintains an otherworldly quality. The magi enter to the accompaniment of a chorus, voicing their hope that the new king for whom they look will satisfy their deepest longings: "That the fierce be kind," "That greed be for the things of Heaven / And that the world's injustice be made even," and "That man may see God making fair / Each daily thing; God helping man; / And Death a wisdom in the plan." As the magi exit, the three shepherds enter and discuss the injustices they suffer. Eventually, the curtain at the top of the choir steps opens to reveal the Mother and child, to whom the three kings and three shepherds offer gifts. Joined by the choir, they move out into the transept as the Mercy, the Light, the Sword, and the Power speak of God's leading and urge the audience to worship.

While the success of *The Coming of Christ* enabled George Bell to launch the Canterbury Festival and eventually paved the way for important twentieth century biblical drama festivals in other English towns, including Coventry, Chester, Wakefield, and Tewkesbury, the play did draw criticism. The best-known of the play's detractors was T. S. Eliot, who challenged Masefield's theological orthodoxy and asked in *The Criterion* "whether such an entertainment serves any cause of religion or art." Eliot was more approving of many of the Festival plays that followed, among them his own *Murder in the Cathedral* in 1935, poet Charles Williams's *Thomas Cranmer of Canterbury* in 1936, and detective novelist Dorothy L. Sayers's *The Zeal of Thy House* in 1937 and *The Devil to Pay* in 1939.

Although their Canterbury plays were not strictly biblical dramas, both Charles Williams and Dorothy L. Sayers did write other scripts based on biblical texts: his *Seed of Adam* and her nativity play *He That Should Come* and radio drama cycle *The Man Born to Be King*. While *The Seed of Adam* is largely a footnote in drama history, Sayers's plays had considerable social and theological significance. *He That Should Come* first was performed as a British Broadcasting Corporation radio play on Christmas Day, 1938, and was soon published with directions for stage production. The play was noteworthy for its rustic setting and casual, sometimes slangy language. Sayers explains her approach in her "Note to Producers":

> I feel sure that it is in the interests of a true reverence towards the Incarnate Godhead to show that His Manhood was a real manhood, subject to the common realities of daily life; that the men and women surrounding Him were living human beings, not just characters in a story; that, in short, He was born, not into "the Bible," but into the world.

After hearing *He That Should Come*, a rural BBC listener observed that "it's nice to think that people in the Bible were folks like us."

Sayers's use of vernacular speech contributed significantly to the success of *He That Should Come*, but it created challenges for her as she worked on her next radio project. Pleased with the reception of *The Man Born to Be King*, the BBC's Director of Religious Broadcasting asked Sayers in early 1940 to write a series of 30-minute plays for broadcast during the Sunday evening *Children's Hour*. Sayers replied that she had long wanted to dramatize Christ's life but that the proscription against depicting any member of the Trinity on stage had been an obstacle. Perhaps radio would be the medium in which she could pursue this possibility—using "natural speech." The Director affirmed Sayers's position and outlined their project for the Censor of Plays at the Lord Chamberlain's Office, who granted his permission. Although the press cautioned the public against the production with such headlines such "BBC 'Life of Christ' in Slang" and "Gangsterisms in the Bible Play," the biblical radio cycle, which aired between Dec. 21, 1941 and Oct. 18, 1942, proved a remarkable success. Slightly over twelve percent of adult BBC listeners tuned in to the second installment of the children's series, and the Director estimated that more than two million adults listened over the next year. BBC historian Kenneth M. Wolfe asserted in 1984 that " [t]he Sayers cycle rooted the lectionary of the Church of England in storytelling and theatre.... It was colloquial and perhaps convincing: above all it was popular, and the common people heard it gladly. That it was the most astonishing and far-reaching innovation in all religious broadcasting so far is beyond dispute."

In *The Man Born to Be King,* her effort to present the biblical account of Jesus's life to a twentieth-century radio audience, Sayers strove for realism and particularity. Her high regard for the material world as the site of divine activity necessitated an emphasis on Christ's fully human existence in a particular place and time, signaled by his and the other characters' use of vernacular speech. In an article published eleven years after *The Man Born To Be King,* Sayers explained that her artistic precedents, the medieval mysteries, were "always in contemporary idiom," "comedy was freely permitted; and there was no aesthetic mystique about simplicity and stylization: the aim was the greatest possible realism and a determination to show the events as living historical fact." In adopting the medieval dramatists' strategies, Sayers made the events of Jesus's life seem newly relevant for twentieth century listeners.

BIBLICAL DRAMA IN THE UNITED STATES

Plays in the First Half of the Twentieth Century

Across the Atlantic, playwrights were attempting to show the relevance of biblical stories in other ways. Ridgely Torrence and Marc Connelly each used Bible-based plays to build bridges between black and white Americans. Torrence's

Simon the Cyrenian (1917) and Connelly's *Green Pastures* (1930), gospel drama-tizations with all-black casts, challenged audiences to consider whether Christianity really is a faith that transcends race—one in which, as the apostle Paul claims in Galatians 3:28, "there is neither Jew nor Greek." Their efforts inspired—or provoked—the renowned African American poet Langston Hughes to adopt the genre, as well.

Ironically, the two dramatists who so powerfully used biblical material to promote racial equality in the theater and in the Church were neither black nor Christian. Moreover, both Torrence and Connelly have been criticized for misun-derstanding and misrepresenting black life in America. Torrence's *Simon the Cyrenian* and Connelly's *Green Pastures* were, however, groundbreaking plays in their day, extending new theatrical opportunities to African Americans and launching debates about race and faith.

John Masefield himself read Torrence's groundbreaking biblical play shortly after his *Good Friday* opened in London, writing in a November 2, 1917, letter to Margaret Bridges, "I've also got '3 plays for a negro theater' which may be rather fun." Among Torrence's *Plays For A Negro Theater* was *Simon the Cyrenian*, a one-act about Christ's crucifixion. Although Masefield does not describe to Bridges the play's impression on him, *Simon the Cyrenian* and its companion plays had a profound effect on the American theater. The African American activ-ist and editor W. E. B. Du Bois quoted reviewer Percy MacKaye in the June 1917 issue of *The Crisis* as having described the trilogy's New York opening on April 5, 1917, as "indeed an historic happening. Probably for the first time, in any compa-rable degree, both races are here brought together upon a plane utterly devoid of all racial antagonisms—a plane of art in which audience and actors are happily peers, mutually cordial to each other's gifts of appreciation and interpretation."

Produced by Emilie Hapgood and directed by the young scene designer Robert Edmond Jones, *Simon the Cyrenian* opened with its companion one-acts, *Granny Maumee* and *The Rider of Dreams*, at the Garden Theatre. Somewhat surprisingly, even the trilogy's black crucifixion drama initially escaped harsh criticism. Simply staging any professional biblical play was still a risky venture; although the American theater had no Lord Chamberlain to ban potentially blasphemous plays, professional playwrights in the United States were generally as cautious as their English counterparts. Audiences in 1917 could well have been expected to object to productions that did anything more than present cautious re-tellings of the Christian story.

At first glance, Ridgely Torrence's *Simon the Cyrenian* is a fairly cautious religious play. Like most biblical dramas emerging at the time, Torrence's play fea-tures a set that could have come from a Sunday School text illustration. Its diction is elevated, and it respectfully refrains from having an actor portray Jesus himself. Torrence distinguishes his play from other biblical dramas, however, by writing it for black actors. Although Christian tradition has recognized Simon of Cyrene, Jesus's cross-bearer, to be African, Torrence's stage notes indicate that all the play's characters are black. Writing about *Plays For A Negro Theater*, African American poet and anthologist James Weldon Johnson marveled "how Mr. Torrence, a white man, could write plays of Negro life with such intimate knowledge, with such deep insight and sympathy."

Although its characters are black, making it an appropriate companion piece to *Granny Maumee* and *The Rider of Dreams*, *Simon the Cyrenian* is the only verse drama among the three one-acts (although with little rhyme and a relatively free meter). Furthermore, its subject matter and dialogue reflect an experience unlike that of the more stereotypical African American characters in *Granny Maumee* or *The Rider of Dreams*. Its exotic setting and themes give it a majestic rather than a domestic quality, and it focuses on historical figures instead of on characters inspired by Torrence's black neighbors in Xenia, Ohio. In the play, Pilate's wife Procula frets in her garden over her dreams of Jesus of Nazareth. She enlists the aid of the Egyptian queen Acte in sending for the revolutionary Simon of Cyrene, hoping he will start a riot to deliver Jesus from the Romans. Having been moved by a glimpse of Jesus, Simon tells Acte that Jesus—not a black revolutionary—will save Africa. When Acte accuses him of losing his zeal for freeing their continent, Simon explains that Jesus is the representative of universal suffering. Offstage, cries for Jesus's crucifixion grow louder, and three mockers bearing a scourge, a crown of thorns, and a scarlet robe cross the stage on their way to execute Jesus. Preparing to rush offstage to rescue Jesus from his Roman captors, Simon obeys a mysterious voice that directs him to put away his weapon, warning that "they that take the sword shall perish with the sword." Simon takes up his sword again when the mockers enter and taunt him for following Jesus, but the voice rebukes him, this time saying, "Overcome evil with good. Forgive your enemy." Simon then submits to his mockers, who dress him in the robe in which they had earlier dressed Jesus. They pretend to crown him with thorns, calling him "King of the Africans." As the voice declares, "If any man will come after me let him take up the cross and follow me," Roman soldiers place Jesus's cross on Simon's back. Retrieving the crown of thorns his mockers have tossed aside, Simon places it on his own head and declares, "I will wear this, I will bear this till he comes into his own." Then the curtain falls.

In depicting Simon's victimization, the play reveals Torrence's obvious concern about injustices being done to African Americans. The playwright knew that most members of his New York audience would be white, and his play implies that the mistreatment of the African Simon is the equivalent of abusing Christ. In addition to commenting on America's race problem, however, Torrence also used *Simon* to promote pacifism to a nation on the brink of World War. Unfortunately, few people had the opportunity to hear his message; the production folded after only ten days at the Garden and another week at the Garrick. Despite the brevity of their run, *Three Plays for a Negro Theater* made a mighty impression on James Weldon Johnson, who called April 5, 1917 "the date of the most important single event in the entire history of the Negro in the American theatre" and asserted that "nothing that has been done since has afforded Negro performers such a wide gamut for their powers." Edith J.R. Isaacs wrote in *The Negro in the American Theatre* that *Simon the Cyrenian* and its companion plays "[mark]...a turning point in Negro theatre history. They broke completely with all theatre stereotypes of Negro character....They made Negroes welcome in the audience. They showed that Negroes could appreciate a white man's contribution to the literature of their life, if it were written in truth and beauty."

Marc Connelly followed Torrence's lead with *The Green Pastures,* a biblical play that depicts events leading to Christ's crucifixion. Connelly, however, was to take a step further than Torrence in casting a black actor as the Lord God. While neither Connelly nor Torrence chose to show Jesus, having their crucifixion scenes take place offstage, Connelly's African American Lord God was his play's central character. Connelly could have chosen a safer course had he stuck more closely to his source, Roark Bradford's *Ol' Man Adam and His Chillun,* a re-telling of biblical stories published in 1928, but one of Connelly's most significant changes to Bradford's book was making God the Father black.

For Connelly, the adaptation of Christian faith to everyday African American life also yielded a heaven of fried catfish, cigars, and boiled custard, a vision that drama critics have found increasingly problematic. Even at the time of the initial production, the renowned black actor Richard B. Harrison hesitated before accepting the role of the Lord God. A devout Episcopalian, Harrison's misgivings about the play rose from both his religious convictions and his sense of ethnic loyalty. Not only was he worried that audiences might consider his portraying God blasphemous, but he was also uncomfortable with the play's depiction of African American folk life. After consulting with a prominent Episcopal clergyman, however, Harrison accepted the lead role. Robert Edmond Jones, who had directed Torrence's *Three Plays for a Negro Theater,* was to design sets and costumes; Hall Johnson would lead the music; and Connelly would direct the play himself.

After five weeks of rehearsal, *The Green Pastures* opened on February 26, 1930, in New York's Mansfield Theater. Concerns about negative public reaction proved unfounded; the show was a hit. The next morning's reviews were unanimously positive, with *The World* theater critic Robert Littell's explaining that his article would appear in the following day's paper because he had stayed to see the end of the show instead of leaving to submit his review. "In the meantime," he urged, "don't let anything delay you from running to the Mansfield Theater to buy tickets." Officials of the Roman Catholic Cardinal Newman Fund must have heeded his advice: on the morning after the show opened, they bought all the seats for the first benefit performance. Church leaders who might have been expected to balk at the play's handling of biblical material had instead given it their full support.

The play itself is set in an African American church in rural Louisiana, where Mr. Deshee, an elderly preacher, teaches his young pupils Bible stories. When the children ask about God and the Creation, the kindly minister responds in terms they can understand. His lesson gives way to a series of seventeen scenes leading to Christ's crucifixion. As a whole, the play is both comical and comic—comical in its depiction of human frailty and comic in presenting a struggle that leads to redemption. The play's comic struggle is not only human, however; Connelly's Lord God develops compassion through an encounter with an insightful human being.

By the play's conclusion, *The Green Pastures'* highly anthropomorphized deity has progressed from being an amiable but somewhat inept and impetuous creator to being a god who suffers alongside his people. In the August 13, 1930, issue of *The Christian Century*, drama critic Edward Steiner asserts that the Lord God's tentative quality is the source of *The Green Pastures'* appeal. Comparing Connelly's work to the celebrated Oberammergau Passion Play in Germany, Steiner writes:

> I am under no illusions. "The Green Pastures" has not softened the hard, grey pavement of Broadway, or perhaps made even a dent, but I felt that I and many in the crowded theater had something of a religious experience—a very simple one. We had a glimpse of a naive, kindly, perplexed God, and he touched our hearts as no God dissected by the philosophers or interpreted by the theologians has.

In "God on Stage: A Problem in Characterization (Marc Connelly's *Green Pastures*)," Paul T. Nolan asserts that Connelly's using *The Green Pastures* to work out his idea of God distinguishes it from more orthodox biblical drama. He explains:

> Connelly's achievement in *Green Pastures* is a remarkable one, but not...because he succeeded with a religious play in a secular age, but rather because he so completely secularized religious concepts that he made his auditors review, and perhaps revise, their social and humanistic beliefs in the light of the implications of their religious principles.

Nolan suggests that the play encourages humans to judge their own behavior rightly rather than reminding us of an inevitable divine judgment, traditional religious drama would have. In Connelly's Lord God's transformation, we see a very different repentance from that which Eleanor Prosser believes the medieval mystery plays prompted.

Alan S. Downer points out other differences between *The Green Pastures* and the older biblical plays, asserting similarities that seem to link Connelly's work to

English biblical drama serve a different purpose. He writes, "The anachronisms in the medieval plays were for the purpose of communication, to make plain the meaning of the stories. *The Green Pastures* is not concerned with the meaning of the stories it retells as much as with the manner of their retelling." John Mason Brown, however, makes no such distinction, writing, "When the Custard Maker offers de Lawd a ten-cent seegar, he is following precisely the same impulse which prompted the adoring shepherds in The Pageant of the Shearman and Tailors to present the Christ Child with mittens, a pipe, and a hat." Robert Withington agrees that the similarities are worth noting, asserting that particularities of time and place add realism to both the medieval drama and *The Green Pastures*. Pointing out that Connelly expressed surprise at the apparent inability of the English Lord Chamberlain who banned the stage version of *The Green Pastures* to "distinguish between orthodox sacrilege and a simple miracle play," Withington insists that Connelly knew the earlier tradition. Withington suggests that while he followed the episodic formula of the medieval biblical cycles, Connelly followed a more modern dramatic course in developing his characters. He concludes that the play's success demonstrates the Bible's lasting appeal and notes that while "the play was written with the spirit of the medieval dramatist[,]...the spirit of the public has changed, and cannot be restored to that of the Middle Ages."

For many, the treatment of race in *The Green Pastures* was revelatory enough to make it truly good news—a social gospel if not a theological one. Connelly's play presents in the African American experience a model of spiritual sensitivity and compassion to which every viewer could aspire. W. E. B. Du Bois, whose sociological study of the black Church would likely have equipped him to point out flaws in the play's handling of either African American life or religious experience, called *The Green Pastures* "an extraordinarily appealing and beautiful play based on the folk religion of Negroes." James Weldon Johnson described *The Green Pastures* as "something very little short of a miracle." Theater critic Brooks Atkinson praised Connelly for transcending "Negro comedy" to apprehend the timeless and universal, pronouncing the play a "divine comedy of the modern theater."

The Green Pastures' popular and critical success led to its running for a year and a half in New York's Mansfield Theatre before touring North America and returning to New York in 1936. The play won Connelly the Pulitzer Prize in 1930 and lead actor Richard B. Harrison the NAACP's 1931 Spingarn Medal for making the year's most significant contribution to his race. It was made into a Warner Brothers film in 1936 and revived in New York in 1951; *The Hallmark Hall of Fame* produced a version for television in 1957.

The play's popularity did, however, wane over time. The Broadway revival in 1951 ran for less than a month, and in 1970, Connelly acknowledged that the play would not withstand another production. "It could never be revived now, under the present climate," he said. "God, no. The Negro's picture of himself right now, in this unconscious snobbism in which he is existing, wouldn't allow it. He would denigrate the play, would say that this is Uncle Tomism, that this is what we're trying to get rid of." Increasingly, *The Green Pastures has* faced charges of Uncle Tomism. The 1936 film has become the subject of considerable study, most of it sharply critical.

Black Dramatists

The American theatrical tradition Connelly and Torrence helped establish, however, served as a springboard for the black writers who followed them. As early as 1935, Willis Richardson and May Miller called African Americans to take on the project white playwrights had initiated, writing, "Why does not the Negro dramatize his own life and bring the world unto him? Paul Green, Eugene O'Neill, and Marc Connelly cannot do it. They see that the thing is possible, and they are trying to do it; but at best they misunderstand the Negro because they cannot think black." Leslie Catherine Sanders explains that the work of such white playwrights "provided black dramatists with an irritant as well as a model."

Chief among the black dramatists who saw black drama by whites as both an irritant and a model was Harlem Renaissance poet Langston Hughes. Some critics believe that Hughes wrote his play *Mulatto* in response to Ridgely Torrence's *Granny Maumee*. Whether or not he was specifically responding to either Torrence or Connelly, Hughes wrote his own African American biblical drama, *Black Nativity*, in 1961, interweaving his original poetry with traditional Gospel music. Although it offers more music than script, *Black Nativity* continues to enjoy regular performances during the holidays.

Plays in the Second Half of the Twentieth Century in the United States and United Kingdom

Aside from Maxwell Anderson's *The Journey to Jerusalem,* an unmemorable blank-verse drama about the young Jesus (1940), and Archibald MacLeish's far more impressive *J.B.,* a re-telling of the story of Job (1958), commercial biblical plays were still slow in coming to the stage in the mid-twentieth century. Two more significant biblical musicals did, however, appear a decade after Langston Hughes's: Stephen Schwartz's *Godspell,* which opened off-Broadway at the Cherry Lane Theatre on May 17, 1971, before moving to the Promenade on Broadway, and Tim Rice and Andrew Lloyd Webber's *Jesus Christ Superstar,* which opened in New York's Hellenger Theatre on October 12 of the same year. Although *Superstar* was the younger of the two productions, Rice and Lloyd Webber had been working on their rock opera for several years, releasing the first song as a single in Great Britain in 1969. They wrote the rest of the show and then completed an entire album recording in July 1970. The American public's enthusiastic reception for the album gave them the confidence to stage the show in New York the following year. *Superstar* opened at London's Palace Theatre in its writers' native England on August 9, 1972.

Both *Godspell* and *Jesus Christ Superstar* depict the life of Jesus, emphasizing his humanity and minimizing (if not altogether ignoring) his divinity. *Godspell* envisions Jesus and his followers as a troupe of clowns in a cityscape and focuses more on his parables from the Gospel of Matthew than on his actual life. One of Jesus' followers, Judas, does betray him as in biblical accounts, but instead of being crucified, Jesus is killed on a fence. Unlike the Jesus in Matthew, *Godspell*'s Jesus experiences no resurrection, but his followers conclude the play by singing an increasingly spirited rendition of a reprise of the hit song "Day By Day" that begins with the new lyrics "Long Live God." In declining to depict the resurrection, and in suggesting that Jesus's post-crucifixion presence in the world rests in the convictions of his followers, *Godspell* reflects the Death of God theology William Hamilton and Thomas J.J. Altizer had outlined in their 1966 book *Radical Theology and the Death of God*. *Jesus Christ Superstar* also has roots in its contemporary culture; the Who's treatment of the Messiah myth in the 1969 rock opera *Tommy* was a likely influence. The central figure in *Jesus Christ Superstar* really is Jesus, though—an all-too human Jesus misunderstood and betrayed by Judas. Whatever their theological irregularities, both musicals became blockbusters, with *Godspell* running for 2,651 performances in New York and *Jesus Christ Superstar* for 720 in New York and 3,358 in London. Both musicals became films in 1973.

As if to make up for the centuries religious drama had missed, increasing numbers of playwrights in Britain and North America turned to the Bible for material in 1980s and 1990s. Small-scale, purely devotional drama had never completely died out in individual churches, and that tradition yielded much larger public productions targeting religious audiences across the United States. Individual churches began staging religious plays on ever-grander scales, some of which drew crowds from far beyond their communities. St. Agnes Church in Atlantic Highlands, New Jersey; Hopewell United Methodist Church in Downington, Pennsylvania; First Baptist Church in Atlanta, Georgia; the Word of Life Bible Institute in Hudson, Florida; and the Roman Catholic Diocese of Santa Rosa, California, were only a few of the religious groups that advertised their elaborate biblical plays on the Worldwide Web as the twenty-first century began. The Mystery Players, a youth drama ministry with chapters in New Hampshire, New Jersey, and New York, performed for their home communities across the northeastern United States, drew viewers from Canada, and went on the road. Holy Family Church in Union City, New Jersey, produced the oldest of the American church-sponsored passion plays, billing its Easter drama as "America's Oberammergau." Established in 1915 as a "living prayer" for peace during World War I, the Holy Family Passion

Play ran weekends in March and April for audiences from New Jersey, New York, Pennsylvania, and Connecticut.

Even larger-scale, longer-running seasonal biblical plays, many of which developed out of church dramas, still take place annually across the United States. Thirteen of the 114 summer productions tracked by the Institute of Outdoor Drama are religious. *The Black Hills Passion Play* in Spearfish, South Dakota; *The Great Passion Play* in Eureka Springs, Arkansas; *Jesus of Nazareth* in Puyallup, Washington; *The Life of Christ Passion Play* in Townsend, Tennessee; *The Living Word* in Cambridge, Ohio; *The Louisiana Passion Play* in Ruston, LA; *Mid-Ohio Valley's Outdoor Passion Drama* in Parkersburg, West Virginia; *Worthy Is the Lamb* in Swansboro, North Carolina; and *Two Thieves and A Savior* in Fort Mill, South Carolina, are straightforward depictions of events in the life of Christ. *Two Thieves and a Savior* runs alternately with *The Deliverer,* which presents Christ's life alongside that of Barabbas, and *Anno Domini,* which dramatizes the story of Stephen, the first Christian martyr. *The Man Who Ran* (Disney, Oklahoma) presents the Old Testament story of Jonah alongside Christ's resurrection, and *The Promise* (Glen Rose, Texas) provides the narrative frame of a grandfather and grandchildren who discuss and sing about biblical days. *The Hill Cumorah Pageant* (Palmyra, New York) adds stories from the Book of Mormon to its dramatization of biblical events, and *The Mormon Miracle Pageant* (Manti, Utah) chronicles the early days of the Mormon church. Although they have charted a general decline in the popularity of outdoor dramas in recent years, the Institute reports that the 2000 attendance at the thirteen religious productions was nevertheless an impressive 475,389.

English communities staged cycle plays, as well, hoping to increase tourism and cultivate civic pride. Revivals of historic cycle plays in such cities as York began as early as the 1950s and provided new material for academic study. At Wakefield's Bretton Hall College, Martial Rose experimented with the Towneley Plays in 1958. Translating the manuscript into modern English, he staged twenty of the cycle's thirty-two plays that year. Nine years later, in 1967, John Hodgson performed the entire cycle at Bretton Hall College on Corpus Christi Day. In the same year, the Centre for Medieval Studies' Poculi Ludique Societas at the University of Toronto began producing medieval and early modern plays, many of which were in Middle English. Such educational productions, including landmark performances at Leeds and Lancaster in the 1970s, tested staging theories. A new academic field was developing from the work of scholars such as Richard Southern, who published *The Medieval Theatre in the Round* in 1957; Glynne Wickham, who published *Early English Stages* in 1959; and Rose, whose *Wakefield Cycle* translation appeared in 1961.

Professional theater people quickly saw promise in the mystery plays as they moved from the cathedral to the academy. Scholarly interest in the medieval biblical drama also inspired professional dramatists who sought innovative creative challenges. Tony Harrison and Bill Bryden's *The Mysteries* (1985) and Edward Kemp and Katie Mitchell's *The Mysteries* (1997) both re-presented medieval biblical drama for contemporary British audiences, struggling to update ancient material in the interest of their own social, artistic, and religious agendas. Although both Bryden and Mitchell directed their productions on thrust stages, Bryden's staging at London's Lyceum invited audience members to move among the performers. In contrast, Mitchell's staging at the Royal Shakespeare Company's Other Place was more formal. Instead of focusing on physical inclusivity, director Mitchell and dramaturg Edward Kemp used their play to highlight the gospel's wide social inclusivity. While playwright Harrison had written for and to his native northern England's working class, Mitchell and Kemp sought to address the concerns of even larger groups of marginalized peoples. The 1997 production cast a black actress as Eve and Mary, suggesting that the biblical message transcends racial barriers. Mitchell and Kemp also attempted to restore Jewish elements removed or twisted in the medieval mystery cycles. Mitchell and Kemp overturn the medieval plays' treatment of gender by minimizing the follies of Eve and Mrs. Noah and by highlighting admirable minor female characters such as Anne, the mother of Mary, and the prophetess Anna. A female Gabriel impregnated Mary in the 1997 stage version, and characters of the same sex kiss one another.

Challenging Views within Biblical Themes

Across the Atlantic a year later, two more playwrights used biblical drama to challenge traditional views of gender and sexuality. Terrence McNally's *Corpus Christi* opened at the Manhattan Theatre Club on October 13, 1998, and Paul Rudnick's *The Most Fabulous Story Ever Told* at the New York Theater Workshop on December 14 of the same year, both packing theaters and provoking picketers. While *Most Fabulous* re-envisions the Old Testament story of Adam and Eve as being about Adam and Steve, two gay men, and Jane and Mabel, their lesbian counterparts, *Corpus Christi* goes so far as to depict Jesus and some of his disciples as sexually active gay men.

While neither play made full use of its writer's full abilities, both showed the degree to which late twentieth century dramatists were willing to use biblical material to promote a social and political agenda—and the power biblical material still has to sell tickets. At the cinema, Australian actor and producer Mel Gibson demonstrated the same capacity with his far more orthodox but still controversial film, *The Passion of the Christ*, which grossed over $125 million during the first five days of its 2004 first run. What accounts for the continuing popularity of biblical drama after so many centuries? Dorothy L. Sayers lauds the

Christian story's dramatic potential in her 1949 essay "The Greatest Drama Ever Staged":

> So that is the outline of the official story—the tale of the time when God was the under-dog and got beaten, when He submitted to the conditions He had laid down and became a man like the men He had made, and the men He had made broke Him and killed Him. This is the dogma which we find so dull—this terrifying drama of which God is the victim and hero. If this is dull, then what, in Heaven's name, is worthy to be called exciting?

Over half a century after Sayers's pronouncement, two millennia after the birth of Christ, the Bible's account of his life, death, and resurrection remain compelling enough to intrigue dramatists and directors yet resilient enough to withstand the theological and artistic gymnastics through which they put it.

FURTHER READING

Atkinson, Brooks. "New Negro Drama of Sublime Beauty." *New York Times* February 27, 1930: 9,26.

Bevington, David. *Medieval Drama*. Chicago: Houghton-Mifflin, 1975. p. 228

Brown, John Mason. "The Ever Green Pastures." *Dramatis Personae: A Retrospective Show.* New York: Viking, 1963. 85–89.

Connelly, Marc. *Voices Offstage: A Book of Memoirs.* New York: Holt, Rinehart, and Winston, 1968.

Downer, Alan S. *Fifty Years of American Drama*. Chicago: Henry Regnery, 1951.

Du Bois, W. E. B. "Dramatis Personae: *The Green Pastures*." *The Crisis* 37:5 (May 1930) 162, 177–78.

———. "The New Negro Theatre." *The Crisis* 14:6 (June 1917): 80–81.

Eliot, T.S. Review of *The Coming of Christ*. *The Criterion* 7:4 (June 1928): 5–6.

Isaacs, Edith J. R. *The Negro in the American Theatre.* College Park, Maryland: McGrath, 1968.

Johnson, James Weldon. *Black Manhattan*. New York: Knopf, 1930.

Kolve, V. A. *The Play Called Corpus Christi.* Stanford: Stanford University Press, 1966.

Masefield, John. *The Coming of Christ.* New York: Macmillan, 1928.

———. *Letters to Margaret Bridges (1915–1919).* Edited by Donald Stanford. Manchester: Carcant, 1984.

"More History Plays Show Attendance Gains: Total Attendance Declines, But at Slower Rate," *U.S. Outdoor Drama* (Winter 2000): 1–2.

Nolan, Paul T. "God on Stage: A Problem in Characterization (Marc Connelly's *Green Pastures*)." *Xavier University Studies* 4:2 (May 1965): 74-84.

Prosser, Eleanor. *Drama and Religion in the English Mystery Plays.* Stanford: Stanford University Press, 1961.

Richardson, Willis, and May Miller. *Negro History in Thirteen Plays.* Washington: Associated Publishers, 1935.

Roston, Murray. *Biblical Drama in England.* Evanston: Northwestern University Press, 1968.

Sanders, Leslie Catherine. *The Development of Black Theater in America: From Shadows to Selves.* Baton Rouge and London: Louisiana State University Press, 1988.

Sayers, Dorothy L. "The Greatest Drama Ever Staged." *Creed or Chaos?* New York: Harcourt, Brace, 1949. p. 3–7.

———. *He That Should Come.* In *Two Plays About God and Man.* Norton, Connecticut: Vineyard, 1977. pp. 130–86.

———. "Types of Christian Drama: With Some Notes on Production," *Seven* 2 (March 1981): 88.

Steiner, Edward. "The Fashion Play of 1930." *Christian Century* (13 August 1930): 985–6.

Torrence, Ridgely. *Simon the Cyrenian.* In *Plays for a Negro Theater.* New York: Macmillan, 1917. 78–111.

Weales, Gerald. *Religion in Modern English Drama.* Philadelphia: University of Pennsylvania Press, 1961.

Withington, Robert. "Notes on the Corpus Christi Plays and 'The Green Pastures.'" *The Shakespeare Association Bulletin* 9 (Fall 1934): 193–97.

Wolfe, Kenneth M. *The Churches and the British Broadcasting Corporation, 1922–1956.* London: SCM, 1984.

Gay Drama

James Fisher

The term "gay drama," which most often refers to plays written by and for homosexuals, was coined in the mid-1960s as various marginalized groups—women, African Americans, Latinos, among others—sought liberation from the social constraints which denied them opportunity and equality in American life. Homosexual men, lesbians, bisexuals, and transgendered individuals are traditionally grouped together as "gay" within the realm of drama, but in the past few decades the term has also come to refer to a gay sensibility, meaning simply a collective means of viewing the world through the lens of gay culture. With the onset of the AIDS pandemic in the early 1980s, gay dramas have more overtly explored serious questions inherent in being homosexual in America and, to a significant extent, gay drama has dominated American stages in the last twenty years. Most gay dramas achieving mainstream acclaim have been by and about gay men, with the other sub-groups making strides in off-Broadway and fringe theaters. Alfred Kazin writes, "'The love that dare not speak its name' (in the nineteenth century) cannot, in the twentieth, shut up," but the emergence of a vigorous gay drama demonstrates that there is much to say on a subject about which the stage has been silent for centuries.

In reflecting on the history of homosexuals in American theater, Tony Kushner, author of *Angels in America,* arguably the most acclaimed "gay drama" of the late twentieth century, believes "there's a natural proclivity for gay people—who historically have often spent their lives hiding—to feel an affinity for the extended make-believe and donning of roles that is part of theater. It's reverberant with some of the central facts of our lives." Kushner identifies at least one of the reasons homosexuals find refuge and a necessary means of expression in drama, although even in theater homosexuals were as consigned to the "closet" as gays in other walks of American life prior to the liberated and liberating 1960s.

EARLY GAY DRAMAS IN THE UNITED STATES

Reaching back to the origins of theater and drama, gay playwrights have always been present (if not verifiably identified), but few chose, or were permitted, to present gay themes and characters. In America prior to the mid-twentieth century, openly gay dramatists or explorations of the subject in drama were socially unacceptable, although many gay dramatists were at work on U.S. stages, including leading figures like Clyde Fitch (1865–1909), a close friend and possible lover of Oscar Wilde, and Avery Hopwood (1882–1928), the most popular purveyor of stage farces in the 1910s and 1920s. Actors and designers were similarly compelled to keep their sexual "deviance" from public view and overt depictions of homosexuality in text or imagery were, quite simply, taboo.

From the Renaissance to the beginning of the twentieth century, theatrical history provides relatively subtle dramatic examples of homoeroticism and ambivalence toward traditional gender divisions, but little direct discussion of sexual difference can be found. In the eras of classical and Renaissance drama, sexual confusion was expressed in cross-dressing, a practice in which a performer appearing in drag (as a member of the opposite sex) blurs male/female boundaries. This enduring tradition spread across cultures and through the centuries to the present day, but did little to inspire serious dramatic explorations of the obvious, and not so obvious, issues of gender difference. By the late nineteenth century, dramatists occasionally depicted gay characters, although these were typically hidden by descriptions requiring the viewer to recognize a character's sexual preference without overt identification. Such hidden gay characters were usually peripheral to the main action of the play, sometimes as comic "sissies" or as an obstacle to the main action. Even these characters were few and far between until well into the twentieth century; the taboo of homosexuality in public discourse was so pervasive that any hint of it was too scandalous for theatrical presentations, and in offstage life as well. The late 1890s indecency trials of playwright Oscar Wilde were a tragic scandal that destroyed Wilde's life, but they served the essential purpose of bringing discussion of homosexuality into the open. Prior to the mid-1920s, however, few dramas in the English-speaking theater dealt with homosexuality in any manner.

GAY DRAMA IN THE TWENTIETH CENTURY

The first American play to feature homosexuality may be *The Drag* (1927) by Mae West (1892–1980), but it generated so much controversy that it closed prior to completing a tumultuous pre-Broadway tour. West's exploitive play, which features an onstage drag ball, set the stage for her next, *The Pleasure Man* (1928), which also included gay characters. West was a small part of a pervasive post-World War I movement of writers and artists inclined to delve into previously taboo subjects, ranging from sexuality and interracial marriage to politics and women's rights. In New York, local authorities successfully outlawed any depiction of "sex degeneracy, or sex perversion" on stages from 1927 to 1967, but some plays with gay characters or themes were reluctantly received, including British dramatist Mordaunt Shairp's *The Green Bay Tree* (1933). Shairp presents a homosexual character as a sinister figure, unfortunately instigating a trend of depicting gays as villains, pathetic deviants, or effeminate comic stereotypes.

In *The Children's Hour* (1934) by Lillian Hellman (1906–84), the question of a possible lesbian relationship between two teachers at a private girls' school inspired its climax, but Hellman stressed that her intention was to explore the corrosive power of a lie, not homosexuality. Secondary gay characters appear in a few American plays of the 1930s and 1940s, but they are rarely identified as such. Simon Stimson, the alcoholic choirmaster of *Our Town* (1938) by Thornton Wilder (1897–1975), is an example of such types in that he is comparatively unimportant to the play's main action and that he is depicted as a victim of a society to which he cannot conform. Wilder, a closeted gay man, led a discreet private life and many of his intimates believed homosexuality was a burden to him. In any case, Wilder's contemporaries would not have accepted any public acknowledgment of his sexual preferences even if he had been inclined to "come out." Gay characters do not otherwise appear in Wilder's work, and it can certainly be argued that Stimson's problems have nothing to do with sexuality since not a single word in the play suggests he is or is not a closeted gay man. Stimson is simply a character who does not fit in Wilder's conventional turn-of-the-century small-town setting; he is an outsider who may simply represent all those in marginalized or ostracized groups within American society of the early twentieth century.

Tennessee Williams

The dilemma of being a gay dramatist in the middle of the twentieth century is most evident in the life and work of one of America's finest dramatists, Tennessee Williams (1911–83). Simply put, Williams is the transitional figure of gay drama, moving the stage from avoidance to contemplation of homosexuals and their world, in and out of the closet. In short, Williams liberated sexuality from the invisible list of taboo subjects. His first important play, *The Glass Menagerie* (1944), includes no references to homosexuality (or sexuality in general) despite Williams's own sexual preferences and the fact that this "memory play" is at least partly autobiographical. Williams's alter-ego, Tom Wingfield, is a sensitive young man forced to work in a factory to support his domineering mother and fragile, repressed sister. Tom struggles to be a writer, a profession often serving as a stage or screen metaphor for homosexuals well into the 1960s. Williams subsequently explored the complex relationship of sex and love in a variety of forms, including a fraught dramatic conversation about homosexuality that seems to mirror American society's evolving attitudes. Williams's most characteristic plays feature darkly poetic imagery reflecting the philosophical questions of human existence, particularly in the struggle of romantic, emotionally fragile, or deeply damaged individuals striving to survive brutalizing reality. These characters are expressed through a stage language at once naturalistic and lyrical. In pondering the distance between illusion and reality in the Pirandellian sense, Williams's characters are caught up in personal struggles placing them in conflict with the accepted norms of their society.

Williams's plays, particularly his earliest, are ambivalent on the question of homosexuality, but over time his gay characters become more visible, opinionated, and certainly more diverse. In an interview, Williams stressed that, "Sexuality is part of my work, of course, because sexuality is a part of my life and everyone's life. I see no essential difference between the love of two men for each other and the love of a man for a woman; no essential difference, and that's why I've examined both." Williams's characters, gay or straight, feel the absence of love and exhibit a profound need for connection, but there is little doubt that, as a rule, Williams was writing about love not gender. Constraints on sexuality in Williams's time meant that his sexually confused characters—gay, straight, or something in between—are fugitives from mainstream society who can only be fulfilled through transgression against its strictures. These transgressions come, in the final analysis, at great personal cost that typically elevates Williams's plays to the level of tragedy.

Williams's Pulitzer Prize-winning *A Streetcar Named Desire* (1947) was a seismic event in its exploration of sexuality on stage, depicting a central female character who is promiscuous to the point of criminality, but who is also a tragic victim raped by her brutish brother-in-law, Stanley Kowalski. Blanche DuBois has sought sex as a replacement for love with increasing desperation and from increasingly younger men, a problem resulting from a harrowing death in Blanche's troubled past—the suicide of her young husband, Allan. Following their marriage, Allan's repressed homosexuality can only be understood as some unexplained weakness by the immature, sexually naive Blanche. She remembers that

> There was something different about the boy, a nervousness, a softness and tenderness which wasn't like a man's, although he wasn't the least bit effeminate looking—still—that thing was there....

Blanche, unable to comprehend the situation, fell into a deep confusion until she learned the truth "in the worst of all possible ways" by "coming suddenly into a room that I thought was empty—which wasn't empty, but had two people in it... the boy I had married and an older man who had been his friend for years..." Shocked and disoriented, Blanche expressed her "disgust" to the humiliated Allan. Cornered, Allan subsequently shot himself in despair and shame, setting Blanche's descent in motion. The fatal shot replays continually in her disturbed mind and, as a result, Allan's homosexuality is at the root of her sexual dysfunction. Despite desperate dalliances with countless others, Blanche is unable to escape the guilt she feels and the painful loss of a first love she cannot truly replace.

Williams's next produced play, *Summer and Smoke* (1948), does not deal directly with homosexuality, but centrally explores the relationship of sex and love. Alma Winemiller fears and rejects sexuality, which she equates with bestiality. Her confusing physical attraction for Dr. John Buchanan, whose view of sex is purely biological, sorely tests Alma's beliefs. For much of the play, the puritanical Alma retreats behind small-town proprieties and the safety of a weak suitor, Roger Doremus, an unacknowledged gay man who, she instinctively understands, poses no sexual threat to her. Ultimately, Alma's despair after John changes his views and marries a virtuous young girl instead of turning to Alma, leads her to a complete abandonment of resistance to sexuality, moving, as Williams explained in an interview, "from puritanical shackles to, well, complete profligacy."

In terms of homosexuality, Williams's controversial Broadway failure, *Camino Real* (1953), adopts a gay sensibility in its plea for a romanticized attitude toward life. Williams intermingles literary and historical characters in a phantasmagoric world combining Spanish folklore, Christian iconography, and the labyrinths of literary history. One of the characters, Baron de Charlus, borrowed from Proust, is an avowed homosexual and pointedly effeminate, a trait Williams himself claimed to dislike. More overtly masculine characters of ambiguous sexuality appear in Williams's plays of the mid-1950s and beyond with greater frequency. In *Orpheus Descending* (1957), Williams's protagonist, Val Xavier, a modern Orpheus, is a sensual poet inarticulately yearning for transcendence, either through art or sex. A less poetic version of this type is Chance Wayne, the young male hustler of *Sweet Bird of Youth* (1959), but it is Brick Pollitt, the alcoholic ex-athlete of Williams's Pulitzer Prize-winning *Cat on a Hot Tin Roof* (1955), that Williams's depiction of homosexuality begins to evolve.

Brick hates "fairies" and mocks the memory of the deceased gay couple who formerly owned his family's Southern plantation. Brick's athletic prowess is taken as a sign of hyper-masculinity, but Maggie, his sexually frustrated wife, knows otherwise and is distressed by his reckless drinking. It is not the end of Brick's athletic career that has brought on his drinking, but fears that his confused feelings for his deceased best friend, Skipper, who was a homosexual, suggest that he might be "a queer," as he puts it. Williams explained in an interview that Brick "went no further in physical expression than clasping Skipper's hand across the space between their twin beds in hotel rooms—and yet his sexual nature was not innately 'normal'." Brick also feels disgust for the "mendacity" that he finds around him, and finally comes to recognize within himself. Character and author meet in this attitude, for Williams understood as a gay man in 1950s America that mendacity, as Brick explains, is "a system that we live in." To some extent, Williams tries to have it both ways in *Cat*, for Brick is ultimately lured back to the marriage bed, leaving the thorny question of his true sexual nature unanswered.

Williams's long one-act drama, *Suddenly Last Summer* (1958), sketches a bleaker vision of homosexuality. The play begins in the aftermath of the violent and mysterious death of Violet Venable's poet son, Sebastian. She attempts to convince Dr. Cukrowicz to perform a lobotomy on her niece, Catherine, a witness to Sebastian's death at the hands of a mob of young men Sebastian sexually exploited. Devoured by his own promiscuous appetites in a frightening cosmos where only the most efficient predators survive, Sebastian is Williams's darkest image of a homosexual, but beginning with *Small Craft Warnings* (1972) his viewpoint undergoes a further evolution. Critics generally dismissed this play, but pointed out the embittered view of homosexuality expressed by Quentin, a middle-aged, second-rate screenwriter and avowed homosexual. The play, which is written in a series of connected confessional arias, allows Quentin to reflect on his way of life: "There's a coarseness, a deadening coarseness, in the experience of most homosexuals....Their act of love is like the jabbing of a hypodermic needle to which they're addicted but which is more and more empty of real interest and surprise."

Quentin also expresses amazement that Bobby, a young hustler, has "the capacity for being surprised by what he sees, hears and feels in this kingdom of earth" and painfully acknowledges that he himself has "lost the ability to say: 'My God!' instead of just: 'Oh, well'." Bobby presents an image of youthful wonder and a joy in his unexamined sexuality balancing Quentin's world-weariness. Critics seemed eager to believe that Quentin's disillusionment was some sort of final statement on homosexuality by Williams, ignoring the fact that he presents alternative opinions in the play, as in Bobby's erotic recollection of a bisexual encounter.

In two of his final plays, Williams returns to the subject of homosexuality. *The Notebook of Trigorin* (1981), Williams's free adaptation of Anton Chekhov's *The Seagull*, is largely faithful to its source except in that Williams converts the bored, middle-aged writer Boris Trigorin into a bisexual whose relationship with the imperious actress, Madame Arkadina, is merely a mask for his true desires. Similarly, Trigorin's relationship with Nina, an aspiring actress, is transformed by Williams into a casual affair intended to alleviate Trigorin's boredom which, like Quentin's, has a deadening quality. More significantly, in *Something Cloudy, Something Clear* (1981), Williams returns to the autobiographical "memory play" approach of *The Glass Menagerie*, converting his alter-ego from that play, Tom Wingfield, into an aspiring playwright named August who has left home and is living on a shoestring in Cape Cod exploring his homosexual desires and attempting to understand their relationship to his art.

Mid-Century Dramas

Williams's frequent attention to matters of sexuality broke down barriers about the subject, particularly in regard to homosexuality, in American drama, encouraging early 1950s playwrights to follow his lead. *Tea and Sympathy* (1953) by Robert Anderson (b. 1917) is more notable for its great commercial success than for the play itself, which is little more than a well-crafted drama with ideas of homosexuality firmly rooted in the bourgeois, conformist attitudes of 1950s America. However, its popularity on stage and screen suggest that audiences were at least willing to entertain the subject. In *Tea and Sympathy*, Tom Lee, a sensitive young man at private school, is brutally treated by his fellow students and a homophobic, hyper-masculine headmaster. Tom is "saved" by the headmaster's unhappy wife, who takes Tom to bed to prove his heterosexuality. Other playwrights occasionally introduced gay characters and issues, but generally not in their most visible work. William Inge (1913–73), inspired to become a playwright by Williams, avoided openly homosexual characters in his major plays, although his subject matter, as in *The Dark at the Top of the Stairs* (1957), frequently assails bigotry in any form. Inge features gay characters in his lesser-known one-acts, including *The Tiny Closet* (1959), in which a man living in a boarding house is victimized by a nosy landlady who breaks into his padlocked closet to discover an array of women's hats. The landlady's violation, and the presumption that she will cause him public disgrace, leaves the man's fate in question. Similarly, in *The Boy in the Basement* (1962), an undertaker's assistant secretly attracted to a local youth is forced to receive the boy's body after an accident. His emotional reaction to the death of the object of his unspoken affection reveals the secret sufferings of closeted gay men in a sympathetic light.

Mid-twentieth century American dramatists employed various techniques to present gay characters and themes, but one device, "transference," the act of disguising homosexual characters and situations behind a mask of heterosexuality, generated controversy. Edward Albee (b. 1928), often accused of transference in the writing of such plays as *Who's Afraid of Virginia Woolf?* (1962), is a gay

dramatist who emerged in Williams's wake, but only occasionally featured identified gay characters in his plays until late in his career. Transference inspired *New
York Times* critic Stanley Kauffmann to "out" three unnamed gay playwrights in a
1966 article, "Homosexual Drama and Its Disguises." Kauffmann did not need to
name names, for it is unmistakable that he is pointing to Williams, Inge, and
Albee. Implying that homosexual writers have no business to write about anything except acknowledged gay characters, Kauffmann insists that puritanical
conventions forced homosexuals to wear masks for generations, to hate themselves, and thus to hate those who make them hate themselves. Now that they
have a certain relative freedom, they vent their feelings in camouflaged form. They
emphasize manner and style because these elements of art, at which they are
often adept, are legal tender in their transactions with the world. These elements
are, or can be, esthetically divorced from such other considerations as character
and idea.

Kauffmann's article reflects homophobic attitudes of the period and Albee,
who dealt directly with homosexuality in *Everything in the Garden* (1967), and
in later plays, has refuted the notion that he, Williams, or other playwrights
would consciously indulge in transference. Techniques aside, homosexual characters and themes found voice through the racial divisions of the Civil Rights
era in *The Toilet* (1964) by Amiri Baraka (LeRoi Jones; b. 1934), a savage depiction of the impact of bigotry set in a high school lavatory. Straight dramatists also
occasionally explored issues of male sexuality, including Arthur Miller (1915–
2005) in *A View From the Bridge* (1955), in which a violent male-on-male kiss sets
in motion the downfall of homophobic longshoreman Eddie Carbone. In the
1960s, off-Broadway increasingly presented works by openly gay playwrights on
gay themes, but the resistance expressed by Kauffmann continued, particularly
in the realm of mainstream Broadway drama.

A Turning Point for Gay Drama

Two years after Kauffmann's article, a true breakthrough gay play appeared,
generating new controversy. *The Boys in the Band* (1968) by Mart Crowley
(b. 1935) simultaneously won praise for depicting more realistic images of homosexuals and criticism for indulging in outmoded stereotypes. The play's lasting
value may be its warning against a life lived in the closet—or in the attempts of
gay men to hide their secret gay lives behind a public facade of "straight" lives—
and in comparatively progressive views of the gay lifestyle and the particular
dilemmas facing effeminate gays unable to hide their sexual orientation. Critic
Clive Barnes, writing at the time of the play's premiere, found it to be "by far the
frankest treatment of homosexuality I have ever seen on the stage," noting that
it "is not a play about a homosexual, but a play that takes the homosexual milieu,

and the homosexual way of life, totally for granted and uses this as a valid basis of human experience."

The critical appreciation and commercial success of *The Boys in the Band* on stage, and in a subsequent film version, provided opportunities for more serious depictions of gay life, but stereotypes continued in such plays as Terrence McNally's *The Ritz* (1974), a lunatic farce set in a gay bathhouse that scored an off-Broadway hit (and subsequent film version), as well as a range of mainstream Broadway dramas featuring stereotypical gay characters. A more complex, realistic portrayal of a serious gay relationship is central to the critically-applauded *5th of July* (1978) by Lanford Wilson (b. 1937), a drama exploring the disillusionments of the Vietnam generation, and Wilson, a gay writer, often featured homosexuals in the large canon of his plays.

Beginning in the early 1960s, off-Broadway proved a generally welcoming venue for openly gay dramatists and plays featuring homosexual characters and themes. Caffe Cino in Greenwich Village is an example of one such a forum and, following the Stonewall riot in 1969, off-Broadway gay dramatists took on a more activist sensibility in responding to homosexual concerns and in deconstructing gender stereotypes. Robert Patrick (b. 1937), one of the playwrights emerging from Caffe Cino, won some critical acclaim in off- and off-off-Broadway theaters before resisting its growing commercialization. However, Patrick's most acclaimed play, *Kennedy's Children* (1974), ironically became his most visible work when it was produced in large commercial theater in England and America. Most of Patrick's prolific output, including the gay-themed *T-shirts* (1976), *Michaelangelo's Models* (1981), *The Trial of Socrates* (1986), *Untold Decades* (1988), *Un-tied States* (1990), *Evan of Earth* (1991), and *Bread Alone* (1993), were presented in smaller venues and chronicled the history and evolution of gay lives more frankly than was possible in most mainstream theaters prior to the 1980s.

Changes were in the offing by the mid-1970s, and gay dramatists began to present more diverse portraits of gay characters. Drag actor/playwright Charles Ludlam (1943–87) and his Ridiculous Theatrical Company created outrageous camp spoofs reflecting a more confident gay sensibility. In his adaptation of Dumas's *Camille* (1974) and in his own Gothic farce, *The Mystery of Irma Vep* (1984), among others, Ludlam smashed stereotypes by celebrating them through a kaleidescope of popular culture clichés from art, movies, and nineteenth century romantic theater. On the other side of the spectrum, actor/playwright Harvey Fierstein (b. 1954) coupled gay pride with a realistic depiction of the personal life of a drag performer struggling to find love in a still-homophobic society in *Torch Song Trilogy* (1981). This plea for tolerance surprisingly resonated with Broadway audiences after productions in off-Broadway theaters. Its stage success led to a film version, also scripted by Fierstein. His subsequent book for the hit musical *La Cage aux Folles* (1984) similarly set contemporary gay characters against the backdrop of middle America's traditionally homophobic responses with optimistic visions of a progressive society capable of embracing the gay "other." A darker view emerges in the grim drama *Bent* (1978), in which Martin Sherman (b. 1938) examines the tragic fate of homosexuals during the Holocaust, drawing parallels between that era and the homophobia present in contemporary American society.

Larry Kramer and the Appearance of AIDS in Drama

Ludlam's early death from AIDS signaled the next major transition in gay drama: depictions of the personal struggles and divisive social questions arising from the AIDS crisis. In *As Is* (1985), William Hoffman (b. 1939) immersed his audience in the personal horrors of what became an international pandemic, but no playwright in the 1980s addressed AIDS and its attendant issues as directly as Larry Kramer (b. 1935). His scathing indictment of American society's failure to respond to the mounting cataclysm was embodied in his vigorous offstage activism and, most particularly, in his documentary-style drama *The Normal Heart* (1985). Kramer, a screenwriter and novelist, wrote his first off-Broadway play, *Sissies' Scrapbook*, in 1973, but he remains an ambivalent playwright, less interested in the medium than the message. *The Normal Heart* (1985) is set between July 1981 and May 1984 and is intended to document the era in which AIDS was first identified as a "gay cancer." Indeed, the play's first line, spoken by a young gay man sitting in a doctor's waiting room sets the overall tone: "I know something's wrong." *The Normal Heart* probes experiences of several gay men, but the connecting thread in this ambitious, fiery work is Ned Weeks, a thinly-veiled portrait of Kramer himself. In conversations with Dr. Emma Brookner, a committed health-care professional, Weeks learns to his horror that she believes the mysterious illness is transmitted sexually. "And you want me to tell every gay man in New York to stop having sex?" Weeks asks in shock, and Brookner insists that he must do so: the government and medical establishment are in denial, she believes, and gay activism may be the only effective response.

Weeks's temperamental outbursts in dealing with officials and medical authorities, compatriots in his own activist organization, and within his own family serve to isolate him. His lover, Felix, tries to be understanding, but in reflecting on Weeks's behavior and his own quiet battle with AIDS and the lack of response to the disease, Felix tells Weeks's brother Ben that "there's not a good word to be said for anybody's behavior in this whole mess." Weeks has an uneasy relationship with his older brother, a father figure who also serves as society's disapproving voice on the "gay lifestyle." By the play's end, Ben moves beyond his prejudices to accept his younger brother, a symbolic image suggesting Kramer's hopes for American society in general.

Following *The Normal Heart,* Kramer's next play, *Just Say No. A Play about a Farce* (1988), was a critical disappointment. Focused on sexual hypocrisy in high places (again during the Reagan presidency), it features an imperious First Lady, her gay son, and the closeted gay Mayor of America's "largest northeastern city." The Reagans and New York City mayor Ed Koch are the obvious targets, but Kramer weaves in references to many aspects of contemporary American culture, particularly in regard to homosexuality, AIDS, and politics. Seven years after *The Normal Heart,* Kramer completed a sequel, *The Destiny of Me* (1992), which shifts attention to Weeks's personal history. Focusing on his own family history within the context of late twentieth century American life, and using AIDS as a dramatic catalyst, Kramer creates a wrenching exploration of Weeks's traumatic sexual awakening and his mounting sense of purpose. Despite its connection to the long tradition of realistic American family dramas, Kramer recounts Weeks's life through a wide variety of postmodern theatrical devices. Various periods overlap as characters float in and out of the action presenting key situations in Weeks's life, but again the message matters more than the medium as Kramer demands response to the AIDS crisis and a greater sensitivity to those living with the disease and the lingering homophobic attitudes in the United States.

Critical and Commercial Success: Terrence McNally

In the same era, a less confrontational gay dramatist balanced Kramer's diatribes. Terrence McNally (b. 1939), who had his first major success with the aforementioned 1970s off-Broadway hit *The Ritz,* had endured failure in the previous decade. McNally's *And Things That Go Bump In the Night* (1964) dealt with a crazed mother and her sadistic, bisexual son, but critics were not appreciative of this effort. McNally's subsequent prolific output ultimately won critical and commercial favor, and his work is burnished by a late twentieth century gay sensibility. McNally's work increasingly featured openly gay characters and themes after the 1970s. *The Lisbon Traviata* (1985), for example, focuses on Mendy, a fanatical (and obviously gay) opera fan, who begs his friend Stephen to loan him a rare pirated copy of Maria Callas performing *La Traviata* in Lisbon. Their encounter over the recording exposes the profound unhappiness of both men, who define themselves exclusively through the larger-than-life but artificial passions of opera.

In the late 1980s, McNally adapted Manuel Puig's novel, *Kiss of the Spider Woman,* which had previously been an acclaimed film, into a Broadway musical with a score by John Kander and Fred Ebb. After a long gestation period, the musical *Kiss of the Spider Woman* (1993) received several Tony Awards, including one for McNally's libretto. McNally focuses Puig's story through the eyes of one of its central characters, Molina, a gay department store window dresser jailed in a Latin American prison, who escapes his fears through fantasies of his favorite movie star, known only as The Spider Woman. Valentin, a defiant political prisoner and hyper-masculine male, joins the politically ambivalent Molina in a cell and they achieve a level of mutual respect which helps both face tragic fates. McNally told *New York Times* critic David Richards that what *Kiss of the Spider Woman* "says about a gay man is very important, although he's not just a gay man. He's a small person who says, 'My life is trivial, I'm inconsequential' and who learns he's not, that we all matter."

McNally's assimilationist sensibility is reflected in most of his post-1980s plays, including *Lips Together, Teeth Apart* (1991), a four-character comedy-drama involving Sally, a woman who has recently inherited a Fire Island beach house from her brother, who died of AIDS. Sally and Sam, her husband, invite Sam's sister Chloe and her husband John for the Fourth of July weekend, during which comic and tragic memories, past relationships, and the unseen presence of their gay neighbors release unspoken feelings. Homophobic John is so fearful of AIDS that he will not swim because so many gay men live nearby, prompting Sally, thinking of her brother, to respond sarcastically, "I think we're very brave to dangle our feet like this. They may fall off." John attacks Sam for his inability to rein in Sally's sarcasm, which only fuels her ire. Drinking a handful of water, she shouts, "Then let's all get AIDS and die!" Injecting straight characters into a gay world, as he had similarly done more superficially in *The Ritz*, allows McNally to explore current attitudes about homosexuality and AIDS.

This approach is most evident in *Love! Valour! Compassion!* (1994), for which McNally received the Pulitzer Prize. A bittersweet comedy about the close friendships of eight gay New Yorkers who spend holiday weekends at the country home of one of them, *Love! Valour! Compassion!* explores gay relationships of all sorts set against the problems of living with AIDS. Gregory, a celebrated choreographer, and his sweet-natured blind lover Bobby, live in a farmhouse where Gregory has his dance studio. Their guests include Arthur and Perry, who have been a couple for fourteen years; "We're role models. It's very stressful," quips the acerbic Perry. HIV-positive Buzz Hauser, another guest, is a flamboyant musical comedy buff and costumer for Gregory's dance troupe. Viciously sarcastic John, a British rehearsal pianist, is flooded with jealousy about the professional and personal success of the others and brings along Ramon, an ambitious young dancer who aspires to eclipse Gregory's achievements. Ramon also attempts to woo Bobby from Gregory. John's twin brother James, a gentle man dying of AIDS, joins the group and develops a close relationship with Buzz. The spectre of AIDS hangs heavily over all of the characters, and their fears and losses exacerbate their individual longings for love and commitment. Even John, who is often a pariah, and Ramon, who severely damages Gregory's relationship with Bobby, expose their deepest fears and longings, but remain a part of this tightly knit group of friends who recognize that true community may be a form of redemption.

The announcement of McNally's *Corpus Christi* (1998) set off a firestorm of controversy at the time of its premiere at the Manhattan Theatre Club. *Corpus Christi* focuses on a group of gay men in Texas putting on a passion play about Jesus Christ's life. It was attacked by various groups ostensibly concerned by the play's connection of contemporary gay lives with Christ's. Bomb threats and pickets accompanied the play's opening, but the publicity only served to attract more interest in *Corpus Christi* than would have otherwise existed. In the play, thirteen actors play various biblical roles, debating varied beliefs about the lessons of the Bible's account of Christ's life. The intersection of biblical figures with the lives of the actors playing them permits McNally an opportunity of simultaneously revealing the stories of each character/actor. This wedding of the traditional and the contemporary, the "straight" version of the Bible and the "gay response" to it, is the play's true purpose. In a preface to the published version of *Corpus Christi*, McNally writes that "I'm a playwright, not a theologian," adding that the "level of dislike of gay men and the vehemence of the denial of any claim they might make for spiritual parity with their Christian 'brothers' that *Corpus Christi* revealed was disheartening." In describing the work, McNally says that it is a "passion play" beginning with "the familiar dialogue with ourselves: Do I love my neighbor? Am I contributing good to the society in which I operate or nil? Do I, in fact, matter? Nothing more, nothing less. The play is more religious ritual than a play" and one that questions not only what was done to Christ, but what "they did one cold October night to a young man in Wyoming as well. Jesus Christ died again when Matthew Shepard did." Curiously, only months after the *Corpus Christi* controversy, a similar play, *The Most Fabulous Story Ever Told* (1998) by Paul Rudnick (b. 1958), opened at the New York Theatre Workshop to virtually no public outcry. Rudnick had previously written *Jeffrey* (1995), a chronicle of a gay Everyman in contemporary America, and perhaps the play's debut in a small off-Broadway venue kept it out of the media spotlight.

Activism in the Theater: Tony Kushner

Despite the controversy engendered by *Corpus Christi*, it caused less furor than that which had accompanied productions of a previous gay-themed drama, *Angels in America: A Gay Fantasia on National Themes*, an epic work consisting of two long plays, the Pulitzer Prize-winning *Millennium Approaches* (1991) and *Perestroika* (1992). Its author, Tony Kushner (b. 1956), was well-established as a director, adaptor, and playwright in regional theaters prior to *Angels*, but he was thrust into the forefront of American drama when *Angels* reached Broadway following critically acclaimed runs at San Francisco's Eureka Theatre, Los Angeles's Mark Taper Forum, and the Royal National Theatre of Great Britain. *Angels* raises complex questions regarding the future of American society in the wake of

Reagan's presidency, particularly in the areas of morality, politics, and sexuality. Kushner wonders if a nation can be considered truly moral if it oppresses any of its citizenry. *Angels* suggests the inevitability of change and, with a mixture of outrageous humor and heartrending drama, Kushner peers into the unknown future to ponder whether apocalypse is inevitable or a brighter, more progressive tomorrow is possible. Examining a few individuals in the intimacy of their private lives at moments of profound personal crisis, Kushner considers the impact of history, as well as prevailing societal and political conditions, on their troubled lives. *Angels* features a range of gay characters—some closeted, some not—dealing with the problems of being homosexual in the darkest hours of the mounting AIDS crisis and at the height of the neo-conservative Reagan revolution.

Kushner, who came of age in an era of profound change in the American cultural landscape, is inspired, in part, by dramatists of the Stonewall generation and after, as well as classical German romanticisim, Bertolt Brecht's epic theater, and the poetic realism of mid-twentieth century American drama as exemplified by Williams. Kushner also found inspiration in the messages of activist gay organizations ACT UP and Queer Nation, whose chant, "We're here, we're queer, we're fabulous," pervades *Angels*. Contemporary American society is in an age of intellectual and moral stagnation, Kushner believes, an era of staggering political and social crisis, and *Angels* insists that the moral emptiness experienced in postmodern America results from an abandonment of its founding principles of justice, compassion, and liberty.

Angels in America

The first part of the play, *Millennium Approaches*, begins at the funeral of an elderly Jewish woman, Sarah Ironson, described by the presiding rabbi as an exemplar of Old World values. Having established the death of past certitudes which are the foundation of accepted values, Kushner sets his characters adrift with only the wreckage of the past to both guide and burden them. The play focuses on Joe and Harper Pitt, an unhappily married Mormon couple, and Prior Walter and Louis Ironson (the grandson of the deceased woman), a gay couple. These characters are all enduring personal crises when their lives intersect with historical figure Roy Cohn, who won fame (or infamy) as primary aide to Senator Joseph McCarthy during the House Un-American Activities Committee anticommunist "witchhunts" of the 1950s. Early in the play, Cohn, now a prominent New York divorce lawyer, learns he is suffering from full-blown AIDS.

Joe, a conservative lawyer, is encouraged by Cohn, who hopes to place Joe in a Justice Department job as his man in Washington, but Joe is caught up in a personal struggle with his long-repressed homosexuality. He has been raised with traditional values: to be a family man, devoutly religious, and politically conservative. However, it is all slipping away as his true nature surfaces. In an agonized plea to Harper, who demands that Joe tell her whether or not he is, in fact, a homosexual, Joe exclaims: "Does it make any difference? That I might be one thing deep within, no matter how wrong or ugly that thing is, so long as I have fought, with everything I have, to kill it. What do you want from me, Harper? More than that? For God's sake, there's nothing left, I'm a shell. There's nothing left to kill. As long as my behavior is what I know it has to be. Decent. Correct. That alone in the eyes of God."

When Joe finally acknowledges his homosexuality, he telephones his mother, Hannah, in the middle of the night, painfully revealing his secret in a scene that mirrors the experiences of many homosexuals—Kushner himself has said that this scene is taken directly from his own "coming out" experience. Joe subsequently meets Louis, who is in a desperate flight of fear from his longtime lover Prior, who has revealed that he is HIV-positive. Racked with guilt, the liberal Louis reflects on the Reagan era which he sees as a metaphor for his own bad faith. Meanwhile, Harper, addicted to Valium, and Prior, delirious as he becomes sicker, meet in a mutual hallucination where Harper comes to terms with Joe's true sexual nature. Prior attempts to find hope despite his physical ills and emotional despair, employing camp humor to cope with his suffering. He insists that he is not a "typical homosexual," jokingly adding that he is "stereo-typical."

Kushner imbues Cohn with a darker brand of humor drawn from his rapacious corruption. Cohn's self-loathing is at the heart of the play's most unsettling depiction of homosexuality, manifested in Cohn's deep, angry denial: "Like all labels they tell you one thing and one thing only: where does an individual so identified fit in the food chain, in the pecking order? Not ideology, or sexual taste, but something much simpler: clout." Suggesting that he could not possibly be considered a homosexual because he is a political force, Cohn sneers that "Homosexuals are not men who sleep with other men. Homosexuals are men who in fifteen years of trying cannot get a pissant antidiscrimination bill through City Council. Homosexuals are men who know nobody and who nobody knows."

Kushner's scathing view of Cohn as an exemplar of the excesses of twentieth century American conservatism is balanced by a similarly harsh view of Louis's liberal politics, which he finds self-righteous and ineffectual. Louis meets his match in Belize, a gay African American nurse and close friend of Prior, who also becomes Cohn's caregiver in *Perestroika*. Angry at the inherent bigotry and homophobia he finds on both sides of the political spectrum, Belize tells Louis: "I hate this country. It's just big ideas, and stories, and people dying, and people like you. The white cracker who wrote the national anthem knew what he was doing. He set the word 'free' to a note so high nobody can reach it." And of Louis specifically, Belize proposes that his liberalism has him "Up in the air, just like that angel, too far off the earth to pick out the details" or, presumably, to respond to them in any effective way, either personally or politically.

Throughout both plays, Prior grapples with the politics of existence humanely and compassionately, transcending the traditionally adversarial poles of conservatism or liberalism. At the end of *Millennium Approaches,* an angel appears to Prior in his delirium, bringing either death or redemption. Frightened, Prior resists his fears in a speech Kushner clearly intends to destroy stereotypes of weakness expressed earlier in the play by Cohn. "I can handle pressure, I am a gay man and I am used to pressure, to trouble, I am tough and strong," Prior proclaims, and this viewpoint is reiterated in the final scene of *Perestroika,* which is set five years after the rest of *Angels.* Some of the characters meet at the Bethesda fountain in Central Park, with its statue of an angel, a figure commemorating death but suggesting "a world without dying." Prior, whose AIDS symptoms have stabilized, points out that the healing waters of the fountain are not presently flowing, but he hopes to be around to see the day the waters flow again. Speaking for those gay characters who have come before him and for those suffering in the age of AIDS, Prior says, "This disease will be the end of many of us, but not nearly all, and the dead will be commemorated and will struggle on with the living, and we are not going away. We won't die secret deaths anymore. The world only spins forward. We will be citizens. The time has come."

RECENT GAY DRAMA

Gay-themed plays proliferated after the mid-1990s, although most subsequent playwrights have followed models created by Williams, Fierstein, Kramer, McNally, and Kushner. Standing out among more recent gay dramatists is Richard Greenberg (b. 1958), whose acclaimed *Take Me Out* (2003) mixes drama and comedy to imagine what might happen if a popular major league baseball player publicly announced his homosexuality. *Take Me Out* drew large audiences, tapping into changing American attitudes about gays at the dawn of the twenty-first century. Like the acclaimed film *Brokeback Mountain* (2005), which explores homosexuality among traditionally hyper-masculine cowboys, *Take Me Out* brings American gay drama full circle. Like many of the gay plays of the past decade, it makes clear that gay men and women are present in all walks of American life; some are noble, others are not, but the long process of disposing of the "closet" may be ending in the transition to the new millennium.

FURTHER READING

Baker, Rob. *The Art of AIDS.* New York: Continuum, 1994.

Bernstein, Robin. *Cast Out: Queer Lives in Theater.* Ann Arbor, Michigan: University of Michigan Press, 2006.

Clum, John M. *Acting Gay: Male Homosexuality in Modern Drama*. New York: Columbia University Press, 1992.

———. *Still Acting Gay: Male Homosexuality in Modern Drama*. New York: Palgrave/ Macmillan 2000.

Curtin, Kaier. *"We Can Always Call Them Bulgarians": The Emergence of Lesbians and Gay Men on the American Stage*. Boston: Alyson, 1987.

Fisher, James. *The Theatre of Tony Kushner: Living Past Hope*. New York: Routledge, 2001.

———, ed. *Tony Kushner: New Essays on the Art and Politics of the Plays*. Jefferson, North Carolina: McFarland Publishers, Inc., 2006.

Frantzen, Allen J. *Before the Closet: Same-Sex Love From Beowulf to Angels in America*. Chicago: University of Chicago, 1998.

Geis, Deborah R. and Steven F. Kruger, eds. *Approaching the Millennium: Essays on Angels in America*. Ann Arbor, Michigan: University of Michigan Press, 1997.

Harbin, Billy J., Kim Marra, and Robert A. Schanke. *The Gay & Lesbian Theatrical Legacy*. Ann Arbor, Michigan: University of Michigan Press, 2005.

Kauffmann, Stanley, "Homosexual Drama and Its Disguises." *New York Times* January 23, 1966, Section 2, p. 1.

Kaufman, David. *Ridiculous! The Theatrical Life and Times of Charles Ludlam*. New York: Applause Books, 2002.

Kolin, Philip C., ed. *The Undiscovered Country: The Later Plays of Tennessee Williams*. New York: Peter Lang, 2002.

Kolin, Philip C., and Colby H. Kullman. *Speaking on Stage. Interviews with Contemporary American Playwrights*. Tuscaloosa, Alabama: The University of Alabama Press, 1996.

Kramer, Larry. *Reports from the Holocaust: The Story of an AIDS Activist*. New York: St. Martin's Press, 1994.

Ludlam, Charles, and Steven Samuels. *Ridiculous Theatre: Scourge of Human Folly: The Essays and Opinions of Charles Ludlam*. New York: Theatre Communications Group, Inc., 1992.

Mass, Lawrence D. *We Must Love One Another or Die: The Life and Legacies of Larry Kramer*. New York: Palgrave/Macmillan, 1999.

McDonough, Carla J. *Staging Masculinity. Male Identity in Contemporary American Drama*. Jefferson, North Carolina and London: McFarland & Co., Inc., Publishers, 1997.

McRuer, Robert. *The Queer Renaissance: Contemporary American Literature and the Reinvention of Lesbian and Gay Identities*. New York: New York University Press, 1997.

Paller, Michael. *Gentlemen Callers: Tennessee Williams, Homosexuality, and Mid-Twentieth Century Drama*. New York: Palgrave/Macmillan, 2005.

Román, David. *Acts of Intervention. Performance, Gay Culture, and AIDS*. Bloomington and Indianapolis, Indiana: Indiana University Press, 1998.

Savran, David. *Communists, Cowboys, and Queers: The Politics of Masculinity in the Work of Arthur Miller and Tennessee Williams*. Minneapolis, Minnesota: University of Minnesota, 1992.

Schanke, Robert A., and Kimberly B. Marra. *Staging Desire: Queer Readings of American Theatre History*. Ann Arbor, Michigan: University of Michigan Press, 2002.

Schulman, Sarah. *Stagestruck: Theater, AIDS, and the Marketing of Gay America*. Durham, North Carolina: Duke University Press, 1998.

Sinfield, Alan. *Out on Stage: Lesbian and Gay Theatre in the Twentieth Century.* New Haven, Connecticut: Yale University Press, 1999.

Solomon, Alisa. *Re-Dressing the Canon. Essays on Theater and Gender.* London and New York: Routledge, 1997.

Solomon, Alisa and Framji Minwalla. *The Queerest Art: Essays on Lesbian and Gay Theater.* New York: New York University Press, 2002.

Vorlicky, Robert H. *Act Like a Man: Challenging Masculinities in American Drama.* Ann Arbor, Michigan: University of Michigan Press, 1994.

————, ed. *Tony Kushner in Conversation.* Ann Arbor, Michigan: University of Michigan Press, 1997.

Williams, Tennessee. *Memoirs.* New York: Doubleday, 1975.

————. *Where I Live. Selected Essays.* Edited by Christine R. Day and Bob Woods. New York: A New Directions Books, 1978. p. 72.

Zimna, Silverman. *Terrence McNally: A Casebook.* New York: Garland, 1997.

ॐ

Gender and Theater

Gwendolyn N. Hale

Wendy Wasserstein captured the plight of gender and theater when she stated, "[T]here aren't enough plays by women—by and about women." Those plays authored by and concerning women often bear the unfair burden of being representative of all female plays and characters. Such a title is simply unfair. In fact, female playwrights such as Wasserstein often find themselves the target of many feminist criticisms for not being more "feminist." While theater has certainly freed itself from many of the heavier, confining shackles of gender stereotypes and limitations such as the way in which women and men are portrayed and written about, gender roles are continually being defined and renegotiated on the stage. The theater has become a tricky medium for gender and sex as both continue to be volatile subjects politically and, in turn, artistically. Male and female playwrights alike tackle the issues associated with gender in a variety of fashions. Interesting, however, are the ways in which contemporary female dramatists approach masculine and feminine roles within their drama. Leading the charge (perhaps unintentionally) of female playwrights engaging gender and gender biases within their works are Naomi Wallace, Paula Vogel, and Marsha Norman.

NAOMI WALLACE

The issue of gender is not a simple one, and it extends far beyond costumes and character assignments. In fact, both men and women write plays for and about other men and women. A great deal of the difficulty in defining gender in today's theater comes from audiences' limited and arbitrary language. Most audiences still define gender as strictly male or female and pay no mind to those whose gender defies the absolute and confining labels of male and female. Naomi Wallace's *The Trestle at Pope Lick Creek*, while it does not set out to solely address issues of gender, does touch on gender roles with its two main characters Dalton and Pace. With Dalton and Pace, Wallace effectively blurs the boundaries between traditional male and female roles and characteristics.

For Pace, trauma has blurred all real distinctions in her life. Through apparent ridicule and even emotional neglect, Pace Creagan has become tough both emotionally and physically. In one of the first scenes of the play, Dalton points out Pace's apparent lack of female characteristics. Not only does she bring a pair of her brother's pants to wear to run the trestle, Dalton tells her, "You don't talk like a girl. Should." Ignoring the ridicule in Dalton's observation, Pace thanks him for it. This scene is one of the first indications that Pace is relatively free from the confines of gender as her world cannot harbor femininity or any other trait that might be construed as a weakness given the time period and its perceptions of gender.

Along with her absence of femininity, we also find a profound lack of connection with other females. She talks about their friend Mary Ellen much like a male would with comments such as, "I'd say she was on the menu. Front, back, and in reverse." Pace does not mention other females very much except that even when she pays Mary Ellen a compliment, she couples it with a memory of how she could exert control over Mary Ellen. Pace would instruct her to take off her clothes and Mary Ellen would comply. Gender is a luxury that would allow Pace a clearly defined role by which to conform. However, Pace's world, while free from the fetters of stereotypical gender roles, is complicated by the fact that she must forge her own path. No one in her life can instruct her on how to be a strong, independent female. She is in a purgatory of gender roles in that she is neither wholly male nor female, and she must define who she is independently of any previous definitions ignoring Dalton's expectations and anger.

The cause of Dalton's anger is profound sexual frustration. In one scene prior to her running the trestle, Pace refuses to kiss Dalton on the mouth because "that's common," so she kisses him on the back of the knee for ten seconds as she makes Dalton count. Pace also tells Dalton to take off his clothes so she can merely look at him. Again, his hopes for sex are destroyed when Pace tells him to get dressed. Dalton desperately wants Pace to be like other girls, but Pace sees Dalton as a very nice boy who will have to be, sooner or later, "[broken] in half," and she assumes the duty of doing so. She makes Dalton feel like a fool even though she does not mean to. Dalton is at Pace's mercy in that she defies the characteristics of the typical girls Dalton knows. The life Dalton wants is one in which Pace allows him to be the dominant partner and one in which she acquiesces to sex. Pace has her own ideas about sex and love, and Dalton cannot reconcile her ideas with his own sexual frustration. Pace opens up a Pandora's Box of sorts for Dalton in that she has told him of another way to live but given him no instruction or hope as to how to go about living this life. In her effort to "break Dalton in half," Pace withholds such information. No matter how much Dalton would like to go back to his former ignorance, he cannot, and therefore he hates Pace.

Toward the end of the play, Wallace blurs the distinctions between Pace and Dalton, fiction and reality, and male and female. For possibly the first time in his life, Dalton feels intensely: love, pain, frustration, and anger. During this scene, Pace is actually "in" Dalton in a reverse act of sexual intercourse. Before all this, Pace has refused to kiss Dalton because "that's common." Now, as Claudia Barnett comments, in the play's "most provocative *gestus*, she stands still and instructs him to close his eyes and touch himself as if he were touching her." She instructs: "Yes. There....And do this. Go on....Now close your eyes. And touch me....Go on. Open your legs. Do it....Can you feel me? I'm hard. I want to be inside you." As Barnett points out, this is the only instance when Pace does not require a witness because seeing would be meaningless in that all this occurs within their minds. As Pace is dead and Dalton has come to view the world differently, the distinctions between male and female are pointless in this instance.

PAULA VOGEL

Where Wallace's Pace exerts control and power, Paula Vogel's character Li'l Bit, in *How I Learned to Drive*, is an intelligent woman whose possibilities and experiences have been limited because of sexual abuse from her uncle and fire-and-brimstone talks from her grandmother regarding sex. Like Pace, Li'l Bit is held captive by limitations. While Pace's prison stems from socioeconomics, Li'l Bit's results from her own femininity. That which makes her a woman perplexes her and makes her self-conscious. When her mother and grandmother are discussing sex, Li'l Bit asks, "Why does everything have to hurt for girls? Why is there always blood?" Li'l Bit's seemingly simple and innocent questions are met with opposing answers. The mother attempts to be honest and inform her daughter that there is some discomfort, but sex is beautiful if it occurs with someone Li'l Bit is in love with. Still, the grandmother's retorts are from a darker, stricter time as she tells her granddaughter about sex: "You'll bleed like stuck pig! And you lay there and say, 'Why O Lord, have you forsaken me?!'" With her uncle sexually abusing her from age eleven and her grandmother and mother offering conflicting views about sex, it is little wonder Li'l Bit finds her own womanhood burdensome.

Li'l Bit's breasts are much larger than most of the girls in her school. Her breasts are an outward manifestation of her sexual maturity, yet Li'l Bit is not sexually mature in the least. Her questions go unanswered, and the only clues she is given are the sexual advances from her uncle. Her uncle has stunted her sexual maturation by taking advantage of her at a very young age. Her breasts, as Li'l Bit points out, are cumbersome, and most boys only want to dance with her so they can watch them jiggle. Not only do the boys tease her about them, but so do the girls in her gym class. Betrayed by both her male and female counterparts, Li'l Bit retreats back into the arms of her abusive Uncle Peck.

Uncle Peck embodies the manipulation experiences throughout her childhood and adolescence. Uncle Peck is the one person in Li'l Bit's life who tells her she is beautiful and attempts to explain the ways of the world, particularly her peers' reactions to her breasts and beauty. Li'l Bit is manipulated by a pedophile, a desperate man clinging to his youth by attempting to win the love of a much younger girl. As Uncle Peck showers Li'l Bit with gifts and attention, the most damaging actions come from those who tell Li'l Bit how she should and should not act: Never drink on an empty stomach; throw up in the ladies' room if intoxicated; don't have sex; wear a skin-tight girdle. With all this instruction, no one tells Li'l Bit the reasoning behind such precautions and actions. She remains naive, confused, and unfocused.

Li'l Bit is intelligent and wants to "rise above [her] cracker background." However, when she tells her family of her plans, they negate her confidence and aspirations by reverting the conversation back to her body. Her grandfather argues, "Shakespeare is really going to help you in life.... How is Shakespeare going to help [you] lie on [your] back in the dark?" Here, along with her uncle's abuse, men's reactions to her, and women's reactions to her, Li'l Bit finds all emphasis placed on her body, and her value as a woman is measured by her body and sexuality. Further, any anger and betrayal Li'l Bit may feel is replaced by guilt and social restrictions. When she becomes angry in high school for Jerome grabbing her breasts and insinuating her bra is padded, the Teenage Greek Chorus blames her: "Rage is not attractive in a girl" Then, just before the first time Li'l Bit is molested by her uncle, her mother unknowingly affixes permanent guilt and silence onto her daughter by stating, "I'm warning you—if anything happens, I hold you responsible." From this day forward, Li'l Bit must accept her fate as she is responsible for what happens to her even though she has never been armed with the weapons by which to defend herself. This lack of defense is a natural progression for Li'l Bit because Li'l Bit's grandmother told her mother the same thing when she (Lucy) got pregnant. She forced her to have the baby on her own saying, "I hold you responsible." Vogel utilizes the abuse by the uncle and the ways in which men and women are taught to drive, the former aggressively and the latter submissively and apologetically, to demonstrate the victimization of women through long-held beliefs and societal indoctrination.

MARSHA NORMAN

In Marsha Norman's 'Night, Mother, victimization is demonstrated on the domestic front without the physical presence of males. The play begins as an innocuous account of a mother-daughter relationship that eventually manifests itself as a power struggle between two women. Jessie's life is one of limitation and stagnation; she lives with her mother after he marriage fails and her son turns out to be a thief. Further, Jessie is haunted by epilepsy and a life of unfulfilled dreams. As the play opens, Jessie asks her mother for her dead father's revolver, and she calmly announces she is going to kill herself. Jessie's mother, like everyone else in Jessie's life, does not take her seriously when she clearly states she is going to end her own life.

Initially, Jessie exhibits profound female characteristics. Of the two residing in the house, Jessie is the maternal one; she takes charge of all the details of her mother's life. This role-reversal is cruel in that no one ever nurtures Jessie. Her strength never wanes as she makes list after list of things her mother needs. The play opens with her mother relying wholly on Jessie for her happiness: "Jessie, it's the last snowball, sugar. Put it on the list, O.K.? And we're out of Hershey bars and where's that peanut brittle?" The mother has regressed to the mentality of a child, and she lives in the moment. She relies on the sensual pleasures and instant gratification of candy and has little interaction with other humans other than her children, Agnes and Dawson. Mostly, however, she just has TV. Jessie has ceased to be a daughter and has been cast in the role of servant. While Jessie prepares to kill herself in the least messy way possible, Mama reminds Jessie that it is Saturday night and her nails need to be done. Jessie responds, "I know. I got it on the schedule." Jessie's world revolves around serving her mother.

Cleaning and attending to her mother's every whim, Jessie exhibits stereotypical feminine characteristics as she must get everything in order before committing suicide. She gathers old towels and plastic in order to cover the floor of her bedroom so that she does not make a mess for her mother. Jessie spends the last hours of her life getting everything in order for her mother who has never really had to care for herself. Soon, Jessie blurs the boundaries of masculinity and femininity when she tells her mother to wash her hands so she can give her a manicure. In the meantime, she is going up to get her father's gun from the attic. This revolver is the only thing her father has really left her, and it is a means by which to end her miserable life. Next, Jessie begins cleaning the gun very skillfully much as a man would do: "Jessie sits with the gun and starts cleaning it, pushing the cylinder out, checking to see that the chambers and barrel are empty, then putting some oil on a small patch of cloth and pushing it through the barrel with the push rod that was in the box." Jessie intends to kill herself with her father's revolver. A firearm is a profoundly masculine way to kill oneself, and there is little chance for Jessie to be saved from a self-inflicted bullet wound.

With Jessie's suicide comes a power struggle. Jessie struggles under the weight of her past, memories of her family, and the life that has ceased to be hers. First, although all the characters on the stage are female, male characters permeate the present, thus becoming presences. Jessie's son, Ricky, is a thief, and their relationship has been destroyed beyond repair. Further, Jessie's brother, Dawson, is dominating and exerts power over her and her mother. He uses his money as a means of maintaining dominance and power over his mother and sister. Finally, Jessie's father was the one person she could relate to, and her mother despised him. Jessie attempts to defend her father within the last moments of her life, and her mother replies, "How could I love him, Jessie. I didn't have a thing he wanted....You loved him enough for both of us." All Jessie has are memories, and even those are not that great. The only control Jessie has of her own life is to end it; all other aspects are controlled by someone else. Still, Mama refuses to acknowledge the fact that Jessie is her own woman and no longer needs this world or her trivial, small life with her mother.

The play culminates in heartbreak. Jessie's will prevails, and she whispers, "'Night, Mother" (Norman 1983,57). Separated by Jessie's locked bedroom door, Mama is emotionally no closer to Jessie now than when Jessie was alive. Mama threatens to do things against Jessie's orders in a selfish attempt to keep her around and to not have to feel the guilt that Jessie's suicide will bring. Mama screams, "Jessie!...I didn't know! I was here with you all the time. How could I know you were so alone?...I thought you were mine." With the sound of a gunshot, Mama makes a phone call to Dawson to come and take care of the details of Jessie's death. The play and Jessie's life come to a conclusion.

While gender does not directly impact the course of events of Norman's play, Norman does examine the dynamics of a mother-daughter relationship that has reversed itself. Jessie, a woman who has never had control of her own life, asserts herself in death. Like Pace Creagan in *The Trestle at Pope Lick Creek*, Jessie is able to free herself from the confines of her life and her gender. Power and gender seem to play an integral role in many of the plays of female dramatists. The three aforementioned plays all demonstrate a power struggle of sorts, and often gender factors into the struggle. Pace and Dalton struggle to free themselves from the confines of their socioeconomic status as Pace attempts to define gender is some way that allows her to be the person she longs to be. Li'l Bit struggles with her blossoming womanhood as her uncle molests her by exerting control over her. Because of Uncle Peck's sexual dominance over Li'l Bit, she perpetuates the cycle and exercises dominance over her sexual partners. For Li'l Bit, sex becomes a weapon by which to gain power and control. Finally, for Jessie, she struggles with her mother for the right to kill herself. Her mother has always dominated the relationship, and Mama cannot stand the idea that she will not be able to control her daughter any longer.

GENDER'S MANY ROLES IN DRAMA

Few would argue that all relationships are based on some sort of power hierarchy. Male and female playwrights often focus on such power structures and bring them to the stage in an attempt to address such conflicts in everyday life. Gender is a terrifically fluid term, particularly when used with regards to drama, and often brings to the fore different tensions. Moreover, many still believe that one is either born male or female. According to Judith Butler, however, gender is unnatural as well as a social construction. No matter the intent behind the use of gender, the politics of masculinity and femininity are present. Whether a character is oppressed by her gender, imprisoned by her sexuality, or simply struggling with her role in the family, expectations of males and females remain. Whether a play is feminist or is simply dealing with everyday issues, gender is inescapable; its manifestations simply beg the audience to examine the play and their own long-held beliefs in a new way.

FURTHER READING

Barnett, Claudia. "Dialectic and the Drama of Naomi Wallace." *Southern Women Playwrights: New Essays in Literary History and Criticism.* Edited by Robert L. McDonald and Linda Rohrer Paige. Tuscaloosa, Alabama: University of Alabama Press, 2002.

Butler, Judith. "Variations on Sex and Gender." *The Judith Butler Reader.* Edited by Sara Salih and Judith Butler. Malden, Massachusetts: Blackwell Publishing, 2004.

Norman, Marsha. *'Night, Mother.* New York: Dramatists Play Service Inc., 1983.

Vogel, Paula. *How I Learned to Drive.* New York: Dramatists Play Service Inc., 1998.

Wallace, Naomi. *The Trestle at Pope Lick Creek. In the Heart of America and Other Plays.* New York: Theatre Communications Group, 2001.

Musical Theater

Gary Konas

ORIGINS AND PRECURSORS OF THE AMERICAN MUSICAL

Although the Broadway musical is considered one of America's original art forms, it actually comes from several European sources. John Gay's *The Beggar's Opera* (1728), a British play which mixed dialogue with ballads, is one of the earliest ancestors to the modern musical. The German-born Jacques Offenbach wrote several *opéra-bouffes* performed in Paris, beginning in 1855, which are closer to American-type musical theater. Also, W.S. Gilbert and Arthur Sullivan perfected the form of comic operetta in England with such works as *H. M. S. Pinafore* (1878), *The Pirates of Penzance* (1880), and *The Mikado* (1885). The wild popularity of the New York production of *Pinafore* had a tremendous influence on America's attitude toward musical theater.

The Black Crook (1866) is commonly thought of as being the first American musical. This five-hour extravaganza is still remembered as part of show-business lore, even though it probably had less lasting influence on the American musical than did its European counterparts. Soon after, Edward Harrigan and Tony Hart's *Mulligan Guards* musical plays (1877–85, music by David Braham) featured comic conflicts among Irish, German, and black residents of New York. During the 1890s, European-trained Reginald de Koven enjoyed success on Broadway with such early musicals as *Robin Hood* (1891).

Meanwhile, operetta flourished in Europe. Franz Lehar's *The Merry Widow* (1905) opened in Vienna and became incredibly successful throughout Europe and America, arriving in New York to considerable acclaim in 1907. The twentieth century American musical began with a British import, *Florodora* (1900), which enjoyed great popularity. Victor Herbert composed several memorable "comic operas," including *Babes in Toyland* (1903) and *Naughty Marietta* (1910). George M. Cohan, one of the most popular performers of his day, wrote the book and score for *Little Johnny Jones* (1904), which gave America "The Yankee Doodle Boy" and "Give My Regards to Broadway." By this time the theater district, formerly centered downtown, was moving uptown to Times Square, centered around Broadway between 42nd and 49th Streets.

Along with the musical comedy and European-style operetta, a third form of musical called "revue" developed with *The Passing Show* (1894). Producer Florenz Ziegfeld made this genre world-famous in 1907 with the first of his annual *Follies*. Unlike other musical forms, revues simply presented production numbers, comedy skits, and vaudeville acts. Ziegfeld patterned his shows on the French revue, with its emphasis on topical satire, and he spared no expense when it came to costumes, performers (including Bert Williams and Fanny Brice), and songwriters, most notably Irving Berlin.

THE MUSICAL IN THE TWENTIETH CENTURY

1915–40

During the 1910s Jerome Kern perfected the form of the "book" musical (i.e., one with a libretto that tells a story) with several works, including *Very Good Eddie* (1915) and *Leave It to Jane* (1917). If Kern was the father of the American musical, George Gershwin was its first genius. In his 38 years he wrote not only musical comedy, but also jazz, symphonic music, and opera. With his lyricist brother Ira he wrote outstanding scores for *Lady, Be Good* (1924; such as "Fascinating Rhythm"),[1] *Oh, Kay!* (1926; "Someone to Watch Over Me"), *Funny Face* (1927; "'S Wonderful"), *Girl Crazy* (1930; "I Got Rhythm"), and *Of Thee I Sing* (1931). With Ira and playwright DuBose Heyward, Gershwin created an enduring American opera, *Porgy and Bess* (1935; "Summertime," "Bess, You Is My Woman Now"). Today's greatest songwriter Stephen Sondheim perhaps put it best when he said, "There's *Porgy and Bess,* then there's everything else."

Richard Rodgers and Lorenz Hart rose to prominence during the 1920s and built upon this success during the following decade. Their excellent scores included *A Connecticut Yankee* (1927), *Babes in Arms* (1937; "The Lady Is a Tramp," "My Funny Valentine"), and *The Boys from Syracuse* (1938; "Falling in Love with Love"). Rodgers had a great gift for melody and complex harmonies, while Hart's love-song lyrics (e.g., "Spring Is Here") tended toward cynicism and melancholy, matching his tortured personality. Although musical comedy had always included some dance, *On Your Toes* (1936; "There's a Small Hotel") innovatively included ballet ("Slaughter on Tenth Avenue"), thus paving the way for shows Rodgers would later write with Oscar Hammerstein II.

Rodgers and Hart's last great show, *Pal Joey* (1940; "Bewitched"), was criticized for having an unlikeable main character and was only later fully appreciated for its dramatic quality.

Cole Porter was an American composer-lyricist whose career was slowed by years of party-going in Europe with his wife Linda. He nevertheless managed to write a number of witty, sophisticated scores for *Fifty Million Frenchmen* (1929), *Anything Goes* (1934; "You're the Top"), *Red, Hot, and Blue* (1936; "De-Lovely"), *Leave It to Me* (1938; "My Heart Belongs to Daddy"), *Kiss Me, Kate* (1948; "So in Love"), and *Can-Can* (1953; "I Love Paris"). His multilayered love songs (e.g., "Begin the Beguine") often hid melancholy, despair, *double-entendre*, and/or homosexual longing beneath the happy exterior of his music and lyrics.

Although Broadway built its reputation on the "book" musical during the 1920s and 1930s, revues continued to entertain audiences on Broadway. Ziegfeld's success with his *Follies* brought competition from others, most notably *George White's Scandals* (beginning 1919). Less spectacular revues relying on solid scores included *The Band Wagon* (1931; "Dancing in the Dark"), with music by Arthur Schwartz and lyrics by Howard Dietz. Irving Berlin's *Music Box Revue* (1921; "Say It with Music") and Harold Rome's *Pins and Needles* (1937) also enjoyed solid runs. The comedy sketches in these shows tended to be topical. Berlin, considered the god of American popular song ("God Bless America"), also wrote the memorable musical *Annie Get Your Gun* (1946, "There's No Business Like Show Business").

America's appetite for operetta continued throughout the 1920s, especially in the works of Sigmund Romberg and Rudolf Friml. These shows were often set in mythical Central European countries known collectively as "Ruritania," or else they took place in the distant American past. The lush, romantic scores usually had an operatic vocal sweep. Romberg scored with *Blossom Time* (1921) and *The Student Prince* (1924). Also in 1924, lyricist Oscar Hammerstein II wrote the popular operetta *Rose-Marie* ("Indian Love Call") with Rudolf Friml.

In 1927 Kern and Hammerstein created *Show Boat*, which was a true musical drama and the forerunner to all serious musicals since. The score's songs—which included "Ol' Man River," "Make Believe," and "Can't Help Lovin' Dat Man"—developed character and advanced the plot. The stories for most musicals during this period ran the gamut from silly to forgettable, and before *Show Boat* they did not integrate song with story. *Show Boat* was certainly the first great Broadway musical and the triumph of Kern's career, even though he continued to write solid musicals during the 1930s, most notably *Roberta* (1933; "Smoke Gets in Your Eyes").

British writers wrote decent operettas during the period—most notably, Frederick Norton and Oscar Asche's *Chu Chin Chow* (1916), which ran for over 2,200 performances in London. Overall, 1920s British audiences preferred operettas imported from America, many of which were adapted into at least one successful film. After 1930, however, several British composers rose to prominence. Noel Gay's *Me and My Girl* (1937; "The Lambeth Walk") was popular in its day and reborn in a popular London and New York revival in 1985–86. Ivor Novello was a popular English actor who wrote several musicals, most notably *The Dancing Years* (1939), which remain virtually unknown in America. By contrast, actor-director-playwright-composer-lyricist Noel Coward became well-known in America with such shows as *Bitter Sweet* (1929; "I'll See You Again").

The Musical in the United States and Great Britain, 1940–2000

After breaking up with Lorenz Hart (who soon died), Richard Rodgers established a partnership with librettist-lyricist Oscar Hammerstein, becoming the most successful team in American history. *Oklahoma!* (1943; "Oh, What a Beautiful Morning") reminded wartime America of what they were fighting for, and the show ran for five years. The duo then wrote an even better musical, *Carousel* (1945; "If I Loved You"). They also enjoyed great success with the hit-laden *South Pacific* (1949; "Bali Ha'i," "This Nearly Was Mine"), *The King and I* (1951; "Shall We Dance?"), *Flower Drum Song* (1958; "I Enjoy Being a Girl"), and *The Sound of Music* (1959; "Do Re Mi," "Climb Every Mountain"). All six of these shows have been preserved in relatively faithful film adaptations. These musical dramas, often including dance to help tell the story, took on such serious issues as spousal abuse, racism, and war while remaining very entertaining, thanks to Hammerstein's soul and Rodgers's musical brilliance.

Alan Jay Lerner and German immigrant Frederick Loewe, after warming up with *Brigadoon* (1947) and *Paint Your Wagon* (1951), matched the fame of Rodgers and Hammerstein with *My Fair Lady* (1956). This adaptation of G.B. Shaw's *Pygmalion*, which made a star of Julie Andrews, still belongs on any "Top Five" list of American musicals, with its great story and solid gold score ("I Could Have Danced All Night," "Get Me to the Church on Time," "I've Grown Accustomed to Her Face").

Another German immigrant, Kurt Weill, came to America and wrote the music for several shows, most notably *Lady in the Dark* (1941; "My Ship"). *The Three Penny Opera* (1933), an adaptation of *The Beggar's Opera* written in Germany with Bertolt Brecht, opened Off-Broadway in 1954 in its English translation ("Mack the Knife"), running over 2,200 performances.

Harold Arlen, although a white songwriter, was best known for his blues songs ("Stormy Weather," "Blues in the Night"), along with his score with lyricist E.Y. "Yip" Harburg for the immortal 1939 film *The Wizard of Oz* ("Over the Rainbow"). Harburg and Burton Lane wrote *Finian's Rainbow* (1947), which took a light-hearted poke at Southern racism.

After the postwar "American invasion" of London by Rodgers and Hammerstein musicals, several British songwriters emerged during the 1950s. Sandy Wilson wrote *The Boy Friend* (1954), a love letter to 1920s musical comedies. Lionel Bart had a huge hit in both London and New York with his adaptation of a Dickens novel, *Oliver!* (1960, London, 1963, New York; "Consider Yourself"). Anthony Newley and Leslie Bricusse succeeded in both London and New York with *Stop the World, I Want to Get Off* (1961/62; "What Kind of Fool Am I?"), which also starred Newley.

Back in America, Frank Loesser wrote words and music for what may be Broadway's most perfect musical comedy, *Guys and Dolls* (1950; "Luck Be a Lady"). He also managed to turn office life into a Pulitzer Prize–winning show, *How To Succeed in Business Without Really Trying* (1961; "I Believe in You"). Several of Loesser's protégés produced tuneful hit scores of their own: Robert Wright and George Forrest (*Kismet*, 1953), Richard Adler and Jerry Ross (*The Pajama Game*, 1954 and *Damn Yankees*, 1955), and Meredith Willson (*The Music Man*, 1957). In the 1960s composer-lyricist Jerry Herman began writing his own cheerfully melodic musicals, including *Hello, Dolly!* (1964), *Mame* (1966), and *La Cage aux Folles* (1983; "I Am What I Am").

In contrast to all these traditional shows, the "American tribal love-rock" musical *Hair* (1968; "Good Morning Starshine," "Aquarius"), written by James Rado, Gerome Ragni, and composer Galt MacDermot, seemed very hip and contemporary at the time, but it hardly signaled the end of traditional musicals. More likely, the replacement of hit show tunes by rock-and-roll on radio had a larger effect on the decline of the Broadway musical as an influential popular medium. Nevertheless, the musical has remained the mainstay of Broadway for the past several decades, and shows such as Charles Strouse and Lee Adams's *Bye Bye Birdie* (1960; "Put on a Happy Face") continue to thrive in community and high-school productions.

And when a show really strikes a chord, it can seemingly run forever. Tom Jones and Harvey Schmidt's *The Fantasticks* ("Try to Remember") opened in a small Off-Broadway theater in 1960 and ran there for over 40 years. Jerry Bock and Sheldon Harnick set Broadway longevity records on Broadway with *Fiddler on the Roof* (1964; "If I Were a Rich Man," "Sunrise, Sunset"), which ran for eight years and was successfully revived in 2004. About the time this show closed, the 1950s rock musical *Grease* opened (1972; "Summer Nights"). The only show written by Jim Jacobs and Warren Casey, *Grease* also ran eight years on and off Broadway, spawning the 1978 hit film adaptation. *A Chorus Line* (1975; "What I Did for Love"), by Marvin Hamlisch and Edward Kleban, ran an astounding 15 years, a record later to be eclipsed by Andrew Lloyd Webber's *Cats*. John Kander and Fred Ebb's *Chicago* (1975; "All That Jazz") enjoyed moderate success in its original 1975 production, as had their first hit *Cabaret* (1966), but the 1996 revival of *Chicago* was still running nine years later, even though by 2003 most musical lovers had seen the Oscar-winning film adaptation.

Although most musicals live or die by the quality of their libretto and musical score, several famous musicals are best known for their directors and/or choreographers. Jerome Robbins directed and created dance for a number of memorable musicals, including *On the Town* (1944) and *Fiddler on the Roof*, being universally acknowledged as one of the true geniuses of the theater. Bob Fosse's distinctive dance style (recognizable by his use of hats, hunched shoulders, and toed-in footwork) helped enliven such shows as *Pajama Game, Damn Yankees, How to Succeed, Sweet Charity,* and *Chicago*. Other influential choreographers include Agnes DeMille (*Oklahoma!, Brigadoon*), Jack Cole (*Kismet, Forum*), Michael Kidd (*Guys and Dolls, Can-Can*), and Gower Champion (*Bye Bye Birdie, Hello, Dolly!,* and *42nd Street* [1980]). Currently Susan Stroman, with several recent hits to her credit (most notably *The Producers* [see below]), seems to be today's hottest director-choreographer.

Librettist-lyricists Betty Comden and Adolph Green worked together exclusively from the late 1930s until Green's death in 2002. With composer Leonard Bernstein they wrote *On the Town* (1944) and *Wonderful Town* (1953). They wrote several shows with composer Jule Styne, including *Bells Are Ringing* (1956; "Just in Time," "The Party's Over"). More recently they wrote *On the Twentieth Century* (1978) and *The Will Rogers Follies* (1991) with Cy Coleman. Coleman, who died in 2004 (as did Fred Ebb), was a jazz musician who wrote several sophisticated scores with other lyricists, including Carolyn Leigh (*Wildcat,* 1960; "Hey, Look Me Over"), Dorothy Fields (*Sweet Charity,* 1966; "Big Spender"), and Michael Stewart (*Barnum,* 1980). Styne launched Barbra Streisand's stardom with *Funny Girl* (1964; "People"), but his finest writing came in *Gypsy* (1959; "Everything's Coming Up Roses"), with lyricist Stephen Sondheim.

Although Sondheim started as a lyricist on *West Side Story* (1957; "Maria") with composer Bernstein, after *Gypsy* he pursued his dream to write both music and lyrics with *A Funny Thing Happened on the Way to the Forum* (1962; "Comedy Tonight"). His mentor had been Oscar Hammerstein, who taught him well. Indeed, Sondheim has reigned as the undisputed genius of the musical theater since 1970. Best known for "Send in the Clowns" from *A Little Night Music* (1973), Sondheim wrote the landmark "concept musical" *Company* (1970), a non-linear, episodic exploration of bachelorhood and marriage. Equally bold and innovative were *Follies* (1971; "Broadway Baby"), *Sweeney Todd* (1979), and *Sunday in the Park with George* (1984). His collaboration in the 1970s with producer-director Harold Prince produced amazing work.

Another type of show, one that might be called the "compilation revue," is built around songs associated with one songwriter or performer. The most notable examples include *Jacques Brel Is Alive and Well...* (Brel, 1968), *Side by Side by*

Sondheim (1977), *Ain't Misbehavin'* (Fats Waller, 1978), *Sophisticated Ladies* (Duke Ellington, 1981), and *Smokey Joe's Café* (Lieber and Stoller, 1995). More recently Broadway shows have been built around the collected songs of ABBA (*Mamma Mia!*, 2002) and Billy Joel (*Movin' Out*, 2002).

During what became the "Age of Sondheim" in America, in Great Britain composer Andrew Lloyd Webber wrote *Jesus Christ, Superstar* (1971; "I Don't Know How to Love Him") and *Evita* (1979; "Don't Cry for Me Argentina") with lyricist Tim Rice. During this time a new sub-genre, the "megamusical," became the dominant form. These large-scale shows, often produced in London by Cameron Macintosh, made stage effects the real stars, and several of them had no libretto, relying entirely on songs. Lloyd Webber's *Cats* (1981 London, 1982 New York; "Memory"), a spectacle about singing, dancing cats, ran 21 years in London and 18 years on Broadway. Lloyd Webber's immensely popular *The Phantom of the Opera* (1986 London, 1988 New York; "The Music of the Night"), which "starred" a crashing chandelier, was finally filmed in 2004. Alain Boublil and Claude-Michel Schönberg's *Les Misèrables* (1980 Paris, 1985 London, 1987 New York; "Do You Hear the People Sing?") became a multi-billion-dollar franchise around the world, playing nearly 6,700 performances in New York alone. The team had another hit in London and New York with *Miss Saigon* (1989–91), which featured a helicopter appearing to land on stage. Yet another French musical, *Notre Dame de Paris* (1998), has enjoyed great success in Europe.

Lloyd Webber's star has dimmed lately, with such recent musicals as *The Beautiful Game* (2000) and *The Woman in White* (2004) failing to match his past shows' huge popularity. At age 75 Sondheim also struggled to regain his past magic. His musical comedy *Bounce* failed to show enough promise in its 2004 Chicago and Washington DC productions to lead to a Broadway opening, at least as of 2005.

Two other composer-lyricists must be mentioned. Stephen Schwartz had youthful hits with *Godspell* (1971; "Day by Day") and *Pippin* (1972; "Magic to Do"), and after years of writing scores for Disney films, he has returned to Broadway with the immensely popular *Wicked* (2004), the Oz story told from the witches' perspective. William Finn's witty *Falsettos* (1992), which was a compilation of two earlier one-act musicals, followed gay Jewish characters through various family problems, including AIDS. His 2005 Off-Broadway musical *The 25th Annual Putnam County Spelling Bee* was universally praised, stimulating a move to a larger Broadway theater.

TRENDS AND THE FUTURE FOR THE AMERICAN MUSICAL THEATER

The current trend in America is toward adapting familiar films into musicals. In 2001 Mel Brooks adapted his 1968 film *The Producers* into a blockbuster that struggled somewhat after the exit of its stars Nathan Lane and Matthew Broderick. This success was closely followed by Mark Shaiman and Scott Wittman's *Hairspray*, the biggest hit of 2002–3, which was based on the John Waters film of the same title. The trend continued in 2005 with *Dirty Rotten Scoundrels* and *Monty Python's Spamalot* (based on *Monty Python and the Holy Grail*). With the price of mounting a new musical exceeding $10 million, many producers want to have a bankable title and plot to build upon. The Disney corporation has, indeed, led this trend with its Broadway adaptations of *Beauty and the Beast* (1994) and *The Lion King* (1997), with *Chitty Chitty Bang Bang* (2002) and *Mary Poppins* (2004) flying over to New York from London engagements.

In contrast to these spectaculars, several younger songwriters have devoted themselves to creating more intimate, intelligent musical theater. Jonathan Larson unfortunately died before his breakthrough hit *Rent* (1996; "Seasons of Love") opened. The show is currently moving toward its 4,000th Broadway performance. Most of his contemporaries, including Alan Menken (*Little Shop of Horrors*, 1982), Stephen Flaherty and Lynn Ahrens (*Ragtime*, 1998), Michael John LaChiusa (*The Wild Party*, 2000), Jeanine Tesori (*Violet*, 1996), Jason Robert Brown (*Parade*, 1998), and Adam Guettel (*Floyd Collins*, 1995), have all either shunned or struggled to find commercial success with their earnest, high-minded musicals. However, *Hairspray* reminded everyone that popular musicals can be smart, fun, and lucrative. So has *Avenue Q* (2004), essentially an R-rated Muppet show with a clever score by newcomers Robert Lopez and Jeff Marx.

The American theater has been the "fabulous invalid" for over 100 years. But just as musical theater survived the twentieth century worldwide despite economic pressures, it will probably continue to entertain audiences through the twenty-first century, as long as talented people keep it breathing with song and dance.

NOTE

1. Parenthetical information after show titles includes the year of first production and a key song from the musical.

FURTHER READING

Bordman, Gerald. *American Musical Theatre: A Chronicle*. 3rd ed. New York: Oxford University Press, 2001.

Everett, William A. and Paul R. Laird, eds. *The Cambridge Companion to the Musical*. Cambridge and New York: Cambridge University Press, 2002.

Green, Stanley. *Broadway Musicals Show by Show*. 3rd ed. Milwaukee: Hal Leonard, 1990.

Henderson, Amy and Dwight Blocker Bowers. *Red, Hot, and Blue: A Smithsonian Salute to the American Musical*. Washington: Smithsonian Institution Press, 1996.

Kantor, Michael and Laurence Maslon. *Broadway: The American Musical*. New York: Bulfinch Press, 2004.

Lerner, Alan Jay. *The Musical Theatre*. New York: McGraw Hill, 1986.

Lewis, David H. *Broadway Musicals: A Hundred Year History*. Jefferson, North Carolina: McFarland, 2002.

Outdoor Drama

Eszter A. Julian

There is a particular piece of advice that, although still worthwhile, has been repeated so often that it has become a cliché, to "write what you know." Well-worn it may be, but this advice appears to have worked for playwright Paul Green, who is widely acknowledged as the originator of modern outdoor drama in the United States. Green wisely followed the counsel of Frederick Koch, his professor at the University of North Carolina in Chapel Hill, to write what he knew around him, and to make use of the soil beneath his feet. Throughout his long career, Green wrote plays that revolved around the normal, everyday people he knew best. These "folk dramas" are intrinsically linked to Green's vision of drama as an embodiment of the American democratic ideal, as being of the people, by the people, and for the people. With the vast, sweeping epic outdoor dramas that he created starting in the 1930s, he did, to a certain extent, succeed in creating this democratic drama. In Green and his works lie the beginnings of the unique form that is American outdoor drama, and this essay will attempt to introduce and describe this form to the reader, to examine its distinctiveness, and to peer into its uncertain future.

OUTDOOR DRAMA IN THE UNITED STATES

The concept of outdoor drama, of plays enacted in the open air, is not a new one: the Greeks performed dramas in their great stone amphitheater and later, Elizabethan theater companies and their audiences filled spaces such as the Globe Theatre. For all this illustrious past, the history of outdoor drama in the United States is a relatively brief one. Paul Green's "symphonic drama" *The Lost Colony* is generally accepted as the first modern outdoor drama, and it opened in 1937 in eastern North Carolina. Today, all sorts of different dramas are performed all over the country. Outdoor historical dramas, based on the facts of the past or on legends, are usually the most common. Shakespeare is also regularly performed outdoors, and there are also religious and passion plays scattered across the country, with plots coming from biblical or other sources. The content of the plays can range from these religious, classical, and historical subjects to plays based on well-known novels or music. The Rodgers and Hammerstein musical *Oklahoma!* is performed outdoors at the Discoveryland! Amphitheater in—where else?—Tulsa, Oklahoma during the summer, and Paul Green's *Cross and Sword,* based on the early history of Florida, has been declared the official play of that state. As far away as Alaska's Kodiak Island, the "sounds of balalaikas, Russian folk music and dancers transport audiences back to the tiny settlement whose traces remain in today's Kodiak" in Frank Brink's *Cry of the Wild Ram,* which is set in that state prior to its purchase by the United States from Russia.

Mark Sumner, the former head of the Institute of Outdoor Drama has said that "Spectators…attend these presentations [outdoor historical dramas] for many of the same reasons that the ancient classics were attended: for knowledge and empathy for other people and times." He has also emphasized that these dramas are not merely repetitions of history lessons, but are actually creations for the stage based on historical fact or educated conjecture. Many of the plays are performed annually, during the summer months, and many of them fit into the category of Paul Green's concept of "symphonic drama."

Green coined the term to express his feeling of being a composer, putting together many different instruments and aspects to achieve a harmonious whole. Using all sorts of different theatrical arts, "motifs must be developed, thematic statements made and exploited, and a ferment of symphonic creativity must be kept brewing to self-realization." Symphonic drama is characterized primarily by its profusion of arts; as Green said regarding the development of the concept,

> I was having to call upon nearly all the available elements in modern theatrical art… Folk song and poetry were needed here. Likewise the dance and pantomime and chorus voices. Even the mental speech of the grisly microphone and echo chamber could be used.…Moments…would call for masks. And ever there was the dynamic flow and modulation of light to accompany the human behavior at work.…And always there was music—music!…I found…that by the symphonic use of the various elements of the theater, especially music, there came a freedom and fullness of possible story statement not otherwise to be had in dealing with large groups of people in action.

Although the symphonic drama approach comes very close to a pageant, or a series of separate performances based on a single theme, the goal is that all the elements of "modern theatrical art" will combine to produce one unified whole, and the ideas of the drama will be reinforced through dance, song, mime, and other arts. One author, at least, sees in symphonic drama the danger that characters and plot will fade in importance next to the spectacle of the thing. However, Green's intention was not to produce plays that were merely spectacular, in the sense that a pageant or a circus is spectacular, but rather to create works whose themes were expressed to the audience in more ways than through acting alone.

Although the performance of plays in a natural setting is part of a long tradition, American outdoor drama is distinguished from its predecessors to some extent because outdoor drama here has developed into a separate genre. Most outdoor dramas are not simply plays produced outside, but something slightly different. Shakespeare's plays, for example, are frequently performed outside, as they were in the time of their writer, but they can also be moved indoors without damage to the production.

Outdoor drama, on the other hand, cannot be enclosed. It belongs to an entirely separate category of creations that are part play or symphonic drama, part historical spectacle, and part tourist attraction.

Across the United States, the one thing that most outdoor dramas share is their very difference from "indoor drama"; however, there are other significant differences as well, most of them deriving from the scale and the location of the endeavors. As Sumner put it, "The aim of outdoor drama is, of course, the aim of all drama, except that, in doing it outdoors, it puts it on a grand scale—the natural setting, the combination of several art forms on the stage—to enhance all the emotions connected to the play." Outdoor drama is more sweeping, more epic in nature, and, out of necessity, many of its elements must be correspondingly larger because of its grander setting. Sumner further said that "The creation in that big space of the kind of illusion of reality that you must achieve is very difficult because you're using bigger spaces, more people, and your rehearsals take longer....Most people...aren't trained in the amount of energy that it takes vocally or physically in terms of just moving around the stage and being 'on' for that space of time in that big area. It's more difficult than people think."

Acting in Outdoor Drama

Actors in outdoor dramas have an entirely different set of considerations than those involved in "indoor drama." Good projection is essential, as the theater spaces are often very large. Although many outdoor theaters were designed with acoustics in mind, actors must bear in mind that there are few walls and very little, if any, roof, and sound will simply disappear into the air. Outdoor dramas' actors must also be prepared for long, hot runs, since many of these productions run for most of the summer. While not necessarily longer than runs elsewhere, they do tend to be considerably hotter. Actors have to be able to deal with the humidity, heat, and heavy historical costumes. There are different technical considerations as well: the time and the position of the sunset must be considered when lighting the action, and outdoor dramas often have spectacular special effects that must be carefully controlled. Some outdoor dramas feature animals onstage, such as horses, and there must be people present who can control them. The grandiose, epic nature of outdoor drama is such that all aspects of it must be correspondingly larger.

Production in Outdoor Drama

Although the acting and technical considerations involved in outdoor drama are not too far removed from those of indoor drama, the outdoor variety can certainly provide a unique set of challenges. The natural elements can play a capricious role in the production, either enhancing the production or, on occasion, detracting or distracting from it. Author Philip Hill has claimed that the "opportunity to use the beauties of nature as an element of the dramatic production is one of the real advantages that outdoor drama can offer" and Sumner once said that on occasion "the natural elements get into the act and enhance what you've done," but the outdoor setting can also produce difficulties that are far out of the realm of indoor theater. While a beautiful sunset can be more awesome than any painted backdrop, indoor presentations do not usually have to contend with the possibility of, say, having a skunk wander onstage. Such a thing happened during one production of *Trumpet in the Land:* Sumner relates how the mere sight of the animal caused much of the audience to abandon their seats, and the actors to avoid the part of the stage containing the skunk.

Towering clouds and rumblings of thunder can add atmosphere and a sense of doom to productions; however, they also result in "rain pace," the absurdly fast speed that the actors must assume when inclement weather threatens. Even the night noises of the outdoors, which many take for granted, can become hindrances to the production. Author Mary Nordstrom, in her pictorial guide to American outdoor drama, tells a story regarding *Tecumseh!* that may discomfit environmentalists:

> The environmental complications of staging outdoor drama are emphasized by producer-director W. L. (Rusty) Mundell who enjoys recounting the story of how he dealt with the dilemma of noisy tree frogs. Applying his knowledge of natural selectivity and the nocturnal habits of the cacophonic offenders, he solved the problem by stocking the pond in the stage area with sunfish and bass. The sunfish ate the frog eggs and the bass ate the sunfish. Tree frogs no longer drowned out the dialogue when the 'houselights' go down!

Theaters and Performing Spaces in Outdoor Drama

Naturally, outdoor drama also requires a different type of theater. The theaters tend to be quite large, in accordance with the large casts, the dances, and musicians that they must contain, and they often take an amphitheater-like form.

Author Philip Hill, in his article on theaters for outdoor drama, goes into considerable detail about the sorts of things that must be taken into account before building:

The natural acoustics of the site in question must be reasonably good, and it should be safely removed from the light and noise of highways, towns, athletic areas, or other distractions, while still remaining easily accessible from well-travelled highways. If daytime use of the theater is intended, it should face north, in order to avoid getting direct sunlight in the eyes of either the audience or the actors, but if only night use is contemplated, it should be oriented so the prevailing breeze will blow from the stage to the audience.

Hill also discusses such things as acoustics and how to improve them, dressing room space, laundry facilities, considerations when using body makeup, several examples of seat number to parking place ratios, the average amount of sheltered space per seat in a theater, and other considerations that are definitely unique to outdoor drama.

Despite the challenges of dealing with tree frogs, skunks, or vast amounts of laundry, the aspect of outdoor drama that most distinguishes it from its indoor counterpart is its site specificity. Many of us are used to indoor theaters in which different plays are presented each season, but with outdoor drama, the same play is presented year after year in the same location. The theaters, often built into the landscape itself or using it as a sort of backdrop, are rather permanent, and are frequently designed and built for particular plays, unlike indoor theaters, which tend to be built for plays in general. The subject matter of outdoor historical dramas, whether it is history or legend, is intrinsically linked to the land in the area, for it is often the very site of the experiences of those figures depicted in the play. Harry Davis, in his essay for the 1957 program of *Unto These Hills,* emphasized this by writing that "Another important feature of the historical play is its direct, indigenous relation to the locale in which it is staged. In nearly all instances the dramatized story, rooted in historical fact, is presented on or near the site where the real story took place. This imparts a valuable spiritual quality into the performance, since it becomes a sort of pilgrimage to holy ground."

For example, *Unto These Hills,* a play that takes the history of the Cherokee tribe as its subject, is performed annually on the Cherokee Reservation in western North Carolina. *The Lost Colony,* which is about the mysterious disappearance of the English settlers from Roanoke, is actually played on Roanoke Island, on the site of the settlers' disappearance. The plays tend to emphasize this for their audiences; for example, the character of the Historian in *The Lost Colony* tells the audience that the colonists "took possession of the Indian village on the north end of Roanoke Island where we are gathered tonight." In an interview, Sumner relates an occasion where the idea was put forward that *The Lost Colony* ought to be presented at the site of *Unto These Hills,* and vice versa. It was decided, however, that the proposal was impossible—the cost of altering the theaters to accommodate the play from the opposite end of the state proved to be prohibitive, and the plays lost some significance by not being presented in the location that is the actual location of the play. "That sense of hallowed ground, that sense of pilgrimage, which is so important to an outdoor historical drama, could not take place" in those circumstances.

OUTDOOR DRAMA'S APPEAL

It is their relative permanence—along, perhaps, with the fact that they are often produced in the summer, when weather tends to be more cooperative—that combines with their site specificity to give many of these dramas a distinctive status as tourist attractions. As early as 1955, Kermit Hunter, a writer of outdoor dramas, told his readers that "the real advantages of the outdoor drama are not found at the box office. The return comes from increased tourist trade" and this still holds true today. Scott Parker, the current director of the Institute of Outdoor Drama, makes clear that outdoor dramas play a large role as tourist attractions, stating that the plays "reach for a tourist audience, which means survival and continued community support in areas where their plays could not otherwise exist on a long time basis." Sumner, in saying that "We have a much broader audience in outdoor drama," also emphasizes the "tourist audience." Most outdoor historical dramas, in order to remain viable, must continue to attract audiences of all ages—grandparents and grandchildren alike should be able to enjoy the productions.

As far as the economic impact of outdoor drama, Parker concurred that it is generally much vaster than that associated with indoor theaters. These dramas, he said, are part of the travel and tourism industry, and attract out-of-state residents who spend money in hotels, restaurants, shops, and the like. Indoor theaters, he said, attract mostly local residents. Of course, there may be some exceptions—perhaps Broadway—but in most places, there is no doubt that this is true. People may travel distances of many miles to see a particular outdoor drama, or their visit may be a part of their travels in a particular state, but rarely would a traveler choose to drive a hundred miles or so just to attend an indoor theater in a particular area.

The program for the 2005 season at Snow Camp, North Carolina, also helps clarify how these dramas become, and interact with, tourist attractions. The program tells the reader that some of the main characters from *Sword of Peace* "are buried in the old graveyard at Cane Creek meeting just up the road from the amphitheater," thus making the history shown in the play even more tangible. In addition, the brochure for the 2005 season features a map with numbered sites of historic significance that a visitor can examine, all within walking distance of the actual theater. Sumner adds that "the audience might well the next morning go over to a graveyard where some of the people in the play are actually buried, or they might go to some of the buildings in the town or in the areas where certain things have taken place, and...these [are] a big part of the adventure of attending at outdoor historical drama."

One can hardly discuss outdoor drama, its past and its future, without mentioning the role played by the University of North Carolina at Chapel Hill (UNC-CH). Outdoor drama can be said to have begun there—Paul Green graduated from the university before going on to write Pulitzer Prize-winning dramas as well as *The Lost Colony*, which is often cited as the first outdoor historical drama. In addition, the Institute of Outdoor Drama is based at UNC-CH. Scott Parker, the current director, writes on the organization's web site that the Institute was established in 1963 and is "the only organization in the US providing national leadership in fostering artistic and managerial excellence and expansion of the outdoor drama movement through training, research and advisory programs, and serves as a national clearinghouse for its more that 100 constituent theatre companies across the nation."

The influence of UNC-CH can also be seen in the writing of many authors active during the first years of the outdoor drama movement. These authors tend to indicate that the way to go about producing an outdoor drama was to find a play or request one from a playwright, and then write to the University of North Carolina and for assistance and advice from the experienced professionals there.

Kermit Hunter, himself a well-known writer of outdoor dramas, wrote in his 1955 article about how to go about establishing an outdoor drama. He declares that the person who has the idea "usually writes a letter to Paul Green, or Samuel Selden, someone at the University of North Carolina, and in a rather cautious way requests that he be given some information on a 'pageant'." Green himself wrote that "Hardly a day passes that I don't get a letter from some section of the United States asking me to come and write a symphonic drama and help build a theater to stage it in."

In the early 1900s, plays were produced in the Forest Theatre, a small outdoor amphitheater on the campus of the university. Though it is smaller than a typical theater for outdoor drama, and was not built for a particular play, as many of those theaters are, it still provided challenges similar to those that outdoor dramatists face today. Because of this, expertise in the field of outdoor drama was already present at the University when the time came to build larger theaters and produce different plays, such as *The Lost Colony*. Prototypes for today's outdoor dramas, Parker said, were "here in Chapel Hill." Green's first play, *Surrender to the Enemy*, which he wrote and submitted as part of a contest for original plays, was actually produced at the Forest Theatre on the University of North Carolina campus during his freshman year at the college, 1916–17.

OUTDOOR DRAMA AS "DEMOCRATIC THEATER"

As noted it is impossible to discuss outdoor drama in the United States without significant attention to Paul Green, generally given credit as the originator of modern outdoor drama. In addition, his concept of symphonic drama has widely influenced many of the other outdoor dramas in this country. As author Charles Watson put it, "Green argued that symphonic drama fit the dramatic needs of the American people, but their traditions, exuberant hearts, and even mechanical skill demanded a larger stage than the narrow conventional theater could offer." Watson later seems to suggest that Green achieved this goal; his plays, the author says, "have brought drama to a large cross-section of society, not merely the customary audience for legitimate theater." Or, as Harry Davis wrote in the 1957 Official Program for *Unto These Hills*, "The 'theatre of the people'—drama in the open air—actually was born almost 3,000 years ago. It had its conception in the great amphitheatres of ancient Greece, was nurtured in the Rome of the Caesars, and came of age during the lusty Elizabethan era of England. And then it died. But now...It is being revived through the outdoor historical drama."

In a preface that he wrote to *The Lost Colony*, Green made his ideal of democratic theater clear. The preface takes the form of a dialogue between himself and a theater critic, and when the critic asks him what he means by "a people's theatre," the playwright replies in the following manner: "I mean a theatre in which plays are written, acted, and produced for and by the people—for their enjoyment and enrichment and not for any special monetary profit." His former professor at UNC, Frederick Koch, wrote in the 1938 program for the play that it exemplified "the most democratic of all the arts. In it all may have a part—poets, players, designers, singers, and dancers." Green also said:

> This type of drama which I have elected to call symphonic seems to be fitted to the needs and dramatic genius of the American people. Our richness of tradition, our imaginative folk life, our boundless enthusiasm and health, our singing and dancing and poetry, our lifted hearts and active feet and hands, even our multitudinous mechanical and machine means for self-expression—all are too outpouring for the narrow confines of the usual professional and killingly expensive Broadway play and stage. But they can be put to use in the symphonic drama and its theater. It is wide enough, free enough, and among the people cheap enough for their joy and popular use.

Paradoxically, Green found sources for his democratic drama in old Europe, in Alexis Granowsky's Moscow Jewish Theater and, to some extent, in the work of Bertolt Brecht, in which, according to one author, "the whole story develops through dance, music, films, commentary, or any other device that jars the viewer into awareness, or that relates the events on the stage to the daily happenings of his life." Watson identifies Green's plays having the following characteristics, which can be considered Brechtian: "the progression of scenes is episodic…and the dramatic unities are nowhere to be seen." Green also used music extensively, and one might also consider the fact that, since his plays are frequently based in history, the audience already knows what happened and that they therefore will concentrate on why it is happening, perhaps a variation of Brecht's famous "alienation effect." One can see further parallels in Watson's assertion that Green's outdoor dramas "champion the ideals of freedom and social reform."

Scott Parker, the current head of the Institute of Outdoor Drama , notes that, in the past, people left their houses to seek entertainment such as concerts, theater, film, and other ways of beguiling their time pleasantly, but today's society is more insulated. With films available to us at the touch of a button on our technologically advanced, high definition televisions, with the internet at our fingertips via computers or cell phones, today we could be connected with the outside world more than ever—yet paradoxically, we insulate ourselves, choosing to be entertained at home rather than leaving the house as we did in the past. The decline of audience members throughout all sorts of art forms is now an accepted fact; the question, of course, is how to solve it.

Ironically, Samuel Selden, in his writing in 1952 for the program of *Horn in the West,* wrote the following about the attraction of outdoor drama: he said that people came flocking to see the plays because of the fundamental urge each of us has to escape the confines of our cramped way of living in a modern world. We work in little rooms; we sleep in little rooms; we eat in little rooms, we play, dance, and even watch the movies with our elbows pinned to our sides. But however civilized we have become, we never feel that this crowding is comfortable and right. Both our bodies and our spirits long for freedom.

This freedom, Selden implied, could be found in the experience of attending an epic outdoor drama amidst the beauties of the natural world. His words, though, seem to belong to a different age, one more concerned with manifest destiny and the idea of a frontier people whose love of freedom was overwhelming and formed an integral part of the national character. This desire for the freedom of open spaces, the push to the frontier, is no longer part of the national psyche.

Our changing culture is not the only factor affecting outdoor drama today. The dramas themselves—the plays, the staging, perhaps even the technical aspects—have stayed the same for so many years that they have begun, in a way, to stagnate, with the dramas tied too much to the past. The dropping audience attendance, however, cannot be attributed to any one factor. Instead, it is linked to the changing culture we live in, the availability of electronic entertainment, and the shorter attention spans of audiences today, who may not wish to sit through epic historical presentations. Participation in many activities formerly thought of as communal—anything from bowling to concert and theater attendance to golf—is down, and people are buying fewer newspapers as well. Today we are a more insulated society, and can get whatever entertainment we need from the internet or delivered to our mailboxes to play in our homes. One might think that this would drive us out to seek human companionship, but perhaps that time has not yet arrived.

Many believe that outdoor theaters will have to reinvent themselves for today's culture. Change comes slowly to theaters, and the outdoor drama situation may worsen, to the point of forcing some theaters to close, before it gets better. Theaters may have to change to adjust to the taste of the public, including improving details such as professional acting, lighting and scenery, rather than forcing a change in the general public's taste.

Christopher Zink, the Lighting Designer and Technical Director at Catawba College, who has also worked in outdoor drama, considers that spectacle is a key part of outdoor drama, and when people go to see them, they expect to see spectacle as part of the tourist attraction, and "twirling a fire baton" cannot compare with spectacle as seen in productions such as Cirque du Soleil. While he sees that part of the solution is refurbishing the productions themselves, both technically and script-wise, he proposes a solution: that the venues for outdoor dramas be used at other times for events that have a bigger box-office draw—his suggestion was for bluegrass festivals. These money-making events held in the outdoor dramas' theaters could furnish the funds that the dramas need to continue being produced.

In his article on outdoor drama, playwright Kermit Hunter expressed the opinion that outdoor drama is a unique and distinctly American art form; in writing of the audience's experience, he says, "Thousands of people have sat there watching and listening to a simple story out of the unending panorama of American history; and they have been deeply moved, because it dealt with timeless values." Outdoor drama has descended from European ancestors via Paul Green to become a uniquely American form. Green saw his symphonic dramas as reflections of the ideals and values of the country as a whole. It would seem that in this time of change, the future of outdoor drama is uncertain. We can only hope that the theaters are able to reinvent themselves and their plays, because it would indeed be unfortunate if this unique form were to disappear forever.

FURTHER READING

Adams, Agatha Boyd. *Paul Green of Chapel Hill.* Edited by Richard Walser. Chapel Hill, North Carolina: University of North Carolina Press, 1951.

Free, William J. and Charles B. Lower. *History into Drama: A Source Book on Symphonic Drama Including the Complete Text of Paul Green's The Lost Colony.* New York: Odyssey Press, 1963.

Green, Paul. "Symphonic Drama." *College English.* Vol. 10, no. 7 (April 1949): 359–65.

Hill, Philip G. "A Theatre for the Outdoor Historical Drama." *Educational Theatre Journal.* Vol. 14, no. 4 (December 1962): 312–17.

Hunter, Kermit. "The Theatre Meets the People." *Educational Theatre Journal.* Vol. 7, no. 2 (May 1955): 128–35.

Institute of Outdoor Drama. Web site of the Institute, located at the University of North Carolina at Chapel Hill: http://www.unc.edu/depts/outdoor/index.html.

Kenny, Vincent S. *Paul Green.* New York: Twayne Publishers, 1971.

Nordstrom, Mary. *Outdoor Drama: Pictorial Guide to Over Fifty Annual Productions in the United States.* Chapel Hill, North Carolina: North South Artscope Publications, 1985.

Parker, Scott. "Outdoor Dramas Expand Across the Country." Institute of Outdoor Drama. (http://www.unc.edu/depts/outdoor/scottarticle.html). Accessed May 22, 2006.

Sumner, Mark. "Mark Sumner: Reflections on Rise of Outdoor Historical Dramas." Southern Theatre Summer 1990, pp. 6–15, 20.

Watson, Charles S. *The History of Southern Drama.* Lexington: University Press of Kentucky, 1997.

PART V

Dramatic Genres and Styles

❧

Dada in Drama

Sarah Bay-Cheng

"What is dada? An art? A philosophy? Politics? *Fire insurance?* Or: the state religion? Is dada actual energy? Or is it absolutely nothing?"

These questions, included in an unpublished anthology of Dada literature in 1920, appear at first to explain Dada, but then they confuse. What is Dada? The answers listed here are nonsense. How can something be described as an art, a philosophy, and *fire insurance?* The more one reads about Dada, the more distant the definition. Significantly, the questions posed here were never answered by artists in Dada. Nor were they meant to be. One of the distinguishing characteristics of Dada, unique among artistic and cultural movements of the twentieth century, is its passionate insistence that it never become an artistic, cultural, or political movement. Unlike its successor surrealism, Dada never wanted to be consistent in anything except its inconsistency. Dada aspired to uncertainty, confusion, and anti-establishment ideals. To define Dada was to misrepresent it. Often described by its adherents as "anti-art," Dada attempted to become a movement that was against all movements, to create works of art that privileged the process of creation more than the art object itself, and to break down existing ideas about art and life. In short, the purpose of Dada was to confuse, anger, and incite its audience into a new way of looking at the modern world.

One of the seminal instances of this challenge was the famous presentation of Marcel Duchamp's sculpture, "Fountain" (1917), to the American Society of Independent Artists. Signed only "R. Mutt," the object—more commonly recognizable as a common urinal—immediately caused an uproar. Described as obscene and outrageous, the "Fountain" was banned from the exhibition and prompted an outcry in the art world, even among those who considered themselves avant-garde.

This was almost certainly Duchamp's intention. As a member of the Independent Artists, Duchamp well knew the conventions surrounding art, particularly its presence in galleries and exhibitions and audiences' receptions of modern art. Only a few years earlier, an American critic labeled Duchamp's cubist painting "Nude Descending a Staircase" (1912) "an explosion in a shingle factory." In the years before the Independent Artists show in New York, Duchamp pursued a type of sculpture he called "readymade." Duchamp collected objects such as bicycle wheels and bottle racks on the street or in stores and, without altering the object, presented them as art. Rather than craft something himself, Duchamp found the sculptures already made, hence the term "readymade." With the "Fountain," Duchamp did not alter the art object/urinal other than to turn it on its side and sign a fictitious name. By placing an object of common (and, to some, vulgar) use in the sphere of public viewing, Duchamp deliberately challenged prevailing opinions of art. There is little aesthetic in the presentation of a urinal; the object itself evokes a more functional context, bringing to mind public restrooms and urination in place of considerations of beauty. Moreover, the lack of effort (this was not marble or clay carved into the image of a urinal, but merely a piece of plumbing purchased from a supply store) was roundly denounced by the artistic community of New York.

For the purposes of Dada, especially its thwarted public performance (the urinal was excluded from the public exhibition), both Duchamp's "Fountain" and its reception highlight the key elements of Dada art and performance: namely, the challenging of established conventions and social mores; the revealing (and reveling) of things of daily life commonly thought improper, dirty, or even obscene; and the belief that the best way to affect an audience was by direct, immediate confrontation. This last aspect of Dada would prove especially important to experimental performance throughout Europe in the years between two World Wars. While poetry and painting captured the confusions and horrors of modern life through abstraction and randomness in painting and sculpture, it was through live performance and film that Dada affected its audience with the immediacy and impact it most desired.

BEGINNINGS OF DADA

Given the centrality of the audience and the assault of public propriety, it should come as no surprise that Dada itself began as theatrical performance. In 1916, two young and ambitious theater artists, Hugo Ball and Emmy Hennings, fled to Zurich from Germany to escape World War I. Both Ball and Hennings had worked in theaters in Germany and Austria, and they met while Hennings was performing in the Cabaret Simplizissimus in Munich, 1913. While in Germany, Ball apprenticed alongside the famous German expressionist director Max Reinhardt, and worked as the dramaturg for the Kammerspiele ("intimate" or "little" theater) in Munich in 1915. As a performer, Hennings embodied the energy and aesthetic of many Dada performances to come. In 1912, the journal *Die Aktion* (*Action*) published the following account of Hennings performance:

> She stepped onto the cabaret stage her face waxen, ribboned about the neck, with her cropped yellow hair and stiffly layered ruffles of her skimpy, dark velvet dress, she was separated from humanity...Emmy Hennings, very made-up, hypnotized by Morphine, Absinthe and the bloodly flame of the electric "Gloire" torn in extremist distortion of the Gothic, her voice hops across the corpses and will mock them, soulfully trilling like a yellow canary.

Unlike most popular cabaret of the period, Hennings rejection of beauty, even her humanity, reflected an important shift in the artistic values that would became Dada theater.

In this early performance, many of the guiding principles of Dada were established. Like many Dada artists to follow, Hennings used sexuality in her performances to make her audience uncomfortable and to test the limits of public performance. By distorting her physical body, she distanced herself from a character, and her exaggerated sexuality undermined the usual femininity of cabaret performances. Her appearance as a corpse similarly predicted Dada's future directions; her combination of sex and death foreshadowed its frequent juxtapositions in both Dada and surrealist performances. Georg Grosz, for example, created a character known as "Dadadeath," and skulls and macabre attire became common images of Dada in the years after World War I. Indeed, the war itself served as an important touchstone for European artists as they struggled to create in the wake of the world's first mechanized war. In his ruminations about theater of the early twentieth century, Ball considered macabre performances as accurate, even necessary, reflections of the coming age. As he wrote in his published journal, *Flight out of Time* (written 1916, published 1927):

> The image of the human form is gradually disappearing from the painting of these times and all objects appear only in fragments. This is one more proof of how ugly and worn the human countenance has become, and of how all the objects of our environment have become repulsive to us.

Written in the midst of World War I, Ball's assessment of war-ravaged Europe and the impact on artistic representation directly translated into the performance of the Cabaret Voltaire in Zurich, Switzerland.

Fleeing Germany in 1916, Ball and Hennings arrived in Zurich, a refuge for many artists escaping World War I. Since the war began, Ball had become obsessed with a new kind of performance. Although declared unfit for military service, Ball witnessed for himself the horrors of the world's first mechanized war. In November 1914, Ball travelled to Belgium, where he directly observed soldiers on the front lines. Shocked by the brutality of the war, Ball wrote soon after, "Theatre has no sense any more. Who wants to act now, or even see acting?...I feel about the theatre as a man must feel who has suddenly been decapitated." But this did not quench his desire for performance. Inspired by the Italian futurist manifestoes, which proclaimed the beauty of machines, fragmentation, and the virtues of simultaneous action, Ball and Hennings began openly soliciting for artists to join them in their new performance venture, the Cabaret Voltaire. Named for the hedonist French writer and philosopher, the Cabaret at first presented experimental readings of poetry and exhibitions of art. Music soon became an important part of the Cabaret, including Ball's own sound poems, Richard Huelsenbeck's drumming, and noise. Through its often wild antics and openness to new forms of art, the Cabaret attracted a core group of artists, poets, painters, and playwrights—including the writer Tristan Tzara, and the painters Marcel Janco and Hans Arp—and a rowdy group of spectators. As Arp explained one performance: "Total pandemonium. The people around us are shouting, laughing, and gesticulating. Our replies of love, volleys of hiccups, poems, moos, and miaowing of medieval *Bruitists*." Bruitism, or noise-music, was introduced by futurist F. T. Marinetti and like Marinetti's theories of simultaneity and mechanized performance, Bruitism became an important part of the Dada aesthetic. Described by one member of Dada as "a chorus of typewriters, kettledrums, rattles, and saucepan lids," Bruitism made loud, confrontational music with objects of everyday life, integrating the material of living into art. Audiences of the Cabaret reveled in the chaotic performances, yelling, cheering, and often participating directly on the tiny stage.

Such integration of life and art played a vital role in the wake of the war waging across Europe. The first mechanized war, World War I introduced the world to the power of the automatic machine gun, grenades, and bombs dropped from airplanes. Trench warfare, including gas and chemical weapons, scarred Europe's hillsides. In light of such atrocities as chemical warfare, Dada artists began to rethink the purpose of art. In a world in which the human body could be quickly and efficiently torn to bits, in which the machines of war could destroy vast tracts of land, and in which people could so easily be turned into unwitting machines of death and destruction, what place did the old values of beauty and truth have in the new century? Dada, then, attempted to confront and attack the institutions that made such dehumanization of the soldier possible. While not always explicitly political, Ball and other Dadaists wanted to tear down the society that supported and encouraged the war. By 1917, the Cabaret reflected Ball's belief that the purpose of art was to reject the conventions of the present age, to drown out the boom of wartime cannons with the crash of Dada's big drum.

As the war drew to an end, however, this expressly political purpose gradually evolved into a more artistic enterprise. Indeed, Dada quickly became anti-politics, attacking all belief systems, including pacifism. As Tzara wrote in his "Dada manifesto, 1918," "Every product of disgust that is capable of becoming a negation of the family is *dada*; protest with the fists of one's whole being in destructive action: DADA..."Over time, Dada's performances began to reflect the aesthetic impulses of the young Rumanian writer Tzara, rather than the political and activist ambitions of Hugo Ball. Tzara's aesthetic vision specifically involved destruction. Boxing and smashing windowpanes became features of its performance. Police were regularly called to calm violent outbursts. But even as Dada attacked society, artists also began more widely to publish poems and plays. Tzara began writing Dada plays both for performance and as literature. His first, "The First Celestial Adventure of Mr. Antipyrine" (1916), appeared in the anthology *Collection Dada*. Richard Huelsenbeck, best known as "Dada's drummer," published his sound poetry, and in January 1917, the first public Dada exhibition of art opened at the Galerie Corray, including painting and literary work by Arp, Janco, Adya Van Rees, and Hans Richter. Performance in the Galerie also flourished. Dancer Sophie Taeuber, who had worked with Rudolph von Laban, performed her "Song of the Flying-fish and Seahorses" at the gallery, and other performances included masks, elaborate costumes, and riotous audiences. Such performances, though inspired by the activist impulses of the Cabaret Voltaire, evolved in new, more self-consciously theatrical directions that were simultaneously destructive and life-affirming. "Anti-art" would destroy the old, withered conventions in order to let the new art emerge. As painter and filmmaker Hans Richter remembers, "I assumed...that the name Dada, applied to our movement, had some connection with the joyous Slavonic affirmation, '*da da*' ['yes, yes' in Rumanian and Russian]—and to me this seemed wholly appropriate. Nothing could better express our optimism, ours sensation of newly won freedom, than this powerfully reiterated '*da, da*'—'yes, yes' to life."

In its constant attack on convention, Dada in Zurich eventually fell to its own internal divisions. As the poet Tzara focused on the literary and artistic aspirations of Dada and manifestoes, Ball felt increasingly alienated. Only a year after the opening of Cabaret Voltaire, original founders Ball and Hennings left for the Alps, and Huelsenbeck returned to Germany, calling the new Galerie Dada a "self-conscious little art business, characterized by tea-drinking old ladies trying to revive their vanishing sexual powers with the help of 'something mad.'" Dada followed Huelsenbeck to Berlin, where Expressionist poets Max Herrmann-Neisse and Theodor Däubler and painter George Grosz enthusiastically joined Dada. The first Dada performance in Berlin featured Huelsenbeck wildly beating his cane around the room and Grosz chanting his poetry: "You-sons-of-bitches, materialists/bread-eaters, flesh=eaters=vegetarians!!/professors, butchers' apprentices, pimps!/you bums!" Grosz completed his performance, perhaps thinking of Duchamp, by urinating on an Expressionist painting.

During this time, performance leaked out of the cabarets and galleries where Dada had previously flourished, and began working among the people on the streets. Artists like Grosz dressed in costume and paraded down the streets of Berlin. Raoul Hausmann and his wife, the artist Hannah Höch, joined in costumed performances, while posters throughout the city proclaimed, "Dada kicks you in the behind and you like it!" Word of the Dada insanity (indeed, one member, Johannes Baader was declared legally insane) spread outside the city, and subsequently spectators flocked to witness the "Dada Rebellion." As in Zurich, the role of simultaneous action flourished. Dada performance rejected a linear progression of events, or coherent plot. Dada instead embraced spontaneous action, illogical language, and artists performing without purpose or clear intent. If the modern world seemed to operate according to rules of cruel chance, so too would Dada create a theater that embraced spontaneity, random events, and destruction of old ideals. For example, Grosz sponsored a "Pan-Germanic Poetry Contest," during which twelve poets read their work simultaneously in a kind of race. This race undermined the value of literature—no one could hear the poems being read—while simultaneously articulating the futility of poetry. Poets were no longer solitary individuals, but rather interchangeable machines with pre-programmed emotions. Audiences could no longer concentrate on the work of art, but rather had to fight through a mélange of aggressive sound.

DADA PERFORMANCE IN GERMANY

Dada adapted this style of performance from the theories of collage (from visual art) and montage (borrowed from film). The layering of action and the repetitions of action became key elements of German Dada. Whereas the Italian influence of futurism had most strongly influenced the performances of Hugo Ball, German performance followed the visual aesthetic of photomontage. Artists such as John Heartfield and Hannah Höch produced work that cut and pasted existing images together, forcing new perspectives and new meanings among the images. Just as Duchamp changed the meaning of a common urinal simply by placing it in an art exhibition, German Dadaists attempted to transform the images of daily life—advertising, newspaper articles, posters, magazines—into art that would reflect the impulses and ambitions of modern life, particularly in postwar Germany. Found images placed in radical juxtaposition to one another quickly translated into performances that included existing text, repetition, and a blurring between life and art. Like its Zurich predecessor, German Dada performance borrowed the techniques of the futurists—simultaneity, machines—but placed new emphasis on performances with objects. Words became relatively unimportant as machines deliberately obscured human voices. Indeed, many of the paintings and collages from German Dada combine the human form with machines, often replacing limbs, mouths, and heads with prosthetic devices.

This representation of humans as biomechanical beings dictated much of Berlin performance. For example, in 1920, Grosz and others presented the First Dada Fair. In attendance was the American journalist Ben Hecht (who later wrote the play *The Front Page* [1928]). In his report on the event, Hecht revealed the importance of machines, chaos, and the aggressive interactions between performers and audience. Hecht described a race between a girl at a sewing machine and a girl at a typewriter. There was a race among eleven poets for a prize. All eleven poets recited their poems at the top of their voices and then with the shot of a starter's pistol, stopped. Grosz, appearing in blackface, danced and yelled throughout the performance. Hecht remembered Grosz yelling "Take your foot out of the butter before it is too late." In its absurdity and incomprehensible language and action, Dadafest created a different standard of performance. No "plays" would be written for the stage. There was no dialogue or poetry to remember or recite. No characters appear in these performances. Chaos, non-linearity, and randomness dominate the event. These performances actively engaged spectators in the event. The performers implicated the audience in the performance itself, often arousing spectators to anger, disgust, and sometimes violence. Hecht noted in his report that such violence marked the conclusion of the Dada festival:

> Finally, the audience started its counterrevolution. Officers drew guns and fired at the stage. Police and soldiery appeared. High officers demanded the arrest of the hooligans who had swindled and mocked Berlin's elite. But there was no one to arrest. The Dadaists had melted into the spring night.

Hecht described a perfect end to a Dada performance. The performance succeeds when it offend the sensibilities of the audience, and sufficiently antagonizes the instruments of the state, i.e., the police and soldiers. Most importantly, the Dadaists get away.

In the midst of the postwar German Weimar Republic, the chaotic, aggressive, and sometimes violent Dada performances reflected the political instability of the time. During the Republic (1919–33), there were more than 30 competing political parties, widespread inflation, a rise in prostitution and sexually transmitted diseases, and scores of war veterans, many of whom were amputees and many more who were psychologically scarred by war. It should come as no surprise that the instability of Dada should have taken hold so powerfully in a city itself so unstable. But despite this compatibility, Berlin Dada was relatively short-lived. By the First Dada Fair in 1920, the movement seemed almost exhausted. Huelsenbeck again moved, this time to Hanover; others like playwright Walter Mehring joined what was called literary Dada. Literary Dada largely eschewed public performance, concentrating its efforts on publication. As the Weimar Republic continued, moving ever closer to Hitler's rise in 1933, artists like Grosz became increasingly politicized, and eventually left Dada performance in favor of more explicitly activist theaters like the Proletarian Theatre of director Erwin Piscator.

It is important, however, to remember that Dada defied the usual progression of an artistic movement. Although Dada's original artists moved frequently in the years after World War I, Dada often appeared independently of its founding members. Kurt Schwitters, for example, formed his own version of Dada even though he was rejected for recognized membership in Dada. Despite his formal rejection, Schwitters made many sculptures and performances in keeping with the spirit of Dada, and he clearly looked to other Dada artists for inspiration. For example, Schwitters based his "Ursonate" (1922)—an atonal, repetition of non-verbal sounds—on Raoul Hausmann's sound poetry. A typical excerpt of "Ursonate" reads as follows:

Oooooooooooooooooooooooooooooooooo,
dll rrrrr beeee bö,
dll rrrrr beeee bö fümms bö,
dll rrrrr beeee bö fümms bö wö,
    beeee bö fümms bö wö tää,
      bö fümms bö wö tää zää,
        fümms bö wö tää zää Uu:

In keeping with the randomness espoused by Dada artists like Arp, Schwitters formed his own kind of art, "Merz." The word "merz" is the second half of the German word "Commerz" or commerce, which Schwitter found on a scrap of paper in the trash. Under this rubric, Schwitters created merz-paintings, merz-columns—towering structures of vertical sculpture—and merz-theater. In his "To All the Theatres of the World I Demand the Merz Stage," Schwitters argued that all objects should share equally in performance, both humans and mechanical devices alike.

Other artists left Berlin for Cologne, where Max Ernst, Arp, and Theodor Baargeld created a "Dada-Demonstration." Spectators entered the exhibition through the bathroom of a bar, in which they discovered Baargeld's "Fluid Skeptic," a large aquarium filled with blood-colored water, an alarm clock, a woman's wig, and a wooden arm. Spectators were invited to destroy the art with a hammer, although it was the police who eventually closed the exhibition. Even with these developments outside of Berlin, German Dada soon ended. Though Dada spread quickly in the five years since its inception in 1916, most artists soon reconvened in the new center of Dada, Paris.

DADA IN FRANCE: PERFORMANCE, LITERATURE, AND ART

Although Dada, especially in performance, had a vigorous life before Paris, it is still widely associated with Parisian culture of the 1920s. Most significantly,

Paris Dada created many more documents of performance than in either Zurich or Berlin. By the time Tzara arrived in Paris in 1920, the energy of Dada (lead prominently by Tzara himself) focused on plays, manifestoes, and films, as well as live performances. Paris was also an active center for avant-garde art, particularly theater. Tzara and the other Dadaists who migrated to Paris were met with unusually fertile ground for a theatrical avant-garde. Nearly 25 years earlier Alfred Jarry's famous play *Ubu Roi* (1896) premiered at the Théâtre de l'Ouevre. This play, arguably the first avant-garde drama, shocked and offended its audience from the moment of its opening line. Jarry's satire of Shakespeare's *Macbeth,* opens with a single word, "Merrrde!" Roughly translated as "Shiterrrrr!" the opening remark allegedly caused riots in the theater. William Butler Yeats, who saw the play in 1896, forlornly responded, "After us, the savage gods." Since Jarry's great attack on art, convention, and decency, the Parisian avant-garde continued to thrive, and it was this environment that welcomed Tzara in 1920.

Though Tzara arrived in Paris alone, a group of young writers anxiously awaited the arrival of their "messiah." The young writers who jointly published the magazine *Littérature* discovered Tzara in the midst of their attempt to radically reform and reshape French culture. The young editors, André Breton, Philippe Soupault, and Louis Aragon, were soon joined by Paul Eluard and Roger Vitrac, a poet who would become Dada's most prominent dramatist. Hans Richter recalls the period of Dada in Paris as "the renewal of language," and certainly the amount of drama written during this time greatly outnumbers those in Dada's previous incarnations. Breton, for example, explicitly followed the example of Jean-Pierre Brisset, who compared language with divine consciousness. Breton wrote of Brisset that, "The Word, which is God, has preserved within its folds the history of the human race." Even before Dada formally arrived with Tzara in 1920, Paris was rife with avant-garde literature and drama. Guillaume Apollinaire published his "sur-realist" play, *The Breasts of Tiresias* in 1917, and Georges Ribemont-Dessaignes wrote his Dada-influenced play, *The Mute Canary* in 1919. Modernist and avant-garde literary figures, including James Joyce, Gertrude Stein, T.S. Eliot, Ezra Pound, and others flocked to Paris' left bank, creating an environment of creative experiment that never has been duplicated.

But Paris was by no means exclusively literary. Painters and photographers filled the city, including Picasso, Joan Miró, Georges Braque, and Man Ray, among many others. Nor was performance diminished by the presence of literature. Not only live performance, but also films proliferated throughout Paris Dada. Often, both live performances and films were combined in theatrical events. For example, Man Ray's *Return to Reason* (1923) was created at Tzara's request for the Dada production, *Evening of the Bearded Heart* (1923). Produced very quickly, Ray's film was more or less an extended motion picture version of his "rayographs." Man Ray created his rayographs by covering unexposed film, then exposing the film to light. Asked by Tzara only a day before the soiree, Ray had little time to complete a film. Unable to shoot a complete film, the photographer simply repeated his photographic technique on motion picture film strips. Although the film includes some camera-shot images, Man Ray created much of *Return to Reason* by covering unexposed film with objects, such as salt and nails, and then exposing the film to light. The developed images create haunting combinations of light and dark that when set in motion, create visual frenzies of black and white images.

Despite their originality, Ray's film images were not the most startling aspects of the "bearded heart." Tzara's play *The Gas Heart* (1920) became the source of a violent confrontation. The text itself follows Tzara's stated aim that Dada should destroy the theater as it existed. Consequently, the text removes many of the markers of the usual play; there are no characters, little plot, and the dialogue is almost entirely nonsensical. The play features characters from a face: nose, eye, mouth, ear, neck, and eyebrow. As critic Robert A. Varisco describes it, "When Tzara removed personalities and names, real characters from the stage, he undermined the expectations of every viewer; a veritable bomb was thrown into the seats of the audience." Such a bomb not only struck the audience, but also other Dadaists in attendance. Breton and Benjamin Péret yelled loudly at the performers and even rushed the stage to attack them. As Georges Hugnet remembers, "When the time came for the performance of *Le couer à gaz* [*The Gas Heart*], the actors…were suddenly interrupted by violent protests from the stalls. Then an unexpected interlude: Breton hoisted himself on to the stage and started to belabour the actors." Eventually, the theater descended into chaos: members of the audience attacked the stage. The poet Paul Éluard was crushed under the weight of several people, breaking footlamps under him. Police were called and some actors left with broken limbs. The break within Dada was unmistakable. As Breton wrote after the soirée, "Leave everything. Leave Dada. Leave your wife. Leave your mistress. Leave your hopes and fears."

Dada was dying, but not yet gone. Though many cite the evening of the bearded heart as Dada's last event, one more performance would include its techniques, if not its name. In a final and stunning conclusion, this anarchic and chaotic style of performance burned out in a now-infamous final performance. Although Francis Picabia had formally rejected Dada, his performance *Relâche* in 1924 still incorporated many elements of Dada, and many of the artists who had made Dada notable around the world. Literally translated as "no performance," *Relâche* was conceived by Picabia, with music by Erik Satie and included the film *Entr'acte*, written by Picabia and filmed by Rene Clair. The live performance featured the simultaneity that the Dadaists had appropriated so effectively from the futurists. The performance opened with photographer Man Ray measuring the floor with his feet. At the same time, a fireman poured water from one bucket to another, while smoking cigarettes, one after another. Members of the Swedish Ballet walked on stage and stripped off their tuxedos. In the confrontational style of Dada, spotlights were shone directly into the eyes of the audience. The intermission was the aptly named film, *Entr'acte*. Deliberately nonlinear and nonsensical, the film follows a runaway coffin from a funeral procession, a male dancer in a skirt (shot almost entirely from directly below through glass), and Man Ray and Duchamp playing chess on the roof of the theater in which the performance appeared. Duchamp also appeared in person, posing as a nearly naked Adam (with a well-placed fig leaf) next to a naked Eve. Dancers danced in macabre pairs, while banners announced that "[Erik] Satie is the greatest musician in the world." In his assessment, painter Fernand Léger announced that the performance succeeded in its aim "to bring the stage to life. All prejudices come crashing down."

Well, perhaps not all prejudices. Predictably (if anything in Dada can be called predictable), the evening ended in chaos. The final curtain call featured the creators driving around the stage in a miniature car, while the audience jeered and hissed. Though not as overtly violent as the bearded heart, *Relâche* was nevertheless destructive. Rolf de Maré described the performance as the end of his Swedish ballet company: "it was impossible for us to go forward, to remain on the path that opened in front of us, and equally impossible to turn back. Up to now we had felt the breath of modern life and translated it into dances; but now we had reached the point at which its downward slope was anathema to us."

DADA'S INFLUENCE

By now, Dada had more or less fully collapsed. Artists like Breton, Aragon, and Soupault busily transformed their interest in the unconscious mind and Freud's theory into surrealism. The plays and films after 1924 differed significantly from those of early Dada. Dream imagery, sexual fantasy, and manipulations of language replaced the playful randomness of Dada and its abstractions. In many ways, the end of Dada was the most fitting confirmation of Dada. Unlike its successor surrealism, Dada defied all rules and classifications. As J. E. Blosche predicted in his *Dada Prophesy* (1919), "Dada will survive only by ceasing to exist." The movement that refused to become a movement could only live up to its promise by destroying itself. Once artists reached the limits of their spontaneity and surprise, the movement came to a halt. Or, as Kurt Schwitters wrote in 1922, "Perhaps you will understand better when I tell you that Dada is a virgin microbe which penetrates with the insistence of air into all those spaces that reason has failed to fill with words and conventions." Dada successfully faded before it could become a convention of its own. But it was not without a legacy. By seeping into

the places without reason, Dada launched surrealism, and many other art movements to follow, including Happenings, Pop Art, and punk rock. Both violent and
playful, destructive and life-affirming, Dada was a unique movement in twentieth
century performance, one which reflected the violence of World War I, but refused
to cower in the face of it. Dada is dead, long live Dada.

FURTHER READING

Bay-Cheng, Sarah. *Mama Dada: Gertrude Stein's Avant Garde Theatre*. New York: Routledge, 2005.

Dant, Tim. *Critical Social Theory: Culture, Society and Critique*. London: Sage Publications
Ltd., 2004.

Worthen, W. B. *Print and the Poetics of Modern Drama*. Cambridge: Cambridge University
Press, 2006.

❧

Dramatic Comedy

Miriam M. Chirico

DEFINITIONS

Contrary to popular belief, it is complications, and not laughter, that acts as the defining attribute of comedy. If the audience finds itself delighting in confusion and plot twist, then they have entered the realm of comedy. Admittedly, playwrights and actor have always sought to amuse and entertain; moving an audience to laughter has always been a central goal of comedy. But while the events of the comedy inevitably elicit laughter, the series of misadventures and the characters' ability to fix these blunders is what defines the genre. Characters twist and turn through a series of misunderstandings and mishaps, often compounding their errors before reaching solutions that have been obvious to the spectator all along. Nor can we permit the quintessential "happy ending" to serve as the defining quality, although comedies do, for the most part, end happily. Long-lost relatives are found, a treasure is rewarded, and planned executions are reversed by thirteenth-hour reprieves. Rather it is the attitude of the characters toward their circumstances that indicates to us when we are in the realm of comedy. One must observe how the characters view their predicament and how they plan to go about solving their plight. If the characters seem optimistic and believe they can find a solution to their current troubles, a spirit of comedy is at work. One also detects an attitude of resilience: if we sense that good fortune dallies around the corner, even while the situation appears dire, then comedy reigns. Thus it is the abundance of complications, obstacles, and dilemmas as well as an overall spirit of optimism that qualifies a play as "comedic." As we shall see, comedies exist in various forms, but all share a sense of flexibility and tempered optimism.

The wilder the playwright can make the complications and the closer the characters come to the point of fatality, the better, just as long as the events are resolved before the play is over. The future for the characters may seem bleak; they may be at the point of demise; yet some fortunate coincidence occurs or someone arrives who holds the key to the puzzle and the plot's knotty problems unravel themselves smoothly. In fact, the events of comedies may veer dangerously close to the point of tragedy in order to increase the hilarity and develop the suspense. Masterful comic plotting comes from the playwright's ability to stretch out a succession of interconnected events, each one raising the stakes of discovery and danger until it seems no rescue is likely. Then, some earlier detail disregarded as insignificant turns out to save the day, and we admire the imbroglio that entertained us for so long. As scholar and critic Northrop Frye notes, "Happy endings do not impress us as true, but as desirable, and they are brought about by manipulation." While a realist might find the forced happy ending deceptive in its lack of correspondence to real life, not all art must be an imitation of life. Comedy may instead provide an image of an ideal world that one could imagine and perhaps work toward. Comedy may actually serve our intelligence in ways that tragedy does not, by providing jigsaw puzzles of possibilities that the mind creatively engineers into new scenarios until the missing piece clicks finally into place with a satisfactory snap.

While the majority of comedies end happily, some comedies, notably Beckettian and Chekhovian dramas, do not offer a cheery finale. In order to expand our definition of comedy to be more inclusive of diverse forms, we must instead look for the spirit of resiliency that the characters possess in the face of all odds. The philosopher Susan Langer perceives the rhythms behind comedy as corresponding to the biological rhythms that pulse beneath the surface of all living things. As forms grow, adapt to new environments, and work to preserve their lives, they manifest an energy that can best be described as the "life force." A lizard that loses his tail will instinctively grow a new one, while a tree crowded out by others will remain long and thin until it can reach the tree cover and spread its leaves. And roots kept in a dark cellar will invariably find the one chink of light towards which to grow. This instinctual, biological drive towards righting a problem is the same impulse found in comedy—the belief that any obstacle can be surmounted, any predicament resolved. The Plautine character Pseudolus, when formulating a scheme to rescue his master's girlfriend, optimistically tells the audience: "I can't see how I'm going to do it,—but, if there's one thing I *can* see, it's that I *will* do it." While tragic characters may likewise hunt for solutions, they do so with a spirit of resignation, a belief that larger forces are at work dominating their actions: "There's a divinity that shapes our ends, rough-hew them how we will," Hamlet says, realizing that events must run their course, while Lear bemoans "As flies to wanton boys are we to the gods; They kill us for their sport."

These tragic characters feel controlled by their circumstances. Not so for the comic characters who feel energized by the challenge to turn fate to their own advantage. Langer shows us how comedy reifies the "life feeling"—the biological impulse, the pure sense of living, when she states, "the feeling of comedy is the feeling of heightened vitality, challenged wit and will, engaged in the great game with Chance."

In fact, the comic character rarely considers himself *fated* and speaks more often of *fortune* than fate. Comedy is not governed by the sense of doom that fate implies—the uneasy sensation that the gods have predetermined one's outcome. Rather comedy operates under another goddess, a kind of ebullient spin-the-wheel force whose philosophy consists of a longer view, an awareness that even though one is hard on one's luck, that luck can always change, and what goes down must come up again. While Aristotle defined tragedy as a reversal of events that occurs when those who are placed high are brought low, he might have additionally suggested that comedy follows a series of events from high to low to high again; the trick for the playwright is to end the play when the wheel of fortune hits the zenith and the character stands on top.

Part of what creates the complications in many classical comedies is the institution of an irrevocable law at the onset of the play. An authority figure puts into place a forbidding and inflexible rule, a limit condition that makes life difficult for certain characters. In Roman writer Terence's play, *The Mother-in-Law* (*Hecyra*) the father pressures his son into settling down with the proper woman for his social class, rather than continue to date his beloved prostitute. Similarly the father in *A Midsummer Night's Dream* designates which man his daughter must marry and threatens her with death should she refuse. Beaumarchais's *The Marriage of Figaro* (1775) has the "droit de seigneur" as its opening premise— the legendary right that a nobleman had to have sexual intercourse with a female servant of the household on the night of her wedding. And the Count Carlo Gozzi begins his fairy-tale-like comedy *The Love of the Three Oranges* (1761) with a curse placed upon a Prince that must be undone or else he will die. The actions of all of these comedies requires that the characters either break the law or try to outsmart the authorial figures that established these constraints. We side with the wily underdog or the spirited rebel who envisions a new way of doing things, a new order. We laugh as they plot to outwit the stern group of law-abiding elders and we relish their recklessness because it appeals to our own.

However, the action of many other comedies only begins the moment the restraint is removed, thus enabling a more licentious, playful period to begin. In Aphra Behn's *The Rover* (1677), it is the departure of her father that allows the heroine and her friends the freedom to join the Carnival festivities in Naples and find themselves lovers. Likewise, by spreading the rumor that he is impotent, Horner, a known London libertine in *The Country Wife* (1675), is provided with free access to many married women in London, because he has removed the stricture of surveillance with which many husbands' previously regarded him.

Comedies thrive on laws and breaking the laws: laws that impede the desires of the characters or laws that guard the characters from becoming victims to their own desires. The rules and constraints surrounding these characters delineate notions of civility and orderliness; these rules tell us much about our society and ourselves. Comedy, with its back-and-forth trespassing between civilized and animalistic behavior, between cultivated responses and instinctual, between the urban area and the rural retreat, reveals both the confining nature of laws as well as their functional safeguard from the chaos within. It is through these very conflicts in comedy where laws are flouted and broken, that one gains a clearer vision of the boundaries that structure and organize our communal networks.

Governments establish laws to shape and define a community and by testing these boundaries one discovers the limits and mores of the people residing there. We need only examine Constitutional debates about prayer in school or burning the flag to understand the value systems at play within the United States. In *A Midsummer Night's Dream* (1604), several lovers leave the town and escape into an enchanted forest, where their jealous, petty natures are revealed, only because they are no longer bound by the chivalrous behavior of the court. Once the communal bonds have been broken or people have escaped from the security of civilizing forces, the characters are challenged to examine their world unfettered by conventional value systems. Sometimes an individual enters into a small community, bringing his or her own views or practices, and knocks the community's lives off-kilter, as the Professor Serebryakov does in Chekhov's play *Uncle Vanya* (1894). All of his habits—his keeping late hours, his laziness and irregular meal times—disturb the standard schedule of the family members living on the estate and rekindle old passions and grievances. A comedy will typically move through quarrels and quandaries towards reconciliation, and by the play's end, the society is reorganized around stable relationships: family members are reunited or lovers are married. This new society is similar to the previous one but individuals have a greater understanding of themselves and the rules that govern them. At the end *Uncle Vanya*, the various characters are saddened by the loss of their illusions, but they reassert their sense of purpose in life; Sonya knows her work will light the way for others.

Stock Figures in Comedy

In addition to looking at comedy structurally, we may also note some stock figures prevalent in comedy, primarily as the trickster figure. This archetypal character is a stock figure in many cultural mythologies, from European folktales to Native American stories. Appearing variously as a god, a spirit, a human being, or even an animal, the trickster's central defining quality is his desire to play pranks on others, either out of malice or simply to have fun. Often a wily underdog, he thrives on outwitting his opponents and breaking the rules of law or of nature. As Langer notes, this character symbolizes "human vitality holding its own in the world." An individual who does not succumb to defeat, but thinks on his feet and knows there is more than one way to skin a cat, the trickster figure embodies vitality and the life-force. In Plautus's play *Miles Gloriosus* (The Braggart Soldier 204 B.C.), the trickster character is Palaestrio, the dexterous slave who helps his master, Nautiklus, get his girlfriend back after she has been kidnapped by the soldier. Because of the soldier's vanity, Dexter finds it very easy to trick him, and the audience delights in watching a virtuoso sleight of hand whereby the arrogant authority figure is duped. Early trickster figures appear in medieval farces throughout Europe; *Gammer Gurton's Needle* (c. 1552) is one such Tudor piece that sports a mischief-making character. Diccon, the mentally unstable character who supposedly escaped from the mental institution of Bedlam, wanders into a small town and gets three different people to accuse one another of stealing some prized object, starting with the eponymous needle. The pleasure of the play is the bedlam that ensues—all carefully orchestrated by Diccon himself. For trickster figures delight in creating mischief for mischief's sake. Puck, who serves the fairy King Oberon in *A Midsummer Night's Dream* (c. 1596), revels in his ability to play pranks on people, bragging about pulling out a step-stool from under a milking maid or neighing like a mare to arouse the stallions in the stable. His fame for playing pranks is so renowned that when he accidentally causes two men to fall in love with the same woman, the fairy King Oberon immediately accuses him of tomfoolery: "Thou mistak'st, Or else committ'st thy knaveries willfully." Puck, rather than be abashed at his error, finds amusement in the confusion he has caused: "Lord, what fools these mortals be." And in a much later Restoration piece, *She Stoops to Conquer* (1773), the ne'er-do-well character Tony Lumpkin successfully convinces his sister's suitor into believing the house where he has arrived is an inn. Accordingly, the suitor—who has never met the family before—peremptorily treats the master of the house and the sister as the innkeeper and the maid, making monstrous social gaffes before his error is revealed. Tricksters, on a strictly functional level, may help to advance the plot, but their primary role is to stir up great gales of laughter.

Trickster figures can predominate in comedies because the genre primarily showcases characters of the lower classes. Tragedies, according to Aristotle's definition in the *Poetics* (c. 334–323 B.C.) follow the tribulations of high-placed, noble characters who are brought low by fate. Comedies witness the dilemmas of the common man or woman: "an imitation of persons who are inferior,"

Aristotle writes, "not, however, going all the way to full villainy, but imitating the ugly, of which the ludicrous is one part." Thus servants, petty criminals, prostitutes, errant school children and other members lower on the social ladder can take part in the action because they are the foolish, inferior people that comedy relishes. Nicole, an impertinent servant in Molière's play *Le Bourgeoise Gentilhomme* (1670) chastises her master for all the pretentious skills he is being taught at great expense and with little results: dancing, music, fencing, philosophy. It is comic to see the underling audaciously mocking her master, Monsieur Jourdain, because she inverts the power in the master-servant relationship with great spunk and wit. As Madame Jourdain tartly informs her husband: "Nicole's quite right. She's got more sense than you have. I'd like to know what you think you want with a dancing master at your age."

The clever servant may also assist his or her master, emphasizing the master's idiocy all the more by his complete helplessness or inability to solve the most basic problems. In the famous final scene of Plautus's *Menaechmi* (*The Manaechmi Brothers* 205–184 B.C.), Messenio leads his master and his master's long-lost twin brother through a rigorous deduction process to determine if they are truly related. Even though it is painfully obvious to all that the two brothers look exactly alike, Messenio highlights their idiocy and draws out the hilarity by proving without a doubt they share the same parentage. Such instrumental and cunning servants can be seen in Shakespeare's *Henry IV* (1596–98) or Beaumarchais's *The Barber of Seville*, which introduced clown-like servants that were so popular, namely Falstaff and Figaro, that their reputations prevail over that of their masters'.

Clowns or fools are slightly different than tricksters in that they add to the frivolous atmosphere without necessarily playing tricks on others. They often speak their minds at the risk of insulting their betters. They have special license to speak bluntly, either because their position at court is so low that no one considers them a threat, or because their chief function is to offer witticisms to delight a king or duke. Such freedom to speak one's mind often yields the truth, and these characters do become—if not a spokesperson for the playwright—a voice of wisdom poking through the nonsense. The wise fool figures in tragedies such as *King Lear*, but he also appears to make such pronouncements in comedies like *Twelfth Night*. As the clown, Feste's responsibility is to cheer up his mistress, Olivia, who is mourning her brother's death. He tells her riddles and finally rebukes her by pointing out the illogical reasoning behind her grief; her grief is wasted because her brother is in heaven. Bertolt Brecht's character of Azdak in *The Caucasian Chalk Circle* (1962) represents the wise fool, a man who becomes a judge during a period of war and who makes radical decisions that at first glance seem illogical and wacky. Although the play is not a comedy *per se,* it draws upon romantic folk tales and uses the wise clown as a motif. Azdak turns out to be a Robin Hood character. His judgments favor the peasants who are at the mercy of the wealthy, powerful upper-classes and his bizarre expressions are mixed with wisdom. In brief, tricksters and clowns are figures of fun. They import nonsense into comedies and remind the characters of their own ability to laugh and triumph. Foolishness is necessary to keep life full, vital, and bright, and both tricksters and clowns understand this rejuvenating element. As Santayana states: "Reason cannot stand alone; brute habit and blind play are at the bottom of art and morals, and unless irrational impulses and fancies are kept alive, the life of reason collapses for sheer emptiness."

Comedy's Common Events in Life

Comedy looks at the common events in life, rather than the extraordinary. Tragedy considers the singular plight of the individual and considers the particular event as it pertains to this character and to no other. For example, the troubled lovers in *A Midsummer Night's Dream* understand their predicament by comparing it to a litany of other lovers for whom "The road of true love never did run smooth"—a deliberation not undertaken by Romeo and Juliet who saw their "star-crossed" turmoil as unique. It is no surprise that tragedies often bear the names of individual figures, who are defined by the events that shape them, such as *Oedipus, Hamlet, Cato, The Emperor Jones,* or *Death of a Salesman,* while comedies are often named after collectivities, like *The Birds, The Merry Wives of Windsor, Every Man in His Humor, The School for Scandal, The Learned Ladies,* and more recently, *Uncommon Women.* For comedy emphasizes what keeps us together as a society, not what separates us as individuals; it emphasizes the communal. And laughter tends to increase the feeling of community within the audience. The old adage "laugh and the world laughs with you; cry and you cry alone" holds true, but it is more than the willingness to share good times. Laughter is infectious; it stands in need of an echo, it draws people in emotionally and warms them with feelings of camaraderie and good will.

Comedy, more so than tragedy, breaks into a variety of subgenres. While all of them share basic characteristics, such as a delight in complications, a spirit of resiliency, a law-defining scenario, and an emphasis on community, it is important to recognize how these subgenres differ from one another. Satire, comedy of manners, romantic comedy, farce, and tragicomedy, are some of the varieties of the comic that are considered in this chapter. Other categories of comedy certainly exist, but these five tend to be the essential subgenres which contain the fundamental properties.

FIVES TYPES OF COMEDY

Satire

Satire rises to the top of the list because it is the oldest form of comedy and because most comedies have some element of corrective laughter to them. Aristophanes's highly satirical play *Lysistrata* (411 B.C.) delights in attacking the Athenian government for its involvement in the ongoing Peloponnesian war, suggesting that if women were in power, there would be no more wars. The women take over the Acropolis and deny their husbands any sexual relations until the men agree to a truce with the other warring city-states. Lysistrata brings the men of Greece—literally—to their knees. The satire scoffs at the stupidity of war as much as it derides how men (and women) are driven by their sexual needs. The objective behind satire is to get the audience to recognize their own faults or shortcomings in the onstage characters and, in thus seeing themselves criticized, mend their bad behaviors. We are more likely to adjust a character flaw within ourselves if that flaw is portrayed as the object of derision. *Saturday Night Live* skits, whether they focus on feel-good psychiatry, the work place, or awkward racial relations, can encourage audiences to examine their own behavior by a mocking depiction of others.

Typically, it is the prominent types who find themselves the objects of satire, authority figures who consider themselves too self-important and who have lost the ability to see their own shortcomings. One of the earliest figures of satire, *Miles Gloriosus* (Braggart Soldier), showed himself as vaunting endlessly about his battle deeds, his military dexterity, and his courage, only to run at the slightest sign of aggression. In one scene, the soldier depicts himself as god's gift to women, and the characters pretend to compliment him, while insulting him behind his back. Milphidippa sets up the scene: "An attractive man like you, endowed with such perfect physique and unparalleled prowess in battle. What man could more pass for a god?" But it is Palaestrio's barbed aside that gets the laughs: "He sure can't pass for human. Dear God, a buzzard is more humane." In addition to military men, other authority figures like doctors, lawyers, and professors become the fodder for a satirical onslaught. These highly trained specialists whose knowledge holds them above the average citizen are the likeliest figures to jeer at because they act the most condescending. Their erudition and large fees make them easy to resent, and thus even easier to mock; likely methods of lampoon consist of having the characters speak in nonsensical Latin, or having them offer medical or legal remedies that are so preposterous the characters become no more than buffoons.

Two of the most popular dramatic satirists in early European literature were Ben Jonson and Jean-Louis Poqueline, known as Molière. Jonson's play *Volpone* (1606) showcased the greediness of mankind in its love of money. Volpone opens the play speaking directly to his gold, praising its worth over that of the sun's and describing his pernicious plot to get more money. As he pretends to lie dying, vulture-like men encircle Volpone's deathbed in hope of being his favored heir, proffering him gifts as tokens of their affection, while unknowingly playing right into his hands. Each character appears more foolish than the last, and yet Volpone's manipulations know no bounds: he successfully convinces a man to allow him to rape his wife. The comedy turns darker and more discomfiting as the play transpires; what begins as good fun ends up taking on a sharp edge. Jonson hoped to make his satire sting the audience into recognizing the mercenary greed abounding within the professional class of London and his preface insists that the audiences' cheeks will be "rubbed raw with laughter."

Molière's satires, which appeared fifty years later, have a more buoyant tone and are decidedly less caustic. His plays have a degree of physical clowning and nonsensical word play that comes from a background in improvisational theater; nonetheless, his satirical thrust still cuts deep. George Meredith, in "An Essay on Comedy," says about Molière: "Never did man wield so shrieking a scourge upon vice." For Molière believed in satire's potential to correct bad behavior, as he mentions in the preface of *Tartuffe* (1667):

> If the function of comedy is to correct men's vices, I do not see why any should be exempt....The most forceful lines of a serious moral statement are usually less powerful than those of satire; and nothing will reform most men better than the depiction of their faults. It is a vigorous blow to vices to expose them to public laughter. Criticism is taken lightly, but men will not tolerate satire. They are quite willing to be mean, but they never like to be ridiculed.

In *The Misanthrope*, Molière attacks the hypocrisy of the royal court, but his complex argument also considers the opposite point of view: how a strict sense of honesty can deteriorate the social fabric. The central figure Alceste decides to be completely straightforward with his fellowmen, but his subsequent frank comments end up insulting many people at the court. For example, a poet Oronte arrives at Alceste's house in order to obtain his opinion of his poem. Though he says he wants honest feedback, he is hurt and angered by Alceste's criticism, and Alceste lacks the necessary diplomacy to assuage his feelings. By the play's end, Alceste's candidness has caused a fight with his fiancée and a court indictment and he decides to leave society altogether. Hypocrisy likewise bears the brunt of Molière's attack in *Tartuffe*, but this time the play follows a religious hypocrite who acts so pious and sanctimonious that he earns the keys to the main character's house and heart. Not only does Tartuffe dupe Orgon into letting him take up residency; he convinces Orgon to disinherit his own son and rewrite his will in Tartuffe's name. At the end of such satires, justice prevails; Jonson's Volpone is punished and Tartuffe is put in prison, illustrating the judgment of each playwright.

Satire is a form that appeals to the intellect, particularly when an individual can use a play as a method of self-correction. As George Meredith claims in his "Essay on Comedy": "You may estimate your capacity for comic perception by being able to detect the ridicule of them you love without loving them less; and more by being able to see yourself somewhat ridiculous in dear eyes, and accepting the correction their image of you proposes." But oftentimes satirists ran into trouble with the public who saw themselves too clearly through the satirists' eyes and felt insulted by the image they saw. Molière had to defend his play *Tartuffe* aggressively by insisting it was not a satire against the Catholic Church, but against the tyranny of hypocrites.

The Comedy of Manners

While these stereotypical figures such as the braggart warrior or the miserly old man serve as perfect objects of satire, they did not originate in satirical comedy but rather in another form of classical drama: the comedy of manners. The focus on individual character types in society became the interest of Plautus and Terence, Roman playwrights who had inherited an earlier Greek form known as "New Comedy" from Menander. Referred to simply as "comedy" during the third and second centuries B.C., this next form develops a plot around particular personality types in society—the clever servant, the stodgy parents, the kind-hearted prostitute—and examines how people follow the social conventions and mores of their day and age. The comedy of manners is the forerunner of our modern-day situation comedy, with its fascination for human interactions, whether it be a merchant class of ancient Rome or a group of young professionals living in New York City. Such comedies will scoff at the manners, customs, speech patterns, and rituals of the upper and middle classes in particular, because of the very artificial nature of such behaviors. Henri Bergson, in his important essay on comedy "Laughter," theorizes about possible sources of humor, and suggests that we laugh when we find some mechanical quality in a living human being. Thus the social niceties and good breeding that enable us to mix and mingle in polite society are essentially rigid constructions that we impose upon our more base desires.

William Congreve's Restoration comedy *The Way of the World* (1700) reveals an upper-class culture that uses etiquette and witty language to cover up its dishonorable intentions as the characters manipulate one another. One character's apt name of Fainall (feign-all) implies the simulated nature of all the characters and points to the false world they live in—a world where the play's hero has earlier married off his pregnant lover to his friend by assuring him of a large dowry. An older, sexually desirous woman, Lady Wishfort (wish-for-it), is successfully blackmailed when she over-hastily engages herself to a man who turns out to be a servant disguised as a knight. She must concede to the conspirators' demands or risk being made a public ridicule. In all of these situations, the characters base their actions on how they will appear to society. Their cultivated manners allow them to protect their inner selves against the immorality of others, but at the same time, prohibit them from being honest with one another.

Oscar Wilde's play *The Importance of Being Earnest* (1895) likewise illustrates how the polite veneer of manners can cover up humanity's vulgar desires. In the renowned tea party scene, two women who despise one another for being in love with the same man make a pretense of social felicities under the ritualistic dictates of a tea ceremony. Wilde's play wittily sends up all the customary habits of courtship in which couples partake—not out of love, but out of social necessity. Lady Bracknell, a grand matron in society, inquires about Jack Worthing's residence, financial status, and lineage to ascertain the appropriateness of his marriage to her daughter, engaging him in a series of questions that demonstrates her obsession with class. Wilde's satire shows these formulaic elements of courtship have reduced lovemaking to a series of perfunctory social arrangements. Comedies of manners essentially explore the ways in which social customs undermine the veracity of human relationships. One of George Bernard Shaw's best plays, *Arms and the Man* (1894), pokes fun at how two young lovers require an unrealistic and glorified view of war in order to serve as a background to their romance. The young man must be able to pose as a brave warrior and she as a heroine in order for their affair to appear passionate to themselves. Their illusions and heroic stances are later rendered ridiculous when contrasted to the pragmatic soldier Bluntschli who would rather save his own skin than fight, yet proves to be truly courageous.

Comedies of manners are often preoccupied with the highly artificial and constructed ways in which people speak. Language serves as an artful way of manipulating others or disguising one's true intentions. The characters in both the *Way of the World* and *The Importance of Being Earnest* are masters of verbal dexterity and use words to confuse the truth of the situation and to get what they want. As Wilde's character Algernon wittily states: "The truth is rarely pure and never simple. Modern life would be very tedious if it were either, and modern literature a complete impossibility!" Wit, repartee, and other forms of verbal banter that constitute a comedy of manners are as instrumental as they are decorative. The wordplay is indicative of the character's personality and morals; the one with the shrewdest comeback wins. For wit requires an agility of mind, the ability to perceive the truth about a situation and to express it succinctly. Paradox is one form of wit, whereby a statement can seem false or odd at first, but upon reflection can reveal a deeper truth. Algernon's comment about a widowed friend of the family's whose "hair has turned quite gold from grief" at first seems implausible, until we remember that a woman might benefit handsomely from her husband's demise.

Repartee, or the rapid-fire retorts in a verbal duel, often permeates a comedy of manners, as each character offers smart, quick rejoinders to his colleague's remarks. The speed and aptness of the speaker's reply impresses us in its ability to reverse or to best the person's last remark. In *The Way of the World,* the two lovers are well-suited because of their ability to engage in repartee; the sparks seem to fly from their clever banter as they prove their sharp intellect in a linguistic sword fight. When the young Mirabelle seems particularly pleased that her fiancé finds her beautiful, her lover takes her down a notch: "You are no longer handsome when you've lost your lover," Millamant tells her, because "your beauty dies upon the instant; for beauty is the lover's gift." In this world of surfaces where it is dangerous to reveal one's true feelings and run the risk of being blackmailed, wit allows Millamant the ideal device for hiding his true affections behind a clever defense of words and not getting hurt by a beautiful lover.

The early nineteenth century offered a variation of the comedy of manners that was less bawdy than the early Restoration plays, and more kindly about the potential of the human heart. Sentimental comedies were meant to offer the wit and exuberance of the earlier plays, but with more polished and refined characters. No longer did the antics of lustful rakes like Jack Horner in *The Country Wife* (1675) drive the action, but instead characters were motivated out of genuine concern for one another. Famous English sentimental playwrights were Oliver Goldsmith and Richard Sheridan. Sheridan's play *School for Scandal* (1777), consisted of a "college" of scandalmongers who met for the sole purpose of raking others' reputations over the coals. The dialogue is ripe with the witty quips and aphorisms of earlier Restoration drama. However the play's belief in innate human goodness and the benevolent actions of other characters moves it into the realm of sentimental drama.

In France, where the form was known as *comedie larmoyante,* or tearful comedy, the master practitioner was Marivaux who revealed the inner workings of the human heart with a language infinitely exquisite and tender. Pierre Carlet de Chamblain de Marivaux placed his characters in unique circumstances where they had to carefully examine the psychological workings of their own heart, often with wiser characters eavesdropping on these discoveries. Often they wander with childlike innocence through their affairs, discovering love, jealously, and betrayal and offering charmingly turned phrases to express these sensations. Marivaux wrote for an aristocratic eighteenth century audience preoccupied with affairs of the heart, perpetuated through their courtly literature of poetry, lyrics, and intimate journals. His plays offer introspective pronouncements on romance; the recognition, for example, that we enjoy relationships because we delight in being admired by another, and having society see a lover admiring us. Marivaux was fond of writing about vain, adolescent women; he has one character gleefully in *La Dispute* (1744) delighting in her own beauty: "I shall spend the rest of my life contemplating me, and soon I'll even fall in love with myself." But we can excuse foolish vanity in a comedy; as Santayana writes: "The foolishness of the simple is delightful; only the foolishness of the wise is exasperating." In another of Marivaux's plays, *Le Jeu de l'amour et du hasard* (*The Game of Love and Chance*, 1730), two people find their fathers arranging their marriage, so they disguise themselves as their servants. Meanwhile, their servants have been disguised as their masters. When the two finally do meet, they inevitably fall in love, but because they are under the impression they are in love with another person's servant, they worry about loving someone of a lower class. This *chassé-croisé* unfolds so that each character feels affection for their proper mate, but in the meantime, the characters spend much time in emotional self-torture, examining the natures of their heart and their attitude toward class.

Well into the twentieth century we find other playwrights who continue a tradition that the Restoration writers established: the laughing attack on marriage. The British writer Noel Coward offered atypical perspectives on romantic relationships during the jazz age, often with wry commentary about the usefulness of conventional morality. Coward's play highlights, as most good comedies of manners do, the games that people play with language, and his dialogue glistens with sardonic humor and clever *double entendres*. In one play, *Design for Living* (1933), a love-triangle develops between three good friends, where each act finds the characters involved in a different permutation of their relationship. Another play, *Private Lives* (1930), is inhabited by two newlywed couples who discover, on their honeymoons, that the husband of one couple has been previously married to the other man's wife. They rekindle their own flame and run off to Paris together, leaving their new husband and wife behind. Neither play offers a moral pronouncement against infidelity but rather suggests it as the natural outgrowth of creative minds. Characters, in fact, must discover how to behave based on a new ethical system. One husband remarks: "this situation is entirely without precedent. We have no prescribed etiquette to fall back on." Prescribed etiquette is exactly the target upon which comedy of manners aims its mocking glances.

Romantic Comedy

The third form of comedy, the romantic comedy, is typically the kind most people envision when they hear the word "comedy." In fact, romantic comedies share many of the same conventions with other forms, particularly sentimental comedies in their intense scrutiny of affairs of the heart. Shakespeare is often considered the father of romantic comedies, even though he borrowed many of his plots from the early Roman comedy of manners. The name "romantic comedy" comes not from a preoccupation with romantic love, but rather because the form was based on French medieval poems—the *romans*—which detailed the marvelous adventures of imaginary or idealized heroes. These romances, later adapted into prose form like *The Tales of King Arthur,* were filled with twists and turns and usually required a dashing hero to overcome knotty problems in order to obtain the love of an engaging and beautiful woman. While love may be the focus of romantic comedies, it is only an end result that guides his actions; getting the girl is secondary to the twists and turns of the adventure. Even when the lover himself is incapacitated by the heady, walking-on-air sensation of being in love, his servant or sidekick usually comes to his rescue and assists him in his mission. The exuberance of love, the illusory feeling that one will love "forever and a day," creates the festal feeling in the romantic comedy. But the festive orientation is also countered by the foolishness of the lover, for the lover is subject to passionate emotional swings. The lovers in *A Midsummer Night's Dream* spend the night chasing or being pursued by the wrong lover and quarreling with one another until a magic potion sorts everyone out. Romantic comedy laughs at the foolish behavior of lovers due to the extreme emotions they suffer: jealousy, despondency, elation, enchantment. Immune to human emotions, Puck can sit back and smugly proclaim "Lord, what fools these mortals be" while watching the antics of the four lovers. In *Twelfth Night* we witness characters falling in love not only with the wrong person but with the wrong person's disguise, and the dilemma is only fixed when the Viola, disguised as a man, reveals her identity. A romantic comedy follows the comic tribulations of lovers and their emotional upheavals, exposing to ridicule the passionate and irrational reactions these lovers experience to the most trivial events.

Wife-chasing or husband-catching scenarios are prevalent plots of romantic comedy, where sometimes lovers are unaware of their own emotions until they are gently nudged (or sometimes pushed) in the right direction. In G. B. Shaw's play *Man and Superman* (1907), a charmingly aggressive young woman pursues an iconoclastic political activist who disagrees with the institution of marriage. He delivers tirades against marriage even while the "trap" of matrimony tightens around him. The goal of most romantic comedies is not satirical commentary, character analysis, or a critique of social mores, but entertainment through clever plotting. Modern day romantic comedies include plays by Neil Simon or movies like *When Harry met Sally.* A good romantic comedy must follow the roller-coaster pursuit of courtship and romance and end when the boy has obtained the girl. This is the only logical conclusion for comedy; as Puck notes during *A Midsummer Night's Dream:* "Jack shall have Jill; Nought shall go ill."

Even though romantic comedies exist as forms of pure pleasure, this kind of comedy also provides insights into the human heart. The most recognizable pattern of a romantic comedy consists of a stable, rule-bound society shifting into one of chaos and confusion, before reverting back to stability and order. While this conceptual design applies to many comedies, it predominates within festive or romantic plays. C.L. Barber identifies this shifting pattern from normalcy to holiday spirit as a "saturnalian" pattern, and finds its roots in the Elizabethan periodic observance of sports and feast days. Many of the secular and Church-sanctioned holidays in early Europe offered periods of festivity and merrymaking which gave the citizens a feeling of release from their daily burdens of work, whether the release involved dancing, drinking, eating, or sexual wantonness. While we might call this practice a "safety-valve" mechanism which provided people with a holiday in order to prevent them from bursting under the weight of their everyday work, it is important to realize that this release also led to clarification. This period of uninhibited indulgence in pleasure meant the citizens were free to view the world from a different perspective, through the lens of a "holiday" instead of a "workday." A lover is a typically lazy individual who escapes his work (lazes about) to fantasize about his loved one. This "holiday humor" appears in comedy whenever characters escape from responsibility, class decorum, or even gender roles. Men in Plautine comedies always attempt to flee their wives or get out of civic work in order to be with their concubines, and many a slave finds ways to avoid their masters' assigned tasks. And women in Shakespearean comedies frequently escape the limitations of their gender, as when Viola in *Twelfth Night* dresses like a man as a means of self-preservation.

This division between everyday and holiday, with its emphasis on shedding workday concerns and experiencing greater freedoms, becomes the dominant pattern for most festive comedies. Characters leave their stable-but-problematic society to go to a place free from rules but with ensuing chaos, to return finally to their stable location with greater knowledge. When Demetrius, at the end of *A Midsummer Night's Dream* wakes up from his night in the forest, he says, "methinks I see the world with parted eye, where everything seems double." He now recognizes that the aristocratic space of the court hides another world beneath its polished veneer—a world where uncivil passions lurk. The character of Vivie Warren, in *Mrs. Warren's Profession* (1893), discovers during the course of the play that her mother's wealth came from her previous work as a prostitute, but even this discovery is not all; through the chaotic encounters that ensue, she learns more importantly that much capitalist wealth depends upon the exploitation of women. The final moments of the play, where the daughter negates any further relationship with her mother, are not uplifting, but instructive; Vivie Warren sees her world for what it is and chooses a path morally superior to her mother's.

The role reversal between Vivie and her mother, where the daughter takes on the role of the mature adult, is frequently seen in comedy and can be explained by another medieval Church holiday: the Feast of Fools. This early celebration reversed the hierarchical order of the religious positions within the church. The lower clergy would take on the higher positions in the church for a brief period, and even the youngest boy was permitted to put on the Bishop's robes. This kind of revolution in positions, where a dignified role is occupied by a subordinate for a few hours, provided people with a greater understanding of the responsibilities and right governing Church hierarchy, i.e., why the Bishop was due respect. The religious inversion of roles can be seen within comedies whenever the lower character rises to a superior post and provides a topsy-turvy component to the comedies: a servant besting his master, a child outwitting his parent, a citizen seizing control of the government. Thus the festival patterns at play in romantic comedies create a sensation of a holiday period, a release from daily constraints, which provides the characters with a sense of clarification and enlightenment when they return to their stable environment.

Often this return to stability is underscored by a marriage, dance, or feast. A dance, with its grouping of individuals who are connected hand-in-hand, becomes symbolic of a community's coalescence. Nor is it a static grouping, but suggestive of energy and the life pulse. Aristophanic comedies end in wild, wine-soaked finales, Shakespearen comedies resolve themselves in marriages and festal dances, and many plays end in dance, including the ballet that turns Monsieur Jordain into a Grand Turk in Molière's *The Would-Be Gentleman*. The image of a group of people joining hands in dance signifies community and concord. George Bernard Shaw's romantic comedy *You Never Can Tell* (1900) has a masked ball at the end, signifying that while some issues between the father and his estranged family members can never be fully solved, they are willing to cover up these differences and join hands in reconciliation. Some communities do not extend the hand to maleficent characters and instead forcibly eject them from their gathering, the most famous example being the treatment of Malvolio in *Twelfth Night*. As Malvolio attests, after having been kept alone in a dark cellar: "I have been most notoriously abused." The process whereby a community gathers together only after it has vilified a particular member is called scapegoating and it allows that group to define itself by constructing an image of what *it is not*. In the celebratory atmosphere of *Twelfth Night*, Malvolio represents someone decorous and proper, at odds with the community's desire to be mischievous and jolly. Identifying a scapegoat also allows the community to dispel its negative energy and rancor onto someone outside of itself, rather than keeping it within; scapegoating permits the community to unify against a common enemy and allows a discharge of vitriolic emotions, rather than directing it within.

Farce

The discomfort that underpins *Twelfth Night's* merriment is created by our sympathetic response toward Malvolio; we feel sorry that while everyone else's fortunes have resulted in happiness, Malvolio has been mistreated. This darker side of comedy finds its home in another form of comedy known as farce, where characters are often subject to some painful predicament. Farce originates in a traditional dramatic form based in southern Italy around the 1500's known as *commedia dell'arte,* or comedy of the artisans, i.e., the professional actors. This kind of comedy was largely improvisational and consisted of broad, bawdy humor, that today we consider slapstick. The individual plays were made up of smaller bits of practical jokes, known as *lazzi*. A *lazzo* (singular form) such as stepping on the prongs of a rake and having it swing upward to smack the character in the face, could be interwoven with bits of choreographed horseplay and develop the plot of the improvised story. Physical humor is still the defining element in farce. Farce tends to be a lowbrow comedy, a comedy mainly known for eliciting "belly-laughs" with its knock-about gestures, its quick timing and speed. Farce, more than any kind of comedy, portrays the animalistic side of human beings in their base pursuit for food, money, sex, or sleep, and shows us the potential consequences of these desires. Here especially applies the "safety-valve" theory of comedy by which we might gain some release seeing our fantasies acted out upon the stage. The constraints of position, class, or marriage are lifted off of our shoulders as we watch the characters' rebellious behavior before us. As Eric Bentley notes, "Farce in general offers a special opportunity. We enjoy the privilege of being totally passive while on stage our most treasured unmentionable wishes are fulfilled before our eyes." Thus farce invites us to live vicariously through the characters, whether their desires overturn the social order or remain a simple indulgence in an afternoon's frivolities.

Even the classical Greeks, who are more frequently associated with dignified tragedy than bawdy comedy, participated in farcical displays of the body, using a great deal of padding on the posterior and belly to emphasize how the body can be a source of fun and humiliation. Aristophanes's play *Lysistrata* relied upon a small string device inside the costumes that, when pulled, would lift a phallus and simulate an erection. Mikhail Bakhtin, studying the French writer Rabelais, comes to similar conclusions about the bawdy nature of popular festive forms, and notes in particular how the carnival celebrations in many medieval towns would focus on the genitalia or lower body parts. He reasons that the emphasis on these procreative areas of the body affirms the immortality of the human race, and argues how comedy is a celebration of this life-giving element. Molière's farces involve characters chasing and smacking one another, typical of a Punch and Judy show where the blows are frequent and violent yet seem to cause no harm. In his short farce, *The Doctor in Spite of Himself,* the husband thrashes his wife in the first scene, so she, in revenge, convinces some wandering men in search of a doctor to beat her husband. She explains that her husband is shy about his talents and will only reveal his profession if they thwack him soundly. It may surprise us to find ourselves laughing at another's discomfort, but herein lies another chief element of comedy, the practice of emotionally distancing ourselves from the ongoing violence or an individual's pain, a tendency Henri Bergson labeled "the momentary anesthesia of the heart." The misfortunes that befall Charlie Chaplin and Buster Keaton are further examples of the violence inherent in farce, yet the pain never seems real. A more recent example of farce is Joe Orton's contemporary play *What the Butler Saw*, which abounds in extreme harm to human beings; a woman is placed in a straitjacket and has her hair cut against her will; others are given sedatives or slapped about, and threatening gun shots ring out. We laugh at the antics not because we are unfeeling, but because the behavior of the characters is so frantic that the high speed removes human feeling from the equation. Bergson's idea about the mechanical quality encrusted upon the living [indicated above] is again apt, because automatic quality is imposed upon human beings. The characters begin to seem more like cartoon-figures or robotic individuals than human beings; they are on automatic pilot and unable to make decisions for themselves.

Perhaps the most daring figure of farcical theater of all-time is King Ubu (*Ubu Roi* 1896). This character, a creation of Alfred Jarry, was meant to shock the audiences and explode classical notions of logical, plot-driven theater. With his string of obscenities, his constant threatening, torturing, and killing of those around him, and his crass behavior—which includes brandishing a toilet plunger as a scepter—the bumbling King Ubu manifests the gluttonous desire to usurp power in the most childish, selfish, and heinous way. As King of Poland, he kills off all the noblemen in order to gain their property for himself; he exterminates them all at once by shoving them into a hole in the ground, like getting rid of excess baggage. The entertainment value of King Ubu comes not from sensible plot or well-fashioned dialogue, but in witnessing a grotesque, overblown adolescent annihilate the world around him.

Marriage more often than not serves as the domain of farce. The strict moral laws governing marriage are an easy target for the impish comic spirit. Vows of love and honor, commandments against adultery, and legal ramifications of matrimony establish a limit situation against which the characters' sexual libidos go wild. Comedy in general mocks marriage, from the bantering and badgering between husbands and wives in Roman comedy to the hurtful jabs at marriage in the Restoration play *The Way of the World*. As Mirabell advises his friend Mrs. Fainall: "You should have just so much disgust for your husband as may be sufficient to relish your lover." Many comedies depict the age-old battle between the sexes as something perpetually comical; Terence's play *The Mother-in-Law* is filled with husbands' rants about their trouble-making wives—and wives trying to defend themselves. Sostrata justifies herself to the audience: "I am not guilty! But clearing my name won't be easy. Men are stuck on the notion that mothers-in-law are unjustifiably evil." According to the Roman playwrights, marriage to a woman is such a burden that even the smallest allusion to it will garner great laughs. Marriage jokes continue over the centuries. Watching the opening scene from Sheridan's *The Critic* is to witness both a husband and wife respectively dismayed that their spouse cannot behave. Mrs. Dangle deplores her husband's foray into the theater and believes he is making a fool of himself. When he badgers her to join him, she tartly replies: "Isn't it sufficient to make yourself ridiculous about your passion for the theater, without continually teasing me about to join you?"

With marriage in mind as an ideal target of ridicule, a number of writers began popularizing a form known as bedroom farce at the beginning of the 19th century, the chief among them being Georges Feydeau. This French playwright would place his characters in the most preposterous situation, mix in some sexual raciness and imbroglios, and logically and precisely have all the problems reconciled by the curtain's close. His play *Le Manage de Baril-Ion* (*On the Marry-go-Wrong*, 1907) involves a woman who accidentally marries her son-in-law, only to discover that her husband, who was presumed dead, has returned from his two-year hiatus and now chastises her for becoming a "bigamistress." Many of his plays witness mistresses and lovers dallying in boudoirs only to escape into a closet or through a back door seconds before the arrival of the unexpected spouse. Another play, *A Flea in Her Ear* (*La Puce à l'oreille*, 1909), incorporates a revolving bed which allows a character to push a button and disappear into the next room—a contrivance that results in hilarious and nightmarish consequences. The genre depends on virtuoso, high-speed antics, well-plotted confusion and surprise, and the audience's superior knowledge of the onstage characters' whereabouts. There is also a slight guilty pleasure to be had from living out our secret fantasies on the stage, without suffering the repercussions ourselves. Joe Orton acknowledges this voyeuristic drive inherent in marital farce: he offers us every kind of forbidden desire or sexual perversion in *What the Butler Saw* (1969): necrophilia, exhibitionism, rape, sadomasochism, fetishism, nymphomania, and implied incest. What alleviates our anxiety or guilt about our fantasy life being played out before us the laughter. Rather than experience self-disapproval toward our own fantasies, we let down our censoring mechanisms and laugh uproariously at the characters' antics. Laughter permits us to examine truths about human nature without succumbing to our judgmental super-ego.

Tragicomedy

The final form of comedy is tragicomedy—a form that has decidedly marked the twentieth century. Tragicomedies seem tonally wrong. They might combine a feeling of optimism with a queer underlying worry. The characters may make humorous comments but meanwhile they appear to be suffering through distressful circumstances. Funny events may occur but they lack any clear causal relationship with actions that happened previously and thus our laughter seems out of place. As the name suggests, a tragicomedy can be viewed as mixture of two genres, tragedy and comedy, but more precisely, it is a structured series of tragic events within a comic atmosphere. Robert Corrigan, in a helpful essay on tragicomedy, explains that the world from which tragicomedy emerges is one of ambiguous values; it is the aristocratic Chekhovian drama on the eve of the Russian communist revolution, or the apocalyptic no-man's land of Samuel Beckett's figures following World War II. Chekhov deliberately created no heroes or villains in his plays, and thus there is no ethical system by which to judge the characters; we never know whether the hero or villain "got what they deserved." Beckettian characters are kept in trash cans, or stuck in piles of sand, or left forgotten and stranded. Despite these bleak scenarios these plays are comic because the spirit of optimism reigns, not in a falsely cheery way, but with the characters' wry resignation that one has no choice but to endure.

Tragicomedy examines areas of the human experience that are atypical topics for comedy—death, aging, sickness, consciousness, or regret—and simultaneously showcases the elasticity of the human spirit. This is not to say that tragicomedies are falsely heartening and inspirational, far from it; rather they sardonically convey an attitude of acceptance—the belief that one must take responsibility for one's life. For example, Anton Chekhov's character Uncle Vanya (1899) is greatly disillusioned to discover that his lifelong project doing research for his relative was meaningless when he discovers the professor is a pompous fraud and that his treatises on modern art are self-contradictory and banal. Vanya bemoans his fate so tragically that we share his pain, but we also are moved to laughter at his excessive emotions and dejected self-view: "I am forty-seven years old; I may live to sixty; I still have thirteen years before me; an eternity! What shall I do? How can I fill them? Don't you see, if only I could live the rest of my life in some new way." His speech resounds tragically with regret and bleakness, but it is also a comic moment because he pathetically overdoes his emotions; he makes his plight seem larger-than-life. Tragicomedy, more than other plays, clearly shows characters searching for some meaning in their lives. Beckett's character Clov sarcastically wonders aloud in *Endgame* (1958) "Mean something! You and I, mean something! (*Brief laugh.*) Ah that's a good one!" The peculiar emotional experience of seeing a tragicomedy is an unusual juxtaposition of impressions; one experiences the deep and profound sufferings of the character, but some comic line or gesture goes too far, and pushes the spectator to view the scene with more detachment. And with that detachment comes a philosophical attitude toward life. As George Meredith reminds us, the comic perspective is one of intelligence, not emotion: "The comic, which is the perceptive, is the governing spirit."

We may want to call these plays tragic instead of comic, since the characters suffer from the bleakness of their lives or their dashed dreams, but we must not overlook the crucial feature of these plays: human resiliency. These characters continue to hope for a change of circumstances. Beckett's two tramps in *Waiting for Godot* (1953) will return the next day and the next to await this personage; Chekhov's women in *Three Sisters* (1926) insist on planning their move to Moscow. Tragicomedy gives us characters whose dreams sustain them, even while they cynically consider their circumstances. Beckett's Winnie, entombed up to her waist and then up to her neck in the earth, talks about adaptability: "I used to perspire freely. Now hardly at all. The heat is much greater. The perspiration much less. That is what I find so wonderful. The way man adapts himself. To changing conditions" (*Happy Days* 1961). Winnie makes a conscious decision to continue living each day; the revolver in her purse—which she kisses—is a constant reminder to her (and to us) that she could end her life if she so chose. The fact that she continues to live each day while contemplating the option of suicide is proof enough of the human spirit to endure.

Beckett's theater also forms part of another kind of comedy, termed "Theater of the Absurd" by Martin Esslin. Not an exact sub-genre of comedy *per se*, this style of comedy originated in the 1950s as a response to the atrocities of the two great World Wars and was influenced by a branch of philosophy known as existentialism. These plays often rely upon an absurd premise or absurd logic to explore the human condition, and often look at life through an alien lens. Eugene Ionesco's play *The Bald Soprano* (1958) demonstrates the problematic nature of human language for communication, and his play *The Lesson* (1951), explores the sadistic nature of power. He demonstrates an absurd pedagogical relationship whereby the professor kills his student for not knowing the Neo-Spanish word for "knife." Edward Albee shocked American audiences with an educated American couple, George and Martha, who delighted in torturing one another—and their guests—mentally and emotionally (*Who's Afraid of Virginia Woolf?* 1962), while Harold Pinter in England revealed the darker psychoses underpinning family relationships in *The Homecoming* (1965). The group of playwrights who wrote absurdist dramas is not large, but their body of works left an impression on modern drama by their attack on scientific positivism—the naive belief that the world was a logical place that could be studied and understood. Perhaps Tom Stoppard is the contemporary playwright most influenced by the absurd tradition. His well-known characters Rosencrantz and Guildenstern, borrowed from *Hamlet*, struggle to make sense of the world into which they have been thrust unawares (*Rosencrantz and Guildenstern are Dead* 1967). The simple action that begins the play, the coin-toss that perpetually comes up "heads," exemplifies how laws of chance do not always apply and that the characters' attempt to understand their fate is fruitless. In all cases, theater of the absurd makes us laugh by revealing the very human aspiration to determine a logical explanation for our existence and the fact that the search is ultimately absurd.

COMEDY'S IMPORTANCE

In our final analysis of comedy, we must acknowledge that it is impossible to define the genre by breaking it into subcategories or identifying the traits that differentiate it from tragedy. Many more qualities of comedy exist than those discussed in this essay. Henri Bergson stresses, for example, that comedy is humanistic, that it can only be found in human actions and scenarios: "The comic does not exist outside the pale of what is strictly human." When we laugh at a dog or cat, for example, we laugh at a quality within them that reminds us of human nature. Similarly comedy depends to a great extent on nonverbal elements: on physical pratfalls and facial expressions, to be sure, but also on a quality known as "timing," that is, the particular pacing and length of jokes. Likewise comedy appears to be a quality that does not translate, whether from one culture to another, from one language to another, or even from one generation to another. Whereas tragedy possesses a universal appeal, comedy seems bound not only by nation but by time.

Finally comedy seems to rely upon a sense of incongruity, a recognition that there is a disparity between what is expected from a situation or a person and what is the ensuing result. Freud noted that laughter comes from seeing an individual make movements that were exaggerated and inexpedient and reasoned that the laughter we felt came from a sense of superiority. By comparing ourselves to the person observed, we detect an incongruity between what we would have done and the extra effort the person has displayed. Freud explains that "A person appears comic to us if...he makes too great an expenditure on his bodily functions and too little on his mental ones....In these cases our laughter expresses a pleasurable sense of the superiority which we feel in relation to him." In the play *The Importance of Being Earnest*, the two young women Cecily and Gwendolyn are disturbed by the fact that their fiancés are not called Earnest: "Your Christian names are still an insuperable barrier. That is all." Oscar Wilde has created a scenario where all the characters invest too much energy into inconsequential things, thus the subtitle: "A Trivial Comedy for Serious People."

And yet, comedy, with its lack of serious endeavors, with its concern for the trivial, the absurd, the incongruous, may be the most important genre for manifesting life upon the stage. Tragedy, because of its serious philosophical underpinnings and its search for integral positions in the face of crisis, provides us with a space to feel deeply for the ethical plights and moral dilemmas of our heroes. But comedy provides us with a way to see ourselves out of these plights, whether through clever solutions or moral compromises. It is the genre that acknowledges life's difficulties, frames them with obstacles and shenanigans, yet challenges us to search for a solution or to at least believe, optimistically and faithfully, that the problem will rectify itself with a lucky shake of the dice. This belief, however fanciful, is still necessary, and the culture that finds itself shunning comedy finds itself empty and lifeless within. As Santayana remarks, "Where the spirit of comedy becomes constraint, reserve eats up the spirit, and people fall into a penurious melancholy in their scruple to be always exact, sane, reasonable."

FURTHER READING

Bentley, E. "Farce." *The Life of the Drama*. New York: Atheneum; 1964.

Bergson, Henri. "Laughter." In Sypher, 1956.

Freud, Sigmund. *Jokes and Their Relation to the Unconscious*. London: Hogarth Press; 1960.

Frye, Northrop. "The Mythos of Spring: Comedy." *Anatomy of Criticism: Four Essays*. Princeton, New Jersey: Princeton University Press, 1957.

Langer, Susanne. "The Great Dramatic Forms: The Comic Rhythm." *Feeling and Form: A Theory of Art Developed from* Philosophy in a New Key. New York: Charles Scribner's Sons, 1953.

Meredith, George. "An Essay on Comedy." In Sypher, 1956.

Perry, H.T.E. *Masters of Dramatic Comedy*. Port Washington, New York: Kennikat Press, 1939.

Segal, Erich. *The Death of Comedy*. Cambridge, Massachusetts: Harvard University Press, 2001.

Sypher, Wylie. *Comedy*. Baltimore: Johns Hopkins University Press, 1956.

ℰℬ

Dramatic Comedy: A History of European and American Plays

Reade Dornan

Defining comedy in dramatic literary works (as opposed to stand-up comedy, television sitcoms, vaudeville routines, game shows, and similar forms of popular entertainment) is problematic. First, there is no single uniform definition of the comic structure or the methodological approach to comedy. In its simplest terms, dramatic comedy could be defined as a situation that represents human experience in a stylized, imaginative, or caricature-like manner to arouse laughter and end happily. But some comedy, several of Shakespeare's so-called "comedies "for example, arouses very little laughter and ends with only tenuously held harmony. So critical theorists have not been able to establish a single idea of comedy that they can all agree upon. Second, comedy has a complex of styles, categories, subgenres, and traditions, and many of these subgenres such as satire, farce, or parody have such well-developed forms that folding them into a snappy definition of comedy would hardly do justice to the literature. Third, if we were obliged to consider many of the lesser genres such as a comedy of morals or a comedy of reconciliation, we would cover only a fraction of the subgenres. Fourth, comedic tastes have varied through the centuries, so a single definition would inevitably favor one period's perspectives over the others. To address these multiple issues, we offer instead a brief historical overview with embedded definitions of key terms that indicate their context, as well as a discussion of why and how comedy provokes smiles, laughter, and amusement. In deference to considerations of space, we will focus largely on European traditions in dramatic comedy and touch only on the major shifts in their development.

THE DEVELOPMENT OF DRAMATIC COMEDY

The historical development of European comedy begins with the Greeks. Most historians trace the beginnings of comedy to the performances in Athens at the festival of Dionysus (the City or Great Dionysia) in the fifth century B.C., in the time of Aristophanes (c. 450–380) and the Peloponnesian War between Athens and Sparta (431–404). It is speculated that the term comedy originated in the Greek word for "procession," *komos,* and that early Greek comedy found its origins in the Satyr plays. These were phallic rites with choruses of fat men, satyrs, men masquerading as animals, men on stilts, and processions of men carrying with large phallic symbols on poles. The festivals offered no scripted theater, but occasion for mockery and bawdy celebration. Comedy won its official status in the City Dionysia in 487–486 B.C., around fifty years after tragedy won recognition in 534. Aristophanes was among a handful of writers who wrote "Old Comedy," characterized by their commentary on contemporary politics and social themes, primarily the Peloponnesian War, and lewd humor. Plays were performed in competitions twice a year—in late January and late March. Aristophanes won prizes for eight of his plays, including a lost version of *Clouds, Birds, Lysistrata,* and *Frogs,* which are still among his best known works today.

"New Comedy" turned away from social and political themes toward featuring the everyday dilemmas of ordinary humans. This new style of comedy used the dramatic devices of concealed identity, coincidence, recognition of long lost relatives, and trickery. Some plays were farcical, while others were more seriously moral in tone. The language was neither as elevated nor as frankly salty as it was in Aristophanes' day. Menander (c. 342–291) was a notable writer of New Comedy as were Roman playwrights such Plautus (c. 254–c.184 B.C.) and Terence (c.195 or 185–159 B.C.) . They burlesqued fools, even the gods, and they traded on financial worries, family relationships, and love affairs as subject matter. By the late fourth century B.C., Aristotle's *Poetics* (c. 335–323) had codified the rules for both comedy and tragedy, notably by requiring a unity of action, time, and plot. What Aristotle meant by the unities has been the subject of debate for centuries, but he was generally promoting a tightly knit plot, short time of action, and a single setting, presumably because a play with a coherent theme and focused production values makes a greater impact than episodic narrative. Most of what Aristotle had to say about comedy was presumably spelled out in his lost Second Book, but in the surviving document, he argued that the pleasure in comedy is in imitation of what men do and so the ending should not be painful. He believed in a happy ending. He insisted that comic characters such as slaves, women, buffoons, parasites, impostors, and braggarts should be ludicrous, drawn from the lower or lesser stations in life. He said little about moral lessons, but it is clear that he had social norms in mind when he conceived of using universal themes to mock inappropriate social behavior. This form of comedy is known as indirect satire, which takes its humor from ridiculing the behavior of lesser characters to make its point. It is humor that laughs *at* characters rather than *with* them.

Medieval Comic Tradition

Like the theater of the ancients, the medieval comic tradition grew out of religious performances around church feast days. From these early instances of ritual and ceremony, some comedy theorists contend that religion with its archetypal figures and seasonal rhythms is the wellspring of all comedy. The English cycle plays of the fourteenth and fifteenth centuries reenacted Bible stories of the Old and New Testaments from the birth of Adam to the Day of Judgment. The most famous of the cycle plays were the *Ludus Coventriae* and those named after the towns where they originated—York, Chester, and Wakefield—in about 1375. They were also known as the *mystères,* because they were performed by the various trades or "mysteries." The biblical topics are handled more lightly than one would suppose. The mysteries remain popular for the low comedy that features braggarts, boisterous jokes, drunkards, and shrewish women. Like the plays of the Greeks, the mysteries use stock characters, "conventional character types," such as Noah's nagging wife, a hapless soul named Mak, a braggart who is a coward, the greedy, and the lecherous. Villainous characters are usually embarrassed and the comic heroes eventually triumph over their weaknesses and adversity. These characters enabled medievalists to exploit with obvious delight the fall of Lucifer, the temptation of Eve, the Seven Deadly Sins, and other human failures. In the motif of seasonal regeneration, there are burlesque parodies of sacred events, god figures, gargantuan feasting and perversion of children's games. The themes are based on complaint about adversity, a fear of man's fate and irrational change of fortune, attack on the hierarchy, and ridicule of deviant characters. Spectators could identify with Noah or Joseph as they question divine purpose and grumble about the little annoyances in life. Although these plays are often bitterly realistic and moralistic in intention, they contain enough farce and slapstick, even ribald parody, a barbed mimicking of someone's style that they are highly entertaining even now.

The Renaissance

By the sixteenth century, Italian comedy had its own tradition of populist theater in the *commedia dell'arte* players. This form of theater was known for its low comedy and improvisational style largely based on gesture and particular dialect. It was shaped by the traditions of Greek New Comedy and Roman theater, particularly their themes and popular plot devices, stock characters and visual humor. The plays were fairly simple in structure: the scenario, or plot outline, was written without much embellishment, and the actors improvised their lines guided by these often farcical, often improbable situations. The plots were convoluted and the characters exaggerated; people came to see them plunged into the strangest of situations. Visited by the courtesans and men of rank in disguise, the *commedia dell'arte* eventually developed a wide repertory, and its influence spread throughout Europe and into other art forms. Shakespeare, pantomime, and opera owe much to the characters and plots.

It was an Italian, Francesco Robotello (1516–68), who wrote the first literary commentary on Aristotle. He opened the door for Italians to revive Greek and Roman traditions. It reawakened in Europe an interest in Aristotle's *Poetics*. As directed by Aristotle, "neoclassical comedy" of the seventeenth century sought a more realistic form and coherent form of theater. Stressing verisimilitude, writers restricted characters from the middle or lower classes to comedy and a "superior" folk to tragedy. After debating and redefining the three unities of action, time, and place, they decided that a play needs a single plot, it should take place in less than twenty-four hours. and it must be situated in one place. The aim should be universal themes and moral lesson, imitating behavior that met the expectations of the audience and norms of nature. These Aristotelian rules were rigorously applied to both comedy and tragedy throughout Europe until prominent playwrights proved that the most realistic characters did not always act according to fixed type according to age, rank, and profession.

Shakespeare and Jonson

William Shakespeare (1564–1616) and the Jacobean and Carolinian dramatists of the seventeenth century liberalized the Aristotelian unity of action by adding secondary subplots and redefining the unity of place to say that it would be valid still if characters could move easily from locale to locale. English dramatists generally observed the rules only when it was convenient. Shakespeare blurred the boundaries between comedy and tragedy as he mixed clowns and kings, pain and laughter, farce and death. Many of his so-called dark comedies or problem comedies such as *Measure for Measure* and *All's Well That Ends Well* appear to be miscatalogued as comedy since they depict serious action and sometimes end with a strained truce. Shakespeare's most outrageous characters such as Bottom in *A Midsummer's Night Dream* or Shylock in *A Merchant of Venice*, who are both the wit and butt of the humor, meet their downfall and exit on a sober, even pitiful note. Even so, there is the feeling that the outliers have been welcomed to the fold. Marriage is generally the outcome. Although couples tend to pair off in a predictable pattern, true love is not their object, nor does it seem a likely outcome in some cases. Despite the tensions, Shakespeare's comedies end with greater self-knowledge and understanding of the others, a reconciliation, communal harmony, and some measure of forgiveness. There is always hope in these plays.

Shakespeare's festive comedies are celebratory in tone, enabling movement toward release from restraint and dull burden. They too have been linked to Greek theater. These plays gently ridicule romance, killjoys, the trials of life, and pretentiousness, indeed anything that may be taken seriously. Shakespeare also used hilarious reversals and stock characters of traditional comedy as low humor in short scenes. He borrowed from *commedia dell'arte* for theatrical types such as the rustic clown, the drunkard, the pedant, the gullible father, and loose widow.

Among the Elizabethan playwrights, Ben Jonson (1572–1637) was the most self-conscious adherent of the classical form. His popular comedies—*The Alchemist, Volpone*, and *Bartholomew Fair*—anticipate the moralistic theater of social commentary in the nineteenth and twentieth centuries. Rather than portray lovable rogues, as did Shakespeare, Jonson drew a harsher gallery of characters, whose failings call more for scorn and correction than admiration.

Molière

French playwright Molière (1622–73) was known for his natural style, particularly for his individualistic characters in such plays as *Le Misanthrope* and *Le Malade Imaginaire*. He too moved away from the rigidities of neoclassical comedy to more closely mirror real life. No longer were comic figures drawn only from low life, but he skewered people of all ranks. His people are so realistic that they roused angry attack when audiences suspected that the actors represented actual individuals whose deviant behavior seemed recognizable. Even while aiming at a more truthful reflection of human nature, many of his works are farces in the tradition of the *commedia dell'arte*, and they remain generally faithful to the unities. His sharply drawn, complex comic characters, his satire on manner and custom, and his interior settings (rather than using the out-of-doors) raise the level of dramatic comedy from the mask and improvised theater of the *commedia dell'arte* to a new standard of polished and scripted works.

Restoration Comedy

Restoration Comedy, a period of English drama which shortly followed Shakespeare's time, made its mark with a comedy of manners, known for its sparkling dialogue, clever plot, and caricature of the upper classes. This is a world of intriguers, fops, fools, and foolish lovers. Since their smart mannerisms are exaggerated to highlight character, we cannot take them to be faithful pictures of the life of the people. Even so, there are large elements of reality and their behaviors seem to be portraits of the time. Among the best known playwrights of the comedy of manners were William Congreve (1670–1729) and William Wycherly (1640–1715).

Much later came Richard Brinsley Sheridan (1751–1816) and Oliver Goldsmith (1730?–74). Their plays continue to be loved for their brilliantly witty scenes and flippant treatment of lovers who find themselves preoccupied with suggestive flirtation, seduction, arranged marriage, and moral laxity. This is not the buffoonery, sex, and adultery of Greek theater nor the crude farce of the *commedia dell'arte*, which relied on broad and unsubtle humor. It is high comedy that turns on grace and wit in its gentle satire of human foible and social pretension. A derivation of the comedy of manners is the comedy of intrigue in Spain and Italy with its intricate plots, artificial, contrived situations that are somewhat less engaging because the pieces lack the word play and shiny wit of the English.

European Comedy, 1700–1900

Much of the fare on the stages of the eighteenth and nineteenth century theater in both Europe and the United States was melodrama, which is usually marked by high contrast between good and evil and sensationalism, or burlesque, which an exaggerated form of ridicule either by treating a trivial subject with deep seriousness or by treating a dignified subject frivolously. One exception was John Gay's *The Beggar's Opera* (1728), which both parodied melodrama and painted a cynical picture of corruption in high places and a satire of the operatic form. Mixing popular music with dark comedy, *The Beggar's Opera* is one of the earliest examples of musical theater and expression of the working-class condition. It had a heavy influence on twentieth century dramatists such as Bertolt Brecht who admired its nihilistic tone and emphasis on workers' politics. The theater of Aristophanic political and social criticism reappears only sporadically through the centuries. The mystery plays, which toyed irreverently with a not-so-veiled criticism of the church and its leaders, and *The Beggar's Opera* are examples.

Lasting political satire, or work that uses ridicule to criticize or provoke change in human nature or institutions, did not thrive in English theater until the nineteenth century, when George Bernard Shaw (1856–1950) gained the literary stature to stand up to the various levels of licensing in London. The Lord Chamberlain had virtually total authority to censor or shut down a play in the City of Westminster (London) that was offensive to the court. And Parliament could choose to remove the license of "theatres royal" in specific towns outside London. Even local magistrates had some authority for having control over the themes, mode, and language of entertainment. They often wielded their power arbitrarily and closed down plays without question. Shaw's most important comedies are more serious than not. They are examples of high comedy which employs grace and wit to appeal to the intellect, downplaying emotion and affect. As a Fabian socialist, committed vegetarian, and nudist, Shaw prided himself in unmasking the hypocrisies of Victorians and mocking their illusions and cynicism. Shaw's plays such as *Arms and the Man* and *Major Barbara* comment on the absurd myths we live by, in this case love and war and profit and war. *Mrs. Warren's Profession, Candida,* and *Pygmalion* pose thorny questions about the treatment and roles of women. Because the Victorian theater was generally not prepared for a searching discussion of social problems, it is surprising that both Shaw and Oscar Wilde (1856–1900) enjoyed huge popularity in their time. Like Shaw, Wilde championed the rights and dignity of women in *Lady Windemere's Fan, An Ideal Husband,* and *A Woman of No Importance.* Wilde's *Importance of Being Ernest* is recognized as one of the great plays of English comedy. The play's avowed goal to "treat all the trivial things very seriously and all the serious things of life with sincere and studied triviality" speaks for the comic tradition in England, which had been well honed over the years since the Restoration. Although the charm of these plays mitigated Wilde's sarcasm, the public eventually turned against him for his flagrant disregard of social convention.

In their own way, William Schwenck Gilbert (1836–1911) and Arthur Sullivan (1842–1900) wrote some of the most enduring comedy of the last two centuries. Gilbert wrote the book and Sullivan composed the music for musicals that still enjoy a loyal following. Gilbert and Sullivan constructed the make-believe world of Topsy Turvey, where lighthearted melody evoked both nostalgia for the old British Empire and genial spoof of British institutions—self-important royalty (*The Mikado*), the gnarled legal system (*Trial by Jury*), feminists (*Princess Ida*), aristocratic rank (*H.M.S. Pinafore*), and upper middle class tastes—including the craze for Oscar Wilde and the "Aesthetes" (*Patience*). Most of Gilbert and Sullivan's operettas feature contrived plots with cradle mix-ups and kinship recognition (borrowing a gimmick from the Greeks), the exaggeration of burlesque and a parody of operatic style and other subgenres.

European Comedy, Twentieth Century

Noel Coward (1899–1973) also belongs to the group of socially aware playwrights, even though he had little interest in serious political satire. If anything, Coward's plays about contemporary issues spanned the World Wars and were thus patriotic. Nevertheless he was heir to Shaw and Wilde's penchant for caustic commentary on dubious human behavior, particularly in the battle between the sexes. Coward's contribution to comedy is the twisted attitude of the urbane character who has little interest in sentiment or attachment. Men and women in Coward's plays flaunt their premarital affairs, marry the wrong people, and swap partners. While antimarital English comedy of the seventeenth and eighteenth centuries similarly threatened social stability, they usually ended by reassuringly reestablishing the social order. Sheridan's eighteenth century *The School for Scandal*, for example, reaffirmed marriage even if it suggested more discord to follow. Sometimes called "comedies of bad manners," Coward's *The Vortex, Fallen*

Angels, and *Private Lives* shocked audiences that expected some affirmation of marriage values and conventional relationships, even if the couples went their own way. Licentious sentiments expressed in Coward's plays once again recall the racier examples of Greek and Roman comedy.

A more pointed political satire appeared in the 1960s in the United Kingdom in the form of Agit Prop, a sketch-like form of political theater that commented on the news of the day, and later, leftist theater that, post-World War II, protested the degradation of the environment, the myth of achieving class parity, a rejection of cold-war imperialism, and crude materialism. John McGrath (1935–2002) of the 7:84 Theatre Company and Caryl Churchill (b. 1938) are two playwrights who challenged assumptions about power and economic relationships. McGrath used folk forms such as the Scottish *ceilidh,* a celebration with song, dance, and ribald parody in *The Cheviot, the Stag, and the Black, Black Oil,* to show how power corrupts and to demonstrate that the people could fight back with communal resistance. Churchill continues to write some of the most original comedy on the British stage. Her early work was with Monstrous Regiment, a feminist group that developed scripts out of workshopping through analysis, discussion, and experimentation. *Cloud Nine* linked economic imperialism and sexual imperialism in hilariously unexpected ways. *Top Girls* is an innovative feminist comedy about what women in power must give up. Radical comedy in the United States continues to be mounted by committed theater companies such as La Mama Experimental Theatre, San Francisco Mime Troupe, Marbou Mines, and Omaha Magic Theatre.

The content of the theater of the absurd departed markedly from centuries of social satire and farcical comedy. It bewilders audiences, who cannot understand its antisocial nature and seemingly destructive philosophy. Its plays depict a strange and dislocated world in which "absurd" events confront and mystify the characters and the audience is forced to decide on meaning for themselves. Writers such as Samuel Beckett (1906–89), Eugène Ionesco (1909–1994), Václav Havel (b. 1936), Edward Albee (b. 1928), and Harold Pinter (b. 1930) retained traditional dramatic forms but rejected rational views of the universe. The theater of the absurd was probably suggested by Dadaism and a fascination with Jung's and Freud's investigations of dreams and neuroses, which they believed open windows on the recesses of the unconscious. Dada appeared around 1916 or 1918, when a number of visual artists independently responded to the massive destruction of World War I by creating non-art. European culture had lost all meaning. This nihilistic feeling spread with the spiritual exhaustion at the end of World War II, when they were forced to admit that the humanistic ideals of the Renaissance had been unable to prevent the holocaust and that they should stop pretending that the arts had something to say. About the same time, philosophers Martin Heidegger, Soren Kirkegaard, and Jean-Paul Sartre raised the ideas of existentialism. It grew into a loosely constructed philosophical movement that places a heavy emphasis on individual responsibility and living in the present according to a personally authenticated code of rules for existence. The movement came to its peak in Europe and the United States in the 1950s, a time of abstract expressionist painting, cold-war fear, rampant materialism, and mindless conformity. These trends informed a theater that neither preached nor proposed solutions but described things as they were in scathing metaphor.

The comedy of the theater of the absurd is based on the ludicrous situations that lone characters, isolated from the world and reasoned interaction, must endure, since their stories almost never end happily. Without a past or a future, Beckett's characters inhabit barren landscapes, some are trapped in isolated rooms, others are stuck in garbage cans or buried alive in a hole. They reject cliché and ideology. Pinter's characters live in secret dread. In an interview with Kenneth Tynan, Pinter talked about the absurd, "Everything is funny; the greatest earnestness is funny; even tragedy is funny.…The point about tragedy is that it is *no longer funny*. It is funny, and then it becomes no longer funny." In the theater of the absurd, comedy merges with tragedy once everything seems pointless and relative. These plays are darker than almost any before their time and they make a mockery of the lighthearted themes of comedy—romance, marriage, rogues and tricksters, and sex. This form of comedy is so turned on its head that barriers between the arts break down and one does not know whether to laugh or not.

AMERICAN COMEDIC THEATER

America's comedic theater began long after the Puritan era and developed more in the direction of popular entertainment than dramatic comedy. From the nineteenth century on, minstrel shows, vaudeville, medicine shows, and burlesque filled the stages more than serious comedy. Certainly, there was no author with the historical influence of a Shaw or a Shakespeare. Most American comedies are either straight farce or musical theater, comic in structure with laughter and comic endings, largely based on farce, or "dramatic pieces intended to excite laughter and depending less on plot and character than on improbable situations, the humor arising from gross incongruities, coarse wit, or horseplay." George S. Kauffman (1889–1961) had the reputation of being one of the wittiest writers of his time. He collaborated with Moss Hart (1904–61) to create popular comedies of the 1930s and 1940s—*The Man Who Came to Dinner* and *You Can't Take It With You*. William Saroyan (1900–81) made his fame on likable characters. Neil Simon (b. 1927) similarly has written well-loved works—*Barefoot in the Park, The Odd Couple, Brighton Beach Memoirs* to name a few. Simon's plays are largely romantic comedies, stories about couples who have "obstacles thrown up in the way of true love, but they usually end happily." With a few exceptions, American comedy has found so much profit in farcical themes that it has done little to push the development of dramatic comedy into new directions.

One exception is America's ethnic theater, which has daringly taken on sensitive racial subject matter for two centuries. The humor works both ways—as the exploitation of stereotypes by mainstream culture and as disdain of power by ethnic groups. It has sprung from a variety of traditions. In the Native American theater, the comedy has been rooted for centuries in ritual ceremony and celebration. In the nineteenth century, ethnic theater was a cultural focus for immigrants. A popular topos was poking fun at the "green one," the newcomer to the United States. Often mounted in the language of the community, these productions provided a reason for community. There was a well-established French theater in New Orleans in the early nineteenth century, a Yiddish theater for decades in New York City, Chicago-based Swedish companies, and Finnish companies in mining camps. Chinese theater flourished in San Francisco. Italian comedic theater came from an ages-old love of opera and the *commedia dell'arte* (Seller 1983). Protest theater reached its peak with the waves of immigrants in the late nineteenth and the early twentieth centuries and with the African American Civil Rights Movement. An ongoing subject for ethnic humor is protest against exclusionary institutions and hypocritical attitudes in the mainstream. Ethnic theater continues to preserve folklore, educate the audience to values and community culture, provide a center for the social life, and entertain. August Wilson's cycle plays covering African American twentieth century history is a fine example of this. One of the activist theaters today is the Chicano El Teatro Campesino. Originating in the 1965 grape-picking camps of the United Farm Workers, it traded on slapstick and a fast-paced form of comedy for protest and political satire. It has grown from improvisation to full-length plays and films.

These multivalent forms of dramatic comedy have in common those various elements that make people laugh. From Aristotle on, a common view of comedy was that we find the protagonist funny as a deviant from the social norm. We enjoy feeling superior to the character. It is not enough to regard the poor buffoon as a moral inferior; some writers use his missteps as a reason for moral judgment and correction. This is particularly the case for stock figures that function as types. They sometimes stand for the aberrants that the dramatist can shape a play or scene against. Audiences enjoy the clueless, the rigid, the mechanical, and the outrageous as long as they are not to be pitied. Characters on the edge are funny because we become aware of the gap between them and ourselves. In short it is the proximity between disjunctive objects that is funny. In Freud's *Jokes and Their Relation to the Unconscious* (1905), he explores the idea of incongruity. He is especially interested in the joke as a signal from the unconscious to the conscious mind of difference. He speaks of the "comic process as necessarily an unconscious one," attaching it to dreams and the "lost laughter of childhood." He explains that we become aware of difference and we experience pleasure when we know it is not us. Freud was particularly aware of comedy as a social event and a release from fear. In *The Gay Science* (1882), Friedrich Nietzsche detached comedy from its judgmental and moral overtones, by arguing that the ideal human confronts seriousness as though it were the stuff of laughter. Had Nietzsche lived long enough, he might have endorsed the plays of the theater of the absurd because he saw humor as a way out of atrophying human behavior, as a way of producing new knowledge and disaggregating stultifying conventional values. Nietzsche contended that comedy was not only faultfinding, but exuberant and liberating, pleasurable because it is the playful spirit that puts one in touch with the divine.

FURTHER READING

Barber, C.L. *Shakeskpeare's Festive Comedy: A Study of Dramatic Form and its Relation to Social Custom.* Princeton University Press, 1959.

Brockett, Oscar G. *A History of the Theatre.* 5th Edition. Boston: Allyn and Bacon, 1987.

Hockenson, Jan Walsh. *The Idea of Comedy: History, Theory, Critique.* Madison: Fairleigh Dickinson Press, 2006.

Holman, C. Hugh and William Harmon. *A Handbook to Literature.* 6th edition. Macmillan and Collier Publishing Companies, 1992.

Itzin, Catherine. *Stages in the Revolution: Political Theatre in Britain Since 1968.* London: Eyre Methuen, 1980.

Lauter, Paul, ed. *Theories of Comedy.* New York: Anchor Books, 1964.

Seller, Maxine Schwartz. *Ethnic Theatre in the United States.* Westport, Connecticut, Greenwood Press, 1983.

Styan, J.L. *The Dark Comedy: The Development of Modern Comic Tragedy.* Cambridge University Press, 1968.

❧

Expressionism

Robert F. Gross

In a snow-covered landscape, a man watches as a leafless tree turns into a human skeleton....To the clink of gold pieces, bankers in silk top hats dance the fox trot around the stock exchange....A horde of creditors descend on a funeral procession and strip the corpse naked....Expressionist drama abounds in images of great intensity, violence, raw sexuality, and grotesquerie. Yet these images rarely exist only to shock; they are usually put to the service of highly idealistic visions of a desperate need for social reform and spiritual regeneration in modern society. Rejecting realism, the dominant style of Western theater in the twentieth century, the expressionists responded with a theater of stylized speech, expansive gestures, dreamlike occurrences, masks, choral effects, music, choreographed movement, distorted settings, and innovative lighting techniques to evoke a world of almost unbearable intensity. First flourishing in Germany in the years during and immediately following World War I, both the vision and techniques of expressionist theater have reappeared, often as a form of social protest, throughout the twentieth century and into the twenty-first.

The term "expressionism" was not coined as the name of theatrical movement, nor did it ever denote a strictly defined coterie of theater artists who shared a single, unified aesthetic. The word was actually first applied to developments in the visual arts. Whereas the "impressionist" painters, including Claude Monet, Camille Pissaro, and Pierre Auguste Renoir, had moved their easels out of doors to catch the play of light and color more accurately, artists in the succeeding generation were often less interested in rendering the appearances of the outside world. They were more interested in the challenge of how to convey emotional states in visual form. These artists, including Vincent Van Gogh, Paul Gauguin, and Edvard Munch, embraced an artistic vision of radical subjectivity. Munch's most famous work, "The Scream," was, he explained, his attempt to communicate to the viewer his personal experience of feeling a "scream go through nature." Not concerned with rendering the bridge perspectively, or catching the reflection of sunset on the water, or using the actual proportion of human hands in relationship to the head, or following the actual anatomy of the body, Munch uses line, color, shape, and composition to convey the particular intensity of his experience. In "The Scream," the *impression* of the external world on the eye has given way to the *expression* of intense emotion through the artistic distortion of external phenomena.

THE BEGINNINGS OF EXPRESSIONISM IN DRAMA

Strindberg

In the theater, the beginnings of expressionism can be seen in the work of Swedish playwright August Strindberg (1849–1912). A prolific and relentless experimenter, his works contain instances of almost every style of modern theater: realism, symbolism, surrealism, neo-romanticism, absurdism—and expressionism. Strindberg gained fame and notoriety as the author of plays that still stand among the masterpieces of naturalism, including *The Father* (*Vadren*, 1887) and *Miss Julie* (*Frøken Julie*, 1888). His fascination, however, with intense human drives and his belief that strong personalities can seize and control the minds of weaker individuals—even to the point of committing "psychic murder" by the mere power of suggestion—led Strindberg to portray psychic forces at work on the stage. A series of psychotic episodes between 1894 and 1896, accompanied by a conversion to religious mysticism, further opened his dramaturgy to the representation of subjective states.

In his trilogy, *To Damascus* (*Till Damaskus*, Parts 1 and 2, 1898; Part 3, 1904), he presents a visionary autobiographical drama of his movement toward religious belief. He dramatizes his spiritual quest in a series of disjointed, dreamlike episodes. In one, a boyhood rival appears as the husband of the woman he loves, and as the superintendent of a mental hospital. In another, a formal banquet held in his honor mysteriously degenerates into a sordid event attended by beggars and prostitutes. Strindberg's episodic depiction of his spiritual journey became known as *Stationendrama*, or "station play," after the Catholic devotional practice of the Stations of the Cross, a series of fourteen episodes depicting the suffering, death, and entombment of Jesus. The *Stationendrama* became a major form of expressionist drama.

Presenting himself as "The Stranger," Strindberg encounters such representative types as "The Lady," "The Confessor," "The Beggar," and "The Madman."

Stripped of proper names, and presented as types rather than detailed, realistic characters, these figures often seem to be aspects of The Stranger's psyche, much as they might appear in dreams. The tendency to prefer types over individualized characters became one of the most salient aspects of expressionist dramaturgy.

In *A Dream Play* (*Ett Drömspel*, 1902), Strindberg took his experiments in transformation even further, creating a play in which "anything can happen; anything is possible and probable." The daughter of the god Indra descends to an earth in which everything has the fluidity of a dream and the sole constant is human suffering. Characters move freely across time and space; a castle grows like a plant and, as it is consumed in flames at the final curtain, it bursts into flower, with a huge chrysanthemum at its top. This experimentation with the theater as a place of continual, imaginative transformation would become an important part of American expressionism in the 1960s and 1970s.

In *The Ghost Sonata* (*Spöksonaten*, 1907), Strindberg strips away the veneer of an apparently happy and respectable middle-class household to find it a den of madness, sin, and betrayal, inhabited by a mummy, a vampire, and a beautiful young woman who is mysteriously wasting away. The barrier between life and death becomes insubstantial; a recently deceased consul watches himself being mourned from the balcony of his home. From what he observes in the house, an idealistic student concludes that Jesus's descent into hell was in fact his descent into the madhouse of our world.

Although Strindberg's experimental dramas were not accepted at first, they slowly established themselves, and then became wildly successful in Germany after his death. Between 1913 and 1915, twenty-four of his plays were performed in sixty-two German cities, racking up more than a thousand performances. Strindberg's plays continue to be revived and have attracted the attention of such notable directors as Max Reinhardt, Evgeny Vakhtangov, Olof Molander, Ingmar Bergman, and Robert Wilson.

Early Expressionism in German Drama

Spiritual yearning is replaced by cynicism and satire in the plays of Frank Wedekind (1864–1918), the other major precursor of expressionism. An iconoclast disgusted by sexual repression and prudery, he wrote *Spring's Awakening* (*Frühlingserwachen*) in 1891 but had to wait until 1906 for its premiere, even in a heavily censored version. By turns lyrical and grotesque, the play presents a group of adolescents struggling to reach adulthood in a rigid, hypocritical, and brutally repressive society. Wedekind fractured his dramatic action into a series of intense episodes, some of which deal with masturbation, homosexuality, sexual violence, and abortion—all strictly taboo subjects on the German stage of that era. In the final and most dreamlike scene, Melchior, the young protagonist, finds himself in a cemetery, where he encounters a school friend who had committed suicide by shooting himself. Carrying his head in his hands, the friend tries to persuade Melchior to join him in death, only to be defeated by a rebuttal from the mysterious "Man in a Mask," who represents the forces of life.

Wedekind's *Lulu*, published and performed in two parts, entitled *Earth Spirit* (*Erdgeist*, 1895) and *Pandora's Box* (*Die Büchse der Pandora*, 1904), is a sort of perverse, erotic *Stationendrama*. In it, Lulu survives three husbands—the first dies of a stroke when he finds her in the arms of an artist; the second cuts his throat when he learns of her sexual past, and the third, driven insane by her many admirers, is shot by Lulu herself. Fleeing both the police and a blackmailer, she dies in a London slum, murdered by Jack the Ripper. Not a scheming femme fatale, Lulu is a strangely innocent figure whom Wedekind uses to show up the hypocrisy, possessiveness, and emotional insecurity of the men who flock around her. As with *Spring's Awakening*, the *Lulu* plays offended the censors, and it was not until 1989 that Wedekind's original text was performed.

Dissatisfied with the early performances of his plays, Wedekind, an accomplished cabaret performer, took to the stage himself. Rejecting both the smooth, declamatory style of the classical school of acting and the understated, psychologically based style of the realists, Wedekind created his own powerfully idiosyncratic style. His harsh, grating voice, lurching movements, high energy and abrasive presence, dominated the productions of his plays and fascinated audiences. He became a model for the coming generation of expressionist performers in Germany.

Wedekind's attacks on sexual repressiveness and bourgeois gentility appealed to the anti-establishment—even anarchistic—sensibility of many German expressionists, who celebrated the power of life over tradition and social convention. In a 1906 manifesto, expressionist painter Ernst Kirchner defined the goal of attracting "all the revolutionary and surging elements…and…to create…freedom of life and movement against the long-established older forces," and many of his contemporaries in literature and theater concurred.

Artist Oskar Kokoschka's playlet, *Murder, Hope of Women* (*Mörder, Hoffnung der Frauen*), first produced in Vienna in 1909, is considered the first true expressionist drama. Performed outdoors at night after the briefest of rehearsals by Kokoschka's fellow art students, it caused a sensation and led its author to lose the academic stipend that paid for his schooling. The play's mythic structure, minimal dialogue, violent physicalizations and extreme compression (the script is only five pages long), distilled the dramatic action into a single shockwave unlike anything in the plays of Strindberg and Wedekind.

The play presents a duel-to-the-death between "Man" and "Woman," who are locked in a demonic struggle for dominance, complete with branding and stabbing. It climaxes in the ecstatic death of Woman and a violent surge of energy from Man, who strides through the terrified chorus and "kills them like mosqui-toes and leaves red behind." Kokoschka painted muscles, nerves, and veins on the faces and bodies of the performers, suggesting a primal world of tortured physicality and flayed sensibilities.

Far more influential, and more representative of early expressionist drama than *Murder, Hope of Women* is Reinhard Sorge's *The Beggar* (*Der Bettler*; published 1912, premiered 1917), which adopts the form of *Stationendrama* to tell the story of a young artist's development. Instead of Strindberg's questioning pilgrims, how-ever, Sorge's protagonist is a young firebrand who realizes his poetic vocation with no self-doubt and little opposition from others. Plot and conflict are reduced to a minimum, and the hero often expresses the stages of his spiritual journey in long, declamatory speeches. The protagonist (variously referred to as "the Poet," "the Brother," "the Young Man," and "the Son," as well as "the Beggar" of the title) is the embodiment of all that Sorge finds noble: youth, idealism, creativity, and an unremitting dedication to his vision. He is the first of many examples of the expressionist figure of "The New Man"— a prophetic, sometimes even Messianic figure who represents the values of a utopian future. Often, the New Man is called upon to annihilate the unenlightened *status quo* in the figure of his father. In *The Beggar*, the poet's father—a demented invalid with fantastic dreams of economic development on Mars—is poisoned by the hero in response to his father's entreat-ies. The idea of euthanasia provokes neither ethical conflict nor legal consequen-ces for the son: an example of Sorge's predilection for lyrical abstraction over dramatic suspense and tension. Sorge's strategy is not to sustain dramatic interest through conflict, but through the lyric evocation of the poet's visionary existence.

Early expressionist dramas were often called *Schreidramen*, or "scream plays," summoning up the shattering intensity of Edvard Munch's pictorial idea. Inten-sity, whether elicited by sex, violence, mob experience, or spiritual ecstasy, was set in opposition to the values of middle-class culture. Playwrights experimented with ways of heightening language—whether rhapsodic, free-verse declamations, or short, telegraphic bursts of speech—and the elements of production were used to further boost the emotional effect. Actors were encouraged to stretch their physical and vocal resources to the utmost, and exaggerate vocal contrasts through unexpected shifts in volume, tempo, and rhythm. Claw-like hands, rolling eyes, bared teeth, and trancelike declamations became familiar elements in the expressionist actors' arsenal of techniques. The aim was less to create a character than to channel primal emotional states in all their unadulterated power.

The scream, breaking through the social codes of language with its raw inten-sity, was not only an image for how expressionists saw their art, but was some-times a key moment in their productions. In Karl-Heinz Martin's production of Ernst Toller's *Transfiguration* (*Die Wandlung*, 1919), wounded and mutilated sol-diers complained of their sufferings individually, then screamed in unison, bringing the groaning nurses in the ward to their knees—a moment that left some members of the audience in tears. In Ernst Barlach's *The Deluge* (*Die Suÿakndflut*, 1924), we hear from offstage the repeated screams of a shepherd whose hands have been chopped off in a deliberate gesture of provocation to both the humans and deity who fail to intervene in such atrocities.

At first the provocative themes and aggressive style of expressionist drama kept many of them off the stage, and they were often published in literary journals long before they were performed. In 1916 Dresden became the scene of the first professional production of an expressionist drama: Walter Hasenclever's *The Son* (*Der Sohn*). Another treatment of the popular theme of the son's violent revolt against patriarchy, *The Son* shows a youthful protagonist who is under virtual house arrest and physically abused by his tyrannical father. Breaking free under the mesmerizing influence of his friend (named "the Friend"), he brings an offstage audience to a frenzy as he recounts the story of his oppression and displays his scars—a true *Schrei* performance. Returning home with a pistol, he intends to kill his father. But before he can shoot, the oppressor drops dead of a stroke.

Other expressionist dramatists would continue to ring changes on the theme of father-son conflict. In Anton Wildgans's *Dies Irae*, the confrontation ends with the son's death. In Arnolt Bronnen's notoriously sensational (and very successful) *Patricide* (*Vatermord*, written 1916, published 1920, performed 1922), the son, who is incestuously involved with his mother, murders his father and then, repudiating his sexually overstimulated mother's advances, soars into the heavens.

TWENTIETH CENTURY GERMAN EXPRESSIONISM

The outbreak of World War I soon forced many writers to widen their purview beyond domestic battles. Although some expressionists at first welcomed the war as a relief from the monotonous constraints of bourgeois life, the horrors of the battlefield, trench warfare, and poison gas quickly disabused them of any naive illusions. Some perished in the war, including August Stramm (1874–1915), Reinhard Sorge (1892–1916) and Gustav Sack (1885–1916). Others, including Fritz von Unruh (1885–1975) and Ernst Toller (1843–1939), survived and wrote plays from a pacifist perspective. Toller's *Transfiguration* chronicled the playwright's own conversion from nationalist, pro-war fervor to committed pacifism. Among other notable pacifist plays: Georg Kaiser's *The Burgers of Calais* (*Die Bürger von Calais*, written 1914; performed 1917) Hasenclever's *Antigone* (1917), and Reinhard Goering's *Naval Encounter* (*Seeschlacht*, 1917).

In *Naval Encounter*, Goering rejects the formal expansiveness of *Stationendrama*, achieving intensity by having the play unfold in one uninterrupted act in a single place—the gun turret of a battleship at sea. Their identities minimized by their combat functions, the sailors have no names, and are simply numbered from 1 to 7. Hardened by their work, they wait anxiously for the enemy to appear. Only Sailor 5 realizes what has happened to them:

For two years we have wandered the sea,
Blind and obsessive, killing, finding death
Nobody remembers anything else
No one knows anything else
No one can do anything else
But killing and dying.

He tries to rally his shipmates to mutiny, but suddenly enemy ships are sighted and the intensity of combat is irresistible—he plunges into battle with the others. Further deindividualized in their gas masks, they become indistinguishable from each other, and all meet their deaths in the frenzy of battle. Only in the last moments of his life does Sailor 5 realize how he has been unable to sustain his vision of a better world. Goering dramatizes the exhilarating intensity of warfare, its horrors, and a tragic dichotomy between group experience and individual reflection.

Sailor 5 possesses all the visionary intensity and idealism of the New Man, but lacks the ability to convert others to his enlightened beliefs; even worse, he is incapable of sustaining his own idealism against opposing forces. This disillusion-ment with the prophetic hero can be seen increasingly in later expressionist dramas, along with an increasingly pessimistic vision of contemporary life. No longer is bourgeois repressiveness the enemy, but the increasing dehumanization brought about by modern industrialism, militarism, and urban life.

Although the early expressionist plays of Georg Kaiser (1878–1945) expressed hope in the coming of the New Man, his later work often gave way to despair. In his *Gas* trilogy, composed of *The Coral* (*Die Koralle*, 1917), *Gas I* (1918) and *Gas II* (1920), the workers in the gas factory are not only without proper names; they have been reduced to their function in the industrial process. The man who oper-ates the lever all day is seen as nothing but a hand; the man who works the pedal, a foot; the man who watches the gauge, an eye. But when the New Man, in the person of the factory's idealistic owner, tries to persuade them to reject this perilous and dehumanizing work in favor of an agrarian idyll, they refuse, and the control of the factory is seized by the government, citing its importance to the national defense.

In *Gas II*, the situation has worsened, and the factory runs unceasingly to produce gas for the war between the Blues and the Yellows. When the workers are encouraged to use the latest invention—poison gas—to insure their victory, the great-grandson of the owner opposes them: "Let the kingdom arise which shall reign in you almighty," he desperately entreats them. But when he finds that the masses are intent on this suicidal course of mass destruction, he releases the poison that brings on the final destruction of civilization. The trilogy ends with the factory in ruins, the bleached skeletons of the workers scattered about, and bombs exploding in the distance.

The implications of this apocalyptic ending are ambiguous, and have been debated by critics. Is Kaiser dramatizing a set of disturbing possibilities that he nevertheless believes can be avoided? Or is he expressing his own nihilistic loathing and despair? Certainly Kaiser deeply doubted the possibility of collective enlightenment by this point in his career. In *The Coral* his protagonist observes, "the deepest wisdom is found only by a single mind. And when it is found it is so overwhelming that it cannot become affective." The despairing tone of the *Gas* trilogy is an example of the widespread disillusionment to be found in German expressionist drama of the last years of World War I and its aftermath.

A similar disillusionment can be seen in Ernst Toller's writing. His first play, *Transfiguration,* celebrates the education both of its hero and the masses. His later and most famous work, however, replaces that hopefulness with a tragic awareness of guilt and defeat. Written in prison, where Toller was serving a five-year sentence for his participation in the short-lived communist government in Bavaria, *Man and the Masses* (*Masse-Mensch,* 1921) shows its idealistic heroine opposing both her bourgeois, politically conservative husband and the revolutionary violence of The Nameless One. Despite her devotion to pacifism, she capitulates in the face of passionate revolutionary rhetoric, and much like Goering's Sailor 5, is swept away by the intensity of violent action. When the revolution fails, and she is imprisoned, she realizes the extent of her guilt and refusing the attempts of both her husband and The Nameless One to free her, accepts her death sentence as an act of principle.

The increasingly desperate vision of German expressionism in its final phases has led to its being dubbed "black expressionism," reaching extremes of physical torment and anguished introspection in the works of Hans Henny Jahnn (1894–1959), the last important German playwright to emerge from the movement. In his first published play, the seven-hour *Pastor Ephraim Magnus* (1919), two sons of a highly unorthodox minister follow two different paths to fulfillment, both of them grisly. One becomes a sex killer who dismembers a woman's body in the hopes of finding her soul. The other, submitting to blinding, mutilation, castration, and crucifixion at the hands of his sister, does so in imitation of Jesus who, we are told, takes "all sufferings upon himself without finding salvation." This controversial work was condemned as the artless ravings of a sick and obscene imagination by some, and praised by others for its unremitting exploration of spirituality in a world cut off from the possibility of redemption. Although awarded the prestigious Kleist Prize in 1920, *Pastor Ephraim Magnus* had to wait until 1923 for its drastically shortened stage premiere in a private Berlin club, only to be closed by the authorities before the week was out.

Jahnn gained more popular success with his *Medea* (1926), one of the few German expressionist dramas to enjoy successful revivals in recent years. Jahnn makes the mythic heroine a woman of color, her children by Jason biracial, and uses her tragedy to explore the dilemma of the racial outsider in Western culture. Even here, Jahnn does not hesitate to explore areas of violence and taboo sexuality; Jason is a cynical hedonist, a promiscuous bisexual who admits to finding his own sons more sexually appealing than his wife, and Medea kills her sons while they are having sex together.

With Jahnn, we reach both an extremity of content and a bleakness of vision that marks the end of expressionist experimentation. In the second half of the 1920s, Toller increasingly turned to realism; Hasenclever, to comedy; and the prolific and indefatigable Kaiser, while occasionally returning to expressionism, produced an array of comic satires, mystical romances, and libretti. Overall, the emotional rawness of expressionism gave way to the distance of the New Objectivity (*Neue Sachlichkeit*), another loosely defined movement characterized by a renewed interest in realistic depictions of life, through usually from an ironic and decidedly unsentimental perspective. Marieluise Fliesser (1901–74) and Ödön von Horváth (1901–38) explored the hypocrisies and viciousness of life in small towns and big-city neighborhoods, and Bertolt Brecht (1898–1956) developed a highly influential approach to political drama based on an aesthetic of emotional detachment.

Expressionism's Decline

By the time the Nazis came to power, expressionism had ceased to be a vital movement. Many of the plays were officially condemned and production of them forbidden. Some erstwhile expressionists, like Arnolt Bronnen and Hanns Johst (1890–1978), reworked their style and vision to become successful Nazi playwrights. Others, including Toller, Kaiser, Jahnn and Hasenclever, went abroad. After World War II, there was little interest in reviving expressionism, though Jahnn continued with his anguished intensities, and Wolfgang Borchert's successful radio play, *The Outsider* (*Draußen vor der Tür,* 1947) used expressionist techniques in a story of a traumatized soldier's return from the war.

The legacy of German expressionism to the modern theater is not limited to the works of its playwrights, but to the innovations of its directors and designers as well. In fact, the long-term influence of the movement has actually been greatest in the area of theatrical production. At first directors often did not know how to approach these experimental scripts. The impact of *The Son's* 1916 Dresden premiere, for example, was severely hampered by its director, Adolf Licho, who approached it as a realistic piece and neglected its *Schrei* intensity. It would not be until two years later, in Mannheim, that director Richard Weichert developed a production style that suited Hasenclever's text. Stripping the scenery back to minimal groups of furniture in a surround of black draperies, Weichert placed the Son stage center beneath a harsh light, while the other characters entered through the darkness and addressed him from the shadowy periphery. Without stage makeup, the actors appeared spectral figures in an internal drama, rather than in a social drama in the style of Ibsen. Strongly cast with expressionist actors and visually compelling, this production of *The Son* met with critical and popular success.

Weichert was one of a number of directors who discovered that the best way to present the intense, interior world of expressionist drama was to remove any superfluous details in the staging, sometimes simplifying the productions far beyond the playwright's own stage directions. In 1921, designer Hans Storbach simplified the settings of *Man and the Masses* to a flight of stairs and a few emblematic props, enabling director Jürgen Fehling to create arresting, nonrealistic images with the actors: a clerk on an exaggeratedly high stool at an equally high desk; an enclosure like a birdcage held the crouching heroine in her imprisonment. As in Weichert's production of *The Son*, shafts of light pierced the darkness, and the design made much of the compositional possibilities of bright light and deep shadow. Most importantly, however, Fehling choreographed the crowd scenes to give the sense of the collective having a force and volition far beyond any single individual. Well-documented and reported, Fehling's staging of *Man and the Masses* was the single most influential expressionist production abroad.

The most celebrated advocate of this new scenic austerity was Leopold Jessner, who became famous for reducing scenery to a bare flight of ascending steps and platforms, or, as they are called to this day, "*Jessnertreppen*" (Jessner-steps). On these staircases, the actors were costumed in bright colors, arranged in striking compositions, and often sharply outlined by harsh lighting. The effect of taking them out of a realistic milieu was to stress the timeless, mythic dimension of the action. Not only did Jessner stage new plays in this style, but returned to classic texts as well, including *Othello*, *Macbeth*, and *Richard III*. Richard's rise to power, for example, was reflected in his gradual ascent of the *Jessnertreppen*, climaxing in his coronation, as he stood at the top of the stage, the steps beneath him and his subjects all in red. After this, he descended, finally falling down the steps to be killed by Richmond's soldiers, clad in white.

Not all playwrights, however, were pleased with Jessner's ascetic style. When Jessner undertook the premiere of Ernst Barlach's *The Genuine Sedemunds* (*Die echten Sedemunds*, 1920), the playwright, himself a celebrated sculptor, showed the director the real-life locations that had inspired the play's settings, only to find that the production did away with all of them. Frustrated that Jessner had ignored the specific demands of the script in favor of his own celebrated mise-en-scéne, Barlach avoided seeing subsequent productions of his plays.

Using stark and sometimes distorted scenery, bright colors, the full force of electric lighting against deep shadows, and powerful stage compositions, the experiments of expressionist directors and designers created a harsh, intense aesthetic that expressed both the trauma and alienating impersonality of contemporary life. In so doing, they expanded the stylistic vocabulary of the modern theater.

Moreover, expressionist theater often foregrounded the director's contribution, leading to productions in which the director's vision of the script became more hotly debated than the merits of the script or the performers. The "director's theater" of today is deeply indebted to these innovators of the 1920s.

GERMAN EXPRESSIONISM'S INFLUENCE ON U.S. DRAMA

The experiments of the German expressionists influenced theatrical production throughout Europe, but had their greatest influence in the United States. The Theatre Guild and the Provincetown Players, two producing organizations alert to European developments, brought expressionist plays to the New York stage— to decidedly mixed reviews but great interest, especially among the theatrical community. In 1922, the Theatre Guild presented Georg Kaiser's *From Morn to Midnight* (*Von Morgens bis Mitternachts*, 1916), followed by *Man and the Masses* in 1924, and Franz Werfel's *Goat Song* (*Bockgesang*, 1921) in 1926. The Provincetown Players staged Strindberg's *The Ghost Sonata* in 1924 and Hasenclever's *Beyond* (*Jenseits*, 1920) the following year. But probably no single stage production equalled the influence of Robert Wiene's silent film *The Cabinet of Doctor Caligari* (*Das Kabinett des Dr. Caligari*, 1919). With its distorted, strangely angled scenery, shadowy lighting, grotesquely made-up actors, and the trancelike performance of Conrad Veidt as Cesare the sonnambulist, its 1921 New York showing brought a taste of expressionism to viewers who could not see experimental productions in Germany. Playwright Eugene O'Neill (1888–1953) found the film a revelation, and it inspired him in his experiments with expressionist devices in the 1920s and early 1930s.

By the time expressionism had begun to make its influence felt on the American stage, however, World War I was over; the plays' protests seemed pointless and their visionary hope for regeneration, passé. American expressionism was less concerned with the ecstatic and revolutionary than it was with the sociological and psychological. The anonymity of the big city and the impersonality of the workplace became major themes, nowhere more clearly than in Elmer Rice's *The Adding Machine* (1923), with its cipher protagonist, Mr. Zero, an accountant locked in a meaningless life with his nagging wife, surrounded by other, equally vapid couples.

The New Man was replaced by the Neurotic. More pathologized than prophetic, the hysterical and sexually repressed heroines of Sophie Treadwell's

Machinal (1928) and Rice's *The Subway* (1929), and the split personalities of Eugene O'Neill reflected the influence of Sigmund Freud and Carl Jung in American artistic circles. O'Neill used a number of devices to dramatize the split psyche: masks in *The Great God Brown* (1925), lengthy asides in *Strange Interlude* (1928), and two actors presenting opposed sides of a single self in *Days without End* (1933).

Although the form of the *Stationendrama* was assimilated to American expressionism, it was not used to dramatize a spiritual quest, but a process of psychological deterioration. Rice's Mr. Zero is jolted out of his colorless existence and murders his boss; Treadwell's Young Woman is driven to kill her coarse husband; both are sent to the electric chair. The protagonist of O'Neill's *The Emperor Jones* (1920) loses every bit of his self-possession and rationality as he flees into a jungle during an uprising, and Yank, the protagonist of O'Neill's most fully realized foray into expressionism, *The Hairy Ape* (1921), finds himself an outcast among humans and finally seeks companionship with the gorilla in the zoo, only to be crushed to death.

Both Susan Glaspell (1876–1948) and Sophie Treadwell (1885–1970) extended the range of expressionism by using it to explore feminist concerns. Although Glaspell's *The Verge* (1921) is mostly realistic, its fascinating second act, set in a shadowy, Caligari-esque tower, uses distorted scenery and exaggerated characters to convey the dilemma of a brilliant female scientist who is hemmed in on all sides by conventional thought. Treadwell's *Machinal* uses broken, telegraphic language to communicate the emotionally brutal, sexually exploitative world of the office that drives the Young Woman into an unfulfilling marriage, and eventually to murder. A critical success in its day, *Machinal* has enjoyed major revivals in London and New York over the past decade, as well as a renewed stage life on many college campuses.

No doubt the most commercially successful and influential work of American expressionism, however, was a comedy. George S. Kaufman and Marc Connelly's *Beggar on Horseback* (1924), played the attack on the bourgeoisie for laughs. A free adaptation of an obscure German original, the play used expressionist devices ingeniously. An aspiring but impoverished composer falls asleep. In his dream, he imagines marrying an idiotic heiress (who carries a bridal bouquet of banknotes) in a jazz ceremony celebrated in a railway station. When she destroys his symphony, he murders her and her obnoxious family, finds himself in a trial conducted as a theatrical performance, and is condemned to a prison in which artists are sentenced to turn out appallingly banal commercial work. Fortunately, of course, it is all a dream, and the composer awakes to find his true love waiting for him. Expressionist devices have been assimilated into a Broadway romantic comedy, complete with whimsical touches, a sentimental love story, and a happy ending. By containing expressionism within the framework of a realistic, commercial play, Kaufman and Connelly achieved its domestication, opening the way to the insipid dream ballet of Richard Rodgers and Oscar Hammerstein's *Oklahoma!* (1943) and its countless imitators, and the overproduced, cloying fantasies of Moss Hart's *Christopher Blake* (1946), which depicts the daydreams of a boy facing his parents' impending divorce. Expressionism, which had begun as a radical protest decades earlier, was safely assimilated on Broadway, and degenerated into cliché.

Broadway's poetic realists of the 1940s and 1950s occasionally used expressionist devices to heighten dramatic moments or add imagistic touches. Arthur Miller's *Death of a Salesman* (1949) is fundamentally realistic, but the appearances of Willy's dead uncle, his boss's unnerving Dictaphone, and the dreamlike aura of certain episodes are all indebted to expressionism. Similarly, in Tennessee Williams's *A Streetcar Named Desire* (1947), the playwright uses the ghostly playing of the "Varsouviana" and the sound of a gun firing to underscore how Blanche is tormented by memories of her husband's suicide. Both plays remain, however, fundamentally realistic in their treatment of behavior, plot, and setting.

THE REVIVAL OF EXPRESSIONISM

The rediscovery of the expressionist impulse in the theater did not come about until the 1960s—and then through an unexpected source. The French theatrical visionary Antonin Artaud (1896–1949) seems not to have been directly influenced by the expressionists— his primary contacts were with the French surrealists— but he shared their enthusiasm for the plays of Strindberg, staging *A Dream Play* in 1928, and his proposals for a "theatre of cruelty," which would break through daily life with a shattering intensity resonate with the visions of the expressionists. Although he eschewed the literary language that of the German playwrights, he shared their fascination with choreography, rhythmic incantation, and the mythic, often violent perspectives of Kokoschka, Bronnen, and Jahnn. As Artaud's writings grew more influential in the theater of the 1960s, an aesthetic developed that, although not calling itself "expressionist," nevertheless has much in common with it.

In the United States, this revival has been centered in the experimental theaters of Off-Off Broadway. The counterculture of the 1960s embraced the impulse to revolt against the status quo that had galvanized the German bohemians decades earlier. The highly influential Living Theatre rediscovered both the raw emotions and anarchic-pacifist philosophy that had inspired many expressionists. The unrelenting intensity of Kenneth Brown's *The Brig*, performed by the collective in 1963, with its characters reduced to numbers, evoked the dehumanization of *Naval Encounter* and *Gas*, while simplifying the language beyond anything to be found in the plays of Goering and Kaiser. Realistic motivation and causal plotting were completely discarded in later pieces such as *Paradise Now* and *Frankenstein* (both 1968), in which actors embodied impulses, rather than portrayed characters. In the latter, the head of Frankenstein's monster became a world prison in which fugitives were imprisoned merely for being alive. Peter Schumann's Bread and Puppet Theatre used larger-than-life puppets and masked figures to create powerful works of social protest. Joseph Chaikin (1935–2003), originally a member of the Living Theatre, used the transformational aesthetics of Strindberg's *A Dream Play* in his own dreamlike, often mythic work, although his pieces rarely aimed at the intensity of expressionism.

In the 1990s, gay playwright and director Reza Abdoh (1963–95) created dense works of violent, often assaultive imagery drawn from contemporary life and popular culture, as in *The Law of Remains* (1992), in which the life of serial killer Jeffrey Dahmer is filmed by Andy Warhol. Abdoh said the play aimed to remind its audience "That it's not enough to think of a world that is more livable...but that you have to act on it."

In England, where expressionism had had little influence between the two World Wars, a theater with many expressionist elements has developed since the late 1960s. The plays of Edward Bond (b. 1934) fuse utopian impulses with denunciations of violence in intense, haunting works of nonrealistic theater. The cannibalism of *Early Morning* (1968), the blinding of Lear and torture of Gloucester in *Lear* (1972), and the apocalyptic landscapes of the War Plays (1985) blend shock and polemic in a manner reminiscent of expressionism. Bond has had a major influence on younger British playwrights, most notably on Howard Barker (b. 1946) a prolific playwright who calls his provocative explorations of the politics of desire, accompanied by dense, poetic language "The Theatre of Catastrophe." Barker, in turn, influenced Sarah Kane (1971–99), whose *Blasted* (1995), a nightmarish drama that includes onstage masturbation, fellatio, rape, blinding, and cannibalism, produced a journalistic furor that easily equalled (if not surpassed) the controversy that surrounded plays by Wedekind, Bronnen, and Jahnn decades earlier. Kane explained that her play was an investigation of male psychology in the contemporary world, which leads not only to rapes in hotel rooms, but to rape camps in Bosnia. She insisted, however, that *Blasted* was a play about hope, since it shows people trying to continue in circumstances that could easily drive one to despair.

In December 2004, the International WOW Company, a multicultural troupe of artists based in Thailand and the United States, presented a new play, written and directed by Josh Fox, at the Ohio Theatre in Manhattan. *The Expense of Spirit* opened to a loud surge of minimalist music as an actor noisily chopped (invisible) vegetables on a clattering metal platter. Marty, the boisterous owner of a vast video store, prepares to host her annual Christmas Eve dinner, while waiting for news of her daughter, stationed with the U.S. military forces in Iraq. Shortly before the party begins, Marty learns her daughter has died but tells no one, and the party goes on as planned. Increasingly loud and frenzied, the grotesque guests move in slow motion one moment, and lurch into a jerky, "fast-forward" the next, growing ever more drunken, gluttonous, and gross. As Marty, actor Deborah Wallace, moving with incredible tension and aggressiveness, hit a high level of intensity early on, and then, astonishingly, surpassed it time and time again, creating an atmosphere of almost unendurable tension. Exploding in vulgar tirades of forced jubilation and rage, Wallace seemed both desperately anguished and indomitable. Then, after a sequence of seeming equanimity, Marty suddenly shoots herself, bringing the play to a jarring halt. In its nonrealistic devices, grotesque touches, aggressive aesthetic, sustained intensity, and antiwar message, *The Expense of Spirit* demonstrates the ongoing vigor, effectiveness, and urgency of the expressionist tradition.

FURTHER READING

Kuhns, David F. *German Expressionist Theatre: The Actor and the Stage.* Cambridge: Cambridge University Press, 1997.

Patterson, Michael. *The Revolution in German Theatre: 1900–1930.* Boston: Routledge, 1981.

Valgemae, Mardi. *Accelerated Grimace: Expressionism in the American Drama of the 1920s.* Carbondale, Illinois: Southern Illinois University Press, 1972.

❧

"In Yer Face" Theater: "Purely through Image" and the Collapse of Language

Luc Gilleman

SARAH KANE'S *BLASTED*

The Necessity of Violence

In *Blasted* (1995), a soldier rapes a man, then sucks out and swallows his eyeballs. Later the mutilated rape victim digs up a dead baby and devours it. The play also features fellatio, anal penetration with a gun, onstage masturbation, micturition, and defecation. *The Daily Mail* in London called *Blasted* "a disgusting feast of filth." Most journalists agreed. It was the first professionally produced play, at the Royal Court Theatre Upstairs, of an unknown young woman, Sarah Kane, who was then 23 years old. She was 28 when, in 1999, she overdosed on pills, was saved, only to hang herself a few days later in the lavatory of the hospital where she was being treated for depression. The newspaper people were understandably shocked and awed, and the critical reception of her plays changed accordingly. The evils of depression became the centerpiece of discussions; her play *4.48 Psychosis*, written in 1999 and performed posthumously in 2000, was widely read as a sort of suicide note, and the violent imagery of her plays was suddenly no longer the result of an immature imagination but an artistic symbol of existential despair.

Violence, especially when it seems gratuitous and excessive, guarantees audience response, though not always of the kind the playwright hopes for. Kane said of *Blasted* that it was "a shocking play, but only in the sense that falling down the

stairs is shocking—it's painful and it makes you aware of your own fragility."
Violence, then, is supposed to heighten awareness. But it doesn't always do so.
The complexity of *Blasted* is often overlooked for the scenes of rape and cannibalism—just as Edward Bond's *Saved* (1965) is remembered mainly as the play where
a baby is stoned to death; Howard Brenton's *Romans in Britain* (1980), as the play
that features a scene of anal rape; and Anthony Neilson's *The Censor* (1997), as
the play where a woman defecates onstage. Violence and obscenity do not
always stimulate thought; they often soak up any subtler meanings the plays
might have.

Serious and incontestably talented playwrights like Kane depict violence on
stage because they feel it has become an unavoidable and crucial ingredient of
any play that claims to be relevant for our time. After all, the twentieth century
was the bloodiest one on count, with some 160 million people killed by state-
organized violence alone, victims of conflicting ideologies and the efficiency of
technologically improved warfare. With this figure in mind, the drawing-room play
seems eerily artificial. This occurred to Kane when in 1993 she was writing the
hotel room scenes in *Blasted*, scenes featuring a couple's private despair, and
Bosnia was the site of indescribable atrocities: "I switched on the television," Kane
recalled. "Srebrenica was under siege. An old woman was looking into the camera,
crying. She said, 'Please, please, somebody help us. Somebody do something.'
I knew nobody was going to do a thing. Suddenly, I was completely uninterested
in the play I was writing. What I wanted to write about was what I'd just seen on
television." Kane could have abandoned the fairly conventional, one-room play
she had been working on for a kind of social documentary about the war in Bosnia.
Instead, she kept the story about the abusive relationship between a jaded tabloid
journalist and a naive young girl but in the second half "blasted" the room open
and, with images of unparalleled violence, let the outside world flood in. The result
was disorienting, but also powerful and deeply unsettling. As the box set collapses,
the nightmare we all do our best to forget, rushes in. After September 11, 2001,
a date that gave the term "global village" a sinister ring, a play like *Blasted* has
become frighteningly relevant.

Theater of Disintegration

Blasted is the result of a careful whittling down and condensing of long drafts
containing comprehensive accounts of characters' background and motivations.
Only surface was allowed to remain, symptoms without authorial diagnosis—all
this in conformance with a performance-based view of "experiential" theater that
eschews narrative explication. There are no easily identifiable authorial comments
in *Blasted*, keys to an interpretive unraveling of its perplexing events. Harold
Pinter—himself a minimalist, well-known for his use of the pause, silence, ellipsis,
non sequitur, and ambivalence—vigorously defended the play against its

detractors. So did Edward Bond, whose dark and violent vision of humankind is closest to Kane's. *Blasted* acknowledges its debt to both of these older playwrights with oblique references to Pinter's *The Birthday Party* (1958) and *The Dumb Waiter* (1960) and to Bond's *Lear* (1971), which, like *Blasted* is a grim rewriting of Shakespeare's *King Lear*.

Because, as Pinter would say, "there is no chorus in this play," *Blasted* offers no interpretive closure. Spectators have to make inferences and establish connections at their own risk, decide what is serendipitous and what deliberate, wondering perhaps whether the author herself always knew what she was doing. As Kane admits, "writing my first play really was a process of groping about in the dark, making connections that I understood on an instinctive level but couldn't (and didn't want to) necessarily articulate." Digressions about Cate's love of soccer or dim references to Ian's past as a secret agent may belong to a former vision of the play, traces of which the playwright failed to erase completely or deliberately included, to confuse rather than to clarify. Such trace elements, undeveloped and apparently unconnected references to an extraneous and not fully integrated reality, compel careful readers or spectators to develop ever more nuanced or comprehensive interpretations. Many, however, lose patience with the play, especially when, near the end, it disintegrates into a series of grotesquely violent, disconnected images, one of which includes Ian's death, after which he implausibly returns back to life. Kane does not make it any easier on her audience when she insists that these episodes should not be staged as a nightmare or hallucination, but that they are "even more real" than the play's realistic beginning. Violence and obscenity definitely stoked the critics' anger, yet much of the derision the play provoked was undoubtedly caused by its refusal to allow the audience to connect all the dots and spell out a moral lesson.

Kane said that she intended the title of her play to refer to the "blasted heath" where Lear is exposed to the tempest, to "cataracts and hurricanoes." Though the phrase "blasted heath" occurs in *Macbeth* (1.3), a play that like *Blasted* is concerned with guilt, *King Lear* is indeed the more obvious model for the disintegration with which Kane's play is concerned. Ian is a 45-year old tabloid journalist, a successful dirt raker, in poor health and obsessed with bad smells. In his view, the world "stinks," but so does his own body, with a smell of decay that bathing cannot obliterate. With only one diseased lung left and all major organs on the point of failure, Ian lives daily with the thought of death, or "non-being," as he calls it. Fearing death, he devotes himself to the frantic pursuit of elementary pleasures, though these have long ceased to be pleasurable and propel him towards the non-being he fears. As he lights a cigarette, swills gin, or hungrily devours slices of bacon, he is racked by spasms of pain. Equally painful are the dreary orgasms he relentlessly pursues through masturbation and rape. Ian's life revolves almost exclusively around excretion and ingestion, including the play's very opening line:

Ian: I've shat in better places than this.

The opening lines, together with the direction that they are spoken in "a very expensive hotel room in Leeds—the kind that is so expensive it could be anywhere in the world," reveal much of what we need to know about Ian and the major themes of the play. Ian's curious association of the sanitary luxury of the room with defecation introduces the audience not only to one of his obsessions but also, more generally, to the scatological meaning of wealth: money, like excrement, is a great equalizer, reducing difference to sameness, quality to quantity, inalienable essences to a common denominator. While "Cate stops at the door, amazed at the classiness of the room," Ian has long lost this capacity for wonder. In his jaded view of the world, all is endlessly exchangeable, valuable only in as far as it can be quickly and casually consumed. After tossing down the gin, he turns to the next source of pleasure. His habitual sexual scheming is hinted at by the non sequitur: "I stink. You want a bath?" Barely in the hotel room and reacquainted with his former girlfriend, he is already envisioning sharing a bath with her. After all, he has little time left: "Enjoy myself while I'm here" is his philosophy.

Ian's casual disdain for others, for foreigners (wog, Paki, nigger, coon, conker, Sooty, whodat), the mentally disabled (retard, spaz, joey), and homosexuals (lesbos, dyke, gash suckers, cocksuckers, queers), extends to Cate, a twenty-one year old with marked regressive tendencies. While she naively wonders what they are celebrating, the money he spent on the room, flowers, and champagne, is meant to buy him the pleasure of her sexual service. At the start of the next scene, the next day, the flowers are scattered, and Cate is bleeding and hurting. During the previous night, she has become the unwilling object of Ian's violent sexual fantasies. But this is not yet another "beauty and the beast" story. Cate is not a Griselda, a symbol of saintly female compliance, or a Justine, the ever white slate of female innocence on which masculine abuse can ceaselessly write itself afresh. She gives as well as she takes, seducing Ian at one point only so that, in revenge, she can bite him where it hurts most. She also learns and adapts quickly. When the room is inexplicably and implausibly transposed into a war zone, Cate escapes through a window, while Ian, though armed and prepared for the worst, is easily overwhelmed. Later, having been reduced to a sightless head sticking out of a hole in the floor, Ian, who was afraid of "non-being," begs for death. Cate, who, as Ian thought, was too stupid to even look after herself, resolutely chooses for life: she adapts to the new order, eating the meat she previously scorned and drinking the gin she gained through prostitution. In Cate, the essence of humanity survives, expressing itself in simple acts of decency: an attempt to save a child, to give it a proper burial when it dies, and to look after Ian when he becomes helpless.

The Wages of Sin

Arthur Miller once said that the theater he liked and practiced portrays the "wages of sin." It derives its creative impetus from a moral and ethical vision of shared human values and explores what happens when we ignore or fail to live up to those. *Blasted* shares this utopian belief in humankind, though violence and obscenity tend to overshadow its hopefulness. Whereas Ian's first words are "I've shat," his last are a simple and decent "thank you." At least, he has taken to heart the soldier's ironic advice that he "learn some manners." When intense physical suffering strips him of his habitual cynicism, Ian stands revealed as a father worrying about the welfare of his son. *Blasted* never allows us to forget the pitiful humanity of anyone, even the perpetrators of violence. We see Ian fumbling with his clothes when Cate laughs at the sight of his genitals. We learn that this sexual predator is a puritan at heart, uncomfortable with any frank discussion of sexual matters, as when Cate tells him of her experiences with masturbation, uneasy also at the thought that anyone would suspect him of being gay. Cate believes Ian is "soft," that he is not as tough as he seems to be. The latter could also be said of *Blasted,* which despite its gruesomeness verges on the sentimental. Coming out of one of her "fits," during which Ian masturbates on her helpless body, Cate is said to be "crying her heart out." While raping Ian, the soldier too is "crying his heart out." Reporting about the war devastation outside, Cate says, "everyone in town is crying." And in the end, Ian, embracing "for comfort" the dead body of the man who tortured and raped him, is "crying, huge bloody tears." Violence in the play is invariably accompanied by a sense of loss, of unspeakable regret. The mention of the "heart" is revealing because it suggests an intangible human interiority, a utopian longing that when overcome by an all too intransigent reality expresses itself in a flood of tears.

Water imagery runs through the play, bringing with it a host of metaphysical and religious associations. Every scene ends with the sound of rain, that of spring for scene one, summer for two, autumn for three, and winter for four. Though this effect can hardly be reproduced in production, it indicates that Kane conceived of the events in her play as evolving cyclically, like the seasons. This brings with it expectations of renewal and rebirth, confirmed also in other ways. The quest for absolution and redemption is present in Ian's repeated attempts to wash the "stink" of his body in the bathroom. The latter is the place from where Cate escapes to the outside, when the soldier invades the hotel room, and from where, after Ian's mutilation and the soldier's suicide, she reemerges "soaking wet and carrying a baby." Time is transcended altogether in the final scene, where it simply "rains," without reference to any season. It pours through the roof onto Ian's tortured head, and, in an unwished for miracle, brings him back to life after he dies "with relief." The final impression is one of a world where everything solid has liquefied: as rain is pouring down, blood is "seeping from between [Cate's] legs" and streaming from Ian's eyes; Ian ejaculates and defecates on the floor. We have entered an elemental world. In this watery milieu, things are disintegrating, but perhaps also being incubated: the play ends with Ian's head sticking out of a hole in the floor, eye sockets empty and bloody, being hand-fed by Cate. Stark religious imagery pervades the final scene: the baby, symbol of innocence, has died. Cate gives it an improvised Christian burial, making for it a primitive cross and praying over its body. Ian asks for forgiveness and to be remembered in her prayers. In a caricature of the Holy Communion, Ian devours the baby, and in an equally caricatured representation of the Last Supper, Cate shares sausage and gin with Ian. But if this is meant as a profession of belief, it is indeed a curious one. Ian, who claimed there is no God and that "when you die, it's the end," dies and comes back to life again, but only to have his suffering prolonged. Cate, who believes in God and for that reason refuses to help Ian commit suicide, loses the baby she was trying to save. And while the baby who represents the future dies, the man who carries the burden of the past remains alive so that he can die endlessly.

Kane was a lapsed Evangelical Christian, product of a strict religious upbringing that had left her with an enduring fascination for the dark stories of rape and murder that abound in the Bible. Perhaps for that reason, she tends to pursue moral and ethical issues not within a well-defined realistic context but set against a larger, eschatological canvas. Blasted's vision of violence is apocalyptic, not in its cruelty (which is sadly realistic), but in its nameless and timeless universality. Despite Kane's reference to Bosnia in her account of the genesis of the play, Blasted avoids locating the war in time and space. Ironically, this vagueness has increased the topicality of the play for the post September 11 world. Ian who complains that England is turning into "Wogland," boasts of having worked for the Secret Service, first disposing of bodies and later doing "the real job," which apparently means killing terrorists: "Planting bombs and killing little kiddies, that's wrong. That's what they do. Kids like your brother." Blasted, however, is not concerned with analyzing the political and economic underpinnings of terrorism. The latter stands mainly for the vagueness of the threat and the resulting longing for an impossible clarity, expressed in the kind of jingoistic shorthand that fits on bumper stickers: "Done the jobs they asked. Because I love this land." Lost on Ian, of course, is the irony of posing as the defender of the weak, after having raped Cate and having expressed his disdain for her mentally disabled brother. And what Ian gains is not clarity but guilt and fear of retaliation "for things I've done." The danger now is everywhere, coming not only from unnamed terrorists but also from the Secret Service: "Think they're trying to kill me. Served my purpose."

The Collapse of Language

War enters the play not as specific historical event but as symbol for the precariousness of civilization, the illusion of which depends on maintaining the difference between here and there, inside and outside, private and public. In the course of the play, "there" enters "here," demanding to become also its reality. The violence of war brings to the surface the vileness that is supposed to remain hidden underneath, much as in the blinding scene in *King Lear*, the "vile jelly" is made to erupt from something as smooth and perfect as an eyeball. The war scenes described in *Blasted* focus on similar images: "Insides of people's heads came out of their eyes. Saw a child most of his face blown off, young girl I fucked hand up inside her trying to claw my liquid out..." When the outside world of public violence blasts its way into the luxurious hotel, it proclaims affinity with the secret criminality of the character hiding there and the private acts of sexual abuse that are taking place within those walls. Ian's crimes differ from those of the soldier in degree rather than in kind: like the soldier, he raped, but only once; like the soldier, he killed, but refrained from torturing. As Kane said in an interview, "I do think that the seeds of full-scale war can always be found in peacetime civilization."

"Here" is also where violence is mainly an exciting fantasy; "there" is where it actually happens. Without spelling out any arguments, *Blasted* points to a correlation between an obsession with violence and an inability to conceive of its reality. As a tabloid journalist, Ian gathers sensational stories involving the rape, torture, or ritual murder of teenage girls or young women ("a beautiful redhead with dreams of becoming a model"). As he repeatedly says, these are just "stories," without any news value, invitations to fantasize about the very acts they condemn. It does not, for instance, occur to him that, as a 45-year old who sexually dominates and humiliates a naive young woman of 21, he's not that different from the so-called maniacs, lunatics, and perverts whose exploits he documents. Text is carefully distinguished from reality—at least, in the kind of journalism that Ian practices.

The soldier who inexplicably invades the hotel room, with stories about his participation in a kind of violence that outstrips anything Ian ever reported, reminds Ian that the job of a journalist consists in bridging the gap between story and reality. Ian, he says, should make his story real, "proving it happened": "At home I'm clean. Like it never happened. Tell them you saw me." Although steeped in gory reality, the soldier feels unreal, trapped in an experience so extreme that it cannot be adequately conveyed through words. Ian cannot and will not accommodate his wishes. Later, blind and abused, having become "a nightmare," Ian too will long for the touch of a human being to convince himself of his own reality and will beg Cate to report his existence to the outside world, to his son Matthew:

"Punish me or rescue me makes no difference I love you Cate tell him for me do it for me touch me Cate." And Ian will meet with the same refusal.

The stories the soldier tells Ian differ from the latter's tabloid reports only by the degree of their cruelty: a young boy being shot through the legs, a family murdered, a woman stabbed repeatedly in the groin, a twelve-year old girl sodomized, her brothers strung up by their testicles, etc.—stories of cruelty so extreme as to appear unreal, nightmarish. Kane did not have to invent them: similar reports from the ethnic wars in Bosnia-Herzegovina and Rwanda appeared in the press from the early to the mid-1990s, when Kane was writing *Blasted*. In writing about the horrors of war, Kane was faced with a problem well-known to writers about the Holocaust. Faced with the singularity of an extreme experience, silence is the only adequate response—or, it should be, if it did not entail the possibility of historical erasure and thus the risk of future repetition. Telling, however, means betraying, compromising the singularity of experience with the communality of language, a language that does not contain a separate code for Truth and that therefore cannot differentiate adequately between accounts of actual torture and the lurid fantasies of the human imagination. The soldier finally reverts to the only way of making words real: he acts them out on Ian, kissing him tenderly, as he used to kiss his love; sodomizing and blinding him, as was done to her by the enemy. Through the repetition of such violence, the soldier is writing himself, leaving onto Ian's body the indelible marks of his reality, empathizing both with Col, his "poor love," and with the "poor fucking bastard." who did to her what he himself did to other women. The play too gives up on words, entrusting its message almost entirely to a series of disconnected tableaux, snapshots of horror lighting up briefly in the darkness. As Kane says, "it got to the point where I didn't know what words to use any more, and it was a complete breakdown of language. I thought I'm going to have to do this purely through image, which I'm happier doing anyway."

KANE IN CONTEXT: TOWARD A SPECTACULAR THEATER

Now almost forty years ago, social critics from Herbert Marcuse to R.D. Laing declared that modern civilized human beings are "demented creatures." "Normality," in their view, is the name we give to the routines that allow us to slide along the surface of experience without getting snagged on unpleasant facts. After all, to live, one must forget. And the more we know, the more we need to suppress in order to carry on with our daily business. Today, we are incessantly bombarded with unpleasant knowledge, from newspapers to the Internet, and our powers of denial have increased proportionally to our increased access to unpleasant realities. Modern playwrights are thus faced with an audience whose "dementia" has reached truly frightening proportions.

Though the idea that art ought to attack the public's weakened sensibilities reaches far back, at least as far as the Dadaists, it became increasingly trendy in the late 1960s. In France, the philosopher of theatrical happenings Jean-Jacques Lebel called for art to become a form of violation, a transgression he did not hesitate to liken to rape: the well-known French phrase "épatez le bourgeois" (impress or shock the bourgeois) became the more pointed "fuck the bourgeois." Following the Dadaists, Lebel also rebelled against the expectation that art should be seemly and sanitary, with the notorious exclamation ART = SHIT. Defecation on stage became almost *de rigueur,* as it was more effectively shocking than nudity. So, by the way, was rape—of men rather than of women, because the latter had been too often eroticized. Lebel shared the view of many innovative artists that nothing is more devastating to art than the notion of art itself. The happenings staged by Lebel, or by the more extreme Hermann Nitsch who littered the stage with bloody carcasses, refused to be the exquisite products awaiting refined consumption that lovers of conventional Art had come to expect.

The Theater of Cruelty

Performance artists like Lebel and Nitsch, who favor image over word, find inspiration in the "Theatre of Cruelty" of Antonin Artaud (1896–1948), a theatrical innovator who claimed that conventional, text-based theater deepens an audience's habitual stupor, preventing them from experiencing reality. "I would like to write a Book which would drive men mad," Artaud declares in "The Umbilicus of Limbo" (1925), "which would be like an open door leading them where they would never have consented to go, in short, a door that opens onto reality." Engaged on an impossible quest for "pure" sounds and gestures that would pierce people's souls, he rejected any theater that relies on argumentation, the reasonable and eloquent articulation of thought: "To save the theater I would even banish Ibsen, because of all those discussions of points of philosophy or morality which do not sufficiently affect the souls of his protagonists *in relation to us.*" Speech, he said, should be used only "in a concrete and spatial sense," as if it were "a solid object." *The Theatre and Its Double (Le Théâtre et son Double,* 1938), Artaud's best-known work, is a plea for an anti-realistic, archetypal theater in which words and thoughts would seek their most perfect material incarnation—a theater, in other words, dominated by director and actor rather than by playwright.

Artaud's vision of a purely physical theater reached Britain in mitigated form, mainly via Peter Brook, who presented it first, in 1964, through a spectacular production of Peter Weiss's *Marat/Sade* and then, in 1968, through a treatise on theater, *The Empty Space,* which supplemented Artaud with insights derived from Bertolt Brecht, Jerzy Grotowski, and Julian Beck. While British theater was to remain firmly text-based, playwrights became more eager to explore its spectacular aspects. The work of one group of playwrights stood out in particular: it was called "neo-Jacobean" because of its frequent recourse to violent imagery. After the abolishment of theatrical censorship in 1968, words lost some of their capacity to shock, as virtually anything could be said on the stage; images, however, remained effective and direct, and could still lead to charges of obscenity. The notoriety of the so-called B-Boys, Edward Bond, Howard Brenton, and Harold Barker, was caused mainly by their use of spectacular images. Bond's career started among the controversy generated by a scene in his second play *Saved* (1965), in which a gang of young people stone to death a baby in its pram—an image that, more effectively than any dialogue, conveys the boredom of these disaffected youths; *Narrow Road to the Deep North* (1968) is dominated by the image of the cut up and wrongly reassembled, naked body of the emperor, a striking embodiment of the transformations of power the play is concerned with; and the relationship between money and death in *Bingo* (1973), a play about Shakespeare's final years, is represented by the putrefying gibbeted body of a beggar woman. In Brenton's *Romans in Britain,* the horror of imperialism is expressed in a drawn-out scene of anal rape, which led to a prosecution on obscenity charges; in Barker's *The Castle* (1985), a rebellious woman is condemned to carry the corpse of her male victim strapped to her waist in mock pregnancy. While thematically relevant, such visual shorthand is also meant to shock. Brenton called it "pissing in the audience's eyeballs," Bond, the "aggro-effect."

The Theater of Panic and Catastrophism

Barker, inspired by Fernando Arrabal's vision of a theater of panic, advocated "catastrophism," a term he used for the liberating disorientation he expects an audience to experience after witnessing an overwhelmingly rich theatrical event. In "Arguments for a Theatre," Barker pitched catastrophic theater against "humanist," mainstream theater. In a contrived and often questionable schematic comparison, he claims that, whereas the humanist theater aims at educating the audience, catastrophic theater tries to make the audience "divided" so that it "goes home disturbed or amazed." Catastrophic theater refrains from articulating a clear message: "the audience cannot grasp everything; nor did the author." This applies to neo-Jacobean plays in general: they are confusing and often upsetting, and generate rather than communicate ideas. Characters in these plays are often grotesque, plots outlandish or absurd, and language poetic in an obscene, baroque, or demented way. The latter flaunts its materiality, in the way Artaud advocated, drawing attention to itself as an artificial construct by refusing to sound "natural." No longer a natural extension of character, words are put on display, enter the arena of performance—or, as Bond puts it, "the language is the play's not the characters'." The right question to ask of such plays is not "what does it mean" but "what could its possible meanings be."

The New Brutalists in Drama

This is also the right question to ask of Sarah Kane's work and that of the "New Brutalists" with which it is often associated. The latter practice what Aleks Sierz calls "In-Yer-Face Theatre" and are influenced both by performance art and by the work of the neo-Jacobeans. "How can you tell if a play is in-yer-face?" Sierz asks in his book *In-Yer-Face Theatre*. "It really isn't difficult: the language is usually filthy, characters talk about unmentionable subjects, take their clothes off, have sex, humiliate each another, experience unpleasant emotions, become suddenly violent." He calls it "a theatre of sensation," written by a new generation of playwrights (most of them men) brought up on Quentin Tarantino, MTV, graphic novels, cartoons, and pornography. The neo-Jacobeans were children of the welfare state, of the high-minded postwar years of socialist nation building; while they believed, with Bond, that "the imagination is political," they did not always trust their highly imaginative plays to the free play of an audience's interpretation and often accompanied them with manifesto-like introductions that hammer the political message home. The New Brutalists, in contrast, are Thatcher's children, products of a more individualistic and politically disillusioned age. They have the reputation of not pussyfooting around, of saying and especially showing things the way they are. Obscenity is one way of doing that, when it is let out of its pornography paddock and allowed to graze among the serious things. In Neilson's *The Censor* a female pornography director tries to save her film from an X-rating by acting out the censor's secret sexual fantasy. So she squats down in front of him and defecates on the floor. There is little lovemaking in these plays, as is evident already from the title of Mark Ravenhill's *Shopping and Fucking* (1996), which features a teenage boy begging to be sodomized with a screwdriver. "Fucking" is escaping the burden of being human, an attempt at becoming elemental and joining the material universe—as simple and devastating as a chemical reaction.

CONCLUSION: "PURELY THROUGH IMAGE"

It is impossible to forget these brief flashes of light during which we see Ian in lonely, unobserved desolation act out the rituals of elementary being—masturbating to the obsessive repetition of the word "cunt," relieving himself on the floor and clumsily trying to clean it up; clutching his hands at his throat in a ludicrous attempt to choke the remaining life out of him. These are private acts one is not supposed to witness—indeed, the kind of acts that drawing room plays, the dramatization of private life, decorously avoid. Watching these silent scenes, one realizes how much the bleakness of the bleakest Shakespeare play is relieved by the consoling beauty of words: "Thou art the thing itself / unaccommodated man is no more but such a poor bare / forked animal as thou art" (*King Lear* 3.4). How eminently quotable misery can be! The deeper the play descends into despair, the more eloquent and poetic it waxes. The felicitous articulation of insights, of which *King Lear* abounds, never ceases to remind us that language can still encompass the extremes of being and accommodate even the "unaccommodated." *Blasted* refuses such consolation. "Every act is a symbol / the weight of which crushes me," a disembodied voice intones in Kane's posthumously produced *4.48 Psychosis* (2000). The weight of reality drove Kane finally to the ultimate silence—or, as she puts it in the same play: "I have become so depressed by the fact of my mortality that I have decided to commit suicide." To watch Ian is to know, if only for a moment, the incredible heaviness of being.

FURTHER READING

Artaud, Antonin. *Antonin Artaud: Selected Writings*. Translated by Helen Weaver. Edited by Susan Sontag. Berkeley: University of California Press, 1976.

Bond, Edward. "Commentary on the War Plays." *Plays: 6*. London: Methuen, 1998. pp. 247–363.

Edgar, David. "Provocative Acts: British Playwriting in the Post-War Era and Beyond." *State of the Play: Playwrights on Playwriting*. London: Faber, 1999. pp. 1–36.

Kane, Sarah. *Blasted*. Complete Plays. London: Methuen, 2001.

———. *4.48 Psychosis*. Complete Plays. London: Methuen, 2001.

Lebel, Jean-Jacques. "On the Necessity of Violation." *The Drama Review* 13.1 (1968): 89–105.

Miller, Arthur. Interview. *Conversations with Arthur Miller*. Edited by Matthew C. Roudané. Jackson, Mississippi and London: University Press of Mississippi, 1987.

Saunders, Graham. *'Love me or kill': Sarah Kane and the Theatre of Extremes*. Manchester University Press, 2002.

———. "'Out vile jelly': Sarah Kane's *Blasted* and Shakespeare's *King Lear*." *NTQ* 20, no. 1 (2004): 69–78.

Sierz, Aleks. *In-Yer-Face Theatre: British Drama Today*. London: Faber, 2001.

Sontag, Susan. "Artaud." In Artaud, 1976. pp. xvii–lix.

♋

Kitchen Sink Drama

Reade Dornan

Newspaper critics in the 1960s hailed the appearance of what they called in Britain "Kitchen Sink drama." Although not a movement or a homogeneous group of like-minded playwrights, this seemingly new direction in theater had its day between 1956 and 1976. Unlike the avant garde theater of Jerzy Grotowski or the theater of the absurd of Samuel Beckett, it had a social message and an ideological stance, which was largely leftist. It drew attention to the conditions of working-class lives: hardships, strong sense of community, and the injustice of limiting their upward mobility. It stood four square against "the establishment." Many of the plays opposed government regulation, corporate conformity, and commercial manipulation. Unlike traditional theater, kitchen sink drama depicted, sometimes with raw realism, the everyday lives of ordinary people in a struggle against the degradation of powerlessness, the loss of community, or the deadening influence of suburbia. Often it dealt with young people in domestic settings who protested with direct, straightforward, outspoken dissatisfaction against the status quo.

Few people outside the press used this term, however. Playwrights such as John Osborne, Arnold Wesker, Shelagh Delaney, and John Arden, who were supposedly part of this movement, never referred to themselves as "Kitchen Sink Dramatists." Arnold Wesker, whose trilogy was closely associated with the term, said, "Kitchen Sink Drama is a lazy description of a group that didn't exist. I certainly was not a conscious party to a 'countermovement to the drawing-room theatre'. We were all so diverse" (e-mail message to author March 2005). The widely varied list of authors and works, many of them not even playwrights that are supposedly part of this movement, are John Braine (*Room at the Top*), Shelagh Delaney (*Taste of*

Honey), Alan Sillitoe (*Loneliness of the Long-Distance Runner*), and Keith Waterhouse (*Billy Liar*). Also mentioned are Ted Hughes, Philip Larkin, John Wain, and Colin Wilson.

The commercial media, however, welcomed the tension in the theater created by the suggestion of kitchen sink drama. Holding the trend up as the promising, new direction in theater, critics took aim at prewar matinee favorites such as Noel Coward and Alan Ayckbourn. Although experimental theater forms had already broken with the British drawing room tradition, critics considered kitchen sink drama more promising because of its greater interest to the regular theater-going crowd. It had a cachet that appealed to post World War II egalitarian audiences bent on further dismantling the rigid class system. With its naturalistic form and gritty realism, its accessibility seemed to support the belief that theater had become a popular form for the arts.

FURTHER READING

Denison, Patricia. *John Osborne: A Casebook*. New York: Garland Publishing, 1997.
Dornan, Reade. *Arnold Wesker: A Casebook*. New York: Garland Publishing, 1998.

ॐ

Language in Play: From "Well-Made" and Absurdist Plays to Talk Drama

Luc Gilleman

ABSURDIST DRAMA

Absurdist drama deals with man's hopeless search for meaning in a meaningless universe. This doesn't have to be as depressing as it sounds; in fact, senselessness and ennui can give rise to great humor. Think of the dialogue between Flaps and Buzzie, the vultures in Disney's animated version of *Jungle Book* (1967), where they keep asking each "What' cha wanna do?," never coming to a resolution.

Flaps and Buzzie are the Vladimir and Estragon of Disney who, like these clowns from Samuel Beckett's *Waiting for Godot* (1952), compensate for their inaction with a prodigious expense of verbal energy, talking about pulling on trousers, and "going," but who in the end do not move.

This music-hall routine concludes a play in which nothing very much happens and nothing is resolved. It is more than just funny, however; it signals a major shift in what we have come to expect of drama since the latter part of the twentieth century. Vladimir and Estragon have been waiting for a certain Godot who has failed to show up. In the end, as at the beginning of the play, they still have nowhere to go and nothing to do.

At least since Aristotle's *Poetics* (fourth century B.C.), we have been accustomed to think of drama as a form of action, a series of plausibly connected events. In the "well-made play," incidents are lined up in such a way as to evoke gradually rising and quickly falling tension separated by a climactic moment that often takes the form of a confrontation between major characters. This is when discoveries are made, unpleasant truths are articulated, and characters gain new insights. The audience is expected to leave the theater, in the words of one famous French practitioner of the *pièce bien faite*, "*bien content*"—that is, satisfied in the knowledge that something of importance has happened and that they got its "point." Eugène Scribe (1791–1861), the playwright here alluded to, made himself a fortune, using this handy plot formula to piece together more than four hundred plays—and today, one only has to switch on television to realize that the formula is alive and well and is still making some people a great deal of money.

This is not to imply that there is something inherently shallow about "well-made plays." In fact, "serious" dramatists, like George Bernard Shaw, Sir Arthur Wing Pinero, Eugene O'Neill, Arthur Miller, Tennessee Williams, and others, continued to construct plays according to this well-tested plot outline if only because it virtually guarantees the audience's emotional involvement in the political or psychological argument of the play. As an added benefit, there is something essentially life-affirming about even the most dismal plays that continue to associate a dramatic reversal in the protagonist's fortunes (what Aristotle referred to as the *peripeteia*) with a moment of intellectual growth ("recognition" or *anagnorisis*). Linking these two confirms what one hopes to be true of life as well—namely, to put a common saying on its head, that there is no pain without at least some gain. In other words, the worldview endorsed by the well-made play suggests that human suffering is not altogether meaningless.

Given the lasting success of this formula, it is then something of a challenge to write a play that offers no clear climax, no true reversal, no discernible confrontation scene, and no definable insight—where, to quote Estragon of *Waiting for Godot*, "nothing happens, nobody comes, nobody goes, it's awful!" To be fair, this is not quite an accurate assessment of *Waiting for Godot*; things do happen in this play: Pozzo and Lucky come by twice, and the second time Pozzo has inexplicably become blind. In Act II, the barren tree of Act I has acquired a few new leaves. Vladimir and Estragon have been presented with certain choices: the choice to help Lucky, for instance, or the choice to move on. Acts of kindness have occurred, as well as acts of brutality. Yet the meaning of these apparently random events and choices is nowhere clearly articulated in the play, and the overall impression is one of almost unbearable stasis, exacerbated rather than relieved by Vladimir and Estragon's endless patter and intermittently punctuated by the hopeless refrain of "We're waiting for Godot," when one of them suggests, "Let's go."

Despite, or rather because of, this "pointlessness," *Waiting for Godot* was quickly recognized as a most moving expression of the existential "crisis" coeval with the advent of modernity and most acutely felt after World War II, when it appeared that neither religion and philosophy, nor advances in technical and scientific knowledge had been able to prevent the horrors of the Holocaust, the death of countless civilians through firebombing, and the nuclear devastation of Hiroshima and Nagasaki. Here was indeed a human tragedy that, despite being enacted in modern times by supposedly "enlightened" Europeans, defied reason and was singularly devoid of *peripeteia* and *anagnorisis*. And it offered neither resolution nor the comfort of a new beginning. The Cold War that followed continued the mindless squandering of human resources in the search for ever-superior methods of mass annihilation. Absurdist drama portrays the desperate existential condition resulting from this failure of the great ideological narratives of human liberation and salvation. As *Waiting for Godot* demonstrates, in the modern world we have become tellers of little stories, to fill the needs of the moment and while away the time that separates us from death.

Absurdist plays, then, are not as pointless as they seem; they are symbolical enactments of particular philosophical insights into modernity. Some playwrights of the 1970s and 1980s, however, seemed interested less in the philosophy than in the technique of absurdism. Because nothing much happens in *Waiting for Godot*, language becomes its main event. The same can be said of a number of other plays that, while borrowing absurdism's foregrounding of language, attempted something altogether less "philosophical." In 1987, an American theater scholar, Timothy Wiles, coined the term "talk drama" to refer to a number of plays of the seventies and eighties that stood out by their unconventional use of language. Wiles emphasized how speech in plays by Sam Shepard, David Mamet, David Rabe, Lanford Wilson, and others no longer played a primarily instrumental function; in other words, it no longer served mainly as a medium to express preexisting truths. The latter, for instance, happens in any conventionally constructed realistic play where characters at some crucial moment communicate their "inner feelings," articulate what they believe to be their true identity, or reveal a shameful secret from their past. Such a scene usually starts off with a character signaling to the audience that it is on the point of entering a moment of unadorned truth and that language is now going to play its purely transitive function. The confrontation scene in Arthur Miller's *Death of a Salesman* (1949) starts with Biff angrily telling his father, "No, you're going to hear the truth—what you are and what I am!" And the most celebrated moment in Henrik Ibsen's *A Doll House* (1879), signaling the emancipation of the long-suffering wife, Nora, begins with the latter telling her husband to "[s]it down. This will take time. I have a lot to say to you." This belief that one can, in Nora's phrase, get "at the bottom of anything" through "serious conversation" is essential for any play that aims at presenting an intellectual argument. In contrast, talk drama conjures up a less comforting world that shares no such belief and where characters can no longer be assumed to mean what they say.

TALK DRAMA

"Talk drama" is by no means a neat category, governed by principles to which certain playwrights pledge allegiance. The term, however, is useful because it suggests a tendency of many plays since, roughly speaking, the 1970s, to avoid privileging certain kinds of speech as more "truthful" than others. In talk drama, everything is inevitably pulled down into "talk"—that is, no character can extricate him or herself from the fray of human interaction in order to deliver an insightful comment and thus, in matter of fact, voice the playwright's "point." The latter happens, for instance, in *Death of a Salesman,* which, despite its innovations in the portrayal of time and space, remains bound by the speech conventions of conventionally realistic drama. At one point, Linda, in a much-quoted speech, neatly summarizes the generative idea of that play: "Willy Loman never made a lot of money. His name was never in the paper. He's not the finest character that ever lived. But he's a human being, and a terrible thing is happening to him. So attention must be paid. He's not to be allowed to fall into his grave like an old dog. Attention, attention must be finally paid to such a person." This is not just Linda telling her sons to take their father's plight seriously; this is Miller telling his audience why he wrote a play about such an insignificant character as Willy Loman. We can think of this as the dramatic equivalent of the omniscient narrator in fiction. In classical tragedy, voicing such comments was the task of the Chorus. It is a tribute to Miller's artistry that he is able to create the emotional climate in which the audience can accept this stylistically heightened articulation of a "truth" as coming from a mere participant in the action and in the course of a common conversation.

Critics who had been trained to search plays for such privileged moments of insight were sorely disappointed when they attended *The Birthday Party* (1958), the first professionally produced full-length play of Harold Pinter, an English actor who had been writing for the stage since 1956. "There is no Chorus in this play," Pinter had warned his director: "The curtain goes up and comes down. Something has happened. Right? Cokeyed, brutish, absurd, with no comment." Critics were now unable to find the play's "point" neatly summarized by a character. Could the play then be a symbolic enactment of a philosophical idea about the search for sense in a senseless universe? Though Pinter had learned his craft from studying Beckett, whom he greatly admired and later befriended, he did not think of his plays as absurdist either, declaring in "Writing for Myself" that "what goes on in my plays is realistic, but what I'm doing is not realism." As he explained: "A character on the stage who can present no convincing argument or information as to his past experience, his present behaviour or his aspirations, nor give a comprehensive analysis of his motives is as legitimate and as worthy of attention as one who, alarmingly, can do all these things. The more acute the experience the less articulate its expression." After all, in real life "we don't carry labels on our chests, and even though they are continually fixed to us by others, they convince nobody. The desire for verification on the part of all of us, with regards to our own experience and the experience of others, is understandable but cannot always be satisfied." Ironically, what frustrated theater critics most was Pinter's insistence on remaining within the constraints imposed by the dramatic genre in which everything is embedded in dialogue so that no gems of insight can be safely extracted from the complexities of interaction. It comes as no surprise to learn that the first production of *The Birthday Party* had to close down after barely a week. It took some time before actors, spectators, and critics were sufficiently accustomed to the new conventions for the play to be recognized as the masterwork it truly is.

What may have eased the assimilation of these new conventions was Pinter's willingness to situate them within a vision about how language functions in "real" life. According to this vision, communication is a hazardous process during which we constantly renegotiate who we think we are with whom we think our interlocutor believes us to be. In theory, this mirror-effect is endless: "what is the other thinking of what I am thinking of him thinking of me thinking of him...?" The inaccessibility of the other's experience—including of that other's experience of one's own experience, and so on—is at the heart of the paranoid universe Pinter's characters inhabit. Applied to the stage, the most important corollary of such a vision is the loss of a long tradition of articulateness in drama. Much of the joy of watching a conventionally realistic play consists in listening to characters who are far more eloquent than we ever manage to be and who therefore are able to voice with precision and beauty what we might only dimly feel. Pinter's characters do not allow us that kind of enjoyment. As Pinter puts it, "you and I, the characters which grow on a page, most of the time we're inexpressive, giving little away, unreliable, elusive, evasive, obstructive, unwilling." Pinter's characters do not like to commit themselves unambiguously to their words because they fear having to pay the penalty of clarity—which is to be weighed and found wanting. But "comedy of menace," the label sometimes applied to Pinter's drama, suggests that a world without certainty can be both threatening and funny. In *The Caretaker*, a homeless bum, Davies, is trying to ingratiate himself to Mick in order to seize control of a room he's now sharing with the latter's mentally troubled brother, Aston. Davies, however, is unsure of Mick's real feelings about his brother, but in an attempt to discuss the brother, starting off with, "Well...he's a funny bloke, your brother," the conversation devolves to Davies agreeing with Mick's statement of "I don't call it funny."

Such moments, when a character sticks out his feelers only to pull them quickly back at the least sign of trouble, abound in Pinter. Pinter's plays are therefore more often about what is left unsaid than what is actually articulated. In other words: whereas conventional drama celebrates eloquence, those moments when characters come fully into being through the perfect articulation of their innermost thoughts and feelings, talk drama explores the dramatic possibilities of inexpressiveness. And whereas conventional drama strives for perfect coherence, suggesting a world in which characters respond to one another fluently, at its best in a polyphony of voices reminiscent of Chekhov, talk drama tends to punctuate each exchange with emphatic pauses that alert us to the gap of misunderstanding that looms between characters who are isolated from one another, each in his or her solipsistic universe.

In the United States, Pinter's experiments with dramatic speech found their most creative application in the plays of David Mamet. Like Pinter and Beckett, Mamet does not care very much about stringing together a series of events in the manner of the well-made play. Mel Gussow refers to Mamet's work as "plays of indirect action," in which most action is concentrated in the language, in what words *do* rather than *say*. In an introduction to *American Buffalo*, Mamet explains the primacy of language as follows: "The way we use [language], its rhythm, actually determines the way we behave, more than the other way around.... Words create behavior...; our rhythms prescribe our actions." And again, as with Pinter, critics have acknowledged the possibly "realistic" nature of such language. As Jack Kroll put it in a February 1977 *Newsweek* review: "Mamet has heard the ultimate Muzak, the dissonant din of people yammering at one another and not connecting. He is a comic eavesdropper who's caught the American aphasia."

The characters' lack of articulateness in talk drama makes us aware of how speech comes into being haltingly, as ideas are constructed and renegotiated on the go—in a conversational battlefield, so to speak. In *Glengarry Glen Ross* (1983), Mamet makes disjointed "stutter speech" emblematic of capitalism itself, of a world in which nothing can escape the workings of the market.

Like Willy Loman, Levene is an aging salesman, down on his luck and intent on getting Williamson, his younger interlocutor in this conversation, to give him preferential access to the best "leads," thus increasing his chances of brokering a successful sale and perhaps saving his job. Put in a similar situation, Loman discovered in his despair the courage to confront his boss unambiguously: "I put thirty-four years into this firm, Howard, and now I can't pay my insurance! You can't eat the orange and throw the peel away—a man is not a piece of fruit!" Levene never reaches a comparable moment of eloquent self-realization. His broken language, a challenge for the actor who has to catch the complex rhythm of such speech, betrays the effort he has to expend in order to maintain control over the interaction. And thus, before he is able to formulate his request, he has already thoroughly disqualified himself.

In *Glengarry Glen Ross*, the salesmen's mantra "Always Be Closing," the ABC of competitive salesmanship, perfectly sums up the new status of language. Nothing transcends the world of buying and selling. Words too have entered the market place; they are being bought and sold, their value determined by market forces. Even a moment of intimacy between characters, an exchange of confidences, sooner or later stands revealed as a form of entrapment and mastery. Much of the humor in this kind of play is based on the characters' insecurity in a world in which the meaning of words is relative and the intent of a conversation can never be properly gauged. This instability of meaning and intent is a boon to the salesman who knows how to let an idea slip imperceptibly into action. In the following dialogue, Moss is deftly manipulating his colleague Aaronow into becoming his accomplice in a robbery of the leads, where he convinces Aaronow that "we're just speaking about it. (*Pause.*) As an *idea.*"

As any shrewd salesman, Moss introduces the robbery as a mere idea, something to talk about "in the abstract," until "just talking" imperceptibly turns into "actual talking," and Aaronow, the weaker salesman, finds himself an "accomplice" in a criminal action he never endorsed.

With *Glengarry Glen Ross*, we have moved far from *Death of a Salesman*. The latter was still built around a longing for inalienable essences, and speech still managed to fill the gap between what one is and what one appears to others. In talk drama, this is, generally speaking, no longer the case. This does not mean that characters in such plays no longer suffer from the hemorrhaging of selfhood that *Death of a Salesman* so movingly portrayed. They do, and that is why we remain interested in them. But we learn it not so much from what they say as from what they are unable to say because they have no way of expressing it "truthfully"—in a way that would transcend the give and take of interaction. For the spectators, this poses a challenge. Faced with a play in which one can never be sure whether what characters are saying is real or fabrication, spectators must at every instance wonder what momentary impulse the language is responding to. In a play where language, not event, becomes the mainspring of stage action, spectators have to examine who tries to control meaning and how language affects issues of territory, power, and strategy. And when speech is used mainly strategically, in the here and now, as a form of continuous self-fashioning rather than self-expression, we should keep in mind that what is being said always depends on how, why, and to whom it is being said. But it is a challenge well worth taking up: as theater emancipated itself from storytelling and evolved from the event-based well-made play to language-based absurdism and talk drama, it learned to make better use not only of the dynamic potential of drama but also of the audience's ability to deal with the resulting increase in interpretive uncertainty. As Pinter put it in a letter to Peter Wood, "There is no end to meaning. Meaning which is resolved, parceled, labeled and ready for export is dead, impertinent—and meaningless." In the final instance, it is up to us, the audience, to keep drama alive.

FURTHER READING

Aristotle. *Poetics*. Translated by Leon Golden. Englewood Cliffs, New Jersey: Prentice-Hall, 1968.

Arvin, Neil Cole. *Eugène Scribe and the French Theatre, 1815–1860*. New York: B. Blom, 1967.

Beckett, Samuel. *Waiting for Godot: A Tragicomedy in Two Acts*. Translated by Samuel Beckett. New York: Grove, 1982.

Esslin, Martin. *The Theatre of the Absurd*. 3rd ed. London and New York: Penguin Books, 1991.

Ibsen, Henrik. *A Doll House. Ibsen's Selected Plays*. Edited by Brian Johnston. Critical Edition. New York and London: W.W. Norton, 2004. 143–206.

Koon, Hélène and Richard Switzer. *Eugène Scribe*. Boston: Twayne, 1980.

Mamet, David. *Glengarry Glen Ross*. New York: Grove, 1983.

Miller, Arthur. *Death of a Salesman: Certain Private Conversations in Two Acts and a Requiem*. New York: Penguin, 1998.

Pinter, Harold. "A Letter to Peter Wood" (1958). *Drama* 142:1981.

———. *The Caretaker. The Caretaker & The Dumb Waiter: Two Plays by Harold Pinter*. New York: Grove, 1988. pp. 7–78.

———. "Writing for Myself" (1961). *Complete Works 2*. New York: Grove Weidenfeld, 1990.

———. "Writing for the Theatre" (1962). *Complete Works 1*. New York: Grove Weidenfeld, 1990.

Taylor, John Russell. *The Rise and Fall of the Well-Made Play*. London: Methuen, 1967.

Wiles, Timothy. "Talk Drama: Recent Writers in the American Theater." *Amerikastudien* 32.1 (1987): 65–79.

ॐ

"Oh, die Angst! die Angst!": *Romeo and Juliet* as Rock Opera

William Hutchings

Even if, as Robert Hapgood maintains, *Hamlet* "has been performed more than any other [play]," *Romeo and Juliet* surely comes in as a close second—and surely surpasses it if the various musicals, ballets, adaptations, and redactions are also included in the total. Its title characters are undoubtedly literature's most iconic: their names and their clandestine balcony liaison have long pervaded popular culture, emblematic of heedlessly passionate young love. More than four centuries of its performance history constitute a surprising and often peculiar chronicle, however, that has only recently come into full recognition as a subject of systematic academic inquiry and assessment quite distinct from scholarly exegesis and textual scrutiny.[1]

THE RICH PERFORMANCE HISTORY OF ONE PLAY

Like Shakespeare's comedies, *Romeo and Juliet* has proven extraordinarily transposable across cultures, settings, and periods. In 1998, a New York production titled simply *Shakespeare's R&J* (adapted and directed by Joe Calarco; John Housman Studio Theatre) presented the play's "star-crossed lovers" as both male, played by students in an all-male Catholic school; at about the same time, the stylized film version directed by Baz Luhrmann was set in a decidedly futuristic, very postmodern Verona Beach where dueling-pistols replace rapiers and a television newscaster delivers the play's prologue. The first major production of the twenty-first century, however, is the French musical version by Gérard Presgurvic—a rendition that was first produced in Paris at the Palais de Congrès in 2001 and has since been seen by over six million theatergoers throughout the world, with productions mounted in Antwerp (September 2002, Standschouwburg Theatre), London (November 2002; Picadilly Theatre), Budapest (January 2004, Budapest Operetta Theatre), Moscow (May 2004, Moscow Operetta Theatre), and Vienna (February 2005, Raimund Theater).[2]

Productions in Italy, Poland, Portugal, Spain, China, Japan, and Korea are currently being planned. Following vituperative reviews of the English-language production in London, however, there are apparently no current plans to bring it to the United States. An examination of it in terms of its relationship to Shakespeare's text, which has preoccupied some reviewers, is a relatively futile exercise; the story has obviously not only been set to music but has also been translated into French, then subsequently retranslated into German and/or back into English and/or into other languages as well, so much of the original poetry has necessarily been lost—and is hardly of significant interest to the decidedly youthful audience for whom the production seems intended anyway. Instead, when considered within the long and often bizarre production history of *Romeo and Juliet*, in both musical and nonmusical forms, this latest incarnation as a rock musical seems to fit within traditional stagings in quite unexpected ways *and* to introduce innovations that have gone unappreciated in its reviews.

MUSICAL VERSIONS OF *ROMEO AND JULIET*

That *Romeo and Juliet* would be transformed into a rock opera is hardly surprising; indeed, the surprise is that it had not happened long before now, given more than five decades of rock history and the play's long history of musical adaptations. Among the earliest were two French musical versions that premiered near the beginning of the Reign of Terror; written by J.-M. B. de Monveil (1792) and J.-A. de Ségur (1793) respectively, they featured happy endings in which the young lovers survive. Vincenzo Bellini's *I Capuleti ed i Montecchi*, the first operatic version of the story, was produced in 1830, but it was a dramatization of Shakespeare's Italian source materials rather than the English play; Romeo is here a captain of the Ghibelline faction in its struggle against the Guelphs. Hector Berlioz's "dramatic symphony" *Roméo et Juliette* (1839) was based on Shakespeare's play (more specifically, a version modified by David Garrick) but rendered the title characters *without dialogue;* though the roles of Mercutio and Friar Lawrence were sung, the lead roles were presented only through "the orchestra['s]...instrumental language." Charles Gounaud's opera version of it (1867), still the most often revived, followed Shakespeare's play more faithfully than any of its predecessors, although Friar Lawrence's potion takes effect during Juliet's wedding to Paris; she and Romeo die simultaneously rather than one after the other, and they sing a duet in the tomb. Pyotr Ilyich Tchaikovsky's version (1869, revised 1888) is purely orchestral; Sergei Prokofiev's ballet (1940) emphasized spectacle and swordplay but also featured an emphasis on state power. Leonard Bernstein's *West Side Story* (1957, originally conceived by Jerome Robbins, libretto by Arthur Laurents), of course, audaciously transposed the story into then-contemporary New York City, the feuding Montagues and Capulets being replaced by street gangs named the Sharks and the Jets. Yet as iconic as that landmark production was and is for their parents, grandparents and perhaps great-grandparents, many of today's generation find its melodies only slightly less quaint—and its gangs only slightly more menacing—than those in Gilbert and Sullivan's *Pirates of Penzance*.

The Rock Opera of *Romeo and Juliet*

Structurally, *Romeo and Juliet* is particularly suitable for adaptation into a rock opera for reasons that were best articulated by the Victorian actor Henry Irving in 1882, quoted by his colleague Ellen Terry: "*Romeo and Juliet* proceeds from picture to picture," he explained, adding that "[e]very line suggests a picture. It is a dramatic poem rather than a drama"—in contrast to *Hamlet,* which "marches from situation to situation." In adapting the play into his rock opera, composer and librettist Gérard Presgurvic realized that it could change scenes with virtually every song, given a suitably versatile set (designed by Duncan Hayler)—and that, indeed, each song could itself advance the plot (which is, after all, so widely known that it can readily be followed even by those who do not know the language in which it is being sung). Accordingly, there are seventeen songs (excluding the overture and the finale but including several reprises) in the each of the two acts, as listed in the play's program. Those marked with an asterisk are the sixteen tracks of the "Cast Album—Wien" released by HitSquad Records (2005):

Act One
    Overture (Ouveture) Prologue
    * Verona (Verona) The Duke & ensemble
    The Conflict (Der Kampf) Instrumental
    * The Hatred (Der Hass) Lady Capulet, Lady Montague & ensemble
    * Once (Einmal) Romeo and Juliet
    The Wedding Plan (Der Heieratsantrag) Paris & Lord Capulet
    Rejoice About the Wedding (Freu Dich auf die Hochzeit) Lady Capulet & The Nurse
    Once (Einmal, reprise) Juliet
    * Men of the World (Herrscher der Welt) Romeo, Mercutio, Benvolio, & ensemble
    * The Angst (Die Angst) Romeo
    * The Ball (Der Ball) 1 Instrumental
    Happiness in Love (Liebesglück) Romeo & Juliet

The Ball (Der Ball) 2 Instrumental
* I am Guiltless (Ich Bin Schuldlos) Tybalt
The Balcony (Der Balcon) Romeo & Juliet
We Are Of Flesh and Blood (Wir Sind Aus Fleisch und Blut) Mercutio, Benvolio,
The Nurse, & ensemble
     * See There, She's In Love (Siehe Da, Sie Liebt) The Nurse
     * Love (Liebe) Romeo & Juliet

Act Two
     Have You Heard (Habt Ihr Schon Gehört) Mercutio, Benvolio, Romeo, &
ensemble
     It's Time (Es Wird Zeit) Tybalt & ensemble
     * The Duel (Das Duell) Tybalt, Mercutio, Romeo, Benvolio, & ensemble
     Mercutio's Death (Mercutios Tod) Mercutio & Romeo
     Revenge (Die Rache) Lord Capulet, Lady Capulet, The Nurse, The Duke, Lady
Montague, Romeo, Benvolio, & ensemble
     * Despair (Die Verzweiflung) Friar Lawrence, Lord Capulet, The Nurse,
     Lady Capulet, Benvolio, Lady Montague, & ensemble
     The Song of the Lark (Der Gesang Der Lerche) Romeo & Juliet
     Not for Long (Nicht Lang) Lord Capulet, Lady Capulet, Paris, The Nurse, Juliet, &
ensemble
     * My Dear Child (Mein Liebes Kind) Lord Capulet
     * Without You (Ohne Sie) Romeo & Juliet
     The Gift (Das Gift) Juliet
     Verona II (Verona II, reprise) The Duke
     * How Do I Tell Him? (Wie Sag Ich's Ihm) Benvolio
     Romeo's Death (Romeos Tod) Romeo
     * Juliet's Death (Julias Tod) Juliet
     * Why? (Warum) Friar Lawrence, Lady Capulet, The Nurse, & Lady Montague
     Guilty (Schuldig) Lady Montague, Lady Capulet, The Nurse, Friar Lawrence, Lord
Capulet, Benvolio, The Nurse, Paris, & ensemble
     Finale

With most songs lasting from three to six minutes, and with each constituting a separate "picture" (in Irving's terms) that necessitates a change of scene, the production requires a highly adaptable and physically moving set. The pace established by the director and choreographer, known only by the single name Redha, was especially well suited to an audience long accustomed to the pacing and aesthetic of music videos and/or Baz Luhrmann's film version of the play.

Designed by Duncan Hayler, the set for the Vienna production proved remarkably versatile and rapidly transformable, while taking full advantage of the cavernous stage space of the Raimund Theater. The cityscape of Verona was represented by four stone towers, each of which was three stories in height. Each of these could be moved or reconfigured as necessary for changes of setting and utilization of stage space: street scenes, the masked ball, the fight on the piazza, etc. Each tower also could be rotated to reveal one or more interior acting areas. Thus, for example, the interior of one of the central towers was used for those scenes taking place in the Capulets' house; Juliet's bedroom was the topmost of the three areas. Friar Lawrence's cell was the interior of the tower located at stage right; it too was rotated into existence only when needed. The entire multi-towered set could be covered by a rotatable "city wall," used to conceal larger set changes (including the removal of all four towers) as the solos are performed on the stage apron. Thus, Romeo's "Die Angst" precedes the full-stage masquerade ball, and the nurse's "Siehe Da, Sie Liebt" takes place immediately before the full-stage full-ensemble finale of Act One. When the audience has become accustomed to the particularly busy and fast-moving set, the stark minimalism of the interior of the Capulets' tomb comes as a visually stunning change: her body, clad in white, lies atop a unadorned black bier at center-stage in front of a solid, bright, blood-red backdrop that extends from floor to ceiling; the bier is surrounded by low white stage-smoke that completely covers the stage floor, and a bare scraggly tree at stage right (suitable for use in a production of *Waiting for Godot*) is the sole other adornment of the entire acting space. At the moment of her death, the red backdrop collapses, leaving only stark blackness visible behind the scene.

DEPARTURES FROM THE SCRIPT

The scene in Juliet's tomb contains one of the rock opera's most flagrant departures from Shakespeare's version of the story: Juliet awakens from her drug-induced not-death just after Romeo has fatally stabbed himself *but before he dies*. This change, which wrings yet more pathos out of their mutual demise, allows not only a love duet that is almost irresistible to composers (this is, of course, the most iconic *Liebestod* of all time) but also a moment of *anagnorisis*, Aristotle's term for the moment when one or more characters come to a realization of the true state of affairs, having been previously in error or ignorance. If she awakens only to find his newly-dead body, Romeo has died without learning the bitterly ironic truth. Theirs is, therefore, a tragedy merely because of misfortunate timing; there is no evidence whatsoever to support the Chorus's contention that they are "star-crossed" lovers (Prologue, line 6), that the "fault" or responsibility is in their stars rather than in what Thomas Hardy, in the poem "He Never Expected Much," termed "just neutral-tinted haps and such." Had Juliet awoken two minutes earlier, before Romeo acted on his mistaken perception that she is actually dead, the play would have the happy ending of all traditional comedy: the happy couple would presumably have ridden off into the night, escaping the tomb to live happily ever after (insofar, of course, as any married couple ever does). Had Friar Lawrence's letter been delivered promptly, Romeo could have waited there however long it took and the happy ending would have been the same. This point is made emphatically within the souvenir program sold at the Vienna production itself—in a full page advertisement extolling the reliability of the Austrian Post Office.

Although this change in Shakespeare's plot often offends purists and (more important) startles theatergoers exactly as intended, it has a surprisingly long and especially distinguished provenance in the play's production history. Specifically, the alteration of the final act was first added by the famed actor and playwright David Garrick in 1750—who defended the scene based on a vital but quite surprising literary precedent:

> [Matteo] Bandello, the Italian novelist from whom Shakespeare has borrow'd the subject of this play, has made Juliet to wake in the tomb before Romeo dies: this circumstance Shakespeare has omitted not perhaps from judgement [sic], but from reading the story in the French or English translation, both [of] which have injudiciously left out this addition to the catastrophe.

The scene is thus a *restoration* of the plot line of the original story that Shakespeare, whether inadvertently or deliberately, omitted from his stage adaptation. Garrick's version added seventy lines of dialogue, in which Romeo explicitly blames the feuding fathers' "flinty hearts" that are unmoved by their children's tears, and he dies cursing his fate. Bellini's opera in 1830 also gave the young lovers a duet in the tomb and a simultaneous death (both roles were played by women). Gounaud's opera in 1867 did the same, although Romeo in this version is portrayed by a male. In the latter half of the twentieth century, the "early awakening" was included in productions at Stratford, Ontario in 1960 (starring Julie Harris, directed by Michael Langham), at the Royal Shakespeare Company in 1976 (directed by Trevor Nunn and Barry Kyle), and in the film directed by Baz Luhrmann in 1996 (starring Leonardo diCaprio and Claire Danes). Although the scene still retains its ability to surprise the audience (and distinctly audible gasps came from audience members at the performance I attended in Vienna), its inclusion in Presgurvic's rock opera has a surprisingly long series of precedents and is less innovative than it may seem.

ACTORS OF THE RIGHT AGE

When considered within the long production history of *Romeo and Juliet*, another aspect of the rock opera is far more radically innovative, even though it is now in fact *de rigeur*: the casting of age-appropriate actors in the roles of the title characters. The problem, as previous generations saw it, was eloquently stated by Emma Stebbins, the companion and biographer of Charlotte Cushman, a noted Victorian actress who played the role of Romeo: "When a man has achieved the experience requisite to *act* Romeo, he has ceased to be young enough to *look* it." Since no casting details survive from the original production of *Romeo and Juliet*, no one knows who originated the role of Romeo—but if, as most authorities speculate, it was Richard Burbage, he would have been nearly thirty at the time of the first performance (circa 1594–96). His Juliet, of course, would have been a prepubescent boy dressed as a girl, as were all other players of female roles in Shakespeare's time. For centuries thereafter, more and less renowned actors of middle age and even older performed the role of Romeo as audiences more or less willingly suspended their disbelief: David Garrick at 44 in 1761; Spranger Barry at 49 in 1768; Edwin Booth at 36 in 1869; Henry Irving at 44 in 1882 (opposite 36-year-old Ellen Terry as Juliet); John Gielgud at 31 in 1935, alternating in the role with Laurence Olivier, then 28. Although it is virtually impossible to determine the oldest Romeo and Juliet ever to trod the stage, the list of prime contenders would surely include the American E.H. Sothern, who performed as Romeo until the age of 65 in 1924, opposite his wife Julia Marlowe, who was then 57; the oldest Juliet, however, may have been the Victorian actress Fanny Kemble (1809–93), who first played Juliet when she was 20 but "continued to give readings of it, public and private, until she was at least seventy." Still other productions gained fame (or notoriety) with unorthodox casting in even more unusual ways: in 1744, for example, Theophilus Cibber played Romeo at age 41 opposite his own 14-year-old daughter Jane (Jenny), provoking a reaction of outrage and scorn long before the now-obvious Freudian qualms about such a pairing had ever been formulated; the American actress Charlotte Cushman (1816–76), who "was the most acclaimed Romeo of the [nineteenth] century—male or female," sometimes played the role opposite her own sister as Juliet. Perhaps the twentieth century's most inapposite casting, however, was 46-year-old Leslie Howard, who was cast as Romeo in the 1936 film adaptation directed by George Cukor; his appearance elicits guffaws from today's college students when it is shown in class.

Given this long if little-known tradition of less-than-youthful casting, the use of age-appropriate actors is a relatively recent innovation—primarily post-1960, when producers and directors, emboldened by the success of *West Side Story* (1957; film, 1961) with its youthful gangs, presented the play as having as much or more to say about violence and hatred as about clandestine love. The earliest production to cast literal teenagers in both leads, however, came in 1905, when William Poel cast Esmé Percy as Romeo and Dorothy Minto as Juliet—a production about which George Bernard Shaw remarked that

> When [Poel] found that a child of fourteen was wanted, his critics claimed, 'Ah—but she was an Italian child, and an Italian child of fourteen looks exactly the same as an Englishwoman of forty-five.' Mr. Poel said 'I do not believe it...I will get a child of fourteen,' and accordingly he produced *Romeo and Juliet* in that way and for the first time it became endurable.

The major transition to the use of teenaged actors, however, came with Franco Zeffirelli's film version of the play in 1968, casting 18-year-old Leonard Whiting and 17-year-old Olivia Hussey in the lead roles—a subject that drew extensive critical attention at the time (much of it unfavorable), as did its brief and now-mild nude scene; composer Nino Rota's "Love Theme" for the film, "A Time for Us," was strongly reminiscent in tone and sentiment to the Bernstein-Sondheim song "Somewhere" from *West Side Story*. Despite many critics' tepid-to-hostile reactions, the film became tremendously popular and virtually iconic, far more influential than any stage productions thereafter; no other film of *Romeo and Juliet* was made until Baz Luhrmann's 1996 version starring 24-year-old Leonardo diCaprio and 17-year-old Claire Danes. Decidedly postmodern despite its retention of Shakespeare's language, it set the play in a dystopian future with corporate skyscrapers labeled Montague and Capulet, handguns instead of swords, hallucinogens, SWAT teams in helicopters, punk fashions, a television newscaster delivering the prologue, numerous witty pop culture allusions, and a locale known as Verona Beach. Its jump-cut editing gave it an aesthetic long familiar to viewers of music videos, and its constant visual inventiveness made the long-familiar play seem quite new. Like Zeffirelli's film before it, it seems likely to remain iconic for its generation—and would necessarily have to have been taken into account in designing Presgurvic's rock opera, since many if not most of its young audience members (as well as numerous older ones) would have to be presumed to have seen it.

The post-Luhrmann effects in the Vienna staging of Presgurvic's rock opera are most evident in its costume design and lighting as well as in its casting. In the costume design by Dominique Borg, the Capulets were costumed entirely in red and the Montagues in blue (as in Zeffirelli's film), with the hues often intensified by lighting of the same colors but in stark contrast to the spotlighting of Romeo and Juliet. The masked ball, however, was costumed entirely in white for as long as the revelers' identities had been concealed; when their Montague or Capulet allegiances came out, a return to colored lighting restored their hues. Serving as the narrator during the opening scene and (of course) remaining neutral between the two colorfully-clad factions, the Duke (cast as being in his twenties at most) wore a silvery greatcoat over what appeared to be black pajamas. Whereas Luhrmann's version was set in a specific future, Borg's designs combined elements from various periods, as if to emphasize that it could be taking place in any era. The women's costumes tended to be more characteristic of the Renaissance than those of the men; the fathers' costumes tended to be more Victorian in style. The street combatants wore jeans—some with Renaissance-style codpieces, some with customary modern fronts—and form-fitting and/or semi-transparent shirts; their major (second) fight was staged shirtless, lit by bright spotlights directly overhead as they "froze" in positions that accentuated the musculature of their forms. Romeo was played by 24-year-old Lukas Perman, who, having been one of twelve finalists on the Austrian television program "Starmania," was readily recognizable to many in the audience and brought to the role all the friskiness that a rocking Romeo

What *Is* a Rock Opera?

As used here, the term "rock opera" denotes a subgenre of the modern stage musical. Although there are several little-known Italian forebears, the first major self-proclaimed "rock opera" to have been staged was Andrew Lloyd Webber's *Jesus Christ Superstar* (album 1970; stage version 1971). The Who's *Tommy,* though released earlier (album 1969) and also self-described as a "rock opera," was filmed in 1975 but not adapted for the stage until 1993. Apart from the obvious distinction that it features rock music (which differentiates it from the works of Rodgers and Hammerstein, Lerner and Loewe, *Les Misérables, Phantom of the Opera,* and countless others before and since), a "rock opera" lacks prose dialogue; consisting entirely of a sung libretto that accompanies a full orchestra, it is thus differentiated from "rock musicals" (such as *Grease,* for example). Its source *may* be a canonical literary or musical text (e.g., Jonathan Larson's *Rent,* based on Puccini's *La Bohème*), but not necessarily so. The term "opera" also connotes stage spectacle and grandeur, though its images may be as iconoclastic in those of Tom O'Horgan's original New York production of *Jesus Christ Superstar* or as untraditional as the pinball wizardry of *Tommy;* due to its subject matter, however, *Rent* is an exception. For further details, including the Italian origins of "rock opera" and the term's coinage by Pete Townshend of The Who, see the entry for "rock opera" at en.wikipedia.org. The German version of Presgorvic's adaptation of *Romeo and Juliet* is simply and straightforwardly subtitled "Das Musical," however, deliberately avoiding the more apposite term—perhaps as a marketing strategy designed to appeal to a demographic for whom the term "opera," rock or not, might be disincentive to attend.

should have as well as a diCaprio-like profile and winsomeness, particularly in his ballad of adolescent lovelorn agony titled "Die Angst"—surely paradigmatic of its kind. As Juliet, Marjan Shaki (also an exceptionally young-looking 24 years old) provided a fine and convincing complement to Perman.

Presumably in the interest of time, a number of Shakespeare's plot details were consolidated or altered. Mercutio and Tybalt died in the same street fight, so there was no murder outside the Capulets' tomb. Strangely, Friar Lawrence's messenger was a white-garbed, cowled, Death-like figure; he and (separately) Romeo were waylaid by ragged, almost Beckettian figures that may or may not have been intended to resemble the Furies. A final distraught aria sung by Friar Lawrence ("Warum[?]" / "Why?") strongly implies that his faith has been severely shaken by the outcome of the plan that he devised; however, the finale ("Schuldig" / "Guilty"), performed by the entire company, suggests that all have been in one way or another complicit in the circumstances that contribute to the young lovers' deaths.

Presgurvic's adaptation of *Romeo and Juliet* may well remain primarily a European or at least non-Anglophone phenomenon, however. The London premiere of its English adaptation, co-written by director David Freeman and lyricist Don Black, was assailed by critics as "a dire pop-rock fiasco" with a set made of "industrial scaffolding," costumes that featured "the tat of sub-Versace," and a ball scene that was "gobsmackingly tacky, with sprayed shop-dummies for gold statues." Reviewers also vied to quote the most egregious lines from Black's "deplorable" lyrics, which featured "false rhymes, no rhymes, and trite rhymes." Among the prime contenders were:

- "...Lord Capulet...lilted: 'My Juliet, so sweet, so small / A smile that could make giants fall'."
- the Nurse sings that "Now she's in love and everything has changed / Her feelings and her hair have all been rearranged," even though her hairstyle was *not* changed at any point in the production.
- " 'You turn my stomick [sic]; I want to be sick,' croons Tybalt."
- "...After the wedding night, as the banished Romeo must leave, he leaps off the balcony with a cheery "It was the night of my life. Thanks."
- "Meanwhile Tybalt informs Lady Capulet: "Your daughter is being stuffed by a Montague."
- "...The feuding gangs...deliver such lines as 'Romeo's dipping his wick in the old man's daughter,' or 'Lady Montague's in a right state'."
- " 'Find a place. Get a priest. And send me a message,' this practical-minded Juliet barks at [Romeo] as he climbs down [from the balcony]."
- "'Here goes,' chirrups Juliet as she downs her poisonous potion."
- "'Forbidden love comes at a price / But it is worth the sacrifice,' the young lovers chorus unconvincingly."

Seldom if ever had there been a musical detailed with more woe than Black and Freeman's Anglicized version of Presgurvic's *Romeo*.[3]

Yet for the remarkably young audience in Vienna, and apparently for many others like it, for many of whom this may well have been their first "adult" musical other than *Starlight Express* or the various Disney productions, it was an entirely different matter. To paraphrase Yeats's famous line from "Among School Children," this was no theater for old men, nor old women. Neither was it their English teachers' revered and lofty poetry, nor their grandparents' beloved musical of a half-century ago. After the play's appropriately solemn finale, with the families duly united in grief and guilt, there came perhaps the most surprising innovation in the staging of the entire show: following a long silent blackout in which the cast reassembled for its curtain-call, there was a lengthy reprise of one of the most rousing songs, as the actors led the audience in a rhythmic clap-along, the two leads encouraging the audience to join in a basic dance step (two claps high, one clap low). Joyously, the audience was soon entirely on its feet, united in a sort of communal ritual whose message is as old as theater itself and as insistent as its pop rock tune: death and solemnity would indeed *not* triumph on *this* occasion at least; youth, exuberantly, was reclaiming its own.

NOTES

1. See, for example, the excellent *Shakespeare in Production* series (Loehlin 2002). All details concerning the production history of *Romeo and Juliet* in this essay refer to this edition.

2. All details about performance in this essay are based on the production of *Romeo & Julia: Das Musical* at the Raimund Theater in Vienna, June 2006. The German translation of the libretto (from the original French) is by Michaela Ronzoni with Julia Sengstschmid. Translations of song titles into English are my own. The production closed on July 8, 2006, after a run of one and a half years.

3. The other prime contender for the worst musical adaptation based on a famous literary work is surely *A Doll's Life* (1982), a purported sequel to Henrik Ibsen's *A Doll's House*. Directed by Hal Prince and written by the legendary musical team of Betty Comden and Adolph Green, it closed after a single performance—and established its reputation as one of the worst flops in Broadway history. For details, see Frank Rich's " 'A Doll's Life': Sequel to Ibsen," *The New York Times*, September 24, 1982, C-3.

FURTHER READING

Bassett, Kate. "From Bard to a Great Deal Worse." *Independent on Sunday* (London). November 10, 2002. Features sec., 7.

———. "Arts Etc.: 2002 Review of the Year: Theatre." *Independent on Sunday* (London). December 22, 2002. Features sec., 4.

Cavendish, Dominic. "Never Was a Musical of More Woe." *The Daily Telegraph* (London). November 5, 2002. 20.

Clapp, Susannah. "...They've Lost the Plot in *Romeo and Juliet: The Musical.*" *The Observer* (London). November 10, 2002. Observer Review Pages, 14.

Gardner, Lyn. "Shakespeare Meets Europop: *Romeo and Juliet: The Musical.*" *The Guardian* (London). 16.

Garrick, David. "To the Reader," 1748 ed., *Romeo and Juliet*, in *Garrick's Adaptations of Shakespeare, 1744–1756*, edited by Henry William Pedicord and Fredrick Louis Bergmann, vol. 3 of *The Plays of David Garrick*. Carbondale: Southern Illinois University Press, 1981. p. 77.

Hemming, Sarah. "A Terrible Tragedy of Errors: *Romeo and Juliet: The Musical.*" *The Financial Times* (London). November 6, 2002. 16.

Loehlin, James N. "Introduction." *Romeo and Juliet*. Shakespeare in Production series. Edited by J.S. Bratton and Julie Hankey. Cambridge: Cambridge University Press, 2002.

Russell, William. "Theatre: *Romeo and Juliet—The Musical." The Herald* (Glasgow). November 15, 2002. 22.

Taylor, Paul. "A Virtually Merit-Free Zone: *Romeo and Juliet: The Musical." The Independent* November 8, 2002. 23.

The Primal Power in Harold Pinter and Edward Albee: The American Dream Destructed

Penelope Prentice

Edward Albee and Harold Pinter, the two greatest living dramatists in their respective countries, the United States and England, born two years apart at almost opposite ends of the economic and social spectrum, exhibit striking parallels in their lives and plays. To appreciate the notable similarities and the significance of their differences is to appreciate the greatness of their work that continues to delight and disturb, to provoke and inspire change.

The primal power in Albee's and Pinter's work, the terrifying, yet wittily delightful, life-and-death conflicts, originates at the conjunction of comedy and conflict. These polar opposites create a breadth and depth captured in Western theater's ancient icons of drama, the laughing and crying masks, emblems of fear and desire. Comedy and conflict representing contradictory yet essential human emotions—terror and joy—drive almost all human thought and action.

Where conflict, the essence of drama and growing tip of life, provokes change, comedy, traditionally defined as truth and pain, discloses how change is possible. Albee and Pinter wed conflict and comedy exposing the American Dream, which America had exported to the world, as a greed-driven hunger in a quest for something greater, love—just love: a love that is just. Unlike a Neil Simon, Albee and Pinter never use humor to distance the self from pain, but to make the terror bearable as they convey unsayable truths. Laughter, as the flash point of insight, illuminates our darkest side allowing us to see in that generosity of light a trust that offers the optimism that change is possible. Comedy and conflict in Albee's and Pinter's work conspire to create that generosity and optimism necessary for productive change.

The human faces of Harold Pinter and Edward Albee allow us to appreciate the common wellspring of values driving the primal qualities—the struggle for respect, love, and ultimately life, a just life.

The two dramatists began life on very different squares yet have delivered plays with a primal power that move us as few dramatists have in the twentieth century. At the Albee Playwrights Conference in Alaska commemorating forty years of off-Broadway, it was easy to see that among all the invited luminaries in attendance, none touched Albee for his delightful and disturbing qualities, and at the 2005 Albee Conference only Tony Kushner appeared as a contender.

THE LIVES AND CAREERS OF ALBEE AND PINTER

In 1928 Albee was born and adopted into a newly wealthy family that owned vaudeville houses across America and lived in the exclusive, Protestant section of Larchmont in suburban New York City, wintering in Palm Beach, summering in the Adirondacks and New Hampshire, and later dividing time in the City in a Park Avenue apartment untouched by the Depression or World War II.

In 1930, two years after Albee's birth, Pinter was born to Jewish parents far from the center of London in bustling Hackney where his father, a ladies tailor, lost his job; then during the war Harold was evacuated alone to the countryside, returning home to see flying bombs chugging down his street and his own back-yard in flames. Both men were largely self educated following high school. While Albee got himself expelled from a number of boarding schools—Lawrenceville and Valley Forge Military Academy, where he claims the two courses taught were "sadism and masochism"—he managed to graduate from Choate where he says he discovered how to teach himself, and spent several years at Trinity before dropping out of college. Harold Pinter distinguished himself as a scholar-writer, athlete, and Shakespearean actor at Hackney Downs Grammar school, but because he did not have Latin could not go to Oxford or Cambridge.

Both men left home to "join the circus," so to speak. Edward Albee, who had begun working at age ten, chauffeured to a local drugstore to work as a delivery boy, left home at twenty-one after a spat with his mother, moved to a cold water flat in the Village among composers and writers in New York City where he received $25 a week from a $100,000 trust fund, and worked delivering telegrams. Harold Pinter, who as a conscientious objector after World War II narrowly escaped prison, dropped out of the Royal Academy of Dramatic Arts (being intimidated by golden haired girls in ankle bracelets), and after attending the Central School of Acting went to school in Shakespeare, joined and performed in two traveling Shakespearean theater companies.

Both men began writing very young. Albee wrote his first play, the *Play About Sex* he claims his mother destroyed, at thirteen. Over thirty years ago Albee's unpublished manuscripts arrived at the Lincoln Center Library for the Performing Arts, revealing eight short plays written in his twenties over a ten year apprenticeship, but displaying almost none of the incisive wit and brilliant turns that would mark *Zoo Story* he wrote at the age of thirty, the one-act prelude to *Who's Afraid of Virginia Woolf* that changed American theater and audiences forever. Harold Pinter's manuscripts and papers have only this past decade arrived at the British Museum. As a young actor he wrote hundreds of poems in his dressing rooms after graduating from Hackney Downs Grammar School where he had written impassioned essays on war, film, theater, and the main topics that would capture his adult focus. Harold Pinter wrote his first play *The Room* at twenty-seven at the instigation of his boyhood friend Henry Woolf, who produced in Bristol Drama School and performed in it then and again later in the revival in a London double bill with Pinter's most recent full-length play *Celebration* (2000). *The Room* was followed by *The Birthday Party,* a play both more delightful and darkly disturbing than anything before in Western drama, a play that would change the face and soul of drama in the world forever.

Both Albee and Pinter drank at the height of their early fame. Pinter listed drinking along with sex, reading, writing, and cricket as among his favorite occupations. Albee was known for his feistiness when he got drunk. He no longer drinks at all, and Pinter limits himself to champagne and white wine. Drinks and drinkers would careen through their early works revealing truth tellers and fools. Both had a first sexual experience at thirteen. Albee slept with boys. If he went to bed with girls, he said, "I never felt the same pleasure from it." Sex, liberated in their work as generosity and a liberality, also dramatizes how loveless lust can destroy.

If magnanimity is the crowning virtue, both men exhibit extraordinary generosity to other, younger writers, supporting other writers and playwrights as few other dramatists this past century. Albee's The Barn, a summer-long artists colony at Montauk, furnishes four writers and two painters with a one-month residency. Albee selects the poets and painters. He teaches in Houston, taught at Johns Hopkins, lectures and gives master classes at the Albee Conference in Alaska. Pinter directs and promotes plays of others and, at Greville Press, publishes poets from around the world. Always fiercely private, he rarely attends conferences, even the London Pinter Festival 2000 except to give a reading and to come to dinner.

Both have had longtime, beloved companions. Albee, after living with composer Ned Rhorem, and playwright Terence McNally, now for many years has lived with Jonathan Thomas, a Canadian painter. Pinter, after a long marriage to Vivian Merchant, the actress who starred in many of his early plays and died in an alcoholic suicide, is now married to writer and historian Lady Antonia Fraser, a brilliant and beautiful woman with six children and over a dozen grandchildren. Yet, in a sense both men are childless in ways that have also entered their plays—Albee has no children and Pinter is estranged from his son Daniel who suffered a breakdown after Pinter left Vivian Merchant. Daniel Pinter now lives as an almost total recluse composing music, supported by Pinter, with whom he has no communication. Neither, perhaps, will have his own children or grandchildren at his deathbed, a scene played out with absent or silent children at the end of Pinter's *Moonlight* and Albee's *Three Tall Women*.

Each man has allowed himself to be the subject of a recent authorized biography, Mel Gussow's *Edward Albee: A Singular Journey* and Michael Billington's *The Life and Work of Harold Pinter*. Both biographies contain public confessions of sexual honesty: Albee speaks openly of his homosexuality and Pinter confesses an affair during his first marriage with journalist Joan Bakewell which informed *Betrayal*. The brutal honesty they demand in their work and permit in these largely laudatory biographies furthers appreciation of the common wellspring of their primal powers—the deadly conflicts in service of love, justice, and life.

Both Albee and Pinter value a fierce honesty in their work and both are extraordinarily funny, often as delightfully playful in life as in their writing. In their plays, they both provoke laughter as the flash point of insight to expose hypocrisy and, for Albee, the lies the American Dream exported to the world. When the visiting woman in Albee's *American Dream* complains of the heat, her host suggests, Why don't you just take off your dress. She does. This simple comic technique, which both use, pushes the clichéd word to an act, unexpected and extreme. In their hands comedy remains fresh, brilliant—revealing the wisdom of comic wit. Yet at some point in both Albee's and Pinter's plays, conflict becomes deadly serious—life literally or metaphorically is at stake. But after Pinter and Albee it seems difficult to take seriously anything that isn't witty.

ALBEE'S AND PINTER'S WORK

Comedy and conflict conspire as the catalyst in their work, like the Zen slap of enlightenment, to produce change. George, in *Who's Afraid of Virginia Woolf*, in his quest for truth leaves no illusions intact, including his own, and demands of characters and audience alike what Richard does at the end of Pinter's *The Lover*, "Change." How? Western drama born of a civilization devoted to reason, twice a year, spring and fall, sought *ecstasis*, a going out of the self in Bachnalian ecstasy, binge orgies, to bring back greater truths to daily life in order to return to the *polis*, to participate in public life. That origin of drama is retained in only a few moments of greatness in Western drama: the Greeks, Shakespeare, and in the last century in Pinter and Albee. A country must come almost of age before it can produce drama—in America the first dramatist Eugene O'Neill appeared only in the twentieth century almost a hundred years after the great fiction writers and poets, Hawthorne, Melville, Whitman, and Dickinson.

The late Alan Schneider, a long time director of Albee's work, claimed all twentieth century drama is about the impossibility of living with illusions and the impossibility of living without illusions. Albee's and Pinter's work seems to ask, "When do dreams become illusions? When do nightmares become delusions?" As in ancient drama, answers lie in the extent to which one knows one's self and faces that self honestly and wholly. But equally, for both Albee and Pinter those questions and conflict also connect to love, or the absence of love, and in their most recent plays they dramatize how the loveless destruct.

There is a significant difference in how Albee and Pinter dramatize conflict, the heartbeat of drama and growing tip of life—Pinter deploys a vison, Albee engages with *memento mori* stories. Yet both execute conflict and action through dialogue with a rapier wit that plays against the grain, delivering an anti-American Dream take on life. Applying words of American political cartoon satirist Sorel, their work dramatizes "keeping the world safe for hypocrisy." In *Who's Afraid of Virginia Woolf*, George asks Martha to show Honey the toilet, "where we keep the euphemism."

Where Albee delivers his drama delightfully and disturbingly through story, narratives that forward the conflict and action, Pinter does so through a vision of paradoxical, primal conflict: the awful paradox at the center of each Pinter drama, each beat, scene, act, and each play as a whole is that the very desire for survival, respect, and ultimately love, when driven by a need to dominate another to prove self-worth, destroys the relationship, the other, and less obviously the self, the community—even, obliquely, the country a character seeks to preserve.

Albee's life-and-death stories, like George's famous bergen story in *Who's Afraid of Virginia Woolf*, about the boy who orders bergen (bourbon) in a bar, sending the entire bar up in gales of laughter, are both funny and terrifying, as in this case where we later learn the boy killed his parents in an automobile accident and ends in an asylum never to speak again. The story may or may not be true, may or may not be George, but reveals the illusive and transformational qualities of laughter on the self and reality. Another witty story that also signals a transformational point of no return occurs in Albee's *Three Tall Women* about a wealthy old woman approaching her final decay, her middle aged keeper and her young attorney, a thinly disguised story of Albee's own recently late, adoptive, shop girl mother who married into wealth. The old woman recalls her younger self seated at her dressing table after a party. She is approached by her husband naked except for a diamond bracelet dangling from his erection, a gift he offers her in exchange for a certain sexual favor, oral sex. She refuses. The disappointed erection drops the bracelet that her husband gives her anyway. In his gesture and her act something is severed—nothing between them will ever be the same again.

Still slightly shocking, amusing to a middle class, middle aged heterosexual audience, his overture might be dismissed as merely a sexual act divorced from love. But Albee's witty, (possibly true) unforgettable gesture becomes a weather vane that points to love contained within the circumference of the diamond bracelet and what it represents—a faithless husband buying (forced to buy?) the favors of sales girls (his wife before their marriage), and the lure and promise of wealth which attracted this woman to that man in a loveless marriage. Albee's real life adoptive mother Frankie says she married Albee's adoptive father because he made her laugh, though Albee retains no memory of his doing that, and only slender memory of the man. In the second act the three women blend into three stages of one woman's life where the young no-nonsense attorney, an optimistic dreamer, cannot imagine nightmare possibilities that await her in middle age and advanced years. *Three Tall Women* thus becomes a play of understanding and forgiveness of a woman who in his private and public life Edward Albee viewed as his adversary and nemesis. In this play he dramatizes both her remarkable strength as a tall woman and how her loveless life destroyed pleasure for others, and ultimately herself, in her bitterness in the end as her silent son sits at her bedside bearing witness without communication, which Albee claims they never had in real life anyway.

This lack of bonding points to a second significant difference in the lives of Albee and Pinter, which, however, produces yet again a similar outcome in their work. Albee grew up in the absence of love—describing himself as someone who was never even touched, or hugged by his adoptive parents, and aside from childhood playmates and one close friend, describes himself as a child as "pathologically shy," a loner, alone and lonely, yet he claims he never doubted his work would be great. In contrast, Pinter is described by a childhood friend as so loved by his parents that he had a supreme confidence and many close friends. As Jennifer Mortimer, who grew up with Pinter, remarked on his position among his closest friends, the gang of five boys at Hackney Down Grammar School, "Harold wasn't fighting for supremacy. He was just floating to the top because of his genuine interest and love and talents. His parents must have been so wonderful to him because he has never, ever really doubted himself." Ultimately, both Albee's and Pinter's focus on love, and the destructiveness of lovelessness, that extends beyond the private self, family, and friends to the world, disclose how lovelessness destroys real and just dreams.

Both dramatists, politically active, confront injustices of the world in their work and with their lives. While Albee's work seemingly remains focused on the private lives of characters, Pinter's recent plays *Celebration* and "Press Conference," reveal public people in their public lives devoted to public and private destruction. Yet both writers dramatize not an intellectual hatred, but a visceral and just repugnance to any self-created sham that does not permit love but strangles it, destroying the self and others. But it is the desiring, dreaming about, longing for, and seeking love in Albee's and Pinter's characters that allows us to care deeply about them, however misguided or abortive their attempts to be loved and respected. That palpable desire for love in the face of the comic and tragic in life, separates the work of these dramatists from the work of other playwrights and exposes lesser life-and-death threat adventure stories as trifling.

Albee and Pinter dramatize desire as a dream far beyond the material promises fundamental to human well-being, growth, and transformation as to concern us all, dancing as we are at the edge of the grave. Their characters who each exist along the continuum of the two poles of drama, the masks of horror and hilarity, show us our own face wholly. The ribald wit of the characters in *Celebration* thinly disguises their lives lived as the living dead. But Albee's and Pinter's plays refuse to allow us any escape through escapist entertainment. *Celebration's* very title resonates with the dramatic irony of other paradoxically celebratory titles throughout the Pinter canon, from *The Birthday Party* and *Homecoming* to *New World Order,* all dramatizing characters whose primary qualities illuminate the opposites as their essential truth. *The Birthday Party* ends in the birthday boy Stanley's psychological destruction; *Homecoming,* in the expulsion of the returning son, Teddy, and *New World Order,* in a relapse into a world viciously primitive.

In *Celebration,* Lambert and Julie, in their forties, celebrate their wedding anniversary with Matt and Prue in a restaurant described as the most expensive in town while at another table Russell, in his thirties, and Suki, in her late twenties, dine together. Later, Lambert points to Suki and announces at his anniversary celebration that he once "fucked her when she was eighteen," invites her over to their table with Russell who, sniffing the power these men possess, proposes a business deal with Matt and Lambert, who, in the end, picks up everyone's tab, and all exit except the Waiter. Significantly, the celebrants remain seated, not taking action, but each clearly revealing insecurities. "They believe in me," are Russell's first words to Suki. And Lambert at his table crows, "I know I'm well liked…I trust my family and my friends…deep down they trust me…they respect me…" Like all self-referential statements in Pinter's work, they each signal just the opposite: Russell's lack of self-confidence and Lambert's self-loathing.

"Do you know how much money I made last year?" Lambert asks his wife. His pride and identity rests solely in his money making prowess as all their insecurities register when they are visited by Richard the owner and Sonia, his hostess, whom almost all trash as lessors. The nameless Waiter offers reminders of power and real fame as he interjects recollections of a remarkable grandfather who, he claims, knew catalogues of early and mid-twentieth century luminaries in literature, the arts, and politics—from Yeats, Eliot, Pound, Auden, Dylan Thomas, D.H. Lawrence, Virginia Woolf, and Hardy, to Clark Gable, Hedy Lamarr, Al Capone, John Dillinger, Gary Cooper, Igor Stravinsky, Picasso, and the Three

Stooges to reveal Mussolini, Hitler, and Churchill all in bed together—with his grandfather and the Archduke, obliquely linking politics and the arts among all those in power. Yet, however impressive the list, its ephemeral qualities shadow all earthly immortality.

In this play nothing seems to happen—except almost every celebrant's line edged with a deadly wit is designed to destroy a previous speaker and in a single stroke slash into multiple others with sustained, almost unreleased tension which brilliantly dramatizes how the loveless destruct; in destroying what they cannot have or create—love—they destroy others, community and almost imperceptibly the self. The women unquestioningly endorse their men's material prowess equated with love, relinquishing their own power. Suki tells Russell "I want you to be rich, believe me, I want you to be rich so that you can buy me houses and panties and I'll know that you really love me."

These people hardly seem evil incarnate. Nobody dies in the end. And we as audience laugh all the way up to the final slow fade—"not...a bang but a whimper." Yet what happens before our eyes is not funny but horrifying, at depth—only if we allow ourselves to look beneath the surface. These men, the power brokers of the world, grocery clerk bureaucrats who run the guns, drugs, and money of the world exchange for millions, scarcely hint at their work. And for good reason. Like Goldberg and McCann who cart Stanley away at the end of *The Birthday Party*, their "job" is required to be conducted clandestinely even from family, except for those in the club who know the code words and have the cash and savvy to enter and play.

Celebration, wedding anniversary as commitment to marriage, reveals human relationships to be a facade, commitment to community, country, even to self, as nonexistent except as practiced at the primal edges of power among the recently moneyed privileged, where power, as the raw assertion of the self when money as power replaces desire for all else, dramatizes the pervasive destruction that results when no ethical basis asserts itself.

These characters exceed the destructive limits of fanatics driven by personal vision even in Pinter's torture plays. These people are driven by no vision. Like Pinter's characters throughout his canon they fight most viciously to maintain what they have rather than gain what they do not. Reflexively fighting the desire to sustain power, they are without conscience. As such, they are extremely dangerous, perhaps the most dangerous of all Pinter's characters.

The sexually brutal language of Pinter's recent torturers has assimilated itself into the dinner table talk: men and women calling one another *fuckpigs*, men calling each other *cunts*—this from the writer who once insisted we use such words sparingly because we have so few vivid intensifiers. But in *Celebration* the language foregrounds the longing for love. Lambert, just before he invites Suki to his table, confesses to his wife, brother and sister-in-law that he once "fell in love.

And was loved." When his wife says, "That must have been me," he says "You?" as if the idea had never occurred to him, "No, not you." Yet it is precisely this longing for love that points up love lacking among all these characters.

Pinter's own ability to Cinderella himself beyond a dream into palaces of princes, presidents, and their bureaucratic attendants has yielded no happily-ever-after endings. Where Chaucer's saving grace of satire reveals corruption in the guise of courtliness among the holy orders centuries ago, Pinter's comic tone unmasks far more than sanctimonious hypocrisy and corruption—showing us the faces of outright destructors, brutally laughing at their deadly deals in the name of "peacekeeping." Pinter most remorselessly attacks the democratic impulse in the American Dream because he values it so highly. Whereas in Pinter's essays, letters, lectures, and in the "NATO Action in Serbia Speech" he delivered just prior to writing *Celebration*, he names America as a ruthless, self-interested, destructive aggressor, in his plays he shows us how comedy in our time can be more deadly serious than tragedy.

Celebration's characters are caught not in the act of overwhelming destruction but of playing. Pinter's comedy remains in the service of exposing the terror as evil: annihilation committed by quite ordinary people, who, despite their extraordinary wealth and delightfully inventive but malicious ribaldry, are not so different from us. How better than through comedy to confront ignorance and inaction, to face it boldly before it is too late? But we are more likely, the recent plays imply, to cling tenaciously like the character Rose to our familiar room or restaurant, getting news of the outside world second hand, or to remain ignorant, than we are to act.

What do these characters—and we—want? The characters in Albee's and Pinter's most recent plays seem to have everything the American Dream can offer: often unimaginable wealth, power, family, seeming friends, but in their lovelessness the goods of that Dream creates only a velvet prison, soul destroying. Albee could deconstruct the American Dream from the inside. After *Who's Afraid of Virginia Woolf* was passed over for a Pulitzer, in fact the prize wasn't even awarded in drama that year, many assumed that Albee would turn it down when he received it for *A Delicate Balance*. He considered doing so, but asked how he could criticize the prize if he did turn it down.

His two recent plays *Sylvia, or the Goat,* and *Occupant* play out his own self-invention. *Occupant* accomplishes this through Albee's friend and mentor Louise Nevelson, via a young man's interview with the dead artist, unmasking the awful evanescence of life and fame and glory in art in our time. In *Sylvia*, a middle-aged middle class suburban husband announces to his wife and gay son he has fallen in love with a goat. In an almost Proustian feat, Albee offers an apology for, in the sense of defense of, homosexuality. Where Proust rails against homosexuality for seven-volumes till we cry "Uncle" and say "What's so bad about that?",

Albee goes further by offering bestial love, till by contrast homosexuality seems quite acceptable while exposing unexamined assumptions and received values that threaten to destroy us all.

When in the end the wife enters bearing in her arms the blue-eyed goat she's slain, the indelible image carries the weight of biblical and ancient Greek sacrifice. (Albee claims the first time he saw a crucified Christ over a church altar he wept). But while animal lovers, such as Albee is famously, might be moved by the dead goat, Albee seems to be questioning not only this woman's love for her husband when jealousy outweighs her understanding, but also notions of sexual exclusivity in marriage, and even the proper object of desire in love. Whatever felt-thought shivers through an audience at the end, the awful finality in this goat's death seems on almost all levels to question the very nature of love. For surely her killing is not an act of love. Her husband's honesty in relating his communion with this animal in their exchanged glances has not destroyed the marriage so much as exposed a marriage not grounded on love. Albee has remained an inside outsider, able to navigate the upper classes and heterosexual marriage, half proud of his privileged background, yet ever aware of those unjustly treated. Yet to others who might envy him, he is always quick to point out how unhappy he was as a child.

The silent son who appears at his mother's deathbed at the end of *Three Tall Women* reflects Albee's own decades of silence and inability to really converse or ever connect with his own adoptive mother. In Albee's late sixties, at the end of her real life in her nineties, he was further estranged from his mother's fortune, almost entirely depleted and except for a small stipend, never passed on to him. But Albee made his own comfortable God-Bless-the-Child-Who's-Got-His-Own existence, to pass the gift of time on to others.

Both Albee and Pinter actively rally in demonstrations, in their writing, letters and signing petitions, in support of PEN, Amnesty, and causes of justice and peace around the world. No Western playwright better dramatizes the causes of human violence than Pinter. However important it is to expose falsity in the American Dream that continues to persist for Americans primarily of a certain class, Albee and Pinter dramatize what Martin Luther King said, "When the world looks back on the twentieth century, they will weep not for the atrocities that took place, but for the silence of the good people." Perhaps that is where their drama brings us, to that point that it tosses the important questions of our time to us, and if we are to have the last laugh, any laughs, to pass that laugh of enlightenment on to others, then surely the questions they raise we must answer with our lives.

Pinter and Albee in the completeness of their work show us the classic faces of both horror and joy—it is all there, the full spectrum of life, that comprehensive soul that can evoke in us all life's terror and pity and that Aristotle knew is what moves us. If tragedy is being overcome by one's strengths and comedy, overcoming one's weaknesses, they combine both in perfect balance—a balance that dramatizes how the strengths of the American Dream that promises everyone a chance to obtain unlimited goods also threatens to destroy us all unless we confront our insecurities and claim courage which is love. As Albee and Pinter traverse the full distance between both poles of comedy and tragedy, their comedy conveys a generosity and optimism necessary to productive action. Despite Pinter's recent announcement that he will write no more plays, both he in his many speeches and essays and Albee in his plays continue to move us somewhere new.

In their new work love and lust butt up against loathing, rejection against intimacy, the familiar against the unexpectedly bizarre, normalcy against nightmare—establishing a dynamic beyond rejecting either/or dichotomies or embracing irony. We can see irony as the article of faith of the fearful and faithless: those who have no trust in themselves and are afraid to be found out as fools cover their butts with irony to say, "See! I didn't mean that at all." But Pinter and Albee through comedy and conflict seem to say, "I meant both; I/we are both, are all: bastard, saint, thug, and angel." To seek truth in a free society requires each of us to be a hero—to claim courage to act with just love.

To define greatness is to attempt to define that ineffable quality, genius—exemplified by those who change the way we feel, think, and, above all, *act*. Pinter has changed the way comedy and melodrama reveal and make the felt, primal terror bearable, to give us courage to recognize our power to act, to act responsibly and productively to counter the forces of hypocrisy, dishonesty, lies, injustice, and destruction everywhere. Albee and Pinter have exposed the terror within the American Dream in ways only genius can. They have made it felt palpably, yet both have invited us into their presence to discover our own genius—to feel, to think, to act with just love.

FURTHER READING

Esslin, Martin. *The Theatre of the Absurd.* Woodstock, New York: Overlook Press, 1973.
Gordon, Lois. *Harold Pinter: A Casebook.* New York: Garland, 1990.
Mann, Bruce. *Edward Albee: A Casebook.* New York: Routledge, 2003.

Realism

Robert F. Gross

Not many years ago, I was seated in an off-Broadway theater, waiting for the performance to begin. On the stage was the living room of an apartment, conservative but elegant. When two other audience members sat down to my left, one of them looked at the set and gasped in astonishment. "Oh my God!" she exclaimed. "That's my father's apartment!"

This woman's response to the set shows the realist impulse at its simplest and most immediate. It also reveals the most basic pleasure we derive from it: the pleasure at the recognition of a correspondence between something onstage and something in the world outside. It may be in props, setting, costumes, lighting, or language. It may be in behavior or motivation. But it gives the thrill of a simple response—"I know that!"

Or it may give us pleasure by showing us something that we know exists in the world, but which we have not witnessed. The spectators at the first production of Sidney Kingsley's *Men in White* (1933) had, by and large, not ever been present at a surgical operation, and were fascinated to observe it in the theater. Most of us have never worked in a big restaurant, but Arnold Wesker's *The Kitchen* (1959) allows us to look behind the scenes and enjoy seeing how a professional kitchen operates. There is a pleasure in simply watching workers erect a large tent onstage during David Storey's *The Contractor* (1969) and see how they do it. Realism takes language, objects, and actions from the world outside the theater to persuade us of the validity of what we are viewing.

At its simplest, realism is not a *style;* it is an *impulse.* It may exist in combination with highly theatrical elements—things we would never see outside the theater. Euripides used chant, poetic meters, masks, and highly elaborate costumes for his actors, but the neurotic and cynical attitudes and behavior of his Electra and Orestes strike us as realistic just the same. Euripides is not interested in *scenic*, but in *psychological* realism.

On the other hand, a production of Eugene Ionesco's *The Bald Soprano* (*La Cantatrice Chauve,* 1950) might have a meticulously rendered setting that absolutely resembles a contemporary living room in every detail, while the play itself is utterly theatrical.

But we are not all equally persuaded by every production. What audiences take to be "realistic" is subject to change over time. Many nineteenth century plays once praised for their fidelity to life now seem too staid and formal in their language and contrived in their plots to be enjoyed as realistic today. Even the spectators at the same performance of a contemporary play may disagree about the extent of a play's realism. To some, David Mamet's gritty exposé of the real estate business in *Glengarry Glen Ross* (1983) exemplifies the pinnacle of realism in the American theater today. For others, its psychological insights are too shallow, its presentation of human beings too limited, and its invective-ridden dialogue too artificial to seem lifelike.

The realistic impulse, therefore, must be understood as working in tension other forces: the need to compress events into a few hours of playing time, the need to make sure the audience understands what is going on, and the desire to stimulate the emotions, intellects and imaginations of the audience. It is useful, therefore, to identify those elements in a play that are realistic, those which are not, and then consider how they interact. In a stage set, the room might have walls (realism) but no ceiling (theatricalism). A dramatist may take a scene founded in realistic behavior and enrich it with heightened language and a rich atmosphere; the result would be *poetic realism*. Or she might underline the economic, political, and social determinants of the action; the result would be *critical realism*. A purely objective, unedited realism can be thought of as a sort of "ground zero" of theatrical representation, which is always being shaped through the selection and heightening of some elements and the muting or omission of others.

REALISM FROM THE RENAISSANCE TO THE NINETEENTH CENTURY

Realism as an impulse makes its presence felt throughout the history of theater. Realism as a style has its roots in the Renaissance, but does not become a conscious and consistent style until the second half of the nineteenth century.

In the Renaissance, the realistic impulse found much greater opportunity in the world of comedy than in tragedy. Renaissance definitions of tragedy and comedy divided the genres along class lines: tragedy was supposed to deal with the fall of monarchs and courtiers; comedy, with the follies and affectations of commoners. The diction and tone of the former was to be exalted and dignified, and usually in verse, while the latter was given much more opportunity to imitate the language and customs of daily life. Even in England, where neoclassical strictures were far less pervasive than on the Continent, comedy was the more realistic genre. In the vibrant citizen comedies of Elizabethan and Jacobean periods, references to the minutiae of merchant-class life abound—commercial law, popular plays, superstitions, fashions—often leaving the twenty-first century reader at a loss without a carefully annotated edition of the play and a map of London to decipher the references. Although the characters are often comic types and the plots improbably contrived (though delightful) webs of confidence tricks, amorous intrigues, disguises, and coincidences, these highly theatrical plays are grounded in observations of contemporary life. As a result, citizen comedies such as Thomas Dekker's *The Shoemaker's Holiday* (1599); Ben Jonson, George Chapman, and John Marston's *Eastward Ho!* (1604); and Thomas Middleton's *A Mad World, My Masters* (c1605) and *A Chaste Maid in Cheapside* (1611) offer us far more insights into the daily lives of their original audiences than the tragedies of their age.

The Eighteenth and Early Nineteenth Centuries

Comedy remained the preferred genre for realistic observation well into the eighteenth century. Although the comic playwrights of the Restoration are mostly celebrated for arch, witty, and highly stylized presentations of amorous intrigue, they conducted interesting forays into realism as well. The protagonist of Thomas Otway's bitterly satiric *Friendship in Fashion* (1678) cynically disposes of discarded mistresses by passing them on to his unsuspecting friends, and eventually provokes his own neglected wife into taking a lover. His *The Soldier's Fortune* (1680) shows the anger and poverty of cashiered soldiers, for whom sexual conquest only partially compensates them for their marginal status. In *The Wife's Excuse* (1691), Thomas Southerne vividly depicts the social whirl of London's elite—musical soirées, private raffles, afternoon teas, and masquerades—and its moral bankruptcy. Southerne is unusually adroit in his realistic handling of social gatherings in which his characters mill about, grouping and re-grouping, exchanging the latest gossip, and strategizing the next seduction in bright, terse dialogue. His realism, however, not only manifests itself in his brilliant sketches of social life, but also in psychological portraiture. Mrs. Friendall, caught in a humiliating marriage to a cowardly, philandering lout, becomes the object of malicious speculation in a world that assumes that any woman in an unhappy marriage will inevitably take a lover. As the play opens, the footmen gamble while their employers revel within, and the footmen take the prospect of Mrs. Friendall's infidelity as inevitable. But Southerne's realistic impulses lead him to undermine the character type of the unfaithful wife so common in the Restoration stage: even when Mrs. Friendall wins a separation from her husband, she is far from happy, and still shows no inclination to choose a lover. Both Southerne and Otway's protagonists are more complex and subtly drawn than those of the citizen comedies—a mark of increasing realism.

As the middle class continued to rise in the eighteenth century, so did the taste for realism. Denis Diderot (1713–84) advocated a drama of bourgeois life that more closely imitated the rhythms of daily speech and more freely mixed genres in its depiction of daily life. In Germany, tragedies of middle-class life began to appear, articulating the difficult rise of the German middle-class against local rulers who were not much different from feudal lords. Gotthold Ephraim Lessing's *Emilia Galotti* (1772), J. M. R. Lenz's *The Soldiers* (*Die Soldaten*, 1776), Friedrich Schiller's *Politics and Passion* (*Kabale und Liebe*, 1784), diverge from the tradition of writing tragedy in verse, insist on the dignity of the bourgeoisie and the importance of its dilemmas.

During the early part of the nineteenth century, the stage was dominated by romanticism, and the movement toward realism halted. It began to gain momentum again, however, around mid-century, when realism became a conscious literary and theatrical movement. Reacting against the fanciful world of popular melodramas, it insisted on characters who were individuals rather than types, and settings that were specific to the action, rather than stock.

In the French theater, social issues began to be treated more straightforwardly, often leading to fights with the censors and intense controversy. Alexandre Dumas, fils (1824–95) dramatized his novel, *The Lady of the Camelias* (*La Dame aux Camélias*), better known as *Camille*, in 1850, but it was not approved for production until 1852. The story of the beautiful and doomed courtesan Marguerite Gautier and her sacrifice for the youthful and impetuous Armand Duval both fascinated and outraged audiences across Europe and the Americas with its depiction of the world of the contemporary courtesan—a milieu hitherto taboo in the theater—but also reduced them to tears through its sentimental and idealized portrait of the "fallen woman." "It is all champagne and tears" observed Henry James, pithily encapsulating the play's long-lasting appeal. Dumas's combination of realism and romance proved well-nigh irresistible, and made it one of the most popular and influential plays of the century.

Less romantic and more morally didactic than Dumas, Emile Augier (1820–89) helped popularize the social drama, taking on such topical issues as the power of the press and the manipulation of the stock exchange. An exponent of traditional values, Augier assailed what he saw as the greed, materialism, and ostentatiousness of the middle class. In *Olympe's Marriage* (*Le Mariage d'Olympe*, 1855), he acerbically commented on the vogue for sentimentalizing the prostitute, initiated by *The Lady of the Camelias*.

A courtesan who reinvents herself as a respectable woman in order to hood-wink the wealthy heir of an old family, Olympe inevitably falls back into her dis-reputable ways. The scene in which she entertains her vulgar mother and louche companions in her husband's absence was considered shocking even decades after its premiere. But time has attenuated its notoriety, and *Olympe's Marriage*, for all its sharp observations of Second Empire manners and mores, strikes read-ers today as more melodramatic in its plot contrivances and villainous protagonist than realistic. Yet Augier's dramaturgy has not vanished. Even today, playwrights and filmmakers graft realistic observations of milieu onto intricate and even improbable plots. The ongoing popularity of intricately contrived suspense plots, whether with detectives, secret agents, or confidence men, is evidence of the continued hybridizing of realism and melodrama.

MODERN REALISM

Ibsen

Henrik Ibsen (1828–1906), popularly known as "the father of modern drama," while using the forms of French social drama, gradually simplified the plotting and deepened the characterizations, doing much to free realistic drama from a dependency on melodramatic devices. Although not completely free of melodra-matic elements—forged documents and blackmail—*A Doll's House* (*Ett Duke-hjem*, 1879) is generally regarded as a major step forward in the development of realism. The blackmailer is not a villainous type, but a sad and desperate charac-ter whose downfall was caused by the same crime, forgery, as the heroine's. Nora Helmer is a brilliant and highly individualized portrait of a woman who has led a protected existence as a "doll," first under the control of her father and, later, under her husband. As Nora's assumptions about herself and her marriage col-lapse, she realizes that her first obligation is not to her husband and children, but to herself. She returns her wedding ring to her husband, releasing him of any marital obligations, and demands the same from him. At the end of the play, in one of the most famous concluding scenes in all of drama, Nora departs, having decided "I can no longer be satisfied with what most people say—or what they write in books. I must think things out for myself—get clear about them." As the curtain falls, we hear the door slam as she disappears into the night. Not only was *A Doll's House* widely interpreted, and often vilified, as a manifesto for the feminist movement, but Ibsen's iconoclastic assertion of the rights of each person to self-fulfillment above all other obligations struck a blow for individualism that led the play to be adopted as a polemic for both liberals and anarchists.

His next play, *Ghosts* (*Gengangare*, 1881), intensified Ibsen's attack on conservative values. The "ghosts" of the title are, as protagonist Helene Alving explains, "not only the things we inherit from our parents—but by the ghosts of innumerable prejudices and beliefs—half-forgotten cruelties and betrayals—we may not even be aware of them—but they're there just the same—and we can't get rid of them. The whole world is haunted by the ghosts of the dead past." Mrs. Alving has devoted her life to keeping her late husband's sexual depravity and death from syphilis a secret from the world. Although she has come to doubt the values of her society, she still feels the need to placate them through acts of hypocrisy. Her attempts to free herself, unlike Nora Helmer's, do not succeed, and she is left at the end, alone with her syphilitic son, unable to decide whether she should euthanize him as he requested.

But Ibsen was both too deeply ironic and iconoclastic to leave his liberal positions unproblematized. In *The Wild Duck* (*Vildanden*, 1884), a young firebrand sets out to free a family from its "ghosts," only to destroy it through his revelations. Here Ibsen questions one of the common assumptions of realism: is the public representation of the unvarnished truth salutary, or do people need illusions to survive? Ibsen's ruminations on this question have stimulated both realists and theatricalists alike: the plays of Luigi Pirandello in Italy, Jean Giraudoux and Jean Anouilh in France, Maxim Gorky's *The Lower Depths* (*Ma dne*, 1902) in Russia, and Eugene O'Neill's *The Iceman Cometh* (1939) and Edward Albee's *Who's Afraid of Virginia Woolf?* (1962) in the United States.

In the last decade of his career, Ibsen's plots grew ever simpler, and his realism became more suffused with symbolism. In his penultimate drama, *John Gabriel Borkman* (1896), most of the action takes place long before the curtain's rise, as it shows the emergence of a disgraced business tycoon from years of self-imposed reclusiveness on the last night of his life. The dramatic action is spare; there is no way to expiate the damage that Borkman has done, neither to himself nor to the two sisters who were rivals for his love. The frigid, nocturnal, Norwegian setting is as much an expression of the characters' congealed emotional lives as a realistic setting. As we hear Borkman's pacing in the upstairs gallery of his house, it is mingled with the strains of Camille Saint-Saëns's "Danse macabre" on the piano, a fitting accompaniment to his death-in-life. The fusion of realistic psychology and setting with symbolism and highly imagistic language—a form of poetic realism—in Ibsen's late plays opened new territory for dramatic experimentation.

Zola

Ibsen was clearly the predominant realistic dramatist of the second half of the century, but he wrote no manifestos on behalf of the new drama. That role fell to Emile Zola (1840–1902), who became not only the most influential polemicist in favor of realistic experimentation, but was the founder of a particular subspecies of realism, called *naturalism*.

Influenced by the growth of scientific method and the positivist theories of Auguste Comte, Zola believed that modern drama needed to become more scientific. He urged a meticulous, emotionally detached observation of all aspects of human life, a recognition of the determination of all human behavior by heredity and environment, and a repudiation of melodramatic contrivance. Coining a much-used term, he argued that the theater should become a "slice of life" (*tranche de vie*). Although his few ventures into drama were largely unsuccessful, and the best-known of them, *Thérése Raquin* (1873), owes its continued revival more to its elements of rip-roaring melodrama than its detached observation of everyday life, Zola's insistence on the importance of environmental and hereditary factors proved to be highly influential.

Hauptmann

Nowhere can Zola's naturalistic theory be seen more clearly than in the early plays of Gerhart Hauptmann (1862–1946). *Before Sunrise* (*Vor Sonnenaufgang,* 1889) not only was the first German naturalistic drama, but remains one of the most theatrically vital examples of the movement. A young socialist doing research on conditions in Silesia falls in love with the radiant, vulnerable daughter of a vulgar, degenerate, and alcoholic farming family. He offers the only escape for her from this sordid environment, but when he learns from the local doctor the story of her family's decline, he flees, fearing her genetic inheritance will inevitably doom her. Abandoned, she stabs herself with her father's hunting knife, as her drunken father is heard approaching, singing a lascivious song. Not only did Hauptmann go beyond Ibsen in his aggressive depiction of sociopathic behavior, but in his meticulous recording and theatrical use of Silesian dialect he is far removed from Ibsen's more decorous, middle-class dialogue.

The Weavers (*Die Weber,* 1892) remains Hauptmann's boldest experiment in naturalism. Based on the unsuccessful uprising of Silesian weavers in 1844, Hauptmann rejects the commonplace notion that a play must have a single protagonist, choosing the weavers and their families as a collective protagonist. He paints their misery in unsparing and disturbing touches: an old man, for example, kills the family dog in order to stave off starvation, only to find that his stomach, long grown unused to meat, cannot keep it down. *The Weavers* rejected the contrivances of melodrama in favor of an epic structure, tied naturalism to the literature of social protest, and asserted the legitimacy of a drama that focused on the downtrodden. Although some later critics have argued that the play's pessimism undercuts its revolutionary potential, this groundbreaking drama remains one of the most influential texts of the modern theater.

Strindberg

Although a follower of Zola only in the early part of his career, August Strindberg (1849–1912) contributed memorably to the naturalist with a handful of one-acts and two full-length dramas. The first, *The Father* (*Fadren*, 1887), develops from a simple observation drawn from human biology: a woman *knows* she is the mother of her child, but a man has no such certainty. This simple fact comes into play as Captain Adolf and his wife Laura fight for control over their daughter's education. Laura suggests that Adolf has no authority in this matter; after all, the child may not be his. The suspicion drives the father to insanity, and he dies in his wife's arms bound in a straitjacket, while she explains that the annihilating suspicions she raised were, in fact, totally unfounded. In *The Father*, the basic animosity between men and women is grounded in biology.

Strindberg's most famous naturalistic drama, *Miss Julie* (*Frøken Julie*, 1888) is notable for its preface as well as the play itself. Strindberg argues that human beings are not simple "characters," defined by a single predominant quality, in the way that Molière's Harpagon in *The Miser* is completely defined by his miserliness. The characters of *Miss Julie* are so complex and psychologically discontinuous that they might better be called "characterless." He explains: "My souls (characters) are conglomerations of past and present cultural phases, bits from books and newspapers, scraps of humanity, pieces torn from fine clothes and become rags, patched together as is the human soul." Decades before the cubists would discover pictorial collage, Strindberg put forward the notion of the dramatic figure as collage.

In *Miss Julie*, Strindberg creates two such collages: the imperious, flighty, and impulsive daughter of an aristocrat, and her father's ambitious, passionate but ultimately servile valet. Strindberg puts these two highly unstable figures into the sexually charged atmosphere of a Midsummer Eve and demonstrates the influence of the milieu on their self-destructive behavior. Not only did Strindberg fundamentally complicate the whole idea of dramatic character, but he also questioned conventional wisdom about heterosexual relationships, suggesting that deep-seated animosities and drives for power might be at least as important as sexual attraction and affection.

Realism in Russian Drama

In Russia, realistic theater developed in opposition to a highly repressive government that employed strong stage censorship. Nikolai Gogol (1809–52) explained the impetus behind his masterpiece, *The Inspector General* (*Revizor*, 1836):

> In *The Inspector General* I had decided to collect into one heap everything I knew
> about what was bad in Russia, all the injustices that were being done at times and
> in places where there was the greatest need for justice; and laugh at it all at once.

Virtually unique in its time for its lack of a single sympathetic character, Gogol creates a provincial town rife with corruption and petty rivalries, and then introduces Khlestakov, a mindless, amoral fop whom the townspeople mistakenly take for a government inspector from St. Petersburg. Falling over themselves to curry favor with Khlestakov, they reveal the depths of their venality, from which he is only too willing to profit, before skipping town. Only too late do the villagers discover that they have been duped, and that the real government inspector is on his way. In its lack of sentimentality, romance, and poetic justice, *The Inspector General* established a tradition of Russian realism independent of French models, more grotesque in its humor, colloquial in its dialogue, and less dependent on intricate plotting.

Deeply influenced by Gogol, Alexander Sukhovo-Kobylin (1817–1903) explored the realm in which realistic observation can uncover a demonic, nightmarish world. Accused of being the murderer of his French mistress, Sukhovo-Kobylin suffered through seven years of arrests, investigations, and trials before being acquitted. In the meantime, he gained firsthand knowledge of the graft, corruption, and bureaucratic horrors of the tsarist justice system. In his trilogy, composed of *Kerechinsky's Wedding* (*Svad'ba Krechinsogo*, 1854), *The Case* (*Delo*, 1861), and *Tarelkin's Death* (*Smert' Tarelkina*, 1869), he starts with the witty intrigue of a French comedy, deepens progressively into realism as he dramatizes the struggles of an innocent man in the grasp of the legal system, and finally passes into grotesque fantasy. This brilliant trilogy, sadly neglected in the English-speaking world, encapsulates much of the history of nineteenth and twentieth century drama, and like Franz Kafka, questions the boundaries commonly placed between realistic depiction and hallucination. Needless to say, the trilogy did not please the censors; it took decades before unexpurgated productions were permitted.

Alexander Ostrovsky (1823–86) remains by far the most prolific of major Russian playwrights, writing comedies, tragedies, historical dramas, fairy tale plays, and adaptations of foreign dramas. His first play, a satire of bankruptcy fraud, did not lead to a production, but to police surveillance instead. His comedies of Moscow life usually chronicle the lives of parvenu merchants and tradespeople who lived on the unfashionable south side of the Moskva river, a reactionary class of petty tyrants who lorded it over their employees at work and their families at home. In *Too Clever by Half*, also known in English as *The Diary of a Scoundrel* (*Na vsiakogao mudresta dovol'no prostoty*, 1868), Gloumov, an impecunious, ingenious, and unprincipled young man, rises up through the vanity, greed, and stupidity of Moscow society while recording his brutally honest impressions in a journal. When the journal is discovered and read aloud, everyone is shocked, and Gloumov castigates them for their hypocrisy—he's written no more, he asserts, than they all habitually say behind each other's backs—and storms out. The next moment, however, they decide to recall Gloumov: after all, who would want to live without such a fascinating young man?

In *The Forest* (*Les*, 1870), Ostrovsky's critique moves to a country estate. Two impoverished itinerant actors arrive at the estate of a wealthy aunt, only to see how monetary concerns stunt the capacity for compassion there. After arranging the betrothal of two young lovers, one of whom was driven to attempt suicide by the soulless machinations around her, the penniless actors depart, but not before delivering a stinging diatribe against the inhuman values they have encountered there—a speech, it is pointed out, memorized from Friedrich Schiller's classic play of revolt, *The Robbers*. At once a scathing satire of commercial values and a heartfelt tribute to the humanizing values of the stage, *The Forest* remains one of Ostrovsky's most widely performed works.

The power of petty tyrants grows lethal in *The Storm* (*Groza*, 1859), Ostrovsky's greatest tragedy. In a backward, uneducated, superstitious town on the Volga river, Katerina's life is made unendurable by her vicious and dictatorial mother-in-law, who maintains that a household can only be kept orderly by fear. Katerina's sister-in-law urges her to live a life of deception. "Our entire household is built on lies," she explains. "I never used to lie, but I learned how to, when I had to." But Katerina, a deeply religious, imaginative, and high-strung woman, is incapable of developing such defenses. She briefly finds romance in an extramarital affair, but breaks down and confesses to her husband and mother-in-law. This confession, set in an old arcade painted with scenes of the Last Judgment, haunted by the hellfire-and-brimstone ravings of an old madwoman, and underscored by the coming of a thunderstorm, pushes realism to the verge of expressionism in its intensity. Unable to live with the brutality that follows her confession, she drowns herself in the Volga. Often praised as Ostrovsky's greatest achievement, it inspired a famous operatic adaptation by Czech composer Leoš Janáček, *Káťa Kabanováá* (1921).

Turgenev

Ivan Turgenev (1818–83) primarily devoted his career to writing fiction, but his delicate, probing comedy, *A Month in the Country* (*Mesyats v derevene*, 1850) creates a nuance and restraint far removed from Ostrovsky's more straightforward dramaturgy. Amidst the routine amusements of a country estate—card games, embroidery, long walks, and gossip—Natalya Petrovna, the bored mistress of the estate, neglected by her husband, gradually discovers that she has become infatuated with the young, unsophisticated student who is tutoring her son. The intensity of her emotion could easily become the stuff of melodrama, but Turgenev's characters are individuals, far removed from the simple types of good and evil common to that genre. Natalya is no exemplar of virtue—she seriously contemplates marrying off her seventeen year-old ward to a gauche and simpleminded old landowner when she suspects her of being a rival—but neither is she a villain, maliciously determined to thwart young love. As it turns out, none of the potential love affairs come to fruition: the suitor and tutor leave, the ward in a fit of pique determines to marry the doltish landowner after all, and Natalya is left alone.

The problems encountered by *A Month in the Country* on its way to theatrical acceptance show how much resistance realist playwrights encountered in nineteenth century Russia. In 1850, Turgenev submitted the play to the censors, who demanded many changes, most importantly that Natalya become a widow, to remove any suggestions of immorality. Even after Turgenev submitted to their demands, it was not allowed to be published until 1855, and not until 1869 was the husband permitted back into the script. When it made its way to the stage in 1872, it was poorly received, and only received acclaim a decade later.

Chekhov

In the four late plays of Anton Chekhov (1860–1904)—*The Seagull* (*Chayka*, 1896), *Uncle Vanya* (*Dyadya Vanya*, 1899), *Three Sisters* (*Tri sestry*, 1901), and *The Cherry Orchard* (*Vishnyovy sad*, 1904)—realism reaches its purest and most profound expression. Characters are highly individualized. Plotting appears both unimportant and effortless. No longer constructing plays around a single protagonist, Chekhov presents households in all their crossed purposes, mixed intentions, and blind spots. It seems at times that we are looking at daily life in all its casual disarray, but closer examination reveals that every moment is exquisitely crafted. The characters are no longer persistently engaged with each other in close conversation; the dialogue is rich in non sequiturs and misunderstandings. They often seem not be conducting interchanges with each other, but constructing simultaneous monologues.

If there is a fundamental conflict in these plays, it is no longer between a hero and a villain, but between human beings and time. The characters feel their powerlessness before the losses that time inevitably exacts. Irina, the youngest of the three Prozorov sisters, feels it intensely at 23:

> Oh where has everything gone? Where is it? Oh my God, my God, I've forgotten everything—everything…everything's confused…I can't remember anything—I forget things everyday. Life is passing me by, never to come back.

Time not only takes things from us, it even takes away the memory of them. The aged bachelor Chebutykin asserts repeatedly that he loved the Prozorovs' mother, but, when asked if she loved him, he cannot remember whether she did or not.

Chekhov enriched the modern theater by his development of subtext, the unarticulated message that lies beneath the spoken text. Before Chekhov, dramatic characters usually mean what they say, unless they are consciously dissembling. But in his plays, people often do not understand what they feel—or what they say. Masha is haunted by some lines in a poem by Pushkin during the first act of *Three Sisters* and does not know why. Yelena has every reason to deceive herself about her feelings for Astrov, the dissipated doctor in *Uncle Vanya*. Chekhov's characters, like us, are incapable of fully understanding either themselves or each other, which is one of the reasons they continue to fascinate us with the illusion of their humanity. Psychological realism can go no further. Chekhov's plays finish demolishing the neoclassical division of genres established in the Renaissance. He encourages us to see the actions and characters in his plays as at once comic and tragic: not a sentimental muddling of the two, but the sharp, simultaneous existence of two contrasting perspectives. In *The Cherry Orchard*, the Ranevskys lose their family estate because they are temperamentally incapable of doing anything to save it. From one perspective, they are self-indulgent, eccentric comic figures: Mme. Ranevsky is scatterbrained and totally impractical, her brother, Gaev, wanders about aimlessly, imagining games of billiards and calling the shots aloud as he "plays." From this point of view, they get nothing less than they deserve. At the same time, however, we feel the full, devastating weight of their loss; it is impossible not to feel deeply for them as they leave their childhood home for the last time. The interpenetration of comedy and tragedy is both complete and seamless, opening a line of development in the modern theater from realism to the absurdism of Samuel Beckett. The predominance of tragicomic mixtures in modern drama, would be unthinkable without Chekhov.

Gorky

Maxim Gorky (1868–1936) was widely seen as Chekhov's successor. First attracting widespread attention with the international success of his slice-of-life drama set in a flophouse, *The Lower Depths* (*Ma dne*, 1902), Gorky grafted Chekhovian techniques onto an explicit political agenda—something his predecessor avoided. The delicate strength of Chekhov is replaced by a harsher, more judgmental tone, but Gorky's relative crudeness (and what dramatist of the twentieth century does not seem crude, compared to Chekhov?) carries sharp psychological and social insights, passion, and theatrical power. Gorky's greatest portraits are not of the workers and peasants, whom he tended to idealize, but of the ineffectual intellectuals, and, above all, the crude, vigorous, brutal merchants and tradespeople, theatrical grandchildren of Ostrovsky's bourgeois dictators. In *The Zykovs* (*Zykoy*, 1903), timber merchant Antipa Zykov meets the innocent, convent-bred lass to whom his son is engaged. Antipa invites her into his office, and a little later makes the announcement that she is not going to wed his son, but himself. For all his coarseness, we are drawn to his honesty and opposition to a stagnant world. The title character in *Vassa Zheleznova* (1910; revised, 1935) has built a shipping company on the Volga with seemingly inexhaustible energy and few scruples. When her brutal, dissipated husband is arrested on a morals charge, she persuades him to commit suicide rather than disgrace the family. In the final scene, Vassa begins to lose her hold over the world she has so single-mindedly constructed, but she fights on relentlessly until dropping dead at her desk of a coronary.

Gorky enthusiastically supported the Russian Revolution, and his realist plays, based on analyses of class conflict, were taken as models of socialist realism, when it was promulgated by Andrey Zhdanov as Communist Party orthodoxy at the First All-Union Congress of Soviet Writers in 1934. The result, a stultified, propagandis-tic drama populated with an idealized proletariat and melodramatic villains, bore little or no resemblance to Gorky's work, was anything but realistic, and left Soviet drama imprisoned in a lifeless schematic for decades.

Austrian Dramatic Realism

Austrian playwright Ödön von Horváth (1901–38) developed a new form of critical realism in his dramatic chronicles of the petty bourgeoisie and proletariat between the two World Wars, including *Tales from the Vienna Woods* (*Geschichte aus dem Wiener Wald*, 1931), *Kasimir und Karoline* (*Kasimir and Karoline*, 1932), and *Glaube Liebe Hoffnung* (*Faith Love Hope*, 1933). An innovator in dramatic dia-logue, Horváth explored the ability of language to deceive; how brutality can lie behind sentimentality, and resentment behind protestations of affection. For him, speech is not the spontaneous and direct expression of thought and feeling; it is something acquired. As a result, what we say may not correspond to what we actually believe, not because we are hypocritical, but because our culture's lan-guage indoctrinates us to our culture's ideology. Horváth's characters cannot express themselves directly. Rather, their minds are cluttered with proverbs, quo-tations, and bromides. Surrounded on all sides by the kitsch, propaganda, and detritus of mass culture, they often find themselves closest to their real feelings not in speech, but in silence. In the pauses that punctuate a Horváth play, we are led to perceive the emotional truth that the language is incapable of conveying—the inarticulate struggle of the unconscious with consciousness. Horváth reveals the hopelessness and cruelty that lurk behind the apparently benign artifacts of popular culture, whether Strauss waltzes in *Tales from the Vienna Woods* or the Oktoberfest in *Kasimir and Karoline*. Lacking the language that would help them come to an understanding of the cultural and economic forces that constrain them, his characters often move in circles, unable to liberate themselves.

Horváth's career was undermined by the rise of the Nazis and cut short by an accident at the age of thirty-seven. His plays were largely forgotten until the late 1960s, when he enjoyed a major renaissance in the German-speaking theater, where he continues to be performed frequently. His insights into the ideological force of language influenced a new generation of critical realist playwrights, including Martin Sperr (b. 1944), Franz Xavier Kroetz (b. 1946), and playwright and filmmaker Rainer Werner Fassbinder (1945–82).

English Dramatic Realism

On the English stage of the late nineteenth and early twentieth century, realism largely followed the French model of Dumas and Augier, with the decorous values of middle-class gentility acting as a brake on realistic experimentation. Naturalism was far too raw to exercise any influence. Although W. Somerset Maugham (1874–1965) showed the influence of French naturalism in his early novels, he carefully kept it out of his commercially successful plays, substituting a cynical detachment that could range from brittle high comedy to trenchant satire. *Lady Frederick* (1907) appalled some and titillated many with its scene in which an adventuress sets out to disillusion her young admirer by showing him how she uses makeup to correct the ravages of time each morning at her dressing table. *The Constant Wife* (1926) played a similar game by showing a wife who unflappably accepts her husband's infidelity and attains sufficient financial independence to do the same, if she pleases. The modern wife, she explains, is nothing but "a prostitute who doesn't deliver the goods." Although *Our Betters* (1917), a satire of American heiresses married to European aristocrats, was kept off the London stage by the censors for its depictions of promiscuity and gained some notoriety for its use of the word "slut," it soon became accepted as one of his finest plays. But critics sometimes argued over whether or not Maugham was a realist at all—was he, rather, a highly skilled contriver of theatrically effective entertainments with the merest veneer of modern fashions and manners?

George Bernard Shaw (1856–1950) claimed to be an "Ibsenite," and was an important defender of the Norwegian playwright in England. But his own plays, with the exception of his early *Plays Unpleasant* (1898), are peopled with hyperarticulate characters who inhabit a world of rhetorical pyrotechnics and intellectual idiosyncrasies that bear little resemblance to realistically conceived portraits.

John Galsworthy (1867–1933) articulated a realist program for himself when he observed that a playwright had three options: (1) following what the audience believes, (2) expressing what he believes, or (3) setting out "no cut-and-dried codes, but the phenomena of life and character, selected and combined, but not distorted, by the dramatist's outlook." The result, at its best, is a somewhat detached, even-handed imaginative consideration of a conflict, similar to Ibsen's social dramas in form, though lacking their psychological depth. *Strife* (1907) invites comparison with Hauptmann's *The Weavers*. While Hauptmann is furiously (and magnificently) partisan in his espousal of the weavers' cause, Galsworthy weighs the merits and defects of both sides, and sees the common besetting fault as a failure to compromise. *The Skin Game* (1920) shows the conflict between landed gentry and new money; both sides become progressively debased morally by their intransigence in a fight over real estate. Although infrequently revived today, Galsworthy's best plays won widespread approval for their compassionate, liberal views and thoughtfulness.

Chekhov's influence can easily be seen in the minimally plotted, finely atmospheric plays of N.C. Hunter (*Waters of the Moon*, 1951, and *A Day By the Sea*, 1953) and J.B. Priestley (*Time and the Conways*, 1934, and *Eden End*, 1937), but both have a tendency toward nostalgia and sentimentality not found in the Russian master. Terence Rattigan (1911–77), a more psychologically probing playwright than either Hunter or Priestley, became the preeminent realistic playwright on the West End stage after World War II. His plays explore the sexual agony and self-hatred of deeply troubled people in dialogue that is deceptively simple, but subtextually rich. *The Browning Version* (1948), a masterpiece of one-act play construction, poignantly dramatizes the last day in the career of a desperately lonely and unloved schoolteacher. Hester Collyer in *The Deep Blue Sea* (1952) has left her husband for a man who is now about to leave her. Tempted by suicide, she is not only devastated by the prospect of being alone, but unable to accept the intensity of her sexual desire. *Separate Tables* (1954), set in a residential hotel for downwardly mobile members of the postwar middle class, makes a plea for toleration of misfits and sexual outsiders.

Rattigan's restrained vision of middle-class gentility was directly challenged by John Osborne (1929–94). *Look Back In Anger* (1956), with its protagonist from the working class spewing diatribe and invective, had a vigor and immediacy that suddenly made Rattigan appear old-fashioned. Osborne opened the way toward a more loosely plotted, less decorous realism that reflected the lives of the disadvantaged and marginalized while, ironically, turning his attention to the affluent and privileged in *The Hotel in Amsterdam* (1968) and *West of Suez* (1971).

From the late 1950s through the 1970s, both the subject matter and forms of British stage realism broadened. The deeply compassionate plays of Arnold Wesker (b. 1932) are best known for combining socialist themes and Chekhovian techniques in such dramas as *Roots* (1959), *The Friends* (1970), and *The Old Ones* (1972). Wesker's plays insist on the need for utopian values despite the failure of all utopian schemes. David Storey (b. 1933) often explores the alienation of upwardly mobile young people from their working-class backgrounds, most notably in *In Celebration* (1969) and *The March on Russia* (1989), yet he also gained praise for *The Changing Room* (1971), a "slice-of-life" set in a locker room during a rugby match. Alan Ayckbourn (b. 1939) infuses highly theatrical dramatic structures with deft sketches of suburbia. In *Absent Friends* (1975), *Just Between Ourselves* (1978), and *Woman in Mind* (1986), farcical techniques exist cheek-by-jowl with cruelty and pathos. As with Maugham, critics disagree as to how much of Ayckbourn's work is due to realistic observation and how much to theatrical contrivance, but his best work renders not merely the surface, but also the psychological depths of suburban claustrophobia and alienation.

Film director and playwright Mike Leigh (b. 1943) also mixes comedy and bleakness in his explorations of middle- and working-class anomie, but his approach avoids the ingenious complexity of Ayckbourn, preferring to produce an air of improvisational openness. Starting with *Bleak Moments* (1970), he actually has developed his plays out of lengthy improvisation periods with his actors, making them collaborators in the development of their characters. Both *Abigail's Party* (1977) and *Ecstasy* (1979) unfold during a single, intimate gathering, and show the characters lurching into embarrassing self-disclosures and emotional eruptions under the pressure of social interaction and the loosening effects of alcohol.

U.S. Dramatic Realism

In the United States, scenic realism was received enthusiastically early on, and at least a veneer of realism quickly became required for most successful commercial drama in the twentieth century. Whether softened with humor and sentiment or energized with touches of melodrama, realistic drama has remained dominant in American theater, movies, and television.

But alongside its commercial dominance, it has served other, sometimes oppositional ends. The influence of Ibsen's social dramas on American theater can be seen in an ongoing American tradition of realistic protest plays. Rachel Crothers used realism to assess the position of women in society and attacked the double standard in *A Man's World* (1910), and she considered the obstacles to a creative woman's career in *He and She* (1920). Susan Glaspell made a chilling point of male obliviousness to domestic abuse in *Trifles* (1916), and attacked abuses of free speech in the name of patriotism in *Inheritors* (1921). Before turning to the romantic verse dramas for which he is best known, Maxwell Anderson collaborated with Laurence Stallings on *What Price Glory?* (1924), a play about the senselessness of war, and with Harold Nickerson on *Gods of the Lightning* (1928), a protest against the trial and executions of Sacco and Vanzetti. John Wexley dramatized conditions on death row in *The Last Mile* (1930) and protested against the Scottsboro case in *They Shall Not Die* (1934). Paul Green's *Hymn to the Rising Sun* (1936) condemned the inhumanity of chain gangs in the Southern penal system. Lillian Hellman's *The Children's Hour* (1934) and Robert Anderson's *Tea and Sympathy* (1953) both approached the topic of homophobia, however gingerly. Arthur Miller used the Salem Witch trials to attack the McCarthy hearings in *The Crucible* (1953). Lorraine Hansberry spoke out against racism in *A Raisin in the Sun* (1959). In the early years of the AIDS pandemic, Larry Kramer's *The Normal Heart* (1985) spoke out against public indifference and prejudice against HIV-positive people. While some of these plays move away from realism in melodramatic confrontations between good and evil, they show the power of realism to function with journalistic immediacy and emotional power.

Other playwrights, no less politically committed, followed the model of Chekhov. The most famous of these is Clifford Odets, who translated Chekhov's non sequiturs and loving attention to minutiae into Brooklynese, and softened Gorky's revolutionary fervor into injunctions like "Do what is in your heart and you carry in yourself a revolution." In *Awake and Sing* and *Paradise Lost* (both 1935) he wedded the vigor of American urban slang to a poignant desire for a life. More intellectually sophisticated than Odets but no less poetic, Theodore Ward revealed Depression-era Americans divided among faith in the American dream, socialism, and Marcus Garvey's Back-to-Africa movement in his unjustly neglected *Big White Fog* (1938).

The two American realist playwrights who have enjoyed the highest critical esteem, however, are not known for social dramas. Eugene O'Neill (1888–1953) was a tireless experimenter, but his best-known and most admired plays are in the naturalist tradition. An admirer of Strindberg and Hauptmann, O'Neill created characters whose fates are determined by forces beyond their control. Plot becomes negligible as the playwright devotes himself to depicting characters who are incapable of change. "The past is the present, isn't it? It's the future too." remarks the drug-addicted mother, Mary Tyrone, in his most fully realized play, *A Long Day's Journey Into Night* (1939–41). "We all try to lie out of that but life won't let us."

Eugene O'Neill

One of many playwrights influenced by Freudian psychoanalytic theory, O'Neill rewrote Aeschylus's *Oresteia* as, above all, the working out of Oedipal conflicts in *Mourning Becomes Electra* (1931). In his reworking of the story of the House of Atreus, set in New England after the Civil War, Electra loves her father and despises her mother, while Orestes does the reverse. After their parents' deaths, brother and sister each increasingly come to resemble their same-sex parent, and their scenes become infused with a barely repressed incestuous desire. One's fate, O'Neill suggests, is to become one's parent.

O'Neill was the son of a successful actor who triumphed in melodramatic portrayals, and O'Neill never rid himself of a penchant for a drama of magnitude that sometimes ill-sorted with his realistic impulses. Of all the major realistic dramatists, none was more driven to invest realism with mythic stature and epic breadth: both *Mourning Becomes Electra* and *Strange Interlude* (1928) are written in nine acts—a trilogy of three-act plays. The size of his vision, however, was not always matched by the depth of his insights. In *Dynamo* (1929), for example, O'Neill tried to comment on modern spirituality by having his protagonist worship a maternal goddess in the form of a huge electric generator. In his greatest achievement, however, he kept a tight rein on his ambitions, reducing the cast to five, the time to a one day, and the setting to a single, realistically rendered parlor.

Long Day's Journey Into Night, his most autobiographical work, uncovers the pattern of unconscious betrayals in the history of a family as it slowly comes to the surface through their interactions. There are no melodramatic revelations, no pistol shots or deaths. The play moves into the depths of night and despair as the fog encircles the house—a masterful example of O'Neill's talent for settings that are at once realistically detailed, revelatory of character, and richly atmospheric.

Tennessee Williams

O'Neill's most notable successor was Tennessee Williams (1911–83), whose critical reputation and frequent success in revivals seems have outstripped his predecessor. Williams takes material that could easily be developed naturalistically—the descent of a genteel schoolteacher into promiscuity, alcoholism, and insanity in *A Streetcar Named Desire* (1947), or the futile efforts of an aging hustler to recapture the dreams of his youth, only to meet the certainty of castration in *Sweet Bird of Youth* (1959)—and transform them into plays of poetic realism through heightened language and lush atmospheres. "Don't you just love those long rainy afternoons in New Orleans," remarks *Streetcar*'s heroine, Blanche DuBois, "when an hour isn't just an hour—but a little piece of eternity dropped into your hands—and who knows what to do with it?" The transformation of sordid reality by the poetic imagination is Williams's major theme, one that perhaps makes him at heart less a realist than a romantic.

Since the 1950s, realism as a style in the American theater has lost its edge. Perhaps its very ubiquity has rendered it insipid. Perhaps it has become so widely accepted that it has lost its ability to surprise us. Certainly no contemporary American realist deserves a place alongside Ibsen, Chekhov, Horváth and the other masters of realism's heyday, from 1850 to 1950. Although there are many skilled writers continuing in the tradition, the theatrical excitement now makes its presence felt in more overtly theatrical styles. But realism as an impulse inevitably remains—and will continue to remain—an important ingredient in theatrical experience.

FURTHER READING

Murphy, Brenda. *American Realism and American Drama, 1880–1940*. Cambridge: Cambridge University Press, 1987.

Styan, J. L. *Modern Drama in Theory and Practice: Realism and Naturalism*. Cambridge: Cambridge University Press, 1981.

Wellek, René. "The Concept of Realism in Literary Scholarship." *Concepts of Criticism*. Edited by Stephen G. Nichols, Jr. New Haven, Connecticut: Yale University Press, 1963.

Realism: A Survey of Modern Plays

Bruce Mann

Realism in drama emerges in full force during the late nineteenth century, propelled by new intellectual currents that focus attention on society and the complexities of human social behavior. Rejecting the conventions of romantic opera and melodrama—heroes and villains, exotic settings, and happy endings—playwrights such as Henrik Ibsen (1828–1906), August Strindberg (1849–1912), and Anton Chekhov (1860–1904) create plays that, in production, give spectators the illusion of eavesdropping on scenes from everyday life. Contributing to this illusion are psychologically complex characters, ordinary prose dialogue, lifelike settings, expressive props, and artfully constructed plots that criticize social conditions and leave audiences with unresolved questions to consider.

The prototypical realistic drama is Ibsen's *A Doll's House* (1879). Its main character, Nora Helmer, brings romantic notions to her marriage with Torvald, a straitlaced pillar of Norwegian society, but during the play, she comes to realize that her father and husband, representatives of society, see her only as a plaything. Nora experiences a profound recognition and slams the door at the end as she leaves her "doll house" and family to learn about herself and the world at large. Brilliantly crafted, although not without vestiges of melodrama, *A Doll's House* inaugurates the mature phase of dramatic realism, with its symbolic, detailed setting and evocative props—a Christmas tree, macaroons, and a dance costume—all of which Ibsen uses to comment on Nora's awareness of society's negative influence on her.

While many realistic plays share a theme of romantic ideas colliding with reality, realism cannot be reduced to a formula. For example, *The Cherry Orchard* (1904), a Russian drama by Chekhov, bears little resemblance to *A Doll's House*.

"Let the things that happen on stage be just as complex and yet as simple as they are in real life," writes the playwright. "For instance, people are having a meal at a table, just having a meal, but at the same time their happiness is being created or their lives are being smashed up." In Chekhov's play, nothing seems to happen, but audiences nevertheless are moved by the loss of an aristocratic family's estate while members of an upwardly mobile class gain in status. Utilizing multiple points of view, changes of focus, an abundance of subtext, and internalized action, Chekhov chronicles a society in transition and communicates the sensation of life as we live it.

Fueling the rise of realism in drama are revolutionary currents of thought in science, philosophy, and the social sciences that find human beings to be less heroic than defenseless and subject to a myriad of determinants beyond their control. In France, Auguste Comte (1798–1857) developed scientific procedures to study social problems, thereby founding modern sociology, and in England, Charles Darwin (1809–92) wrote *The Origin of Species* (1859), arguing that humans, like other animals, depend on heredity and adaptation to survive. In short order, Herbert Spencer eagerly applied Darwin's concept of "survival of the fittest" to the social realm. In *Das Kapital* (1867), political economist Karl Marx (1818–83) predicted social unrest—a class struggle—in capitalist societies, because workers inevitably would overthrow the bourgeoisie. French philosopher Hippolyte Taine (1828–93) claims that human beings are little more than machines, the products of three factors: *la race* (heredity), *le milieu* (environment), and *le moment* (historical situation). And psychologist Sigmund Freud posits the unconscious mind in every individual, filled with irrational, violent needs and desires that can overpower the conscious mind. For serious playwrights, these disturbing insights cry out for dramatic treatment.

Also contributing to the success of realism were numerous theatrical innovations. Smaller theaters, such as the *Théâtre Libre* in Paris (1887), the Independent Theatre in London (1891), and the Provincetown Players on Cape Cod (1915), opened around the world, providing acting spaces suited to the intimate nature of realism. Improved scenography and stage lighting allowed for creation of more realistic and atmospheric settings, and new acting techniques appropriate to realism, most notably by Konstantin Stanislavsky of the Moscow Art Theatre, worked to enhance the appeal and understanding of these kinds of plays.

Other examples of early dramatic realism are Maxim Gorky's *The Lower Depths* (1902) and Strindberg's *Miss Julie* (1888). (Both are also considered examples of "naturalism," a term coined by Emile Zola to designate a more intense form of realism that depicts human beings as suffocated by a hostile society and robbed of their souls.) Later plays containing realistic elements or otherwise indebted to realism could include Susan Glaspell's *Trifles* (1916), Clifford Odets's *Awake and Sing!* (1935), Lillian Hellman's *The Children's Hour* (1934) and *The Autumn*

Garden (1951), Eugene O'Neill's *Long Day's Journey into Night* (1941), Tennessee Williams's *The Glass Menagerie* (1945) and *Cat on a Hot Tin Roof* (1955), Arthur Miller's *Death of a Salesman* (1949), John Osborne's *Look Back in Anger* (1956), Lorraine Hansberry's *A Raisin in the Sun* (1959), Arnold Wesker's *Chicken Soup with Barley* (1960), Marsha Norman's *'night, Mother* (1983), and August Wilson's *Fences* (1985) and *The Piano Lesson* (1987).

More than a century after *A Doll's House,* realism remains a dominant style in today's theater (and perhaps is *the* dominant style in film), even after a host of movements that emerged to oppose it: symbolism, expressionism, surrealism, theatricalism, epic theater, and absurdism. But while realism has proven flexible enough to incorporate aspects of other styles, demonstrating its versatility, it now exerts an undue influence over modern theater, not unlike that of Shakespeare over nineteenth century drama. The ghosts of Ibsen, Strindberg, and Chekhov still hover, recognizably, over contemporary theater. Audiences have become entirely comfortable with realistic plays, and realism's thematic material has become shopworn, limiting its effectiveness as a means of exploring social environments.

FURTHER READING

Drake, Durant and Arthur O. Lovejoy. *Essays in Critical Realism.* London: MacMillan, 1920.

Norris, Christopher. *Truth Matters: Realism, Anti-Realism and Response-Dependence.* Edinburgh: Edinburgh University Press, 2002

Seigel, B.T. *Aesthetic Realism: Three Instances.* New York: Terrain Gallery and Definition Press, 1961.

℘

Surrealism

Robert F. Gross

"Beautiful as the accidental meeting of an umbrella and a sewing machine on the dissection table" exclaimed symbolist poet Comte de Lautréamont. His arresting description of a strange new kind of beauty is often quoted as a prophetic evocation of the surrealist movement that was to come. While classical aesthetics had stressed balance, form, proportion, and above all, the meticulous eye of the artist, Lautréamont praised disjunction, chance, and the objects of mass production. The surrealist looks away from conventional definitions of beauty and meaning, exploring unconventional possibilities elsewhere: in mechanized objects, clichés, transgressive acts, nonsense—and, above all, in dreams.

Surrealist playwrights break the standard rules of dramaturgy taught in schools and parroted by critics. Rather than causally developed plots, they write plays that unfold like dreams or pageants or strange, parodic fragments. Rather than psychologically complex characters, they create figures who are two-dimensional or unfold in continual flux. Rather than rational arguments, they spin out chains of associations. Instead of sketching out a play's plot line in advance, they often allow themselves to be carried away through an uncensored flow of verbal associations known as "automatic writing." The lines between male and female, past and future, life and death, animate and inanimate, are repeatedly dissolved.

Influenced by psychoanalysis, the surrealists were fascinated with how dreams, drug-induced hallucinations, techniques of free association and the workings of chance could reveal the workings of the unconscious. André Breton (1896–1966), the chief apologist for the surrealist movement in France and self-appointed arbiter of surrealist orthodoxy (a strangely contradictory position), explained in the *Surrealist Manifesto* of 1924 that "Surrealism is based on the belief in the superior reality of certain forms of previously neglected associations, in the omnipotence of dream, the disinterested play of thought. It tends to ruin all other psychic mechanisms once and for all, and to substitute itself for them in solving all the principal problems of life." Preferring the poetry of the unconscious to the instrumentality of consciousness, the fundamental impulses of the movement remained anarchic, even though some surrealists, including Breton, tried to link their efforts to communism.

Rejecting all the assumptions of mainstream commercial and academic drama in the twentieth century, surrealism has produced few box-office successes. Indeed, its playwrights—a bright, audacious, and visionary lot—have generally spent their careers on the margins. And yet they have produced some of the most vital, insightful, and innovative theatrical work to appear since the beginning of the last century.

SURREALIST DRAMA AND PLAYWRIGHTS

Strindberg

Theatrical maverick August Strindberg's *A Dream Play* (*Ett Drömspel*, 1902) set the direction for surrealism with its explorations of the fluid and mysterious relationships between human life, theatrical representation, and dream. Rather than following the strict patterns of causality and probability that defined realistic drama, Strindberg explained:

> Anything can happen; everything is possible and probable. Time and space do not exist. Working with some unimportant actual events as a background, the imagination weaves them into new patterns—a mixture of memories, spontaneous notions, impossibilities, and improbabilities.

In *A Dream Play* decades can pass before our eyes in moments. A lawyer's hands can grow stained and cracked with the crimes his clients confess to him. A palace can blossom from the manure of a garden. Strindberg does not merely blur the lines between life, theater, and dream; he renders them identical.

It took more than a decade, however, for Strindberg's visionary experiment to begin to be joined by similar experiments. The first notable examples of surrealism appeared, not in spoken drama, but in the French musical theater. The young poet and jack-of-all-artistic trades, Jean Cocteau (1889–1963) hoped to launch his celebrity by creating a new ballet for Serge Diaghilev's Ballets Russes that would rival the controversy it had unleashed in 1913 with the premiere of Igor Stravinsky's *The Rite of Spring*. Cocteau wrote the scenario, enlisted Erik Satie to write the score, Leonid Massine to choreograph, and Pablo Picasso to design sets and costumes. Although *Parade* (1917) never provoked anywhere near the outrage that *The Rite of Spring* had, it diverged sufficiently from the expectations of the

Ballets Russes's patrons—who had swooned over the lush exoticism of Nikolai Rimsky-Korsakov's *Schéhérazade* and Stravinsky's *The Firebird*—to spark some hostility.

Cocteau

In French, a *parade* is an entertainment put on by circus performers outside the tent to lure customers inside. In Cocteau's *Parade*, the performers include a pair of acrobats, a Chinese magician, and a "little American girl" in a sailor suit resembling the heroine of a silent film adventure serial. Promoting the attractions to be seen inside are the "Managers," oversized three-dimensional cubist collages with hats and pipes, accompanied by Picasso's cubist reinvention of a pantomime horse. Despite all the Managers' efforts, however, they fail to make the customers realize that the "real" show is offstage. Erik Satie's score, drawing on ragtime and popular dance forms, was overlaid (much to his consternation) with the sounds of sirens, whistles, and typewriters.

Parade's provocative intrusion of contemporary popular culture into the elite world of high culture became one of the defining characteristics of surrealist performance. The surrealists rejected what they considered the stultified decorum of bourgeois art to embrace the rougher vitality they found in the circus, music hall, movie theater, boxing ring, and jazz club. They praised the comedy of Charlie Chaplin and the Marx Brothers and the jazz dancing of Josephine Baker. They explored comic strips, silent movie serials, detective magazines, and pornography. The surrealists shared an aversion to high culture and bourgeois values with the contemporaneous Dada movement, but whereas the Dadaists aggressively attacked the status quo with its notions of anti-art, the surrealists were more inclined to champion the transformation of art rather than its obliteration.

The term "surrealism" first appeared in the program notes to *Parade* by Guillaume Apollinaire (1880–1918), arguably the first surrealist poet. Apollinaire praised the production's fusion of decor with choreography in the cubist presentation of the Managers; he wrote that it led to a "kind of super-realism (*sur-réalisme*), in which I see the starting point of a series of manifestations of the new spirit." The new word soon was appropriated as the name of the fledgling artistic movement, though its meaning, as we shall see, quickly grew more complex and contested.

Cocteau followed *Parade* with two further ventures into musical theater. Composer Darius Milhaud had returned from Brazil and had penned a lighthearted rondo inspired by the popular music he had heard there. Its title, *The Ox on the Roof* (*Le Boeuf sur le Toit*, 1920) was appropriated from a Brazilian song, as were some of the tunes. He had hoped that the score might inspire a film script by Charlie Chaplin, but Cocteau persuaded Milhaud to let him write a stage scenario for it. Cocteau set the piece in a fanciful evocation of an American speakeasy, with a boxer, a bookie, a society lady, a cross-dressing woman, and an African American dwarf among the clientele. The gamblers' dice were large cardboard cubes, the cigarette smoke was indicated by five large rings hanging in the air, and the bartender wore a mask taken from a sculpture of the Roman emperor Hadrian's paramour, Antinoüs. When the policeman raided the illegal nightspot, it was suddenly transformed into a milk bar. After the policeman was decapitated by a fan, the woman in male drag danced with his head, à la Salome, before returning it to its body. Resuscitated, he was handed a bill a yard long. Throughout the performance, acrobatic clowns wearing oversized masks moved in slow motion while Milhaud's music rushed ahead cheerfully.

In *The Eiffel Tower Wedding Party* (*Les Mariés de la Tour Eiffel*, 1921), Cocteau collaborated with the group of young composers who called themselves "The Six" (Darius Milhaud, Georges Auric, Arthur Honegger, Francis Poulenc, Louis Durey, and Germaine Tailleferre) to create a theatrical piece that played on the double meanings of the French word "cliché"—"snapshot" and "trite expression." It shows a bourgeois wedding party visiting the first platform on the Eiffel Tower on Bastille Day for a photographic group portrait. Two performers, dressed as phonographs, stand to either side of the stage, narrating the events and declaiming the masked dancers' dialogue. The wedding party is described by the phonographs in a series of clichés:

> The Bride, gentle as a lamb.
> The Father-in-Law, rich as Croesus.
> The Bridegroom, handsome as Apollo.
> The Mother-in-Law, false as a bad penny.
> The General, stupid as a goose.

The party had planned to memorialize itself, but it turns out to be more difficult than anticipated. A hunter appears on the Eiffel Tower, stalking an ostrich that turns out to have emerged from the photographer's camera when he asked a posing subject to "watch the birdie." His attempts to take a photograph are interrupted as figures emerge from his apparatus: a bathing beauty, a lion, and the as yet unconceived child of the bridal pair. When the camera is finally working properly, he "takes" their picture, as they disappear inside. In a final transformation, the camera moves off like a railway train with the wedding party within it, waving their handkerchiefs at the audience as they exit.

In Cocteau's musical theater pieces, plot is reduced to little more than a succession of images. Characters, rather than being individualized, are easily recognizable types. The respectability of the bourgeoisie and figures of authority is mocked, while the louche and exotic are celebrated. The impersonal inventions of the modern world—the photograph and phonograph—are regarded ambivalently; they simultaneously mirror the soulless anonymity of the middle class and provide new forms of enchantment and artistic delight.

Other French Surrealists in Drama

The surrealists would continue to attack such institutions as the family, organized religion, formal education, and the state. Often they would mock the banalities of the commercial stage with its predictable, realistic style and narrow focus on domestic issues and adulterous intrigue. In Raymond Radiguet's *The Pelicans* (*Les Pélican,* 1921), the dilemmas of the Pelican family parody those of domestic drama: the eminently respectable father wants his son to be a poet, only to learn that he wishes to be a jockey. His daughter wins the Christmas Day Swimming Race on the Seine, and incidentally saves a photographer who had tried to drown himself. "Miracle of miracles!" exclaims the overjoyed mother. "My daughter wins the first prize in swimming on the day when the Seine is frozen."

One of the most spritely surrealist send-ups of bourgeois norms was also one of the earliest; Guillaume Apollinaire had worked intermittently since 1903 on his drama, *The Breasts of Tiresias* (*Les Mamelles de Tirésias*), and completed it in 1917. Set in a totally imaginary Zanzibar—inspired by a popular French game of chance, not the island in the Indian Ocean—its bored and discontented heroine opens her blouse to release her breasts, red and blue balloons, which she then explodes with a cigarette lighter. Immediately thereafter, she sprouts a beard and mustache, and takes the name "Tiresias." Her husband, in turn, dresses in her skirts, takes up with a policeman, and soon finds himself able to give birth to 40,050 children a day—a talent that soon threatens Zanzibar with overpopulation. Disaster is averted, however, as husband and wife resume their previous sex roles and reunite.

In *The Mirror-Wardrobe One Fine Evening* (*L'Armoire à Glace Un Beau Soir,* 1923) Louis Aragon (1897–1982) begins with a hackneyed device borrowed from the commercial theater: the wife, wild-eyed, stands between an armoire and her husband, who suspects that her lover is hidden inside it. Expectations are quickly undermined as the conventional roles are reversed: the wife repeatedly urges the husband to open the wardrobe, while he is disinclined to do so. What could be a spoof, however, quickly deepens through Aragon's use of richly imagistic language. The theme of the play becomes the erotic mystery of the Unknown. When the husband finally opens the wardrobe, the characters from the play's prologue mysteriously emerge, hand-in-hand, dance a jig in the twilight, and listen to a song whose lyric summons up a dreamlike vision of desire:

> My arms of bark my arms of birds
> Clasp the air I breathe,
> Her two legs are a scissors
> On which the wind is cut...

Starting with theatrical cliché, Aragon undercuts both plot and character through seemingly unmotivated actions and disjunctive images. In so doing, he achieves the primary goal of the surrealist movement: to transcend everyday consciousness by tapping the unconscious.

The French surrealist movement did little to support experimentation in the theater, due largely to the leadership of André Breton, who saw any collaboration with the theater hopelessly reactionary. He blasted Cocteau as "a notorious false poet, a versifier who happens to debase rather than elevate everything he touches." In his *Second Manifesto* (1930), he expelled the two members of his circle who had been most involved in the theater: Antonin Artaud (1896–1948) and Roger Vitrac (1899–1952). Artaud, creator of the Theatre of Cruelty and author of the volume of visionary essays collected under the title *The Theatre and Its Double,* developed his own highly individual theory of the theater, more expressionist than surrealist, and became the most influential French theater theorist and practitioner of the twentieth century. Roger Vitrac, the author of *The Mysteries of Love* (*Les Mystères de l'Amour,* 1937) and *Victor or Power to the Children* (*Victor ou les Enfants au Pouvoir,* 1937), became the only French surrealist playwright besides Cocteau to enjoy any success in the professional theater.

Witkiewicz and Dramatic Surrealism in Poland

The master of surrealist dramaturgy in the years between World War I and World War II, however, was never involved in the internecine feuds of the Parisian art scene. In the Polish city of Zakopane, living most of his life in one or another of his mother's boarding houses, Stanisław Ignacy Witkiewicz (1885–1939) created the most extensive and stunning corpus of surrealist plays. Eccentric, provocative, and totally at odds with the Polish artistic establishment, Witkiewicz (or "Witkacy," as he often called himself)—novelist, philosopher, painter, photographer, and, above all, dramatist—enjoyed little recognition during his lifetime, and his posthumous recognition was hindered by the authoritarian regimes that controlled cultural life in his native land for decades. It was not until 1956 that one of his plays was revived in Poland, but his work underwent a major rediscovery with the coming of the theater of the absurd and postmodernism. He is increasingly recognized as one of the leading playwrights of the twentieth century, with such masterpieces as *They* (*Oni,* 1920), *Metaphysics of a Two-Headed Calf* (*Metafizyka Dwuglowego Cielecia,* 1921), *The Water Hen* (*Kurka Wodna,,* 1921), *Janulka, Daughter of Fidezko* (*Janulka, Corka Fizdejki,* 1923), and *The Shoemakers* (*Szewcy,* 1934).

Witkiewicz's *The Water Hen* opens with a tableau representative of the playwright-cum-painter's intensely visual imagination. In an open field by the sea, a man in eighteenth century garb aims a shotgun at a woman in a chemise. She stands on a mound of earth, bound to a crimson pole from which hangs an octagonal lantern of green glass. Behind this strange couple, the red setting sun illuminates a sky filled with fantastically shaped clouds. When the man eventually fires his shotgun at the woman, she calmly observes "One miss. The other straight through the heart," and continues to converse with her killer for some time before she expires. Just as Louis Aragon developed *The Mirror-Wardrobe One Fine Evening*, Witkiewicz builds *The Water Hen* out of clichés—in this case the fatal sex war between husband and wife á la Strindberg—but he reinvigorates it through elements of parody, dream, anachronism, and vivid stage imagery.

Witkiewicz believed in the primacy of "Pure Form" in drama. Although drama could never achieve the total abstract form of music or painting, he argued that it was formal elements, not mimetic subject matter, which endow a play with power and a claim to permanence. The mixture of human actions with strongly formal elements, such as the striking stage picture that opens *The Water Hen*, aims to convey the mystery of human existence and elicits metaphysical feelings in the spectator. Pure Form, as the bearer of metaphysical feelings, is the sole weapon to combat the increasing soullessness of modernity.

For Witkiewicz, the modern world is entropic. People are becoming more and more incapable of experiencing the mystery of existence; the interest in and capacity for aesthetic feeling and philosophic thought are steadily diminishing. Instead we turn to narcotics, fads, and the increasingly strident stimulation of the movies. Dwarfed by comparison to figures of the past, we are condemned to be wannabes. The repertoire of past cultural types—whether the romantic artist, the femme fatale, the tyrant, or the Nietzschean superman—have all become hopelessly passé and can only be relived as parodies. At the same time, no new roles present themselves. Witkiewicz's protagonists are often victims of a hypertrophied consciousness which impels them to make ever more extreme choices in the vain pursuit of meaning; choices that only lead them to become increasingly bizarre self-parodies.

Witkiewicz's *Janulka, Daughter of Fidezko* takes a popular piece of nineteenth century Polish historical fiction as its jumping-off point, but collages its fourteenth century setting with references to Picasso, Schönberg, Einstein, and contemporary philosophy. The King of Lithuania's throne room is outfitted with a stylish café serviced by minor nobility ("People of a certain psychological makeup can't live without cafés," the monarch observes). Intrigue, coups, and mass bloodshed lead not to the excitement of a romantic potboiler, but to mounting disillusionment and ennui, as the characters realize that they are thin retreads of historical heroes and heroines of bygone days. The Master of the Teutonic Knights finally removes his armor and walks about in violet pajamas with a matching nightcap. The Princess Janulka wearies of her powerful and ambitious suitors and yearns for an ordinary man. When, in a parody of fairy tale romance, a grotesquely birdlike monster is transformed into the man of Janulka's dreams, he is nothing more than a suave "monster-about-town" in a gray suit and spats, who reminds his inamorata that their romance is inevitably banal: "we know—and so does everybody else—what love is like from all those realistic plays—in French, German, Dutch, Polish, and even Lithuanian and Romanian..." But the lapse into banality does not ensure security, as we see when all the major characters are butchered by a band of Boyars in the final moments of the play, and a new king and queen prepare to ascend the throne. For Witkiewicz, the greatest barbarity exists comfortably alongside the highest achievements of modernity.

Dramatic Surrealism in Belgium

In Belgium, Michel de Ghelderode (1898–1962) relished the excesses, savageries, and strange beauties of the medieval, Renaissance and baroque periods. Like Witkiewicz, Ghelderode aimed to create a sense of mystery in his spectators, and turned away from what he took to be the sadly demystified modern world. He was inspired by biblical tales, medieval legends, the grotesque images of painters Hieronymus Bosch and James Ensor, the circus, the music hall, and above all, the puppet theater. A work of dark eroticism, *Lord Halewyn* (*Sire Halewijn,* 1934) draws on a Flemish folk song, and tells of a serial killer who more than meets his match in the beautiful princess who decapitates him, displays his head triumphantly in her father's court, and dies. His most notorious work, *Chronicles of Hell* (*Fastes d'enfer,* 1929) is set in a decaying episcopal palace with tapestries hanging in shreds and the edges of the chamber heaped with "baroque objects, idols, suns, witches' masks, multicolored devils, totems, stakes, and instruments of torture." The bishop, Jan in Eremo, reputedly the offspring of a mermaid and a monk, stalks the palace in a demonic state between life and death, unable to dislodge the poisoned consecrated host that was given him on his sickbed by a rival cleric.

Other plays of Ghelderode display a bawdy sense of humor or a wistful, melancholy charm. *Christopher Columbus* (*Christophe Colomb,* 1927) is one of the latter. Its title character is an implacable dreamer, delighted with spheres, who is first seen admiring the roundness of the soap bubbles he blows. In his voyage across the Atlantic Ocean, he encounters a siren and his own guardian angel, and finally meets Montezuma, with whom he dances joyfully on ship deck.

U.S. Dramatic Realism Between the World Wars

In the United States, nonrealistic playwrights between the World Wars tended to be more influenced by expressionism than surrealism. One of the few exceptions was E. E. Cummings's (1894–1962) *Him,* an ambitious, sprawling play about a playwright writing a play about a playwright writing a play that remains one of the most admired American surrealist experiments.

Though vastly more prolific in his dramatic output than Cummings, William Saroyan (1908–81) is nevertheless similarly remembered for only one of his plays—*The Time of Your Life* (1939), a gently affectionate study of drifters in a saloon. Most of his other plays enjoyed only brief professional runs or amateur productions, and some remain unperformed. First gaining attention in the commercial theater for gentle dramas of poetic realism, Saroyan developed his own distinct variety of surrealism from the 1940s onward. Without either the irony or sexual menace that often characterize the works of his European counterparts, these whimsical, sometimes sentimental, celebrations of the Common Man and childlike innocence tap a vein of feeling that is distinctly American. When asked to explain one of his plays, Saroyan answered, "The theme of the play is quite simple. It's contemptuous of the phony, that's all."

Saroyan's dramaturgy is distinguished by its disdain for conventional structure and a preference for open-ended, improvisational forms—an approach that has led him to be seen as a precursor of the beatniks and hippies. While *Love's Old Sweet Song* (1940) was in rehearsal, Saroyan was more than willing to write new scenes for any eccentric actors who came to him with ideas. He considered including a woman who wanted to parachute onto the stage, but was dissuaded when he realized the stunt could prove lethal. *Sam, The Highest Jumper of Them All* (1960) developed out of improvisations by the cast during rehearsals. *Sweeney in the Trees* (1939) presents a series of scenes loosely arranged around the conflict between creativity and materialism, while a tree grows mysteriously within the apartment building that serves as the setting. *Jim Dandy, Fat Man in a Famine* (1941) is structured between expressions of joy and despair, set in a transparent eggshell that contains the world in miniature—complete with ruins, a public library, a jail, a circus wagon, and other locales. All of these plays preach the need to embrace life in all its glorious variety and eccentricity, and to love each other. Though largely forgotten, Saroyan's plays remain the most significant body of American surrealist drama to appear before the 1960s, and may well merit reassessment.

Links with Absurdism

In the 1950s and 1960s, playwrights were less influenced by surrealism than by absurdism, with its cooler, more alienated tone and existentialist musings. But the line between the two movements is far from clear-cut. Although Arthur Adamov (1908–70) has been identified with the theater of the absurd, he edited a surrealist journal, and his early plays create a nightmarish atmosphere of dread. *Professor Taranne* (*Le Professeur Taranne*, 1953), a one-act play about a professor accused of a series of offenses including indecent exposure, was based on an actual dream of the playwright's. Eugène Ionesco (1909–94) displayed a fondness for nonsense and oneiric images that often makes him appear closer to his predecessors Cocteau and Vitrac than his absurdist contemporaries Samuel Beckett and Jean Genet. In *Amédée or How to Get Rid of It* (*Amédée ou Comment s'en débarraser*,

1954), the dead love between a married couple is embodied in a corpse that grows larger and larger, filling their apartment. The continual flux between life and death and dream and waking life in *Journeys Among the Dead* (*Voyages chez les morts*, 1982) suggests a strong affinity to Strindberg's *A Dream Play*. In Poland, Slawomir Mrozek's *Tango* (*Tango*, 1964) and Tadeusz Rozewicz's *White Marriage* (*Biale Malzenstwo*, 1979) are only two of many plays that show the influence of Witkiewicz's experiments in the 1920s and 1930s.

British Surrealistic Drama

Although the French surrealists admitted an affinity with those British masters of nonsense Lewis Carroll and Edward Lear, surrealism has had little influence on the British stage until recently. While absurdism influenced the work of Harold Pinter and N. F. Simpson in the late 1950s, the surrealists were ignored. Tom Stoppard (b. 1937) was inspired by the paintings of René Magritte in his one-act, *After Magritte* (1970) and frolicked about with the origins of Dada in *Travesties* (1974) with an impishness far closer in spirit to Cocteau's surrealism than Dada's indignation. Caryl Churchill (b. 1938) has made some forays into surrealist territory, most notably with her reworking of fairy tale motifs in *The Skriker*, a sinister tale of a shapeshifter in modern London. But no British playwright has been as consistently surrealist as the brilliant and sadly underrated Snoo Wilson (b. 1948), who has often been dismissed with faint praise as a "cult author." Wilson's dramatic universe is vast and protean, mixing history, myth, occult lore, dream, and science fiction in a single work. *Moonshine* (1999) begins with a bizarre fact: Sir Arthur Conan Doyle believed that fairies had actually been sighted and photographed in the English countryside. Wilson sets Doyle out on a trip to photograph the fairies, only to encounter Abraxas, the Lord of Heaven, who is trying to save the earth from collision with a meteorite propelled by his malevolent son Moloch (propagated by his father in an unfortunate moment of cosmic masturbation). Moloch is not only the Prince of Darkness, but a malign media tycoon who assumed human form in Australia, bearing a disconcerting and delightful affinity to media tycoon Rupert Murdoch. Unlike Murdoch, however, he also is the father of twin daughters with a growing appetite for human flesh who are "clad in extravagantly bad-taste trailer-trash rag-doll punk." Needless to say, it is up to Doyle to save planet Earth—and he does.

For Wilson, the everyday world depicted in realist dramas is actually propelled by irrational forces that often manifest themselves nakedly in his plays through the unanticipated arrival of figures of mythic proportions. In *Moonshine* it is Abraxas and Moloch. In *Darwin's Flood* (1994), Charles Darwin is visited on the eve of his death by Friedrich Nietzsche and Jesus. The play allows the three to debate philosophical points, but they also manifest incredible energy in less intellectual pursuits. Nietzsche, degenerating into the last stages of syphilis and reduced to travelling in a wheelbarrow pushed by his sister Elizabeth, is determined to be castrated by a male prostitute, but has to settle for the less fierce attentions of Mary Magdalene, who appears as a somewhat blasé professional dominatrix. Jesus, who appears in the form of an Northern Irish long-distance bicyclist, spends much of his visit up in the bedroom with Darwin's devoutly Christian wife, Emma, but proves sadly incapable of committing to a long-term relationship. These eruptions of primal energy, however, are not only manifested in the characters but in moments of stage spectacle: Darwin's father's face appears in the ceiling of his library, eventually crashing to the floor and leaving a hole in the ceiling, allowing Mary Magdalene to make her first entrance lowered down by a helicopter; the ark, portending another deluge, pushes its way up to the surface from beneath Darwin's back lawn. In Wilson's intellectually dense, visually extravagant, and comically inventive work, the energies of magic, sexuality, and artistic creativity repeatedly succeed in escaping from the straitjackets society tailors.

But while surrealist experimentation in England has been relatively scant, the contemporary American theater currently boasts a number of notable playwrights who continue to manifest surrealist impulses in their work. Indeed, there are more playwrights in Manhattan today who can confidently be labeled "surrealist" than could be found in 1930s Paris.

"Nothing is as beautiful as a mystery" remarks Robert Wilson (b. 1941)—a comment that reveals his surrealist proclivities. His position as a successor to the French surrealists was confirmed in 1971, when his eight-and-a-half hour *Deafman Glance* was performed in Paris. After seeing it, Louis Aragon, one of the few surviving first-generation surrealists, enthused, "Bob Wilson is not a surrealist. He is what we, with whom surrealism was born, dreamed would come after us and go beyond us." A highly visual artist, many of Wilson's most important works have been storyboarded rather than written, and the most arresting moments of his productions have usually been visual. In *The King of Spain* (1969), monstrous feline paws, reaching from floor to ceiling, crossed the stage. In his staging of Euripides' *Alcestis* (1986) cypress trees were slowly transformed—first into Corinthian columns, then into smokestacks. Wilson's use of tableaux and slow, sometimes almost imperceptible movements evoke a dreamlike state. Like Lautréamont, he reveals qualities through the juxtaposition of disparate objects. As he has explained, the placement of a baroque candlestick on a baroque table reveals nothing about either, while the placement of the same candlestick on a rock will begin to reveal the properties of both. So, for example, in *The Golden Windows* (1982), an unidentified man hung by his neck against a night sky, as someone breezily whistled "A Bicycle Built For Two." The hanging was completely decontextualized, all the more disturbing for remaining unexplained.

Recent American Surrealistic Drama

Two of the earliest of these new American surrealists remain the most admired and influential. Adrienne Kennedy (b. 1931) has brought a sharp awareness of problems of race and gender to surrealism. *The Funnyhouse of a Negro* (1960) ends with its African American protagonist, Sarah, committing suicide, haunted and drawn to figures of whiteness, such as the plaster statue of Queen Victoria that sits on the stage. *A Movie Star Has to Star in Black and White* (1976) gives a more hopeful version of a similar struggle, as the heroine deals with the images of white Hollywood—taken from *Now Voyager, A Place in the Sun,* and *Viva Zapata*—by learning to write her own plays. Sam Shepard (b. 1943) created a distinctly American surrealist landscape of gangsters, hipsters, and rock 'n rollers in his early works. In *Mad Dog Blues* (1971), for example, a rock star and his side-kick encounter Paul Bunyan, Captain Kidd, and a whip-wielding Marlene Dietrich in their wanderings. Although both Shepard and Kennedy have tended increasingly toward realism in their later work, the surrealist influence remains evident.

Suzan-Lori Parks (b. 1954) has created haunted dreamscapes of the African American experience of racism and violence in *The America Play* and *The Death of the Last Black Man in the Whole World* (both 1990). In his whimsical humor and gentle affection for idiosyncratic drifters, Len Jenkin (b. 1941) can be seen as the successor to William Saroyan. Jenkin's landscape, seen in such plays as *Dark Ride* (1981), *American Notes* (1988), and *Like I Say* (1998) is a sprawling nocturnal expanse of freeways, strip malls, and rundown motels, largely peopled by insomniac drifters whose tales are dreamlike pastiches of weird themes from comic books, pulp fiction, tabloid journalism, and B movies.

Mac Wellman (b. 1945) has satirized the hypocrisy and anti-intellectualism of American conservatism in *Sincerity Forever* (1990) and *Seven Blowjobs* (1991), and has brought space aliens into suburban and small-town America with *Cleveland* (1986) and *Whirligig* (1989). A theatrical poet with an ear for the vernacular, Wellman spins out long arias that expose the panic, anger, and lone-liness that characterize much of contemporary American life: "Now we all, each and every one, are orphans" concludes Mr. William Hard in *The Hyacinth Macaw* (1994). Wellman's essay, "A Chrestomathy of Twenty-Two Answers to Twenty-Two Wholly Unaskable and Unrelated Questions Concerning Political and Poetic Theater" (1993) argues with great humor and insight against the hidebound, neo-Aristotelian "Geezer Theater" of the theatrical establishment in America, and celebrates a "Poetic Theater" that is bold enough to bend time, court chaos, and avoid tedious sermonizing.

David Greenspan (b. 1956) has brought a gay sensibility to American surreal-ism. *Son of a Pioneer* (1994) and *Dead Mother, or Shirley Not All in Vain* (1990) revisit the loneliness and frustration of middle-class domesticity from a gay perspective. The former begins with outside a "nice suburban home" and ends on the wastes of Mars, where the father in the form of a bear forces his son to have oral sex with him. The latter shows a gay son's disturbing ability to channel his deceased, emotionally disturbed and homophobic mother, and sends him to visit her in the underworld, where she sits watching an episode of *Hollywood Squares*. In *The Myopia: An Epic Burlesque of Tragic Proportion* (2003), a domestic drama with fairy tale motifs unfolds within a historical satire. A bravura one-man show performed by its author, *The Myopia* shows a young writer who is trying both to write a play about his parent's miserable marriage and finish his father's uncompleted musical on the life of President Warren G. Harding, with a character reminiscent of musical comedy star Carol Channing serving as play doctor. Like Cummings's *Him, The Myopia* confounds multiple levels of reality and a rich range of genres as it dramatizes the drama of a playwright searching for his drama.

No current theatrical artist more clearly exemplifies the ongoing persistence and creative vitality of the surrealist tradition than playwright, director, designer, and theoretician Richard Foreman (b. 1937), founder and artistic director of the Ontological-Hysteric Theatre. Like his surrealist predecessors, Foreman has written about his productions as dreams: "I try to make plays as hard to remember as a vivid dream which, when awake, you know you have lived with intensity, yet try as you might you can't remember." Working to burst the theatrical straitjackets commonly employed to give every moment in a production a clear and unambiguous meaning—plot, character, theme, and atmosphere—Foreman works on every aspect of a production to open it up to a range of competing, even chaotic impulses. A person who has admitted being annoyed whenever anyone asks him the question "How are you?" because it seems to him unanswerable, Foreman has created a theater that cuts through our habitual responses to uncover the rich anarchy that seethes beneath our most confident formulations.

As a dramatist, he has sometimes revived the practice of automatic writing, putting himself in a state between sleep and waking, and allowing the words to flow from that state. Rather than follow a prepared scenario, he produces notebooks filled with material in the form of prose poems and then assembles them into dramatic texts that develop through strategies of association, disjunction, and, most importantly, contradiction. At the beginning of *Paradise Hotel* (1999), a voice tells us that this title is only a facade for another play, *Hotel Fuck*, which in turn fronts yet another play, *Hotel Beautiful Roses*. Idealization and raunchy physicality coexist and in the course of the performance become increasingly indistinguishable from each other. It is not a matter of a pretty illusion masking a sordid reality. Rather, oppositions in Foreman inevitably elicit and contain each other.

In production, Foreman works to further complicate our responses. A character might say, "How beautiful this is!" but snarl the line with disgust and an aggressive gesture, or back away from the "beautiful" object in horror. Objects themselves often manifest ambivalence; for *The Cure* (1986), Foreman designed upholstered furniture that suggested at once tables and sofas. A seemingly straightforward object may be used in such a way that it comes to evoke unfamiliar associations through its use; a lamp may be used as a weapon, a piece of food, or a sexual organ. The sets are similarly multivalent: the setting for *Film is Evil: Radio is Good* (1987) suggested at once a radio studio, a classroom, and a hotel lobby.

Following the surrealist tradition, Foreman has relied on elements of chance to shape his productions. In the early years of the Ontological-Hysteric Theatre, actors were told to wear whatever they wore to the first rehearsal for the run of the show. A red shirt or a faded pair of blue jeans thus became a "found object" that was incorporated into the visual composition of the production. When a favorite actress said she wanted more lines in a scene, Foreman took the script and transferred some lines written for another character to her.

In one of his essays, Foreman describes what might be the utopian vision behind all surrealist theater: "I can imagine every member of the audience falling asleep and the play continuing to the end, turning into an objectification of the dream of that audience." Through the imaginations of Richard Foreman, Snoo Wilson, David Greenspan, and many others, umbrellas, sewing machines, and as-yet unnamed objects continue to encounter each other on the dissection tables of the theater.

FURTHER READING

Benedikt, Michael and George E. Wellwarth, eds. and trans. *Modern French Theatre: An Anthology of Plays. The Avant-Garde, Dada, and Surrealism.* New York: Dutton, 1966.

Foreman, Richard. *Unbalancing Acts: Foundations for a Theater.* New York: Pantheon Books, 1992.

Witkiewicz, S.I. *The Witkiewicz Reader.* Translated and Edited by Daniel Gerould. Evanston, Illinois: Northwestern University Press, 1992.

❧

Tragedy

Kimball King

Not surprisingly, more audiences are interested in dramatic comedy than in dramatic tragedy. Yet tragic drama is seldom depressing. Beginning in ancient Greece it affirmed the nobility and high stature of characters at the same time that it revealed their doom. Sophocles's King Oedipus is a "tragic" figure but he is also larger than life, creative, inquiring and estimable in many ways.

One can say that Oedipus had a quick temper and that he should have remained home with his foster parents and never married; but it is ultimately revealed that he accidentally kills his own father, whom he had never seen before (as the result of an argument over right-of-way on the road to Delphi), marries his mother, and sires incestuous children. Although his wife/mother commits suicide and he blinds himself for his misdeeds, it is impossible to see him as a completely "bad" person. In *Oedipus The King* the will of the Gods must prevail over man's will and the prophesies of the Gods will come true. Antigone, as the daughter of Oedipus, is also doomed from birth. However, in the play *Antigone* she sacrifices her own life in order to bury her brother properly. Finally in the third play, *Oedipus at Colonnus,* in what is often considered Sophocles's tragic trilogy, the former king is forgiven by the gods and finds a measure of peace.

Centuries later Arthur Miller would say that Willy Loman in *Death of a Salesman* is a "tragic" character. In the middle of the twentieth century as the unhappiness of ordinary men seemed to increase, Willy's eventual suicide indicates the failure of a society to provide attainable goals for the average person. Willy Loman then becomes symbolic, representing all "low-men" who have been deceived into believing that good looks, affability, and athletic talent guarantee wealth and happiness. Everyday protagonists can be seen therefore to have tragic lives, not because their own lives influence others, but because a deeply flawed world has marked them for disappointment. Ironically, a world which presently provides more opportunities for self-realization seems to have produced a passive rather than an active tragic hero or heroine.

Many argue that the true era of tragedy developed in Greece in the fifth century B.C. Foremost among the philosophers who describe tragedy was Aristotle. S.H. Butcher translated Aristotle as saying: "Tragedy is an imitation of an action that is serious, complete, and of a certain magnitude; in language embellished with each kind of artistic ornament, the several kinds being found in separate parts of the play; in the form of action, not of narrative; through pity and fear affecting the proper catharsis or purgation of these emotions."

We must ask ourselves if only pity and fear will be removed when we experience "catharsis" in a tragedy, or if other emotions, possibly destructive, will also be purged. It seems that Greek tragedy suggests that humankind is flawed and will always fail, sometimes quite excruciatingly, to achieve perfection. Coming to terms with imperfection, learning to compromise, learning to accept a humble position in the order of things is one way to avoid becoming a tragic victim. Yet there is a grandeur in the protagonist who refuses to be conventional or ordinary. The ancient Greek Oedipus with his desire to rule with complete authority and wisdom, Macbeth in England's Renaissance wanting to be "number one" in his kingdom, both suffer and are destroyed.

Interestingly, there are always men and women who are "risk-takers," who are willing to face disaster if there is a chance of obtaining grandeur or power. Comic characters share many traits with tragic ones. For example, hubris (arrogance or ego-inflation) could describe not only Sophocles's Oedipus but also Shakespeare's Malvolio in *Twelfth Night*. Malvolio is basically a comic character, a buffoon in the author's eyes. Ultimately Aristotle concentrated on the pity and fear one felt when viewing a tragic play and the sort of relief that is experienced when a protagonist is struck down and man's diminished role, as decided by the Greek gods, is established.

The Roman Seneca also depicted a tragic universe. But his tragedies often concentrated on gruesome behavioral tales—such as forms of cannibalism or vengeance. In the English Renaissance nearly any violent or alarming detail in a play was called "Senecan."

Gotthold Lessing in the eighteenth century mainly continued Aristotle's views of tragedy. He wrote comedies like *Minna Von Barnhelm* but he also believed that the purpose of both comedy and tragedy was moral improvement. The purpose of tragedy, he wrote, was to educate audiences to higher levels of character, to experience compassion and pity for those who had overreached themselves. Fear is a major element in tragedy and possibly an audience derives a secret pleasure from knowing that, because most people avoid risky behavior, they are unlikely to experience catastrophe. Perversely, great tragedies, such as *Agamemnon, Thyestes, Hamlet,* and others tend to restore order to the world and to make audiences feel comfortable with their own mediocrity. However, tragic-comedies or so called "dark" comedies may be more troubling. Beckett's Vladimir and Estragon in *Waiting for Godot* waiting endlessly for a Mr. Godot, who will probably never appear, are more troublesome than a murderer like Shakespeare's *Richard III* who will die in battle and become "the Scourge of God," removing evil from the earth and "cleansing" the British monarchy by his own departure.

People are made uncomfortable by the ambiguities of the theater of the absurd, by the suggestion that humans have learned nothing in their long history and that life is senseless and redemption is unattainable. What could be more "tragic" than the conclusion of Beckett's *Endgame*, where Clov claims he will leave Hamm forever, but he remains in a claustrophobic room because life on the "outside" is physically and emotionally impossible. Tragedy is consoling in a world that believes in hierarchy and divine justice. In a relativistic universe tragedy and comedy blend into an unbearable uneasiness, a permanent sense of insecurity.

FURTHER READING

Campbell, Lewis. *Tragic Drama in Aeschylus, Sophocles and Shakespeare: An Essay.* London: John Murray, 1904.
Leaska, Mitchell A. *The Voice of Tragedy.* New York: Robert Spillor and Sons, 1963.
Wadeck, Peter B. *Weighing Delight and Dole.* Peter Lang: New York, Frankfurt, 1988.

PART VI

Theatrical Essentials

Acting Styles

Julie Fishell

Versatility is the goal of many actors. Inhabiting characters from a wide range of dramatic texts provides a relished opportunity to explore social, historical, political, and personal worlds far different from their own. Most often, it is the stage actor who invests in negotiating a range of plays that feature heightened texts, disparate styles, and content. Many actors commit to advanced or conservatory-based training in order to successfully negotiate plays of style—plays that are of a particular form or typify a distinct period. The contemporary actor when faced with the task of acting in plays of style is wise to recognize the relevance of human experience, cultivate a sensitivity to language, research facts about the text and its time, develop a flexible body and voice, and trust in the vital participation of imagination.

Most contemporary actors are comfortable with realistic texts and modern acting theory. Early theories crafted by Konstantin Stanislavsky (1863–1938) continue to permeate actor training in our universities, conservatories, and professional studios. Stanislavsky believed a truly fine performance was primarily achieved by an actor's ability to relax, relate, and seek clear objectives or goals. Stanislavsky succinctly stated that the actor can easily define her job as playing truthful actions to overcome obstacles and to achieve objectives by personalizing the given circumstances. However, the actor experienced and confident in applying these foundational theories when performing realistic texts such as Henrik Ibsen, Tennessee Williams, Beth Henley, and Marsha Norman may not so easily translate their skills to a heightened or stylized text such as Shakespeare, Molière, Pinter, Beckett, Brecht, Feydeu, or Fornes.

In the mid-twentieth century actor, director, theorist, and educator Michel Saint Denis founded drama schools in England, Canada, and the United States. Saint Denis crafted courses of study that directly addressed the contemporary actor's insufficient ability to live their roles when working on a heightened text. His theories and their practical application continue to influence the curriculum of all major conservatory and professional actor training programs around the globe. For more information on Saint Denis's career see his books *Theatre, a Rediscovery of Style* and *Training for the Theatre: Premises and promises.*

BEGINNING TO ACT

The layperson, student actor, or amateur actor will most likely, misguidedly, start with externals. For some unknown reason, it is not uncommon for an actor to alter posture, usually sitting ramrod straight, turning out a foot, or embroider or overstate behavior and activities when rehearsing. Affectation or pretence often permeate the work and result in added tension and rigidity to the physical and vocal life of the actor in role. One can only speculate that this phenomenon could be the result of seeing performances of plays or films set in specific periods that leave their mark as stiff, methodical, and emotionless productions. Equally possible is that actors who lack vocal and physical training may overcompensate in these areas because of their inexperience with heightened or stylized texts. An actor who is comfortable with contemporary or more realistic texts may unnecessarily discount the value of applying some of Stanislavsky's basic theories to their work.

It order to avoid this trap, actors must identify with their character as an individual with a human qualities and needs within the play. Just as Stanislavsky advised, one must create a relationship to action and circumstance by applying the supposition of "What if?" or the "Magic If" to the work. The contemporary actor may actually be surprised that any role in a play of style unquestionably benefits from recognizing and cultivating specific human urges, whims, wishes, fancies, specific pasts, needs, and inclinations. This assumption will then allow the actor to accept that characters are visceral and contemporary to the world they inhabit. This assumption is essential and without full belief in it actors often fail to contribute richly to a stylized text.

Specific Skills

Sensitivity to Language

When studying any script, the actor must chart each playwright's landscape of images that outline given circumstances including the plot or chain of events, character behavior and logic, actions and themes. An added task when working on stylized texts may be reading the play in several translations. Some original scripts have also been adapted for the stage and reading the original in variation may prove to kindle recognition of the play's essential components. Ultimately, the contemporary actor may need to utilize the resources of a fine library, consult a production dramaturg or contact a local authority in order to grasp the text

- Word choice and substitution: In playwright George Bernard Shaw's *Pygmalion*, character Eliza Doolittle bestows friendship, trust, and gratitude along with distance and rejection using only the words of her name. She addresses the benevolent character of Colonel Pickering, "Do you know what began my real education? Your calling me *Miss Doolittle* that day when I first came to Wimpole Street. . .I should like you to call me *Eliza* now, if you would. And I should like Professor Higgins to call me *Miss Doolittle*." An inexperienced actor may only read these lines as a simple request on the part of Shaw's heroine without slowing down to honor the complexity and depth of Eliza's action. So word choice often provides significant clues to character and motivation.

- Images: Kristin Linklater, respected voice teacher, actor, and director, says that "Becoming aware of images in language is a process of slowing down." An actor must take time with individual words, recognizing the organization of words or the syntax of the writing. An actor must completely concretize and clarify the meaning of tangible and intangible things. Plays of style as well as contemporary plays benefit from the actor's taking time to clarify, specify, and concretize the ideas in the play. For example, the word *home* will provoke personal meaning and present a particular image to an individual actor. So when the idea or image of *home* is referred to within the life of a play, the actor must redefine and clarify meaning specific to character.

- Avoiding pauses: Another trap for the actor most comfortable acting realism is adding unnecessary pauses to heightened or period texts. Often playwrights have structured their scripts with a special kind of symmetry. The plays of Molière, for example, have most successfully been translated in rhyme by playwright Richard Wilbur. Within this rhyme scheme there is a balance and proportion that urges the actor to create life on the words. There is a precision common to heightened texts of varying periods that rely on the text to flow. What a contemporary actor might consider subtext is actually provided in words. And if images are broken up too much, the character's logic completely falls apart. Take for example, the first few lines of Jacques' famous speech from Shakespeare's *As You Like It*:

> All the world's a stage,
> And all the men and women merely players.
> They have their exits and their entrances,
> And one man in his time plays many parts,
> His acts being seven ages.

A little fact-finding will help see two sentences on the page. Therefore, actors need to fight the tendency to stop their thought and speech where each comma falls. If they do this, they will start to clarify how succinctly Jacques develops the metaphor of theater for life in the first four lines of the speech. There is no need to stop the line to create a sense of invention. Jacques is creating or riffing on his idea *out loud*. From "stage" he discovers "players" then "exits"—"entrances"—"plays"—"parts" to "acts." The contemporary actor when performing this speech would do well to avoid "taking a minute"—a famous phrase used as teaching tactic by Lee Strasberg (1901–82), considered by some to be the patriarch of American "method" acting. When performing heightened text from a distinctive period, an actor who imposes breaks or pauses to simulate sincerity, invention, or "reality" often achieves the opposite.

- Resources: Most popular and reliable are the Oxford English Dictionary (OED) and *Encyclopedia Britannica*. When working on Shakespeare, in particular, it is common to spend time with Alexander Schmidt's *Shakespeare Lexicon and Quotation Dictionaries, Volume I and II* and *A Shakespeare Glossary: Enlarged and Revised* by C.T. Onions. Try also Leslie O'Dell's *Shakespearean Scholarship: A Guide for Actors and Students* and Webster's *New Explorer Dictionary and Thesaurus*. These dictionaries define common and uncommon words used by Shakespeare and inventory their use by comedy, tragedy, history, or poem. Pronunciation is also an issue for the actor. Key pronunciation dictionaries include *English Pronunciation Dictionary* by Daniel Jones.

Cultural Curiosity

In order to link oneself to the play in cultural context the actor may find great value in researching key historical, political, literary, philosophical, artistic, religious, scientific, and pedestrian events specific to the play at hand and the playwright's life span. A great resource is Bernard Grun's book *The Timetables of History* based on Werner Stein's "Kulturfahrplan." This book covers world events of note from 4500 B.C. to the 1990s. For example, recognizing that dramatist and writer Anton Chekhov's famous Russian drama *The Seagull* was performed for the first time two years after the last Emperor of Russia, Tsar Nicholas II, took the throne and two years before photos were taken with artificial light. Suddenly these cultural guideposts can assist our imaginations and align our thinking with the world in which Chekhov lived and wrote.

Vocal And Physical Ease And Flexibility

The actor who understands the meaning and motivation of a character must have the physical and vocal ability to convey it. Regardless of the style or genre of the play, without the cooperation and integration of a relaxed body and voice, a character will never fully come to life. As mentioned earlier, it is common for actors to almost subconsciously change their physical carriage, use of gestures, and breathing patterns when working on a heightened text or play from a distinct period. However, the same actor reading a scene from Moises Kaufman's *The Laramie Project* (2000), or even Susan Glaspell's *Trifles* written in 1916, will most likely physically and vocally contribute with ease and integration.

- Developing a neutral physicality is crucial for the actor who desires to tackle a variety of roles in a range of genres. Actors must seek to create a body that is flexible, energized and without habit. The body without habit is centered, easy, and integrated with the emotions and the mind. Actors often train in The Alexander Technique, the Feldenkrais method, and other similar disciplines to release unnecessary tension and maximize coordination and balance. An actor is truly free to create when the slight limp, rounded shoulders, or habitual curl of the lip are adopted as choices for a character and not present as the result of the actor's habit. When cast as Orgon in Molière's *Tartuffe*, the physically relaxed actor can arrive at the costume fitting and wear the clothes of period without the clothes wearing him or her. The corset, long skirt, a fan, monocle, spats, reticule, cravat, or scabbard insinuates movement to the body of the relaxed actor and provokes an altered physicality. There is never a need in the first place to "adopt" or "put on" a false walk or affected placement of the neck. Certainly there are manners and codes of conduct that a director may ask the actor to adopt but for the most part a body sensitive to weights, textures, and silhouette will believably assume life inside stylized costumes. Finally, mask work, as theorized by master teacher Jacque LeCoque, contributes greatly to an actor's expansion of physical skill as does clowning, and physical techniques directly related to acting.

- Developing a supple voice that is well-placed, resonant, and unfaltering. Not only is it important to create enough sound to carry in a theater, but the actor must work to expand vocal range, recognize centers of resonance and master proper vowel and consonant placement. Fine diction distinguishes a great actor and is the responsibility of any performer regardless the genre but especially heightened texts. As mentioned earlier, heightened texts often give an actor complete and complex thought through language. Some writers need twenty lines in reference to one idea, question, or topic. Often, plays of style are also epic plays and demand that playing spaces be uncluttered and easily adapted. There are many reputable systems of vocal training. Numerous practitioners and instructors including Cicily Berry, Kristin Linklater, Robert Neff Williams, Elizabeth Smith, Patsy Rodenburg, Jeffrey Crockett, and Bonnie Raphael have written texts and have contributed to global voice pedagogy and professional practice. The work of famed speech coach, teacher, and Broadway consultant Edith Skinner is featured in the seminal text *Speak With Distinction*. This text, complete with optional tape, is devoted to speech and phonetics with explicit information pertaining to a range of topics including the International Phonetic Alphabet, syllabication, diagrams, and exercises. Additionally, a handy web site for dialects is http://web.ku.edu/idea/.

Imagination: The Most Valuable Asset an Actor Brings

Imagination must be the actors' constant companion when working on any role regardless the text. However, a stage actor fulfilling heightened texts commonly structured in Epic form is often stretched to expand his imagination to concretize multiple locations at breakneck speed. Think of Shakespeare's *As You Like It* where the action moves from an orchard, to the lawn of the palace, to a room in the palace, to the Forest of Arden, back to the palace within the first five scenes. Or consider the daunting task of the classic role of Messenger that must report and thereby actualize emotionally charged, graphic and crucial events in numerous Greek texts. The contemporary actor who relies on a fully realized stage or film set, complete with a plethora of props that provide her with primary or secondary activities, is often lost in a world that features heightened texts and multiple locations. So, the actor must take time to specify locations using the five senses that often prove the road to imaginative play. It may be the smell of a remembered spring day that proves the actor's key to believing the Forest of Arden is three dimensional. It may be the remembered texture of hot, loose sand that is the actor's key to believing they travelled a specific road toward a Greek temple.

FURTHER READING

Grun, Bernard. *The Timetables of History*. New York: Simon and Schuster, 2006.

Jones, Daniel. *English Pronunciation Dictionary*. Cambridge, England, New York: Cambridge University Press, 1991.

Saint Denis, Michel. *Theatre, a Rediscovery of Style*. London: Henemann, 1960.

———. *Training for the Theatre: Premises and Promises*. London: Heinemann, 1982.

Skinner, Edith. *Speak With Distinction*. New York: Applause Theatre Book Publishers, 1990.

☙

Costume Design in the United States

Bobbi Owen

Costume designers are important members of the team of theatrical designers who provide visual spectacle to theatrical productions. They are responsible for all the garments and accessories worn by performers and generally create designs for hair and makeup as well, although design specializations in those areas are emerging. In the United States, costume designers are recognized as integral to successful productions; the European tradition of scenography makes it less common for an individual to specialize in costume design outside North America.

Costume designers come from a variety of backgrounds. Some initially studied to be scenic designers, performers, costume construction specialists, or as artists in complementary fields such as sculpture, painting, and fiber arts. Others began their careers as fashion designers or employees at costume rental houses. More often, however, they are costume design specialists trained through an apprenticeship with another designer or in one of the growing number of graduate programs offering a degree in costume design. Frank Poole Bevan (1903–76) at the Yale School of Drama, Paul Reinhardt and Lucy Barton (1891–1971) at the University of Texas, and Barbara and Cletus Anderson at Carnegie-Mellon are among those individuals instrumental in establishing training programs at universities for designers. The development of the profession, which began toward the end of the nineteenth century, continues through these programs.

EARLY COSTUME DESIGN IN THE UNITED STATES

Prior to the twentieth century, designing original costumes for a new production was unusual. A company of actors who performed a repertory of plays maintained wardrobes and adequately costumed their productions. Established companies amassed large wardrobes and successful costumes were used repeatedly. Because each actor selected his or her own wardrobe, productions rarely possessed visual unity. Some attempt might be made to give period plays a historical look, but this was normally a matter of available garments and conventional taste rather than any overriding concern for consistency.

When actors began to work from production to production instead of remaining with one company for several seasons, wardrobes of costumes could no longer be realistically maintained. Instead, company managers selected costumes, often from rental houses with large inventories [such as the establishment run by Maurice Hermann (1866–1921) in New York City and B.J. Simmons Company in London]. These managers were more likely to dress a character according to the needs of the role rather than the personal preference of performers. If time permitted, a company manager could work toward a unified design of sets, furnishings, and costumes in concert with the intent of the play. Occasionally scenic designers would select or approve costumes, or perhaps even design them once the setting was completed. The few individuals who specialized in costumes seldom received recognition. Among those who did were Caroline Siedle (d. 1907), C. Wilhelm (1858–1925), Percy Anderson (1851–1928), and Mrs. John Alexander (1867–1947) who designed for Maude Adams. In some cases, these costume designers were credited on the title pages of playbills, rather than in the back pages along with acknowledgements for piano tuners and stage curtains.

Specialists in Costume Design

During the early decades of the twentieth century, as the number of theaters in the United States increased, several developments led to the growing recognition of the contribution that a specialist in the costume area might make to a production. These developments included the increased use of assistants in specialized areas, the 1919 strike by actors for better wages and working conditions, union participation by scenic designers, and the availability of funding through the Federal Theatre Project for individuals working on productions. The movement from a single designer for scenery, costumes, and lights to individual ones for each specialty was gradual.

As it became standard practice for a single designer to control all of the visual elements of a production, including scenery, lights, and costumes, assistants began to take responsibility for following the various elements through the construction process. Aline Bernstein (1882–1955), for example, regularly employed

Emeline Clarke Roche (1902–95) as her assistant for scenery and Irene Sharaff (1910–93) as her assistant for costumes. Bernstein began this practice during her association with the Neighborhood Playhouse and at the Civic Repertory Theatre. Over time designers such as Bernstein, Jo Mielziner (1901–76), and Robert Edmond Jones (1997–54) acknowledged the difficulty of maintaining control over this wide range of activities and encouraged their assistants to assume design responsibility.

Robert Edmond Jones is widely credited with launching this new American stagecraft when *The Man Who Married a Dumb Wife* opened on Broadway in 1915. Jo Mielziner, one of the most prolific and creative scene designers of the New York stage in the twentieth century, designed numerous notable premieres of what have become American classics, among them Arthur Miller's *Death of a Salesman*, Lillian Hellmann's *Watch on the Rhine*, and Tennessee Williams's *The Glass Menagerie*. The mainstream theater community paid attention to what these two influential theater professionals did—and often followed suit.

The 1919 Actors' Equity Association strike for better wages and working conditions also aided the trend toward a specialization in costume design. The star system had long been an important aspect of the theater; performers able to draw large audiences have always had special privileges, including costumes specially designed and constructed by professionals. As a result of the 1919 strike, producers were required to provide costumes, wigs, shoes, and stockings for all women in principal roles and in the chorus. Because producers were required to pay for costumes, they increasingly looked to specialists for decisions about costume selections.

In the early 1920s, scenic designers began to join the United Scenic Artists Association. Initially a union for stage painters, the United Scenic Artists Association's union activities helped stabilize the role of design in production. By 1936 United Scenic Artists had a special section for costume designers, although they did not receive voting rights until 1966.

In addition, the Federal Theatre Project influenced the move toward specialization in costume design. Created during the early days of the Depression, the Federal Theatre Project was founded to provide employment for all varieties of theater professionals. Having many different individuals doing specialized jobs meant that more individuals were paid for their work. Once the specializations of costume (and lighting) design were developed, there was little possibility of returning to the old format.

NOTABLE COSTUME DESIGNERS

Many talented artists became costume designers as a result of these developments. By the 1930s, Irene Sharaff (1910–93): *West Side Story, The King and I,*

Flower Drum Song; Raoul Pène Du Bois (1914–85): *Wonderful Town, No, No, Nanette;* Charles LeMaire (1896–1985): *George White's Scandals, Of Thee I Sign;* and Lucinda Ballard (1908–93): *A Streetcar Named Desire, Annie Get Your Gun;* all designed costumes regularly for the thriving Broadway theater. They were joined in the 1940s by designers such as Miles White (1914–2000): *Oklahoma!, Gentlemen Prefer Blondes;* Freddy Wittop (1911–2001): *Hello, Dolly!, Dear World;* and Alvin Colt: *Guys and Dolls, A Touch of the Poet;* joined the rapidly emerging profession. By the 1940s almost half of the playbills for New York productions credited costume designers, compared with one percent at the turn of the twentieth century.

Notable theater artists such as Patton Campbell (*Twenty-seven Wagons Full of Cotton*), Ann Roth (*The Odd Couple, The Tale of the Allergist's Wife*), Theoni V. Adredge (*A Chorus Line*), and Patricia Zipprodt (1925–99) (*Cabaret, Sunday in the Park with George*), began designing costumes in the 1950s. They were joined in the 1960s by Florence Klotz (*Kiss of the Spider Woman*), Willa Kim (*Sophisticated Ladies, Will Rogers Follies*), and Jane Greenwood (*Ballad of a Sad Café*), among others. These costume designers continued to work primarily in the theater but, like most contemporary theater artists, also designed opera, dance, film, television, industrial promotions, and extravaganzas.

More recently costume designers Gregg Barnes (*The Drowsy Chaperone*), Gabriel Berry (La MaMa E.T.C.), Judith Dolan (*Joseph and the Amazing Technicolor Dreamcoat*), Susan Hilferty (*Wicked*), Ann Hould-Ward (*Beauty and the Beast*), Toni-Leslie James (*Jelly's Last Jam*) William Ivey Long (*The Producers, Hairspray*), Martin Pakledinaz (*Kiss Me, Kate*), Robert Perdziola (*The Goodbye Girl*), David Zinn (*A Tale of Two Cities*), and Catherine Zuber (*Light on the Piazza*), have become familiar names in the New York theater. As American theater has become less centralized, many designers—including Jeanne Button, Deborah Dryden, Susan Mickey, Robert Morgan, Steven Rubin, Paul Tazewell, and Susan Tsu—have gained recognition for the high quality of their costume design in major off-Broadway houses, and in regional theaters such as the Oregon Shakespeare Festival, The Goodman Theatre, The Guthrie Theatre, and Hartford Stage.

CURRENT DEVELOPMENTS IN COSTUME DESIGN

The specialization in costume design has enhanced the need for professionals in costume construction and in the related fields of millinery, wig making, and painting and dyeing. Many regional theaters in the United States as well as colleges and universities maintain their own shops for creating costumes, and costume rental houses such as Western Costume Company, Norcostco, Inc., TDF Costume Collection, and Stagecraft Studios are valuable resources. As the prominence of costume designers has increased, so too has that of professional costume makers. Valentina (1899–1989) made costumes for designers under contract to major movie studios, dance companies, and Broadway theaters in the middle of the twentieth century, as have Barbara Matera (d. 2001), Martin Izquierdo, and Sally Anne Parsons, among many, many others.

Some theatrical designers, including Tony Walton and Santo Loquasto continue the practice of designing both sets and costumes for productions whenever possible. Even these noteworthy designers acknowledge, however, the contributions made by specialists in the area of costume design and the value of having a specialization in the area of costume design. All costume designers acknowledge that their primary purpose is to serve a production by designing appropriate and effective costumes. And yet, all of them can also cite important moments created by costumes, such as the entrance of Dolly Gallagher Levi makes, accompanied by the title song, in *Hello, Dolly!* The red satin gown with the beaded overdress that Carol Channing wore when she originated the role has been reproduced over and over again because it is impossible to separate Freddy Wittop's design from the character for whom it was created. The gown is in the permanent collection of the Smithsonian's National Museum of American History in Washington DC.

FURTHER READING

Anderson, Barbara and Cletus Anderson. *Costume Design*. New York: Holt, Rinehart, and Winston, 1984.

Corey, Irene. *The Mask of Reality: An Approach to Design for Theatre*. Anchorage, Kentucky: Anchorage Press, 1968.

Cunningham, Rebecca. *The Magic Garment: Principles of Costume Design*. New York: Longman, 1989.

Owen, Bobbi. *Costume Design on Broadway, Designers and Their Credits: 1915–1985*. Westport, Connecticut: Greenwood, 1987.

Owen, Bobbi. *Broadway Design Roster*. Westport, Connecticut: Greenwood, 2003.

Russell, Douglas. *Stage Costume Design, Theory, Technique and Style*. Englewood Cliffs, New Jersey: Prentice-Hall, 1973, 1985.

Wilmeth, Don B., ed. *Cambridge Guide to American Theatre*. Cambridge: Cambridge University Press, 2007.

❧

Directors and Directing Styles

Kimball King

Since theater has existed there have always been people who were involved in financing a play, selecting a venue, choosing actors, and favoring a playwright. Often a work was funded by a patron, who no doubt exercised some demands upon the playwright and the actors. Someone like Sophocles may have incorporated the attitudes of contemporary philosophers into his writings and managed to convince his actors to do as he expected. Nevertheless, the concept of a "director" as we know it today, originated within the last century and a half. Most theater historians claim that the first modern "director" was George II, Duke of Saxe-Meiningen who supervised his own acting troupe, the Meiningen Players, beginning around 1850. The Duke integrated the written play with other aspects of theatrical arts: the costumes, scenery, actors, and venue.

About the same time the Duke became a director other "directors" emerged in Europe. This possibly had something to do with a prospering economy and a greater interest in the bourgeois life that it facilitated. André Antoine founded the Théatre Libre in France. J. T. Grein in England began the Independent Theatre and the famous Konstantin Stanislavsky in Russia began, with the help of Vladimir Nemirovich, the Moscow Arts Theatre. Stanislavsky is particularly important as he insisted that his actors learn the psychological motives of the characters they played. It is difficult to find an actor today who will play an entirely unsympathetic character. Even if an actor portrays a man as evil as Macbeth, he will attempt to "humanize" his character in some way. The "new" Macbeth may be as deplorable as Shakespeare's in his actions but an audience is more likely to guess at the familial and social dysfunctions that transformed him into a villain.

THE DIRECTOR'S RESPONSIBILITIES

Directors basically have five responsibilities: they hope to unify the play artistically, to preserve the integrity of the playwright's vision, to entertain a specific
audience, to enlighten it philosophically, and to organize a working process that
will result in a satisfying production. Some directors work better than others with
actors, leading their actors to perform more effectively. Others are known for their
adherence to a playwright's thematic credo. Still others are conspicuously
efficient, providing from the outset clearly achievable goals.

Probably a director's greatest challenge is to ensure accurate play analysis and
interpretation. Almost no performances in contemporary theaters lack a director.
Occasionally, the playwright himself or herself will direct the play. Or a playwright
will direct a work written by a friend or competitor.

Toby Cole and Helen Chinoy have assembled an excellent discussion of recent
directors. The selections provide a range of theatrical responsibilities appropriate
to their era and audiences. In addition to George II, the Duke of Saxe-Meiningen
whom they regard as a pioneer of directing, they examine the work of France's
André Antoine, Germany's Otto Brahm, Russia's influential Konstantin Stanislavsky, and America's David Belasco. Later Cole and Chinoy present articles by
Adolphe Appia, Gordon Craig, and George Bernard Shaw. Harley Granville-
Barker, who is also named, actually directed many of Shaw's plays. Granville-
Barker's own plays, *Waste* (1903) and *The Voysey Inheritance* (1905), were often
politically more radical than Shaw's work and seldom produced during his
lifetime. Today they are frequently performed and though modern in feeling seem
relatively "mild."

Directors on Directing also lists noted directors Arthur Hopkins, Jacques
Copeau, Louis Jouvet, Bertholt Brecht, Tyrone Guthrie, Nicholai Okhlophov,
Jean Vitor and Harold Clurman. Among the more famous recent directors are
Richard Eyre, Peter Brook, Peter Hall, and Max Stafford-Clark. Of those listed
by Cole and Chinoy, Berthold Brecht occasions the most analysis. Brecht
claimed he wrote and directed Epic Theatre, in which he revealed that mankind
was a sort of epic hero crushed into submission by adverse political forces.
A devoted Marxist, Brecht's plays continually stressed the inadequacies of
modern institutions. He also believed in the alienation-effect (or the "A-effect"
as it is known in chic circles). An audience is alienated from the conventional
suspension of disbelief and forced to face the social issues of Brecht's plays
intellectually. There is no checking in of one's intelligence at the theater door.
Brecht's plays were banned in Germany during Hitler's regime and he fled to
California, where many of his works were performed at the University of California at Berkeley. After World War II, however, Brecht returned to East Germany
where he directed the famous Berliner Ensemble. In Brecht's plays there are

frequent "expressionistic" elements—onstage placards, narrators, and other means of "distancing" the audience from dramatic involvement.

Sometimes Brecht's attempts to "alienate" are unsuccessful because audiences often prefer to "enter into" an imaginary work and to accept symbolic representation as reality. Directors today, Nobel Prize Winner Harold Pinter among them, frequently emphasize natural speech, a play's subtext and psychological ironies that are not immediately apparent. Still, all directors, as the actor/writer Ivor Novello once remarked, "dislike empty seats."

FURTHER READING

Berger, Sidney. *Playwright versus Director: Authorial Intentions and Performance Interpretations.* Westport, Connecticut: Greenwood Press, 1994.

Brook, Peter, Gabriella Giannachi, and Mary Luckhurst. *On Directing: Interviews with Directors.* Houndmills, England: Palgrave Macmillan, 1999.

Catron, Louis. *The Director's Vision.* Mountain View, California: Mayfield Publishing, 1995.

Cole, Toby and Helen Chinoy. *Directors on Directing: A Source Book of the Modern Theatre.* Indianapolis and New York: Bobbs-Merrill, 1953.

❧

Dramaturgy

Karen Blansfield

What exactly *is* a dramaturg? And what does a dramaturg actually *do?*

These questions came to me from friends, family, students, and others when I first began working in this capacity. Since then, I have come to find that most dramaturgs—whether in professional, university, or community theaters, full time employees or free-lancers—have pretty much had the same experience. Indeed, these are perhaps the central questions that dog the field of dramaturgy, from both within and without. Professor Lenora Inez Brown of the Theatre School at DePaul University noted that despite the growing number of dramaturgy programs being offered, "one would think the battles for this often misunderstood field are over, but they are greater today than ever before." ("You Can't Tell a Dramaturg by Her Title.") James Magruder, who was crucial in garnering support from the Mellon Foundation for Baltimore's Center Stage, wrote in his proposal for funding, "Any dramaturg spends a significant portion of his or her time on the job responding to the question, 'What is a dramaturg?'" And Carrie Ryan, Literary Manager of California's La Jolla Playhouse, commented, "One thing that didn't come with my MFA was an easy definition of dramaturgy...."

The list goes on. But in the end, no solid and final definitions of dramaturgy are really possible. Still, a general understanding of the range of roles in which a dramaturg engages can be broadly drawn.

THE DRAMATURG'S ROLES

Research

One of the most prominent and widespread responsibilities for any dramaturg is serving as a researcher. In this capacity, the dramaturg gathers a wide assortment of information that can encompass the following, and more:

1. background material about the time period in which the play is set and the era's social, political, and cultural environment, as well as any notable events

2. information about previous and particularly noteworthy productions of the work

3. material concerning any historical background, references, or actual persons featured in the play

4. a linguistic guide list that clarifies and contextualizes unfamiliar words, phrases, and colloquialisms

5. an economic outline delineating the cost of living at the time of the play, including grocery prices and average salaries.

While such research is time consuming and can be exhausting, it is also stimulating and informative, providing a fruitful learning experience. For example, in a production of Margaret Edson's *Wit,* I undertook a great amount of research on John Donne's poetry to assist the actor in understanding why the professor she portrayed is so enamored of—indeed, obsessed with—Donne's work and his fixation on death. In Michael Frayn's *Copenhagen,* my dramaturg tentacles arched into the fields of history, nuclear physics, and the atomic bomb, among other realms. In Donald Margulies's *Dinner With Friends,* the director even asked me to find out how long a flight from New York to Martha's Vineyard would take.

Preparing Programs and Study Guides

Another primary service rendered by most dramaturgs is writing and designing the production's program, which may include charts, lists, or other creative material, as well as conventional narratives about the play and the playwright. These writing responsibilities extend to other areas as well, including promotional material and study guides for students of various levels who will attend the production, an endeavor that works in collaboration with the outreach branch of the theatrical organization. Furthermore, and also part of public engagement, the dramaturg often conducts post-show discussions, which provide theatergoers the opportunity to ask questions and offer comments about the staging, rehearsal process, characters, and other elements of the production. In some situations, the dramaturg may even develop seminars centered on the play and its issues.

Assisting Directors

A third crucial responsibility is for the dramaturg to be present during rehearsals, offering his or her individual perspectives of the ongoing process. Making notes for the director regarding such aspects as consistencies in actors' performances, clarity of dialogue, unclear points in the plot, problems of continuity, and other such observations can prove quite helpful. Still, this is territory that a dramaturg must tread upon lightly, being careful not to invade the director's turf. And directors vary greatly: some invite and appreciate the observations that a dramaturg brings, while others see them as mere pests. In fact, a longtime debate has pitted the role of the dramaturg as basically a researcher and writer against one who is involved in the creative process of developing the play, through such duties as working with the playwright, offering critical input to the production process, and providing new perspectives on the play.

This trio of dramaturgical duties is just the underpinning of a much broader stage on which the dramaturg performs. The broad scope of tasks that dramaturgs may undertake include the following:

- Reading and assessing new plays.
- Working with a playwright to develop and refine a play.
- Acting as liaison between playwright and director.
- Assisting the artistic director in developing a season's repertoire.
- Serving as literary managers.
- Considering how plays were produced in their own time.
- Identifying what kind of stage, audience, purpose, and acting for which the play was originally written.
- Translating works from one language to another.
- Filling the rehearsal hall with books, articles, and other pertinent resources for the cast, as well as pasting the wall with maps, photographs, timelines, and any other visual information that will assist the company.

Despite the obvious necessity of fulfilling these various tasks for a production, the importance and the role of a dramaturg—at least in America—continues to be challenged and redefined. Scholar Geoffrey Proehl confronts this controversy when he writes, "The dramaturg...is not finally essential to the rehearsal process. To maintain otherwise would require redefining too much theatre history. Dramaturgy...is, however, inseparable from theatre making, whether or not the word itself is ever used." Furthermore, the role of the dramaturg is often unacknowledged, aside from a cursory mention in the production program.

While complexities infiltrate the contemporary role of the dramaturg, the nature of dramaturgy is hardly new; the ancient Greeks of the fourth and fifth centuries B.C. both wrote and acted in their own plays, inevitably addressing dramaturgical issues in the process. Indeed, Susan Jonas and Geoff Proehl note that the function of dramaturgy itself "is probably as old as theater and fundamentally inseparable from it." However, the modern concept of dramaturgy has undergone its own evolution. Conventional wisdom holds that dramaturgy as a field emerged in late eighteenth or early nineteenth century Germany, although, as Jonas and Proehl note, "it has antecedents throughout theater history (East and West)..." The German model focused primarily on theory and criticism, a model that is still widely held and that has shaped academic studies. But the role of the dramaturg is relatively new in American theater. Early in the twentieth century, several small companies developed the philosophy of dramaturg as playwright, a vision fostered through such venues as the Washington Square Players, the Provincetown Players (who most famously launched Eugene O'Neill), The Theatre Guild, and The Group Theatre, among others. Again, this integration of playwright and dramaturg harks back to the dawn of Western drama. By the 1970s, though, this kinship had broadened considerably, due in large part to the proliferation of classes and programs in dramaturgy being offered by universities, most notably Yale.

Regardless of the slippery nature of the term, dramaturgy continues to burgeon in educational programs as well as in theaters throughout the country. A critical eye continues to be leveled at this ambiguous personage, ranging from wholehearted embracement to supercilious dismissal. James Magruder jokes that he continually reconceives his dramaturgical role, creating such identities as "The Keeper of the Flame of Thespis" to "The Resident Egghead and Cultural Flypaper," while always attempting to avoid cultural stereotyping such as "The Cheese Stands Alone."

Even as dramaturgy continues to proliferate and develop, it is unlikely that the position itself will ever be satisfactorily defined. "Few terms in contemporary theater practice have consistently occasioned more perplexity," write Jonas and Proehl. "Individuals who find themselves listed as dramaturges on theater program often grow tired of explaining just what it is they do...."

That dramaturgs are essential to a production is indisputable. But by what name they shall be known, and by what duties they shall be defined, continues to be a work in progress.

FURTHER READING

Cardullo, Bert, ed.*What is Dramaturgy?* New York: Lang, 1995.

Castagno, Paul C., ed. *Voice of the Dramaturg: Southeastern Theatre Conference.* Tuscaloosa, Alabama: University of Alabama Press, 1995.

"Dramaturgy and Silence." *Theatre Topics* 13:27.

Esslin, Martin. "The Role of the Dramaturg in European Theatre." *Theater* 10.1 (1978): 48.

Hay, Peter. "American Dramaturgy: A Critical Reappraisal." *Performing Arts Journal* 7.3 (1983).

Jonas, Susan, Geoff Proehl, and Michael Lupu, eds. *Dramaturgy in American Theater: A Source Book.* New York: Harcourt Brace, 1997.

Kindelan, Nancy. *Shadows of Realism: Dramaturgy and the Theories and Practices of Modernism.* Westport, Connecticut: Greenwood Press, 1996.

Londré, Felicia Hardison. *Words at Play: Creative Writing and Dramaturgy.* Carbondale, Illinois: Southern Illinois Press, 2005.

Magruder, James. "A Place at the Table." *American Theatre* January 2001: 24.

Morawski, Kalikst. *Jean Cocteau, Dramaturg.* Lublin: 1955.

Proehl, Geoffrey S. "Rehearsing Dramaturgy: Olivia's Moment." *Theatre Topics* 9.2 (1999): 197–205.

———. "Dramaturgy and Silence." *Theatre Topics* 13.1 (2003): 25–33.

Rudakoff, Judith D. and Lynn M. Thomson. *Between the Lines: The Process of Dramaturgy.* Toronto: Playwrights Canada Press, 2002.

Ryan, Carrie. "You Can't Tell a Dramaturg by Her Title." *American Theatre* January 2001: 95.

Schechter, Joel. "American Dramaturgs." *The Drama Review* 20.2 (1976): 89.

Suvin, Darko. *To Brecht and Beyond: Soundings in Modern Dramaturgy.* Totowa, New Jersey: Barnes & Noble, 1984.

Theatre Topics. *Dramaturgy* Special Issue. Vol. 13, no. 1. March 2003.

"You Can't Tell a Dramaturg By Her Title." *American Theatre* Jan. 2001. 22–28.

ঔৎ

Drama's Stages: Theaters and Playhouses in Theatrical History

Milly S. Barranger

At the heart of the theatrical experience, as British director Peter Brook suggested, is the act of seeing and being seen in a special space reserved for performance. The ancient Greeks called this space a *theater*, a word derived from *theatron*, meaning a "seeing place."

At one time or another during the history of Western cultures, this place for seeing has been a primitive dancing circle, an amphitheater, a church nave, a marketplace, a temporary platform, a garage, a street, a proscenium playhouse. Neither the stage's shape, nor its location, nor the building's architecture distinguishes a theater. Rather, the *seeing place* derives from the use of space to *imitate* human experience for audiences to see and contemplate. This seeing place is where spectators perceive the how, the what, and the why of experience enacted by others in a revelation of human behavior.

Theater's three basic components are the actor, the space, and the audience. The history of theater has been, in one sense, the changing physical relationship of actor and audience within the prepared space. Whether the physical space becomes more elaborate or less so, whether the performance occurs indoors or out, the actor-audience relationship is theater's vital ingredient. In one sense, the formula for theater is simple: A man or woman stands in front of an audience in a special or prepared place and imitates human realities designed to entertain and instruct. In this privileged place, audiences share in the revelation of a reality separate from their daily lives, although closely related to it.

Both Western and Eastern theaters have been historically divided into stage and auditorium and developed conventions regarding the relationship of performer to spectator and vice versa. For example, where actors perform and the vantage point from which audiences view performances have been delineated since the earliest recorded performances in Greece and the Far East. Western audiences, for example, have moved from the hillside in the Greek open-air theaters to a place before the Christian altar to standing room around the Elizabethan theater's platform stage, to plush seating before a curtained proscenium stage in a darkened hall, to the floor or scaffolds of a modern environmental production.

In a challenge to theatrical tradition in the mid-twentieth century, a number of theater practitioners set about inverting established conventions separating stage from auditorium—actor from spectator. In an attempt to break down time-honored actor-audience relationships, modern practitioners toyed with conventions, violated them, even turned them upside down, in an attempt to engage audiences in new interactions with performers and to redefine the theatrical experience. The terms *alternative* and *environmental* are frequently used to define modern performances found in nontraditional spaces. In such cases, audiences are arranged as an interactive part of that space for the duration of the performance. Like the actors, they become part of the theatrical event in environmental productions.

Traditional and nontraditional stages are found in almost all modern Western cultures. The earliest stages are found in Greece where dramatists crafted tragedies, comedies, and satyr plays to be performed in open-air theaters as civic and religious occasions.

TRADITIONAL STAGES

All cultures, with the exceptions of Mayan, Aztec, Sumerian, and some Islamic cultures, from early to modern times encouraged theatrical performances and special places for seeing and enacting these events. The earliest theatrical spaces were usually flat circular areas for the enactment of rituals dealing with life and death. The priest or guru performed in a threshing circle, in a hut, or an enclosure shared with onlookers.

For many years, theater historians have connected the origins of theater with agrarian and fertility rites and with *special places* for enactment of these rites. Early societies staged mock battles between death and life in which the king or ruler of the old year, representing death, perished in a duel with the champion of the new year. These early rituals contain the beginnings of modern theatrical conventions—enactment, imitation, and seasonal performances held in special or privileged spaces.

What is certain in these early beginnings is that theater became an enactment performed in permanent structures with two components: stage and auditorium. The first such permanent theater building in Western culture existed in the curve of a hillside in Greece.

Classical Stages

The Theatre of Dionysus, the most celebrated theater of fifth century B.C. Athens, Greece, was a permanent open-air structure located on the slope of the hill below the Acropolis. The dancing circle (or *orchestra*) surrounded by audiences on the hillside (the auditorium) was the earliest feature of this theater. In time, two performance areas evolved: the *orchestra* and the area later backed by a wooden scene building (the *skene*) that formed a neutral background for both actors and chorus evolved. In plays written by the classical Greek playwrights, the two or three speaking actors may have performed in the orchestra, or on a raised wooden stage, although no one knows for sure. The sharing of performance space between chorus and actors and conventions, such as formal entrances, choral odes, and the spoken dialogue, dictated the structure of the plays performed there. The plays of Aeschylus, Sophocles, Euripides, and Aristophanes were shaped as much by the theater's physical arrangement and conventions of choruses and masked actors as by the worldview of the playwrights.

From the classical to the Hellenistic period (c. 490–330 B.C.), the theater in Greece underwent changes: wooden seats were replaced by stone; the addition of the scene building made the actors' areas more complex, providing dressing areas, a neutral scenic background with doors for entrances and exits. A low raised stage was probably added sometime after the fifth century B.C. Nevertheless, theater remained in the open air, with well-defined places for audiences to sit and for actors and chorus to perform. This division of space within the permanent open-air structures in Greece dictated theater architecture, writing, and performance conventions for centuries.

Permanent theaters in Rome (the first was the Theatre of Pompey constructed in 55 B.C.) were larger and more sumptuous structures than their Hellenistic predecessors but replicated the essential features. Moreover, they were not the temporary stages of the notable Roman writers Plautus, Terence, and Seneca, whose plays predate the oldest surviving theaters by over one hundred years. Rather, the permanent structures were for honoring gods and emperors and accommodating spectacle and sensationalism. Many were built on level ground with a large stage house (*scaena*)—the raised stage (*pulpitum*) in the Theatre of Pompey was 300 feet wide—and the auditoriums (*cavea*) were covered by porticos and divided by aisles. The corridors (*vomitoria*) provided passageways into the orchestra and auditorium. The facade (*scaenae frons*) of the stage house was decorated with columns, statues, and porticos and often painted or gilded. These structures met the demands for athletic and circus entertainments, including horseracing, prizefighting, wrestling, wild animals, and so on.

Unlike the theaters of Greece, the Roman structures did not survive the decline of the empire and the rule of foreigners. The last record of a performance in Rome is dated 549.

Medieval Stages

The medieval European stages revived the open-air staging practices of Greek and Roman theaters, although there were few permanent structures. The medieval theater (c. 950–1500) began in churches with Latin playlets performed by priests to teach Christian doctrine and encourage moral behavior among spectators. Gradually, as performances became more concerned with entertainment and spectacle, they moved out of the churches into the marketplaces. Lay performers replaced priests and scripts based on biblical material grew longer and more complex, mixing the serious with the boisterous and farcical.

In time, medieval secular stages took two forms: fixed and moveable. The fixed stages, the most famous of which was located in Valenciennes, France, around 1547, were rectangular platforms erected in marketplaces or town squares to celebrate religious and civic occasions. The stage for the *Valenciennes Passion Play* contained "mansions," or huts that designated locales, and an open playing space, called the *platea*. Actors moved from hut to hut to indicate change in locale and performed for the most part in the *platea*. Mansions representing heaven and hell were placed on either end of the platform with earthly scenes of travail occurring between. The fixed stages, like the moveable stages, encouraged the telling of biblical stories sequentially, beginning with Creation and ending with Judgment Day.

Fixed stages were common in many parts of Europe but in Spain and England portable stages, called *carros* or pageant wagons, were devised. These moveable stages had an opening playing space, a *platea*, and a hut serving as a changing room, a neutral background, or another playing level. Wagons were lined up in the order of the biblical scenes to be enacted and moved through the narrow streets of medieval towns stopping at various places. Audiences stood around the wagons to watch performances of the thirty-two surviving plays of the English Wakefield cycle (c. 1375) based on biblical scenes of Christ's torture at the hands of soldiers, followed by his death on the cross. The cycle plays encouraged continuous action from scene to scene played out from wagon to wagon and influenced the later episodic playwriting of Elizabethan dramatists.

By the late sixteenth century, permanent stages were built in England and Europe to house a new kind of secular entertainment, one focusing more on plays with commercial appeal performed by companies of actors. In 1576, James Burbage built London's first theater, naming it simply "The Theatre." It was an open-air structure that adopted features from various places of entertainment: inn-yards, pageant wagons, banquet halls, fixed platforms, and portable stages.

Elizabethan Stages

The Globe, better known as Shakespeare's theater, was an open-air building with a platform stage in the middle surrounded on three sides by standing room for spectators and a large enclosed balcony topped by one or two smaller roofed galleries. Built in 1599, the stage was backed by a multilevel facade as part of the superstructure, called the *tiring house*, used as dressing rooms, storage areas, workrooms, and for exits and entrances. A roof supported by two columns jutted out above the platform; the underside of the roof, called "the heavens," was decorated with figures of the zodiac—moons, stars, and planets. Like medieval audiences, Elizabethan spectators were never far removed from the performers, especially the groundlings as those were called who stood around the platform stages to view performances.

With minimal scenery and few stage properties, the Globe encouraged continuous action and the spoken word to create illusions of storms, shipwrecks, faraway islands, and castle ramparts. The Globe, The Rose, The Curtain, The Fortune, and nine other open-air playhouses, built between 1567 and 1623, featured the works of William Shakespeare, Christopher Marlowe, Ben Jonson, Thomas Middleton, John Webster, John Ford, and other Elizabethan and Jacobean writers.

Like the stages of Greece and medieval Europe, the Elizabethan open-air stages depicted cosmic dramas that touched all people: peasant, artist, merchant, and nobleman. Moreover, its architecture influenced the structure of the plays performed there. The open stages encouraged continuous action. The upper levels were suggestive of castle battlements and romantic balconies. The two or more levels accommodated curtained inner and upper areas for hiding and discovering people and objects; backstage thunder machines and trapdoors in the stage floor offered cosmic effects, apparitions from the underworld, and opportunities for grave diggers to meditate on mortality. Moreover, the open-air structure reminded audiences of the larger universe in which ordinary men and women were merely players.

Proscenium Theaters and Modern Stages

The prototype for modern proscenium stages officially dates from the Italian Renaissance of the early seventeenth century. The Teatro Farnese at Parma, Italy, built in 1618, was one of the earliest theaters with a permanent proscenium arch.

Theater historians agree that late fifteenth century illustrated editions of Terence's plays contributed to the design of the proscenium arch. The first edition of the Roman playwright's plays in 1493 showed illustrations of what is now called the "Terence Stage." The stage is depicted as a platform backed by a continuous facade, either straight or angled and divided into a series of curtained openings, each representing the house of a different character. Later theaters in Italy were designed with elaborate stage openings with semicircular seating facing the stage. However, it was not until the Teatro Farnese, designed by Giovan Battista Aleotti, was completed in 1618 did the prototype for the modern proscenium stage with arch come into prominence.

In a variation of the Terence Stage, an ornamental arched facade across the front wall framed the Farnese stage, restricted the view of audiences, and separated them from the actors. The frame also had practical uses. It masked the machines and the grooves used for changing scenery (large canvas pieces painted in perspective) and other special effects. The auditorium featured U-shaped stadium seating surrounding a large open area that replicated space previously used for dancing and forms of spectacle in court theaters. Unlike the open-air theaters, the proscenium theaters evolved into stages for scenic illusion, spectacle, and entertainment.

Most of the theaters and opera houses built in the Western world over the last four hundred years have been proscenium theaters with framed stages, moveable scenery, machines, lighting, sound equipment, and orchestra pits for musicians. The stage is usually hidden by a curtain until the play's world is discovered by audiences seated in the orchestra area and tiered balconies of the darkened auditorium. The aim of playwrights (and designers) was to create behind the picture frame the illusion of recognizable worlds with drawing rooms, dining areas, streets, offices, and tenement dwellings.

For over a hundred and fifty years, such playwrights as Anton Chekhov, Henrik Ibsen, George Bernard Shaw, Lillian Hellman, and Arthur Miller have crafted plays for the proscenium stage. Its box sets (three walls with a ceiling) enclosed the world of the play inhabited by middle-class characters in recognizable environs. Responding to the possibilities of recreating the physical realities of recognizable living conditions on stage, dramatists wrote plays dealing with problems of contemporary middle-class life (outdated mores, discriminatory laws, inherited disease, legal chicanery, and exploitation in the workplace) that showed individuals, especially women, victimized by repressive societies—sometimes winning but most often losing in the struggle for dignity and livelihood. Ibsen's *The Doll's House*, Shaw's *Mrs. Warren's Profession*, and Hellman's *The Little Foxes* were written for stages that promised the possibility of the physical quality of real living conditions recreated on stage. Their plays demanded real rooms with transparent fourth walls, and actors dressed and moving in truthful fashion among familiar furnishings and authentic stage properties.

The fusion of the "real" in writing and staging practices resulted in pictorial illusion as the modern theater's chief stylistic characteristic. Playwrights readily responded to the possibilities for truthful depictions of contemporary life on stage.

In general, modern Western stages reflect their prototypes in Elizabethan open stages or European indoor playhouses. Thrust or open stages are found in contemporary festival theaters celebrating Shakespeare's work, such as the Oregon

Shakespeare Festival in Ashland and the Utah Shakespearean Festival in Cedar City, and in plays and pageants celebrating historical events staged in outdoor amphitheaters. Moreover, modern thrust stages are also found in indoor theaters located in Minneapolis (the Guthrie Theater) and in Stratford, Ontario (the Shakespearean Festival Theatre). Nevertheless, proscenium stages remain in the majority with their framed, recessed stages and technology for moveable scenery, motorized lighting, and surround sound. Both types of stages offer challenges to modern playwrights creating well-made dramas or sweeping epics or musical books in the manner of August Wilson's *Fences*, Tony Kushner's *Angels in America*, and Arthur Laurents's *West Side Story*.

NONTRADITIONAL STAGES

All performers who have appeared singly or in groups wherever an audience could be gathered are background to the modern interest in alternative performance spaces. Although international in practice, nontraditional stages found in the United States and Europe are associated with political protests in the sixties in opposition to the Vietnam War.

Within the last five decades, the creative works of Jerzy Grotowski (the Polish Laboratory Theatre), Julian Beck and Judith Malina (the Living Theatre), John O'Neal and Gilbert Moses (the Free Southern Theatre), Ariane Mnouchkine (Théâtre du Soleil), and Peter Schumann (the Bread and Puppet Theatre) have been labeled alternative or environmental theater. This type of theatrical performance rejects the conventional seating of proscenium playhouses and amphitheaters and arranges the audience as part of the playing space.

European Forerunners

In modern Russia and Germany, such leaders as the inventive Vsevolod Meyerhold (1874–c.1940) and Max Reinhardt (1873–1943) developed unorthodox production methods and uses of theatrical space. They are forerunners of many of the twentieth century experiments in nontraditional performance styles and the use of alternative spaces.

In the 1930s in Moscow, Russian director Vsevolod Meyerhold, an associate of Konstantin Stanislavsky at the Moscow Art Theatre, rejected the proscenium arch as too confining for actors. He removed the front curtain, the footlights, and the proscenium. Stagehands changed scenery and properties in full view of audiences and actors performed on trapezes, slides, platforms, and ramps to arouse feelings of exhilaration in both performers and audiences. Meyerhold's most famous production was an adaptation of Nikolai Gogol's *The Inspector General* (1926). In the most striking scene, the director arranged fifteen doors around the stage and a provincial official emerged simultaneously from each door to offer the inspector a bribe.

In turn, Max Reinhardt explored vast acting areas, such as circus arenas to stage *Oedipus the King* (1910) in Berlin's Circus Schumann remodeled into the Grosses Schauspielhouse, called his "theatre of the five thousand." He dreamed of a theater on the scale of the Roman amphitheaters used to stage spectacles, circus games, and chariot races for emperors and mass audiences. In 1920, Reinhardt created his most famous spectacle based on the English morality play *Jedermann* (*Everyman*) in the square before the Salzburg Cathedral in Austria. Town criers called from the church towers, spectators became communicants, and the church square was transformed into a ritual performance.

During the last fifty years, especially in the United States, many theater directors and designers looked for new theatrical spaces in warehouses, garages, factories, lofts, and abandoned churches to create new venues for performance. They reshaped all of the space available, thereby making their audiences an essential part of the theatrical event. Leading the international movement toward alternative venues for performance were Jerzy Grotowski in Poland, Julian Beck and Judith Malina in New York City, Ariane Mnouchkine in Paris, and Peter Schumann in the fields of pastoral Vermont.

Environmental Theater

By definition, environmental theater rejects conventional seating and includes audiences in the arrangement of the physical space. Each performance created by Jerzy Grotowski (1933–99) at the Polish Laboratory Theatre in Opole (and then in Wroclaw) in the late 1950s began with redesigning the entire space to find the proper spectator-actor relationship. *Akropolis* (1962) takes place in a large room outfitted with platforms (for spectators) and passageways circling the platforms and a large boxlike structure in the center of the room (for actors). Wire struts for hanging objects, such as metal stovepipes, as reminders of events in Europe's wartime concentration camps crisscrossed the ceiling of the room. Within the confined space, the actors in ragged shirts and trousers, wearing heavy wooden shoes and anonymous berets, build a modern extermination camp. Spectators and actors engage in contrasting Western ideals of love and human dignity with the degradation of the death camps. *Akropolis* ends with a procession of the condemned inmates disappearing one by one down an opening in the large box followed by silence.

In order to answer the question "What is theater?" Grotowski evolved a concept that he called "poor" theater. He became convinced that theater could happen without costumes, scenery, makeup, lighting, and mechanical sound effects. Grotowski's research eliminated everything not truly required by the actor in communion with the audience in order to arrive at deeper understandings of personal and social truths. He wrote about his methods in *Towards a Poor Theatre* (1968) and continued to explore for another thirty years how theater in different cultures conveys performance "truths."

The Living Theatre, the oldest of the collective groups in the United States, began in 1948 in a basement on Wooster Street in New York City. The talents and zeal of Julian Beck (1925–85) and Judith Malina (b. 1926) were directed toward unorthodox productions that encouraged nonviolent revolution against the policies of the U.S. government. In a dazzling act of rebellion in 1963 against both political and theatrical establishments, the Living Theatre staged *The Brig*, written by Kenneth Brown about a day in a Marine Corps prison for military offenders. The production replicated the caged wire, the dormitory bunk beds, overhead industrial lights, and the floor sectioned off by painted white lines demarking the restrictions imposed in the military prison. Spectators sat around the wire cage as witnesses to the dehumanizing of the eleven soldiers and as participants in society's responsibility for sanctioning the humiliation and abuse of other human beings.

Touring in the United States, Europe, and South America for almost forty years, the Living Theatre's activities aroused controversy and debate over the role of art in society. After Julian Beck's death in 1985, Judith Malina reformed the company on a smaller scale. The significance of the group's work rests on its naturalistic environmental productions (*The Connection* and *The Brig*) and experimentations with altered texts promoting anarchy and social change (*Frankenstein* and *Paradise Now*). Their latter-day performances made use of nudity and athleticism, assaulted audience sensibilities with human voices and cacophonous sounds, and confronted audiences with calls for revolution in the service of Julian Beck's mandate for a performance art dedicated to changing audience perceptions of the world.

The Free Southern Theatre grew out of the civil rights movement to address issues of freedom, justice, equality, and voting rights in the American South. In 1963, John O'Neal, Gilbert Moses, and Doris Derby—all staff members of the Student Nonviolent Coordinating Committee (SNCC)—discussed ideas for a "freedom theatre" in the rural South. That year in the state of Mississippi, they founded the Free Southern Theatre (FST), the American South's first legitimate black liberation theater organized to tour poor rural areas, give free performances ("No tickets needed," a sign read), and train black artists in workshops. They received the energetic support of another co-producer, Richard Schechner, editor of *The Drama Review* and a stage director who was teaching at Tulane University in New Orleans at the time and later started the controversial environmental Performance Group, located in the Performing Garage in lower Manhattan.

Started as an experiment during the height of the civil rights movement and antiwar expressions, the aim of the Free Southern Theatre was to promote black theater for the African American community—black artists and audiences. The first production, Martin Duberman's *In White America*, toured to communities and towns from Tougaloo, Mississippi, to New Orleans, Louisiana, in 1964. That summer three civil rights workers (James Chaney, Andrew Goodman, and Michael Schwerner) were brutally murdered in Mississippi. Against this backdrop of violence, FST toured a play to black communities about a legacy of pain and intolerance. Based on historical documents dating from the slave trade to the Freedom Rides and bus boycotts of the late fifties, Duberman's play resonated with rural black audiences. Moreover, the material was readily adaptable to performances on porches of rural farmhouses, in cotton fields, local churches, and community centers.

Largely youthful black audiences, many seeing a play for the first time, sat in the afternoon sun on folding chairs, benches, cots, and in back yards behind small frame houses in rural Mississippi to see *In White America* performed by six actors (four men and two women) and a musician. The back porches became stages; actors made entrances around corners and through screen doors leading into the houses. At times, a pickup truck with a policeman at the wheel drove by the site trolling for trouble.

The first tour of *In White America* took the group to thirteen Mississippi towns during three weeks. Audiences applauded the speeches of black Americans (Booker T. Washington and W. E. B. Du Bois) and joined spontaneously in singing with the cast. Traveling by car and van in the second season, FST toured with established plays written by black and white artists: the popular *Purlie Victorious* by Ossie Davis and the confounding *Waiting for Godot* by Samuel Beckett.

As an extension of the civil rights movement in the sixties, the company waxed and waned over the years as political ideology came into conflict with aesthetic standards. Finally, after seventeen years, with its leadership and monetary sources exhausted, the Free Southern Theatre disbanded in 1980.

Théâtre du Soleil (Theatre of the Sun) is another group that engaged in environmental production styles in Europe in the early sixties. Founded in Paris in 1964 by Ariane Mnouchkine (b. 1939) and a group of politically committed individuals, the Théâtre du Soleil was established as an egalitarian commune. The notion of collaborative creations and democratic participation permeated all levels of decision-making. All members shared responsibilities of research, writing, interpretation, design, construction, and housekeeping in an effort to abolish the theatrical hierarchy of traditional companies. Nevertheless, Théâtre du Soleil is identified with its artistic director Ariane Mnouchkine and with the environmental stagings of *L'Age d'Or* (*The Age of Gold*) and *Tambours Sur La Digue* (*Drums on the Dike*) and Asian-inspired modes of theatrical presentation in classical and Shakespearean revivals of *Les Atrides,* a four-part cycle of Greek plays, and *Richard II, Twelfth Night,* and *Henry IV, Part 1.*

In 1970, the company took up residence in a former munitions factory outside of Paris (the Cartoucherie in Vincennes) where they staged environmental productions that reflected the company's commitment to left-wing political beliefs. Their productions dealt with historical revolutions and modern political theory and featured improvisations and audience participation. Nevertheless, as political fervor waned worldwide with the winding down of the Vietnam War, Théâtre du Soleil turned to other forms of artistic expression that overshadowed "environmental" trendiness or the political and social messages contained in their earlier works. Most notable was the cycle of Greek plays, called *Les Atrides,* and based on Euripides' *Iphigeneia at Aulis* and Aeschylus' *The Oresteia* that further challenged contemporary notions of theatrical presentation by incorporating ancient Indian traditions of *Kutiyattam* and Kathakali dance drama, and Japanese Bunraku puppetry.

Another group in the sixties, Peter Schumann's Bread and Puppet Theatre, located in Glover, Vermont, did not create an environment *per se* but rather performed in almost any setting: streets, fields, gravel pits, gyms, churches, and only sometimes in theaters.

Born in 1934 in Silesia, Schumann emigrated from Germany to the United States in 1961. Within two years he founded the Bread and Puppet Theatre in New York City. His artistic collaborations with his wife, Elka Scott, began with the creation of street performances and antiwar parades featuring giant puppets. Mistrusting the power of words, Schumann used puppets to simplify and caricature the horrors of living in a time of potential global annihilation.

Invited to take up residence at Goddard College in Vermont, Schumann assembled a troupe of puppeteers, designers, musicians, and volunteers. Each August in Glover, Vermont, at harvest time, the troupe performed in grassed-over gravel pits with strolling jazz bands, rope walkers, and fire jugglers. Schumann baked sour dough rye bread (a heritage from his Silesian childhood) to share with audiences. When everyone had tasted bread in an act of social and spiritual communion, the performance began. Thus, audiences and performers participated in a time-honored ritual: the sharing of bread—the staff of life and symbol of humanity's most basic need.

In a Bread and Puppet performance, the stories are simple, the giant puppets riveting, and the tempo majestically slow. Schumann's troupe is best known for his early antiwar and nuclear disarmament pieces: *Fire, The Gray Lady Cantata, The Stations of the Cross,* and *A Man Says Goodbye to His Mother.* More recently, *The Domestic Resurrection Circus,* performed each August, reinforced death and resurrection themes with twenty-foot effigies and head-sized masks of mythical monsters and gods. A tall, careworn Madonna Godface with a cryptic smile and hair woven of milkweed and goldenrod dominated the landscape together with white birds with fifteen-foot wingspans (flown by three puppeteers holding long poles). They travelled across the fields as the moon rose above pinewoods reflected in the last rays of a Vermont sunset.

Peter Schumann's puppet theater employs dolls, effigies, and puppets to represent universal issues of life, death, and resurrection.

For 2,500 years, drama's stages have influenced artists and writers working within open air and indoor theaters on platform, thrust, and proscenium stages. The enclosed structures of the proscenium playhouses and the open areas of the outdoor theaters account in large measure for the types of plays written for these ancient and modern theaters. For the last quarter of the twentieth century, avant-garde groups set about rethinking, reshaping, and recreating the theatrical experience in improvised spaces for actors and audiences. Whether street performances or small rectangular rooms, the avant-garde used different kinds of space to herald alternative modes to truth-seeking within theatrical performance.

The use of traditional and nontraditional stages in the twenty-first century follows the many precedents in writing and performance that frequently began with the organization of space for audiences to see and performers to be seen. To follow the ancient Greek meaning of theater, the "seeing places" in use today around the world are as eclectic as the writing, production styles, and audiences found in the theaters themselves.

FURTHER READING

Barranger, Milly. *Theatre: A Way of Seeing*. Belmont, California: Thomson/ Wadsworth, 2006

Malpede, Karen. *People's Theatre in Amerika*. New York: Drama Books, 1972.

Shank, Theodore. *Beyond the Boundaries: American Alternative Theatre*. Ann Arbor, Michigan: University of Michigan Press, 2002.

Theater Voice Coaching

Bonnie N. Raphael

Theater voice coaches come from a number of different backgrounds and in a number of different varieties. It is their job to tend to the various vocal demands inherent in any theater production. Areas of such demand might include breathing for speech, active relaxation, voice production, loudness, range, rhythm, articulation, accents and dialects, microphone technique, vocal characterization, text analysis, heightened text, phrasing, pronunciation, accent elimination, and even singing.

In an academic environment, a voice coach would most likely be a faculty member who teaches in the theater department and coaches whatever productions are presented in connection with the training program. In a professional theater environment, the voice coach would be hired either by the theater—to be at the service of all incoming directors—or by a particular director—to be in charge of all vocal areas on any production which that particular director directs. In addition, there are voice coaches who work individually with actors to help them to build their voices and perhaps to lessen a regional accent or acquire a suitable accent or other skills in order to prepare for a particular audition or role, and there are voice coaches who work with film and television actors or singing actors to help them hone their speaking capabilities for work on camera, onstage, or outdoors.

Although voice coaching is perceived as a fairly specialized field of endeavor, it involves several different skills in diverse areas. Most often, the theater voice coach's training is in theater performance, with allied interests and/or course work in vocal anatomy and physiology, and/or phonetics, and/or rhetoric and communication, and/or dramatic literature, and perhaps even singing or Alexander Technique. Some voice coaches have completed extensive work in voice therapy as well, in order to be able to help an actor to avoid injury when he or she is asked to do potentially harmful things onstage (e.g., screaming, choking, coughing, speaking over a great deal of crowd or battle noise, speaking loudly while in awkward physical positions, etc.)

On the most basic level, the theater voice coach is a facilitator:

- The voice coach might help the *director* achieve his or her vision of what is needed from the actors. For example, the coach might help the director choose what sounds might be most appropriate for a given production (General American? American Stage Speech? Plantation Southern Dialect? Belfast, Northern Ireland Irish?) and might then help the actors achieve that sound. Even relatively unsophisticated audience members will sense that something is "off" if members of the same onstage family unit don't sound alike in some basic ways, or if characters who have never left a small town in rural Georgia do not speak similarly.

- The coach might help the *actors* better understand what a particular director is asking of them and might help those actors achieve the appropriate behavioral responses. For example, an actor might be asked to allow the voice to increase in age (e.g., *Cyrano de Bergerac*) or to sound progressively more educated during the course of a particular play (e.g., *Pygmalion*). By "translating" a given director's descriptive terms or images into specific vocal language for the actors, and by providing exercises and strategies that will best facilitate behavioral change, the coach can mediate between these creative artists in order to help them to achieve shared goals. For example: if a director were to say that a particular character needed to be darker or more dangerous, the voice coach might suggest that the actor investigate what happens if he or she were to deepen the voice or to use less vocal range or were to speak a bit more slowly. Rather than directing the actor, the coach will present different choices and will help the actor to explore them until the best solution to the theatrical challenge is found.

- The coach is frequently asked to help the actors to relax and to breathe and speak more freely in *moments of "crisis"* within the story of the play. Even if a character is dying or murdering another character or in the heat of a sword fight or trying desperately to break out of prison or to rescue a member of his or her onstage family from a fire, his or her lines must communicate clearly to a listening audience. This might require the voice coach to teach actors different breathing techniques or a new way of projecting the voice or even how best to imitate a well-known political figure's voice and speech patterns, or how to play more than one role in the same production without being recognized, if necessary.

- The coach makes it possible for the *audience* to have a more enjoyable experience in the theater by helping the actors to become more intelligible or to phrase their lines for easier listening or to pronounce proper names and places the same way as the other actors do, in order to minimize confusion or misunderstanding for the listeners. In order to achieve the latter, the voice coach might research pronunciations, check with the play's director to make sure that they are in agreement, and then provide the actors with a summary of these pronunciations at the first cast read-through of the play. Then, during the course of rehearsals, the coach would serve as the "pronunciation police" in order to bring all the actors into unity.

- When a production moves out of the rehearsal room and onto the stage for technical rehearsals, the voice coach facilitates this transition. The actors may discover that they need to project more or to be more intelligible to the audience over background music or scene shifts. Or the voice coach might help the actors determine their minimum loudness levels for any given theater, so that they can be heard even in their quietest or most intimate moments.

- The voice coach is often called on to be an *advocate* for the actors and a mediator and facilitator between them and directors, designers, producers, physicians, or even voice therapists if and when such advocacy is called for. For instance, if an actor is playing a very large role that makes considerable demands on his or her voice, the voice coach might request the director to allow that actor to "mark" the most demanding scenes if they are to be rehearsed over and over again on a particular day. If an actor is playing a role that requires him to wear some challenging headware or masks (e.g., a donkey's head for the actor playing Bottom in Shakespeare's *A Midsummer Night's Dream*), then the voice coach might consult with the costume designer to better insure that the actors won't strain their voices in order to make their lines heard. If an actor is speaking over amplified music, the voice coach might consult with the director and the sound designer to make sure that reasonable loudness levels are set in the underscoring. If an actor cannot be heard in a particularly dark scene in a play, the voice coach might ask the director to have the lighting designer provide a bit more light so that the audience members might hear more easily. And if, by some chance, an actor were to incur an illness that affects the voice, the voice coach might recommend a qualified local physician and then mediate between the medical team, the theater and the actor in order to produce the best result in the most efficient way.

- Voice coaches qualified to do so may be asked to *train choruses* to speak in unison for a Greek tragedy or to sing in unison for plays like *A Christmas Carol*, for example. They might train members of the cast of a particular production to imitate jungle sounds or schoolyard sounds or even wind and weather noises. They might assist when actors are asked to record voice-over sequences on microphone, or may help members of an acting company create and perform war cries or even speak in a foreign or an invented language.

Not every theater department or professional company will have a voice coach on its payroll but when one is part of the production team, the results are most often very significant. When there is no voice coach available to the actors in rehearsals, they might be told that they will be required to learn a Spanish accent or a New England accent and they are expected to do so on their own. An excellent source of available dialects materials can be found at IDEA, the International Dialects of English Archive http://web.ku.edu/idea/. Or an actor needing vocal help can go to the web site of the Voice and Speech Trainers Association: http://www.vasta.org to find a qualified professional in his or her location.

FURTHER READING

Becker, F. *And the Stars Spoke Back: A Dialogue Coach Remembers Hollywood Players of the Sixties in Paris.* Lanheim, Maryland: Scarecrow Press, 2004.

Da Vera, Rocco, ed. *Standard Speech and Other Contemporary Issues in Professional Voice and Speech Training.* New York: Applause, 2000.

Bibliography

Allensworth, Carl. *The Complete Play Production Handbook.* New York: Harper and Row, 1969.

Banks, Rosemarie K. *Theatre Culture in America, 1825–1860.* Cambridge, UK: Cambridge University Press, 1997.

Barnes, Philip. *A Companion to Post-War British Theatre.* Totowa, New Jersey: Barnes and Noble, 1986.

Barranger, Milly. *Understanding Plays,* 3rd ed. New York: Pearson, 2004.

Biet, Christian and Christopho Trian. *Qu'est-ce que de Theatre.* Paris, France: Gallimard, 2006.

Bryer, Jackson and Mary C. Hartig. *The Facts on File Companion to American Drama.* New York: Facts on File, 2005.

Burdick, Jacques. *Theater.* New York: Newsweek Books, 1974.

Cannan, Paul. *The Emergence of Dramatic Criticism in England: From Jonson to Pope.* New York: Palgrave Macmillan, 2006.

Chambers, Colin and Mike Prior. *Playwrights' Progress.* Oxford, UK: Amber Lane, 1987.

Dillon, Janette. *The Cambridge Introduction to Early English Theatre.* Cambridge, UK: Cambridge University Press, 2006.

Hartman, William. *A Handbook to Literature.* Upper Saddle River, New Jersey: Pearson/Prentice Hall, 2006.

Hartnoll, Phyllis. *The Oxford Companion to the Theatre.* (London, UK: Oxford University Press, 1951.

King, Kimball, ed. *Modern Dramatists: A Casebook of Major British, Irish and American Playwrights.* New York: Routledge, 2001.

Kullman, Colby H. and William C. Young. *Theatre Companies of the World, Vol 1 and 2.* Westport, Connecticut: Greenwood Press, 1986.

Londré, Felicia Hardison. *The History of World Theater.* New York: Continuum, 1991.

Meserve, Walter J. *American Drama to 1900: A Guide to Information Sources.* Detroit, Michigan: Gale, 1980.

Murray, Timothy. *Theatrical Legitimation*. Oxford, UK: Oxford University Press, 1987.

Nicoll, Allardyce. *The Development of the Theatre: A Study of Theatrical Art from the Beginnings to the Present Day*. New York: Harcourt Brace and World, 1966.

———, ed. *World Drama: From Aeschylus to Anouilh*. New York: Harper and Row, 1936.

Powell, Henry, ed. *The Cambridge Companion to Victorian and Edwardian Theatre*. Cambridge, UK: Cambridge University Press, 2004.

Quinn, Arthur Hobson. *A History of American Drama: From the Beginning to the Civil War*, 2nd ed. New York: Appleton-Century-Crofts, 1951.

Sobel, Bernard. *The Theatre Handbook and Digest of Plays*. New York: Crown Publishers, 1948.

Taylor, John Russell. *The Penguin Dictionary of Theatre*. Harmondsworth: Penguin, 1966.

Wells, Stanley, ed. *The Oxford Companion to William Shakespeare*. Oxford: Oxford University Press, 2001.

Wickham, Glynne. *A History of the Theatre*. Cambridge, UK: Cambridge University Press, 1988.

Williams, Gordon. *British Theatre in the Great War: A Revaluation*. London: Continuum, 2003.

Index

About the Editor and Contributors

EDITOR

Kimball King has authored or edited thirteen books on American literature and on contemporary British and American Drama. He is Adjunct Professor of Dramatic Arts at the University of North Carolina, Chapel Hill.

CONTRIBUTORS

Andrew Ade is Assistant Professor of English at Westminster College in Pennsylvania. His teaching and research interests include narratology, world drama, theory of drama, and theater history and performance.

Veronika Ambros is an Associate Professor in the Department of Slavic Languages and Literatures, University of Toronto. She has written *Kohout und die Metamorphosen des Sozialistischen Realismus* (1933), as well as many chapters in books. She also has written about Prague's experimental stage and Czech women writers.

Milly S. Barranger, Alumni Distinguished Professor Emerita of the University of North Carolina at Chapel Hill, is an author, producer, and educator. She has written fifteen books on theater and drama, including *Margaret Webster: A Life in the Theater, Understanding Plays, Theatre: A Way of Seeing*, and *Theatre: Past and Present*. She is the author of books on theater history and dramatic criticism, reference works, and play anthologies. An earlier version of this essay on theatrical space appeared in the fifth edition of Barranger's *Theatre: A Way of Seeing* (2002).

Sarah Bay-Cheng is an assistant professor of theater and media studies at the University at Buffalo/SUNY, pursuing research in avant-garde theater and film, modernism, and intermedia performance. She is the author of *Mama Dada: Gertrude Stein's Avant-Garde Theater* (2004) and is currently working on an anthology of modernist drama.

Jeffrey T. Bersett is an Assistant Professor of Spanish and Film Studies at Westminster College in Pennsylvania. He has written on Spanish drama and culture, most notably in his study of theatrical appropriations of José Zorrilla's *Don Juan Tenorio*. Bersett is also the author of *The Baker from Madrigal*, a play adapted from Zorrilla's *Traidor, inconfeso y mártir*.

Karen Blansfield teaches at the University of North Carolina at Chapel Hill. She edited the student Methuen edition of *Glengarry Glen Ross*. She has published articles in several major journals including *South Atlantic Review, Journal of American Drama & Theatre,* and *Studies in American Humor.*

Miriam M. Chirico is Associate Professor of English Literature at Eastern Connecticut State University, with a specialty in twentieth century drama. She has written on G. B. Shaw, Wendy Wasserstein, and John Leguizamo among other comic playwrights.

Reade Dornan is an Associate Professor of English at Michigan State University. She has written widely on contemporary theater—Caryl Churchill, Haruki Murakami, Omaha Magic Theatre, African American playwrights. Her books are *Arnold Wesker Revisited* and *Arnold Wesker: A Casebook.*

Martha Greene Eads is Associate Professor of English and Chair of the Language and Literature Department at Eastern Mennonite University in Harrisonburg, Virginia. Her essays on drama and fiction have appeared in *Christianity and Literature, The Cresset, Modern Drama,* and *Theology.*

Katherine Egerton is an Assistant Professor in the Department of English, Theatre, and Speech Communication at Berea College. Her work in Scandinavian Studies has focused on Henrik Ibsen and his influence on contemporary British and American playwrights. She is currently writing a book on the late plays of Arthur Miller.

Julie Fishell teaches acting and directing in the Department of Dramatic Art at the University of North Carolina at Chapel Hill where she received the Tanner Award for Teaching Excellence. Professor Fishell is also a resident company member of PlayMakers Repertory Company and is a graduate of The Juilliard Drama Division where she was awarded the Michel and Suria Saint-Denis Prize. She is a featured author in *Early Gifts: Recognizing and Nurturing Children's Talents*.

James Fisher, Professor and Theatre Head, Department of Theatre, University of North Carolina at Greensboro, is the author of four books. He has held several research fellowships and has published articles and reviews in numerous periodicals. He edits *The Puppetry Yearbook* and he is book review editor of the *Journal of Dramatic Theory and Criticism*.

Luc Gilleman teaches Modern Drama in the English Department and the Comparative Literature program at Smith College. He is the author of *John Osborne: Vituperative Artist* (2002).

Artur Grabowski is Associate Professor at the Jagiellonian University and a visiting professor at the University of Illinois, Chicago. He teaches Modern Polish and Comparative Literature and theater, Poetics and Creative Writing. He has published four books of poetry, a collection of plays, literary essays on European Modernism as well as numerous articles on literature and theater theory.

Robert F. Gross teaches drama at Hobart and William Smith Colleges. He has published books and articles on a variety of modern playwrights, from Henrik Ibsen and August Strindberg to A. R. Gurney, Caryl Churchill, John Guare, and Tennessee Williams.

Gwendolyn N. Hale is an Assistant Professor of English and the director of the Writing Center at Fisk University in Nashville, Tennessee. She has edited Fountainhead Press's *Core Curriculum Writing Guide* and is currently working on an anthology concerning racial passing as it is portrayed in film and text. She is also working with another professor in an effort to publish a critical text on the drama of Naomi Wallace.

William Hutchings is a Professor of English at the University of Alabama at Birmingham. He is the author of two books on playwright David Storey in addition to numerous essays and reviews on twentieth-century drama and fiction. His most recent book is Samuel Beckett's *Waiting for Godot: A Reference Guide* (Praeger, 2005).

Eszter A. Julian assists for the Technical Director at Temple Theatre in Sanford, North Carolina, and recently graduated Phi Beta Kappa from the University of

North Carolina at Chapel Hill. Her most recent accomplishment was assistant stage managing Theatre Or's production of *Hard Love* at Victory Gardens in Chicago.

Edward Donald Kennedy is Professor of English and Comparative Literature at the University of North Carolina at Chapel Hill. His publications include *Chronicles and other Historical Writing* (vol. 8 of *A Manual of the Writings in Middle English*), *King Arthur: A Casebook* (Garland, 1996: rep. Routledge, 2002), and numerous articles and reviews, primarily on Arthurian subjects and medieval chronicles. He is currently collaborating on an edition of short Scottish chronicles and serving as subject editor for English and Scottish chronicles for the forthcoming *Brill Encyclopedia of the Medieval Chronicle*. He is editor of *Studies in Philology*.

William Kerwin is an associate professor of English at the University of Missouri-Columbia, where he teaches Renaissance literature and Irish studies. He is the editor of *Brian Friel: A Casebook* (Garland, 1997) and *Beyond the Body: The Boundaries of Medicine and English Renaissance Drama* (University of Massachusetts Press, 2005), and is currently writing a book about English Renaissance satire and urban culture.

Gary Konas is an Associate Professor of English at the University of Wisconsin-La Crosse. He is editor of *Neil Simon: A Casebook* (Garland, 1997) and his primary area of research is musical theater.

Ralph Lindheim is Professor Emeritus of Slavic Languages and Literatures, University of Toronto. He is also the editor of *The Bulletin of the North American Chekhov Society*.

Bruce Mann is Dean of Liberal Arts at Northern Virginia Community College (Annandale Campus). For 20 years, he taught drama and modern literature at Oakland University in Rochester, Michigan. He is the editor of *Edward Albee: A Casebook* and the author of articles on Tennessee Williams, Eugene O'Neill, Arthur Miller, and Sam Shepard.

Lurana Donnels O'Malley is Professor in the Department of Theatre and Dance at the University of Hawaii at Manoa. Her teaching includes European and American theater history, research methods and directing. Her recent book (Ashgate, 2006) is *The Dramatic Works of Catherine the Great: Theatre and Politics in Eighteenth-Century Russia*.

Bobbi Owen is Professor of Dramatic Art at the University of North Carolina at Chapel Hill. She has written widely about theatrical designers, including hundreds of articles and five books, most recently, *The Designs of Willa Kim* (New York: 2003).

Penelope Prentice is Professor Emeritus from D'Youville College. She has had a dozen plays performed worldwide including *Thriller, Collector of Beautiful Men, Lady and the Cowboy, Transformational Country Dances, Love Letter to a Friend,* and most recently, *Love Play.* She is the recipient of an Edward Albee Fellowship and a MacDowell Fellowship for playwriting, and she was awarded New York Foundation of the Arts Sponsorships for *Thriller* and *Loveplay.* Her books include *The Pinter Ethic: The Erotic Aesthetic.* "Original Light," poetry from her book *Capturing the Light,* set to music by composer Eric Ewazen, premiered at the Julliard at Lincoln Center.

Bonnie N. Raphael is the resident voice, speech, text and dialect coach for Play-Maker's Repertory Theatre in Chapel Hill. As a professor at the University of North Carolina at Chapel Hill, she teaches voice, speech, text and dialects for graduate theater students enrolled in the Professional Actor Training Program. She is one of the founders of VASTA, the Voice and Speech Trainers Association.

Ennio Italo Rao is Associate Professor of Italian at the University of North Carolina at Chapel Hill. His specializations are the Italian Renaissance and Dialectology. He has published mainly on the literature of the fifteenth-century Humanities, particularly their invectives.

Brett M. Rogers is Franklin Postdoctoral teaching fellow in the Department of Classics at the University of Georgia. He is currently working on his first book, a study of representations of teaching and learning in archaic and classical Greek poetry, in which he seeks to explain why tyrants talk like teachers in Greek drama. He also teaches and lectures on the ancient novel and on classical mythology in relation to intellectual history, literary theory and modern media.

Richard Rankin Russell teaches English and Irish Literature at Baylor University in Texas. He has published essays in journals such as *Modern Drama, Journal of Modern Literature,* and *Eire-Ireland,* and his edited collection of essays by various hands on the Irish playwright Martin McDonagh will be published by Routledge in 2007.

Kay E.B. Ruth is an assistant professor at Wake Technical College in Greensboro, North Carolina. Her Web site on "The Harlem Renaissance," created while she was a teaching assistant in an American literature survey course at the University of North Carolina, has been adapted by major universities on both coasts of the United States.